Optical Networking:
A Beginner's Guide

ABOUT THE AUTHORS

Robert C. Elsenpeter is an author, Web content writer, award-winning journalist, and co-author of *eBusiness: A Beginner's Guide*.

Toby J. Velte, Ph.D., MCSE+I, CCNA, and CCDA, is a respected industry leader in the field of networking and has co-founded several high tech start-ups. Dr. Velte is the author of *Cisco®: A Beginner's Guide, Cisco® Internetworking with Windows® NT and 2000,* and *eBusiness: A Beginner's Guide.*

Optical Networking: A Beginner's Guide

ROBERT C. **ELSENPETER**
TOBY J. **VELTE**

McGraw-Hill/Osborne

New York   Chicago   San Francisco
Lisbon   London   Madrid   Mexico City   Milan
New Delhi   San Juan   Seoul   Singapore   Sydney   Toronto

McGraw-Hill/Osborne
2600 Tenth Street
Berkeley, California 94710
U.S.A.

To arrange bulk purchase discounts for sales promotions, premiums, or fund-raisers, please contact McGraw-Hill/Osborne at the above address. For information on translations or book distributors outside the U.S.A., please see the International Contact Information page immediately following the index of this book.

Optical Networking: A Beginner's Guide

1234567890 CUS CUS 01987654321

ISBN 0-07-219398-0

Publisher
    Brandon A. Nordin
Vice President & Associate Publisher
    Scott Rogers
Acquisitions Editor
    Francis Kelly
Senior Project Editor
    Carolyn Welch
Acquisitions Coordinator
    Alex Corona
Technical Editor
    Mac McVicker
Copy Editor
    Bob Campbell

Proofreader
    Pat Mannion
Indexer
    Claire Splan
Computer Designers
    Lauren McCarthy
    Carie Abrew
Illustrators
    Jackie Sieben
    Richard Coda
Cover Series Design
    Amparo Del Rio
Series Design
    Peter F. Hancik

This book was composed with Corel VENTURA™ Publisher.

For Mom and Dad,
who nurtured my inner geek
by giving me a VIC-20
for my 13th birthday.

AT A GLANCE

CONTENTS

Part I
Networking at the Speed of Light

Part II

Optical Networking Tools, Applications, and Vendors

Part III

Practical Optical Networking

ACKNOWLEDGMENTS

When it comes down to writing a book this size, it is important to thank all the people who work to make sure all the pieces fit together. Franny Kelly coordinated the whole effort and is always a pleasure to work with. Alex Corona kept things in order while Carolyn Welch crossed the 't's and dotted the 'i's. We are indebted to our technical editor Mac McVicker and Bob Campbell our copy editor. They both did a top-notch job under very tight time constraints.

A special thanks goes out to Walter Goralski who allowed us to use figures from his excellent book, *Optical Networking and WDM*.

INTRODUCTION

Try to imagine a time when one lone cable will be able to carry

▼ One million DVD or high-definition television signals

■ Six million high-speed Internet connections

▲ One hundred million dialup Internet connections

If this sounds like the type of data and video networking that only your grand-children will be able to enjoy, don't be too despondent. The truth of the matter is that fiber optics makes this capacity possible today—on just a single strand of fiber!

The capacities of fiber optics are amazing, and every day there seems to be new ways to pack even more data on fiber. One day, your grandchildren might look back and ask, "Fiber could *only* carry a million HDTV channels at the turn of the century?" Although fiber optic systems were first conceived early in the twentieth century (the basics of light and fiber a couple hundred years before that), it wasn't until the mid-1970s that fiber optics were first deployed for communications. Since then, fiber-based communications have been getting more robust, and it is only now that optical networking is coming into its own.

It should come as no surprise that networks are getting faster and faster. If you ask anyone if their network is fast enough, they'll tell you "no." This need for speed is spurred by beefier applications and the changing role of data in modern networks. It isn't sufficient for a network to simply transfer a text file from the server to a client. Now, it is necessary to send video files halfway around the globe and conduct online telephone conversations without any disruption in service.

A way to make networks and computing run faster and with more capacity is to employ an optical system. Optical networks are quite similar to conventional electrical networks. However, optical devices (like routers and switches) are used in place of electrical devices, and miles and miles of extremely thin glass fiber have supplanted copper wire. On the surface, it would seem that spans of glass just a few microns across would be incapable of carrying anything. Quite the opposite is true. Optical networks are able to carry data much faster and in greater quantities than their electrical counterparts.

This book examines optical networking from a variety of angles. We talk about optical networking basics, optical switching and routing, how to design and manage your optical network, and how you can keep everything safe and secure.

OPTICAL NETWORKING AND YOUR ORGANIZATION

Building an optical network is loaded with the same challenges inherent in electrical networks. However, the physics and operation of optical networks make the process hard to get a grasp on sometimes.

No matter how you deploy an optical network, your organization will benefit from it. As networks become more powerful, so do the applications that run on those networks. And as applications demand more bandwidth, the network must grow to match. This is a never-ending circle, but you can get a good jump on network speed and capacity if you employ an optical design.

Optical networks are conventionally thought of as something just for phone companies or Microsoft. The truth of the matter is that organizations of any size can implement an optical solution. Whether your organization needs to transmit video and data across the sea or if you just need high-capacity links in a local area network, optical networking can provide a solution.

Of course, there is a financial reality to optical networks. They tend to be more expensive than their electrical counterparts; however, when you weigh the initial costs of an optical network with the ongoing costs of an electrical network, the cost savings come in on the side of the optical network.

WHO SHOULD READ THIS BOOK

This book is written for a range of people in your organization or for anyone with an interest in optical networking. First and foremost, it is meant for the chief decision maker who will be implementing an optical networking solution. But the content is also appropriate for IT staffers, CEOs, and anyone else with an interest or stake in your organization's optical goals. Anyone reading this book will be able to understand the principles, theories, and applications behind the optical issues presented within.

But this isn't to suggest that individuals with a higher level of technological expertise can't glean valuable information from this book. The world of networking is changing rapidly, and—because of the nature of optical networking—there are different concepts and ways to use technology that are unique to optical deployments. We discuss those issues here.

WHAT THIS BOOK COVERS

Optical Networking: A Beginner's Guide is organized into three parts. Each part presents an important facet about optical networking in an easy-to-follow manner. For example, if you're looking for information about optical networking basics, you can refer to the first three chapters in Part I. If you want to read about putting optical networks into practical deployment, Part III contains chapters germane to that issue. The following describes the sections and the chapters within those sections.

Part I: Networking at the Speed of Light. In the first section, the first three chapters examine the basics of optical transmission, how optics were even considered as a transmission platform, and how networks are built based on optical technology. The chapters in this section are:

▼ **Chapter 1: Optical Networking Theory**   This chapter is really Fiber Optics 101. We cover the basics behind optical networking, including how optical fiber works, amplification, loss, and how light moves through a span of optical fiber.

■ **Chapter 2: History of Optical Networking**   In this chapter we pause for a moment to consider the history of optical networks. We talk about how pioneers like Charles Vernon Boys made the first uniform threads of glass and how Swiss physicist Daniel Colladon and French physicist Jacques Babinet simultaneously discovered that light would follow the flow of water from a fountain. Finally, we wrap up our discussion with a look at former high-speed, last mile designs and what went wrong. Then, we examine passive optical networks (PONs) and see how they could be the answer to the last mile problem.

▲ **Chapter 3: Optical Architectures**   In Chapter 3, we get back to the nitty gritty of optical networking. In this chapter we talk about the types of optical networks that are responsible for the transmission of optical bits and bytes. Our discussion includes Synchronous Optical Networks (also known as SONET) and Dense Wavelength Division Multiplexing (DWDM).

Part II: Optical Networking, Tools, Applications, and Vendors. In this section, we look at how you might design an optical network to suit your particular needs, how optical routing and switching occur, what optical vendors have to sell, and which applications are best suited for an optical network. The chapters in this section are:

▼ **Chapter 4: Optical Networking Design** This chapter focuses on the design of your optical network. Whether you need a large-scale deployment or something smaller, this chapter explains how optical networks are designed. First, we talk about some networking basics; then we apply that knowledge to the world of fiber optics.

■ **Chapter 5: Optical Switching and Routing** In this chapter, we talk about routing and switching. Both are extremely important in the construction of networks and internetworks, both electrical and optical. In an optical deployment, the requirements of a router or a switch are little different, especially when truly all-optical devices are introduced. This chapter not only looks at how routing and switching work, but also how they will work when truly all-optical devices are developed.

■ **Chapter 6: Vendors and their Wares** This chapter examines the various vendors out there who offer optical equipment. We cover the most prevalent vendors in the optical world, talk about their place in it, and also discuss the equipment they offer.

▲ **Chapter 7: Optical Networking Applications** It's all well and good to build an optical network, but what would you use it for? This chapter discusses the applications for which an optical network would be best suited. Topics include Voice over IP (VoIP), storage area networks (SANs), and submarine systems.

Part III: Practical Optical Networking. The final section puts the knowledge of optical networks into practical application. We've moved from designing an optical network to building it. Once an optical network is built, you need to manage it, tune it, and protect it. Further, we talk about the different types of fiber on the market and why you would choose one type over another. Chapters in this section are:

▼ **Chapter 8: Building Optical Networks** This chapter explains how optical networks can be built. Topics include the ever-increasing capacity of Ethernet and Fiber Distributed Data Interface (FDDI) and which technologies would be best for your optical deployment.

■ **Chapter 9: Optical Network Management** Network management is important in any network and this is no less true in optical networks. This chapter looks at issues relevant to the management of optical networks and suggests ways you can manage your own optical networks.

■ **Chapter 10: Optical Maintenance and Tuning** Once a network is built, it does not continue to work, error free, for years on end by itself. Maintenance and tuning are constant chores that information technology professionals must deal with. This chapter discusses issues of optical network management and tuning and also suggests some third-party resources that can help you tune your optical network.

■ **Chapter 11: Optical Fiber**   When it comes time to build an optical network, you need to know what types of fiber are out there, how they're connected, and how you can keep safe. Even though there isn't electrical current coursing through optical fiber, lit fiber can still be hazardous, potentially blinding. In this chapter, we discuss safety from a lit fiber standpoint, as well as the handling and disposal of fiber shards.

▲ **Chapter 12: Optical Network Security**   The last chapter focuses on optical network security. We start with a discussion of security that covers both electrical and optical networks, then move to issues specifically related to optical networks. Not only do we talk about the things you can do to prevent your network from falling prey to a hacker or being accessed by the wrong people, we also discuss the physical things you can do to keep your network from being damaged.

HOW TO READ THIS BOOK

This book has been written with beginners in mind. It is designed so that you can pick it up, flip to any chapter, and find the information you need. We do assume, however, that you have some very basic understanding of networking, computers, and the Internet. If you are looking for something specific (like information about optical routing), you can just flip to that chapter. If you want specific information on security, for example, you can easily turn to that chapter.

PART I

Networking at the Speed of Light

CHAPTER 1

Optical Networking
Theory

When primitive man first figured out how to make fire, he was concerned with keeping warm and cooking food. After a while, he learned to use fire to turn night into day, and then he put it into an engine to make trains and cars run. As we begin the twenty-first century, we're using a form of fire to communicate across great distances and share an abundance of information in a way that our hairy, knuckle-dragging ancestors never conceived of (no, I'm not talking about Uncle Cletus). The advent of the laser and its subsequent application to fiber optic cabling is moving untold gigabits of information every second across continents and under seas.

In this chapter, we look at what makes optical networking happen. We discuss the concepts, and we look at how those concepts are put into practical application. Even though optical networking is discussed in terms of what you can do with it, we also look at the other side of the coin, specifically, what its limitations are.

THE BASICS

In its purest essence, optical networking is some flashing light moving back and forth across a glass rod. This flashing light carries the information traveling between networking components, such as optical switches and routers. As Figure 1-1 shows, think of this process as two ships signaling each other on a cold dark night in the north Atlantic.

But where our two mariner friends are sharing such quick, short messages as "where are we?" and "is that a hole in your bow?" optical networking can send billions of bits of information in a second. An optical network can send pages of text, images, music, and movies in the blink of an eye.

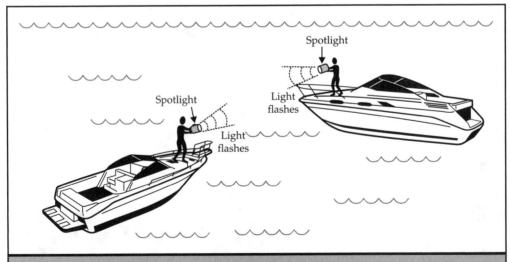

Figure 1-1.   Optical networking is much like ships flashing Morse Code messages to each other

In a conventional internetwork, this information would be transmitted across great distances using twisted-pair copper wire, across a wide area network (WAN) or even a local area network (LAN). As useful and utilitarian as twisted-pair cabling and an electrical network have been, fiber optics allows information to be transferred at immensely higher rates. In the past, when computers shared only brief conversations across the miles, electrical networks could handle the load. But now, as information is shared as it has never been shared before, there is a clear need for an upgrade in network capacities.

Let's go back to our examination of what, exactly, comprises an optical network. As Figure 1-2 illustrates, an optical network is a glass rod connecting networking devices (routers, switches, and so forth) in different locations. Clearly, large glass rods spanning the continents and oceans are not a viable solution. So how, then, are light pulses delivered across such a fragile medium? Amazingly thin strands of glass (even thinner than one of the strands of hair in your Uncle Phil's comb-over) that can be thousands of miles long are used to deliver the optical network's payload. Even though these strands of glass are remarkably strong—even stronger than a similar sized piece of steel wire—they are encased in a surrounding cable and buried underground or even submerged on the ocean floor.

Let's say you've got a short length of a glass rod and you shine a flashlight in one end. Even though you would see the light in the end of the rod, the truth of the matter is that very little of the originating light would make it all the way to the other end. This is because as clear and clean as glass may look, it is still chock-full of impurities. These impurities block the light before it gets to the other end.

So how, you might be wondering, does light make it across thousands of miles on a strand of glass thinner than the human hair? Optical networking is enabled because of two improvements in the field of shining a flashlight in one end of a glass rod:

▼   The glass used in fiber optics is specially designed so that it is low in impurities. Further, within the fiber itself, the light can bounce around and propagate to the far end.

▲   Very powerful lights called *lasers* are capable of traveling much farther than regular light.

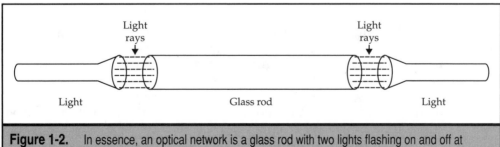

Figure 1-2.   In essence, an optical network is a glass rod with two lights flashing on and off at each end

Like the Morse Code being sent between the two ships in Figure 1-1, the laser light flashes in an optical network represent the information that networking devices are sharing between one another. On the other end of the fiber is the receiver. This receiver keeps up with the flashes of light.

The quicker the lasers can flash on and off, the quicker the information can be transmitted. This speed is known as the *bit rate* and is commonly talked about as bits per second (bps). The most common bit rate going across conventional optical networks is 10 gigabits per second, which breaks down to about 10 billion flashes of light per second. For the sake of comparison, the preeminent electrical networks top out at 1 Gbps, but most commonly operate at 10 or 100 million bits per second (megabits per second).

Though 10 Gbps is impressive, the next step in optical networking speed is 40 Gbps, and some vendors are experimenting with 1.6 terabits per second (1.6 trillion bits per second). To put this all in perspective, using a 10 Gbps optical network, you could transmit the text of 1000 books in just one second.

The Promise of Optical Networking

It's no secret that as industry and society increase their dependence on technology, the capabilities of existing technology will be taxed. Conventionally speaking, information in an internetwork courses through copper wire, be it across LAN connections or across a leased WAN link. Unfortunately, copper wire has its limitations.

Optical networking, on the other hand, offers enhancements over conventional networking because it provides three important network performance improvements: speed, capacity, and distance.

Speed

Comparing the bit rates in electrical networks to optical networks is like putting Woody Allen in a prison yard fist fight with Mike Tyson—there's just no comparison (unless Woody whined neurotically at Mike long enough to give him an aneurysm, but let's stay on track here). The greatest thing that optical networking has going for it is raw speed.

Common WAN links that move across electrical networks are T-1 (1.544 Mbps) and T-3 (45 Mbps). On the LAN front, things get a little better. Most organizations use 10 or 100 Mbps Ethernet. The top-of-the-line Ethernet clocks in at 1 Gbps. However, once fiber optics gets into the race, look out.

At their slowest, fiber optic networks speed along much faster than a T-1 or a T-3. Once fiber shifts out of first gear, there ceases to be a comparison. When discussing optical networking speeds, you'll hear the terminology change from T-1 or T-3 to OC. OC stands for *optical carrier*. OC takes over where T leaves off. Once the optical carrier gets involved, speeds not only reach 1 Gbps but even leave 1 Gbps in the rearview mirror.

Table 1-1 shows how optical networking line speeds increase.

As you can see, the speed rates in optical networks (not to mention their development) are increasing at an amazing velocity. OC-192 is the current top end in optical networking, although OC-768 is soon to be a reality. On the horizon, however, is the

Designation	Speed
OC-12	622 Mbps
OC-24	1.244 Gbps
OC-48	2.488 Gbps
OC-192	9.952 Gbps
OC-768	40 Gbps

OC3 - 156mbps

Table 1-1.   Optical Networking Speeds

networking equivalent of breaking the sound barrier—1.6 *terabits* per second. Breaking the terabit barrier on a single fiber is due thanks to *dense wavelength division multiplexing (DWDM)* and ever- increasing line rates.

NOTE: We talk more about DWDM in Chapter 3.

Capacity

Going hand-in-hand with speed is the notion of capacity. Think of capacity as a garden hose. Let's say that you are trying to water your lawn using a standard, green garden hose available at any lawn and garden store. The hose is good for the job, but what if your house catches on fire? When the fire department shows up, they don't start unrolling lengths of garden hose. Instead, they use hoses that have a much wider diameter. These hoses can deliver more water than your garden hose. The same holds true for networking. The wider the "pipe," the more data can get through.

To think about capacity, it's useful to think about your computer and how you use it. If you receive an e-mail message, it could have come through a 640 Kbps Ethernet connection with no problem whatsoever. Think of this as the garden hose. But what if you want to watch a large video over a WAN or over the Internet? Your 640 Kbps garden hose just won't be able to accommodate your needs. It will get clogged up, you'll drop frames, and the video will be unwatchable. On the other hand, if you use an OC-192 optical network, that's like backing a pumper truck to your burning house. The large volume of video traffic will come through clearly because the link has enough capacity.

Capacity is also helpful if you are trying to develop an IP Telephony solution, for instance. If you are trying to connect a large company to an IP Telephony solution using 10/100 Ethernet, you will run into problems. However, using an optical network ameliorates that problem.

The future of motion pictures will owe a lot to optical networking, as well. Now that more and more motion pictures are being filmed and edited digitally, the next step is to project the film digitally. Rather than mail a disc with the movie to theaters around the country, the movie studios want to electronically transmit the movie to the theaters. This allows the movie to be presented digitally and eliminates the need to ship spools of celluloid cross-country to thousands of theaters. But it also illustrates the need for a high-capacity internetwork.

Distance

One of the key benefits of fiber optics is its ability to span a few feet or thousands of miles. Depending on the quality of the fiber and the hardware, a stretch of fiber a thousand miles long needs no repeater or amplification hardware. This is rare, however, and most stretches of fiber require periodic boosts in signal strength.

NOTE: We talk about the ins and outs of optical networking amplification later in this chapter.

You probably use a fiber optical network day in and day out, but aren't aware of it. When you make a long distance phone call or access a Web site in Europe, for example, the signal has to find a way to hop the pond. But the bulk of the communications aren't being beamed to satellites to make the jump—they cross the oceans using submarine fiber optic cabling.

In order to locate thousands of miles of optical fiber on the ocean floor, the fiber is encased in a very durable material, along with an amplifier as needed, and placed. In order to put the cable on the seabed as safely as possible, a very detailed map of the ocean floor is used, then the cable placement is determined, using a route that takes it out of the way of any obstacles, such as oil platforms or fishing lanes. The place where submarine lines are most often damaged is not out in the deepest part of the ocean. Rather, it is in shallow harbors where boats can snag the line.

How Optical Networking Works

When you buy all the components for an optical network, you don't really need to hire Mr. Wizard to act as a consultant to understand the physics behind the thing. You don't *need* to know how refraction and diffusion occur within your system. However, a little primer on some basics will give you a better understanding of the system and what's going on inside those expensive boxes of circuitry.

Light Reflection and Refraction

The main job of optical fibers is to guide light waves without losing too much light. Within a run of fiber optic cable, light is transmitted at about two-thirds the speed of light in a vacuum. The transmission of light in optical fiber is most commonly explained using the principle of *total internal reflection (TIR)*.

This means that 100 percent of light that strikes a surface is reflected. For means of comparison, a mirror reflects about 90 percent of the light that strikes it, so you can see that TIR is a high standard to meet.

When light is emitted—be it from a powerful laser or from candlelight—the radiated light can bounce, assuming it strikes the right material. Light can be manipulated in two basically different ways:

▼ **Reflection** means that the light bounces back.

▲ **Refraction** means that the light's angle is altered as it passes through a different medium (like a glass of water, a prism, or a fiber). The angle is determined by the *angle of incidence*. The angle of incidence is the angle at which light strikes the interface between an optically denser material and an optically thinner one.

For TIR to occur, the following conditions must be present:

▼ Beams of light must pass from a dense material to a less dense material.

▲ The incident angle must be less than the *critical angle*. The critical angle is the angle of incidence at which light stops being refracted and is instead totally reflected.

Figure 1-3 illustrates the principle of total internal reflection within a fiber core. As you see, the core has a higher refractive index than the surrounding cladding, thus allowing the beam of light to strike the surface at less than the critical angle. The second beam does not meet the critical angle requirement and is refracted.

As you remember from our earlier discussion about fiber, the core and cladding are constructed out of optically denser and optically thinner types of highly pure silica glass.

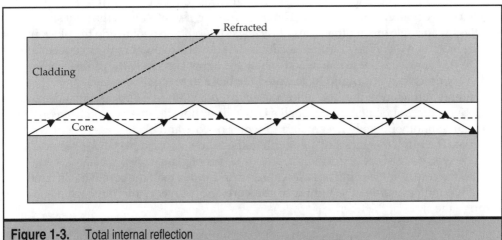

Figure 1-3.   Total internal reflection

These components are mixed with components called *dopants* (like erbium), which adjusts their refractive indices. The difference between the refractive indices of the two different kinds of glass causes most of the emitted light to bounce off the cladding and stay within the core, traveling to the endpoint.

The critical angle requirement is met by controlling the angle at which light is beamed into the core.

Optical Fibers

Earlier in this chapter, we told you that glass (as you know it) is not the best for use in optical networking. Because of its composition and the manufacturing process, it is loaded with impurities, no matter how crystal clear it appears. For optical networking to happen, it must use a fantastically pure kind of glass. In this case, silica glass is the blend of choice. Even though it is exceptionally pure, there is still a little loss of light as the light travels through. The loss, however, is much less pronounced than with ordinary glass.

Pure glass isn't the end of the discussion on how to get information through the fiber without obstacles, especially when it comes to sending information through hundreds or thousands of miles. The key to sending a flash of light across a continent or beneath the ocean is in simple physics. Let's talk about refraction a bit more. Think back to seventh grade science class when the teacher was talking about light and refraction and blah, blah, blah… is this going to be on the final? Anyway, you may remember a demonstration where the teacher held a pencil behind a glass of water. As a jaded teenager, you may have expected just to see the pencil behind the glass. Instead, it was bent at an odd angle. This is how refraction manifests itself. Sure, it wasn't as cool as the baking soda and vinegar volcano or cooking a hot dog with tin foil, but can you send 10 Gbps with baking soda and vinegar?

Another junior high science classic is when you shined a light into a block of glass and rather than coming out of the opposite side, it bent and shot out at a funky angle. We see this in Figure 1-4. This happens because the light was refracted when it left the glass. As you may have noticed when you experimented further, if you beamed the light source into the glass at an angle greater than the *critical angle,* it would be bent inside the block until it left the block at a seemingly random location. The departure point may have seemed random to you; however, if you managed to shine the light at precisely the same location each and every time, the light would have exited the block at precisely the same spot.

Light is refracted within the block (and within a strand of optical fiber) because of refractive indices and Snell's Law. Snell's Law tells us how light—moving from one environment to another, like between air and water or core and cladding—is bent within a material. The refractive index of a material tells us how dense a particular material is.

Once you have a core of pure silica, an extra layer of glass (called *cladding*) is wrapped around the core. The cladding has a lower refractive index than the core. The difference in refractive indices guides the light into the core and prevents the light from escaping through the sides of the fiber.

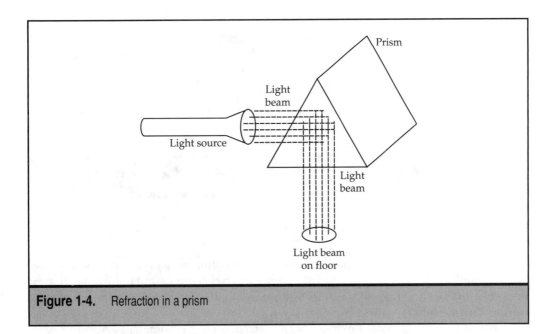

Figure 1-4.   Refraction in a prism

Earlier, we said that large glass rods weren't the ideal way to send information across an optical network. But that doesn't mean that all fiber has to be the smallest diameter object made by man. There can be (and are) varying diameters of fiber core. The size of a fiber's core will determine how light travels through it. A wave of light has a physical size. We may not be able to see it with the human eye, but as Figure 1-5 shows, a wavelength of light has a physical dimension that must be accommodated by the size of the optical fiber. If the fiber is too narrow, the wavelength won't be able to fit inside. An optical signal can generate many different light waves, which can travel through the fiber simultaneously.

This is the method used in *multimode* fibers (which provides a medium over which a number of concurrent transmissions can be sent). Unfortunately, this can also cause problems as the waves arrive at the end of the fiber and are out of sync. Most optical networks use *single-mode* fiber, which has a rather small fiber core (about 9 micrometers—a micrometer is a millionth of a meter), thus ensuring that only a single light wave traverses the fiber, alleviating receiving problems.

NOTE: To get an idea of just how tiny a nanometer is, look at the letter "o" anywhere on this page. That letter is about a millimeter across (using scientific notation, this is expressed as 10^{-3} meters).

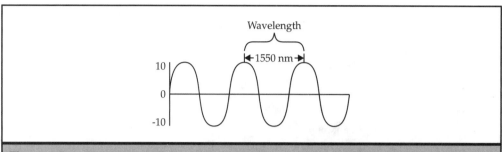

Figure 1-5. Though invisible to the human eye, a wavelength of light has a physical size

Fiber 101

In a nonoptical networking scenario, the wires connecting networking components are simple lengths of copper wire. The most prevalent is twisted pair, but there are still some networks out there using coaxial cable. But optical networks, on the other hand, connect components with fiber optic cabling.

Fiber optic cables contain extremely thin strands (10 micrometers across) of silica glass, which are then encased in a thicker, denser layer of silica glass (about 125 micrometers across). Once a protective wrap is applied, the fiber optic cable is a quarter of a millimeter in diameter. As you remember from our earlier discussion, the glass used within the fiber is highly pure, thus ensuring that the photons keep moving. Also, these strands of glass can be hundreds or thousands of miles long.

A number of factors go into the design and construction of optical fiber. This section takes a closer look at such issues as size, construction, and design.

Design

Optical fiber is composed of three parts:

▼ The *core*, which carries the light

■ *Cladding*, which traps the light in the core, causing total internal reflection

▲ The *Buffer*, which is the insulating wrap protecting the fiber

Figure 1-6 shows how these parts fit together to make fiber optic cabling.

NOTE: The difference between the optical density of a given material and a vacuum is the material's *refractive index*.

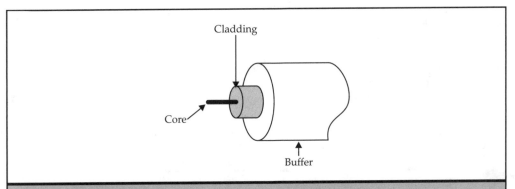

Figure 1-6.   The components that make up a piece of fiber optic cabling

To get a better understanding of how fiber works, let's follow a few photons from their origins, across the fiber to their final destination. Figure 1-7 shows our photonic friends as they make this journey.

1. First, the light source (in this case a laser) converts the network's electrical signal into pulses of light.
2. The light is injected into the core of the fiber.
3. The photons bounce off of the border between the core and the cladding. Because the core and the cladding have different refractive indices, the photons are bounced back into the core.
4. The photons continue through the length of the fiber.
5. Ultimately, they exit the fiber and are converted back into electrical signals by the light detector.
6. Because the fiber doesn't exist in a harm-free environment, the core and cladding are encased in a protective wrap called the buffer. The buffer makes the fiber more durable and easy to handle.

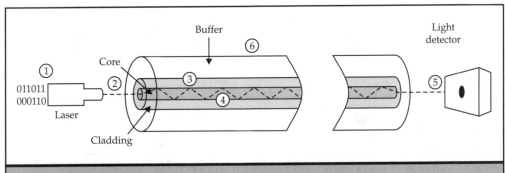

Figure 1-7.   How light travels through fiber optic cabling

Types of Fiber

Fiber comes in two basic types, single-mode and multimode. Figure 1-8 illustrates the difference between these types of fiber.

▼ **Single-mode fiber** has a core size of only about six times the wavelength of the fiber. In turn, this causes all the light to travel across a single path (in optical networking parlance, a path is referred to a *mode*). Single-mode fiber is useful because modal dispersion disappears and the bandwidth of the fiber is at least 100 times greater than graded index fiber.

NOTE: Modal dispersion occurs when an optical pulse is broadened due to different fiber modes traveling at different speeds.

▲ **Multimode fiber** allows light to travel across several different paths through the core of the fiber, which enter and leave the fiber at various angles.

Multimode fiber can further be broken down into two different types of fiber. They differ based on the index. Two types of multimode fiber exist, distinguished by the index

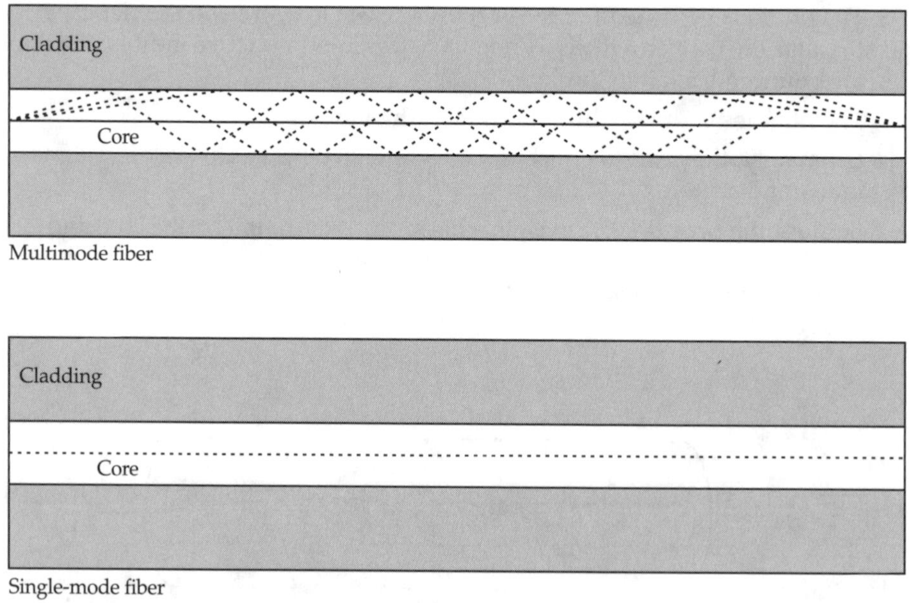

Cladding

Core

Multimode fiber

Cladding

Core

Single-mode fiber

Figure 1-8.   How single-mode and multimode fiber types differ

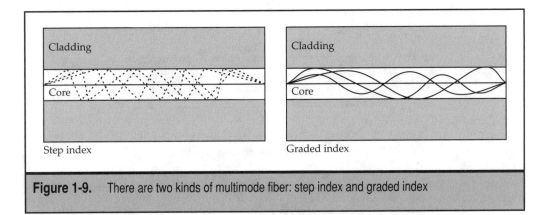

Figure 1-9.   There are two kinds of multimode fiber: step index and graded index

profile of their cores and how light travels in them. Figure 1-9 above illustrates the differences between these types of fiber.

▼   **Step index** fiber has a core made from a single type of glass. Light within the fiber travels in straight lines and reflects off the cladding. Step index fiber has a numerical aperture that is determined by the differences in the indices of refraction of the core and cladding. Because each mode of light travels a different path, a pulse of light is dispersed while traveling through the fiber, thereby restricting the bandwidth of step index fiber.

▲   **Graded index** fiber has a core that is composed of many different layers of glass. The layers differ because of their densities, thereby transmitting light along a parabolic path. In glass with a lower index of refraction, light travels faster as it approaches the outside of the core. Conversely, light traveling closest to the core will travel at the slowest pace. Since the fiber contains these different layers of glass, the bandwidth capacity of the fiber is 100 times greater than for step index fiber.

Size Matters

Fiber can also be categorized by its size. The most popular fiber in multimode today is 62.5/125. As Figure 1-10 shows, this is a measurement of the diameter of the core (62.5 micrometers) and the cladding (125 micrometers).

The first multimode fiber in wide use was 50/125. Telephone companies needing more bandwidth for long-distance uses were the first to adopt this type of fiber. Because it has a small core and a low numeric aperture, it was difficult to connect to LED sources. Because of this difficulty, a move was made to 100/140 fiber. It worked well, but because the core was so large, it was expensive to manufacture. Further, it had a unique cladding that required connector manufacturers to develop connectors specifically for it. The next popular size of fiber was 85/125. It provided connectivity to LED sources but used the same connectors as other fibers. Finally, 62.5/125 became the *de facto* standard for when

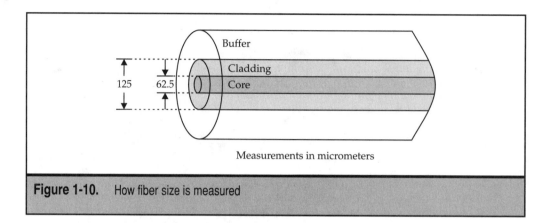

Figure 1-10. How fiber size is measured

IBM turned to 62.5/125 for its fiber optic hardware. When this occurred, other types of fiber have dropped away, leaving 62.5/125 as the industry standard.

In most deployments, you'll find single-mode fiber, because of its better performance at higher bit rates and its lower loss; it allows faster and longer links (without having to install amplifiers) for long-distance telecommunications. Single-mode fiber is also used in CATV, since analog CATV networks use laser sources designed for single-mode fiber. A number of other high-speed networks use single-mode fiber either in support of gigabit data rates or to carry links across long distances. Table 1-2 shows some of common sizes of fiber optic cabling for different types of fiber.

Fiber Type	Core/Cladding Diameter (in microns)
Step index	200/240
Multimode	50/125
Graded index	62.5/125
	85/125 (no longer used)
	100/140 (no longer used)
Single-mode	8-9/125

Table 1-2. Sizes of Various Types of Fiber Optic Cabling

LET THERE BE LIGHT

The center of all optical networking is something all around us—light. Without the ability to harness the light, concentrate it, and tell it what it needs to do, there would be no way to transmit at such high rates of speed.

In this section, we take a closer look at light—not just the stuff that radiates off the sun or buzzes overhead in our offices, but the kind of light that makes optical networks happen. We'll examine the building blocks of light (photons) and talk about how they differ from the electrons in conventional, electrically based networks. Next, we'll take a look at the sources of light that generate those photons. Finally, we'll talk about what happens to the light once it gets where it needs to go.

Photons Versus Electrons

In this corner, weighing in with a mass of 9.1×10^{-28} grams and a radius of less than 10^{-18} meters, the electron! And in this corner, weighing in at nothing and having the same size as an atom, the photon! Contestants, go to your corner and come out propagating!

In the battle between photons and electrons, the electron will always hit the mat first. Unlike a fistfight between two human combatants, size isn't on the electron's side in this bout. Because photons are so much smaller and zippier than electrons, photons are able to move faster, thereby making them perfect for high-speed networking.

Photons are particles with no electrical charge and no mass, but they do have energy and momentum, a property that allows photons to affect other particles when they collide with them. Photons travel at the speed of light, which is about 186,000 miles per second.

Conversely, electrons do have a mass—albeit an extremely tiny mass. That, however, is where the difference becomes important, because that is how the photon beats the electron. Photons move at the ultimate speed—the speed of light—and they leave electrons spinning in the dust, because they travel at just two-thirds the speed of light. Only objects without mass can travel at the speed of light. Objects with mass must travel at slower speeds, and nothing can travel at speeds faster than the speed of light.

Light Sources

Light emitters and light detectors are active devices at opposite ends of an optical network. Light sources, or light emitters, are transmit-side devices that convert electrical signals to light pulses. The process of this conversion, also known as *modulation*, and shown in Figure 1-11, can be accomplished by externally modulating a continuous wave of light or by using a device that can generate modulated light directly.

Once light comes in to the receiving end, as Figure 1-12 shows, *light detectors* perform the opposite function of light emitters. They are receive-side opto-electronic devices that convert light pulses into electrical signals.

The source of light in an optical network must have very specific traits for it to be effective. Additionally, the type of light source you use is an important consideration, because depending on its characteristics, it can be a limiting factor on your optical link's

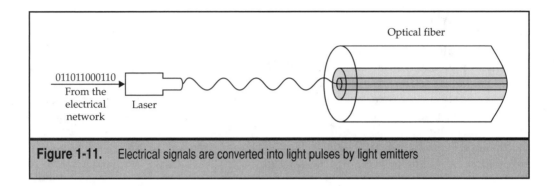

Figure 1-11. Electrical signals are converted into light pulses by light emitters

performance. In order for a light source to be effective, it must be compact, stable, long lasting, and monochromatic.

NOTE: Monochromatic is a relative term. Light sources only exist within a specific range. A light source's stability is a measure of how constant its intensity and wavelength are.

Two general types of light sources are used in optical networking: light emitting diodes (LEDs) and laser diodes or semiconductor lasers.

LEDs

LEDs are slow devices, best suited for speeds less than 1 Gbps. They exhibit a high spectrum width and transmit light in a wide cone. An advantage of LEDs is that they are inexpensive, and they are often used in multimode fiber communications.

NOTE: Of course, calling LEDs slow when they can transmit 1 Gpbs may sound silly—1 Gbps is pretty fast. However, when you compare them to lasers, you can see the distinction.

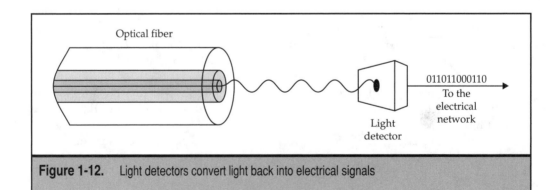

Figure 1-12. Light detectors convert light back into electrical signals

You see LEDs around you every day. The indicator light on your computer's hard drive is probably an LED, and the light on your cellular telephone that blinks when a call comes in is also an LED.

Lasers

According to Hollywood, lasers (Light Amplification by the Stimulated Emission of Radiation) can be used to cut James Bond in half, shoot at Romulans, or blow up planets from the comfort of the Death Star. In reality, however, most lasers are far more benign. Rather than being tools of destruction, lasers are used in such devices as:

▼ Compact disc (CD) players

■ Digital video disc (DVD) players

■ CD-ROM players/burners

■ Law enforcement speed guns (okay, that's an evil application)

▲ Grocery store bar code readers

Blowing up peaceful worlds as a means to get under the Princess's skin is one application of a laser; a more earthly function is to transmit data at extremely high speeds across an optical network.

Unlike a flashlight whose beam dissipates into the night sky, a laser concentrates light so that it can shoot through a fiber for 500 kilometers or more before it has to be amplified or regenerated. When a digital electrical signal is converted to laser pulses, an optical fiber becomes an extraordinarily fast and high-volume way to transmit data.

Physically speaking, when we think of lasers, the tiniest devices that come to mind are the laser pointers only the hippest execs use during board meetings. But in optical networking, the lasers are incredibly tiny—about the size of a grain of sand—and made out of the same materials used for semiconductors. Once they are packaged and ready to ship, the entire laser device is smaller than a nine-volt battery.

Whereas LEDs are best suited for multimode optical networking, lasers are better suited for single-mode fiber applications. Figure 1-13 illustrates how laser light is introduced into fiber. The laser chip diode emits a beam of light in one direction to be focused by the lens onto the fiber; in the other direction, the light is directed to a photodiode. The photodiode is angled to reduce back reflections into the laser cavity and provides a way of monitoring the laser's output, providing data so that adjustments can be made.

To work in an optical network, lasers must have:

▼ Precise wavelength

■ Narrow spectrum width

■ Sufficient power

▲ Control of the change in frequency of a signal over time (known as *chirp*)

Lasers satisfy the first three requirements, but chirp can be influenced by the means used to modulate the signal.

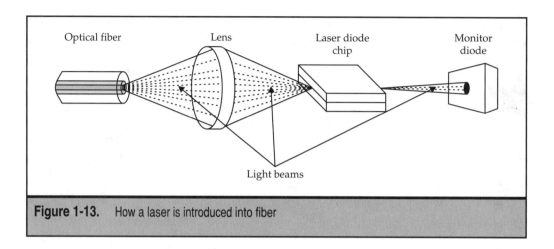

Figure 1-13.   How a laser is introduced into fiber

Directly modulated lasers modulate light internally, while external modulation is achieved with an external device. When lasers are directly modulated, chirp can become a limiting factor at bit rates exceeding 10 Gbps. External modulation, however, helps limit chirp.

Light Detectors

Once the photons have traversed the optical fiber, the end device must receive them. After their receipt, they must be converted from photons back into electrons and sent into the electrical network. To accomplish this task, a light detector is employed. Light detectors are small devices called *photodiodes*. Photodiodes absorb light, then convert the light flashes into electrons that can be read by computers and other devices.

There are two types of light detectors in popular use:

▼   **Positive-intrinsic-negative (PIN) photodiode**   PIN photodiodes work on principles similar to, but the reverse of, LEDs. Rather than emitting light, they absorb it, and photons are converted back into electrons on a 1:1 relationship.

▲   **Avalanche photodiode (APD)**   APDs are similar devices to PIN photodiodes but provide gain through an amplification process: One photon acting on the device releases many electrons.

PIN photodiodes have many advantages, including low cost and reliability, but APDs have higher sensitivity and accuracy. On the other hand, APDs are more expensive than PIN photodiodes, they can have very high current requirements, and they are temperature sensitive.

AMPLIFICATION

You can see the stands are full of people standing and cheering on this sun-dappled afternoon. Even though there are thousands of fans in the bleachers, you can't hear them over the whine of the finely tuned engine in the ultra-sleek craft you're piloting. It's 95 degrees outside, but the rushing blacktop underneath your tires kicks the heat up another half dozen degrees. What's worse is that all the flame retardant gear isn't helping matters any. You've had your racecar teasing 200 mph for the past hour and you're not even halfway through the race. Tired and low on fuel, you can't even see out of the windshield anymore because of all the gunk that has accumulated. If you don't refuel and replenish soon, you'll be dead on the racetrack. The next stop: the pit.

Though this is a scenario NASCAR drivers encounter every Sunday on television, bits charging across a fiber optic network need their own pit stops. After jetting through miles and miles of optical fiber, the photons lose their momentum to things like dispersion and attenuation. In order to get back up to speed, optical pulses don't stop in for new tires and a slug of Gatorade; instead, as Figure 1-14 shows, their pit stops take place in amplifiers. Once the light pulse exits, it is as strong as it was when it originated.

Get a Boost

Let's say that on the racetrack, cars run on two different types of fuel—leaded and unleaded. If you are whizzing along the track, you must ensure that you stop into the correct pit. If your car uses unleaded fuel and you pull into a pit with leaded fuel, your car might as well be towed around the track by Elmer the mule.

Optical networks face the same scenario. The light pulses won't be helped if they are channeled through an amplifier that handles electrical signals. Rather, they must go through an amplifier that is meant especially for optical signals. Furthermore, optical

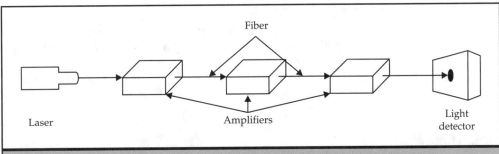

Figure 1-14.   Amplifiers give the photons a boost of energy to continue through the fiber

amplification removes a step that would slow down the process. If the light were to be amplified via an electrical amplifier, first the signal would have to be converted from photons back into electrons, amplified, then turned from electrons back into photons and retransmitted.

But as your car turns in to the correct pit and your fuel is replenished, unfortunately so is something else. The exhaust of your engine gets a little bit thicker with each stop at the pit. As you make more pit stops, the exhaust becomes thicker and more acrid. In an optical network, this kind of amplification is known as *gain* and is measured in units called *decibels (dB)*.

> **NOTE:** A decibel is calculated as one tenth of the logarithm of the output power divided by the input power.

Like NASCAR racing, optical signals can get a boost a few different places in the network. For instance:

▼ At the beginning of a race, the car will have been inspected with a fine-toothed comb and tuned within an inch of its life. Optical signals can get a similar boost immediately after leaving the laser. This is called *power amplification.*

■ In the middle of the race, the car can swing into the pit for fuel, for air, and to get the bugs scraped off the windshield. In optical networking, this kind of boost is known as *line amplification.*

▲ At the very end of the race, the driver may decide just to floor it, not worry about fuel conservation or upcoming curves in the road. With the checkered flag in sight, he or she might just go for the gusto. This type of amplification at the end of the optical pulses' journey is known as *preamplification.*

Erbium-Doped Fiber Amplifiers (EDFAs)

One way to replenish those bits is by *doping* the fiber. An erbium-doped fiber amplifier (EDFA) is a few meters of optical fiber that has been doped—or infused—with a few atoms of the rare earth element *erbium.*

As Figure 1-15 shows, the optical signal enters this length of fiber, along with additional light from a *pump* laser. The pump laser is designed to stimulate the erbium ions and beef up the data-carrying signal.

How They Work

Remember that kid from high school who bounced off the walls every time he ate a bag of Skittles? Now, do you remember how he was usually eating a bag of Skittles, which caused him to work everyone's last nerve? Think of erbium-doped fiber as that kid—let's call him Lester. His body chemistry was such that consuming sugar turned him into a whirling dervish, which usually caused him to act the most like a doof when you were trying to impress one of the cheerleaders.

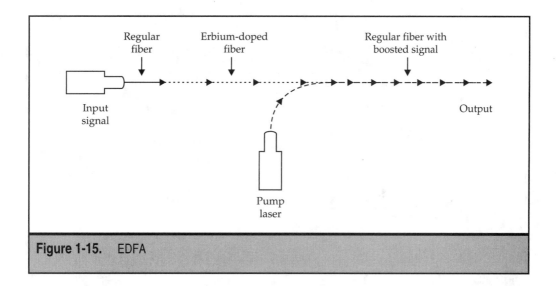

Figure 1-15.   EDFA

Now, think about regular optical fiber. Since you probably never got into any kind of trouble—sugar induced or otherwise—you're that nice, plain, dutiful, functional fiber making up the rest of the network.

When you give Lester a giant bag of Skittles, he gets even more excited, thanks to the sugar rush. This is much like what happens to the erbium ions when the pump laser hits them. If you continue to pump Skittles into Lester (and the erbium-doped fiber with laser light), they both get so excited they can't possibly get any more worked up.

Now, think of an incoming data transmission as a bottle of Mountain Dew. As soon as that super-sugary pop hits Lester's gullet, it's coming back out and it's not coming out alone. Because Lester is so sugared up, it is accompanied by all the material from earlier pumpings. This, in its essence, is how EDFA works. As the optical signal is expelled through the EDFA, it has been increased in intensity many times over.

Erbium gets excited at a number of energy levels, but its ions rest in the *ground state* (they are unexcited). The ions can only be excited (or pumped up with sugar) when they get hit with a 1480 nm pump laser. This gets them to the first excited state, as shown in Figure 1-16.

If erbium ions stay in their excited state long enough, they will eventually fall back to the ground state—much like the mellow Lester after a long day of sugaring it up.

As the ions return to the ground state, they have some extra energy to get rid of, which manifests itself as a photon. This phenomenon is known as *spontaneous emission* because as the ions return to the ground state, they expel photons without any outside impetus. These emissions can build up in the amplifier and are known as *amplified spontaneous emission (ASE)*. Like the build-up of smoke and stink from the NASCARs we talked about earlier, ASE adds noise to the amplification system.

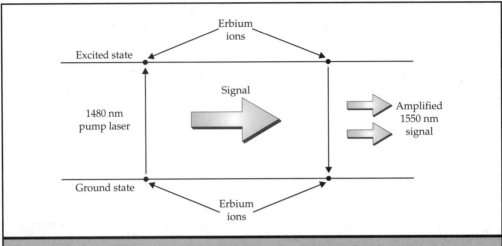

Figure 1-16.   Erbium ions get excited when a 1480 nm pump laser strikes them

Kicking It Up a Notch

Earlier, we established that the ideal wavelength for an optical signal is 1550 nm. Since the visible spectrum for humans is between roughly 400 to 700 nm, we can't see light emanating at 1550 nm. If a signal comes into the EDFA at that wavelength, then it can cause some excited ions to return to the ground state and give off photons. This is called *stimulated* emission, because it is the signal itself causing the photonic emissions. Because the photons are emitted at precisely the same wavelength as the incoming signal, those photons become a part of the signal.

This isn't a bad thing, however. The signal now has more photons than when it entered the EDFA; it has been amplified. This can continue down the remaining few feet of fiber, until many photons have joined the signal photons and the signal has been amplified greatly. This can occur at a number of wavelengths between 1530 nm and 1580 nm. This is known as *conventional-band* or *C-band* amplification. EDFAs can also be designed to provide amplification between 1580 nm and 1610 nm. This is known as *long-band* or *L-band* amplification.

Think of a 1480 nm pump laser as a firecracker. You light the fuse, it blows up with a respectable little explosion. A 980 nm laser pump, on the other hand, can be thought of as an M-80. As Figure 1-17 shows, the 980 nm laser pump blows the erbium ions into a much higher state of excitement than the little 1480 nm pump. But the higher the ions are shot into the sky, the less time they will spend at that altitude. They will stay at that excited state for only nanoseconds before they drop down to the next state. Once they reach the next state, they stay at that level much longer than the ions that were excited by the 1480 nm laser pump—milliseconds, this time. And the longer they stay at the excited state, the more likely that the signal will come along and generate stimulated emission.

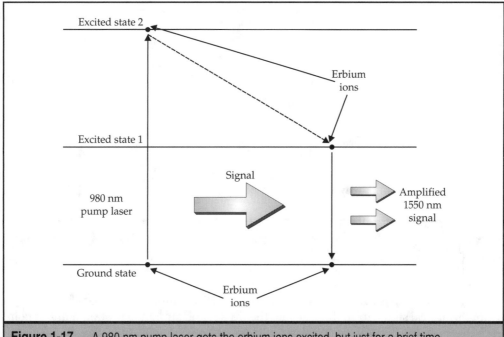

Figure 1-17. A 980 nm pump laser gets the erbium ions excited, but just for a brief time

Furthermore, this reduces unwanted spontaneous emissions that cause noise to be injected into the photon stream. Because of this behavior, a 980 nm pump provides greater amplification efficiency and is the favored pump wavelength for most EDFAs.

EDFA is used most often in submarine systems, where optical signals must travel for thousands of miles in the briny deep. EDFAs can be manufactured and placed in waterproof boxes at 50-mile intervals. To assure reliability, these EDFAs incorporate a simple design. Though popular on the ocean floor, EDFAs are also gaining popularity on dry land.

Semiconductor Optical Amplifiers

A semiconductor optical amplifier works a lot like a basic laser. They share a common structure, each with two hunks of semiconductor material sandwiching another material in between them. The "meat" of this semiconductor sandwich forms the *active layer*. This is shown in Figure 1-18. When an electrical current is run through the device, the electrons get excited but then fall back to the nonexcited ground state (a similar process to EDFAs), sending out photons.

However, there are two major differences between a standard laser and a semiconductor optical amplifier. In a standard laser, the goal is to keep light bouncing back and forth within the cavity. In a standard laser, this is accomplished by bouncing the optical

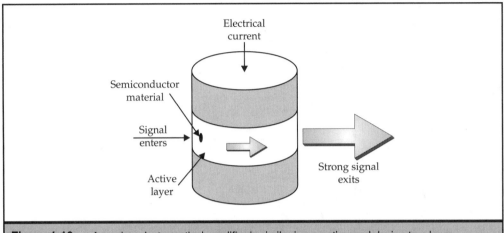

Figure 1-18. A semiconductor optical amplifier is similar in operation and design to a laser

signal between two mirrors. In a semiconductor optical amplifier, on the other hand, we want the optical signal to go directly into the cavity, and straight back out, without being reflected back into the cavity. Thus, no mirrors are used to reflect the signal.

Further, we want a specific wavelength to be issued from the standard laser. In a semiconductor optical amplifier, we want to amplify light at as many wavelengths as possible. This is necessary because it is possible in the optical network that the signal may come in on many different wavelengths. By covering a range of wavelengths, it is possible to amplify them simultaneously.

Now, the incoming light from the optical signals moving down to their ground states stimulates the electrons within the semiconductor. As they make this transition, they send out a photon, which just happens to match the photon that caused the emission in the first place. The amount of photons representing a section of a signal has doubled, and that's how semiconductor optical amplification occurs.

Semiconductor optical amplifiers don't provide as much amplification as EDFAs at the most common 1550 nm–range wavelengths. They can, however, be used to amplify signals in the 1300 nm transmission range. This range is becoming more and more popular, and as demand for more wavelengths grows, look for semiconductor optical amplifiers to become more prevalent.

Raman Amplification

You and a few buddies are out having a great time. Your college football team just won the big homecoming game, and you're ready to have a makeshift party in the street. You guys are stoked, you're full of pride (and a few pints), and you just want to share your joy with the world. You could say that you're in an excited state. You're just like laser light injected from a Raman pump laser, coursing though a length of optical fiber.

But as you walk through the streets of your college town, you notice some other students who aren't in such a celebratory mood. Maybe they have to study for exams the next morning; maybe (gulp) they aren't football fans. Whatever the case, they're just not very excited. Party people that you and your buddies are, you're determined to get them in good cheer.

If you, your friends, and the bystanders were light, the fact that the bystanders have less energy that you would mean that they have a longer wavelength—around 1550 nm. Because you and your posse are in such an excited state, your wavelength is shorter—about 1450 nm. But as you and your friends run down the street, hoping to stop into a local bar and hoist a few in celebration, you suddenly notice that all the bars are closed. Even worse, there are police cars all over, so you can't even work up a good, old-fashioned, post-game riot. After all these obstacles, your mood dips down to the level of the people in the crowd. What happened is that you gave up some of your energy to the closed bars and the vigilant police force, causing you to have the same amount of energy as the crowd. And as the crowd goes on its merry way, so do you. Now you've become part of the 1550 nm crowd. This is what happens in *stimulated Raman scattering.*

The idea behind Raman scattering is that a shorter-wavelength pump laser traveling through optical fiber, along with a signal wavelength, scatters some atoms in the fiber, loses some of its energy to the atoms, and continues on its journey, this time at the same wavelength as the signal. Now, the signal has additional photons added to it, thereby amplifying the signal. This is illustrated in Figure 1-19.

Raman amplification is different from EDFA, because there is no need to specially dope the fiber. Amplification usually occurs within the entire length of the fiber, rather than in one particular place, within a special device, like EDFA. Amplification within the length of fiber is known as *distributed amplification.* To the fiber carrying your signal, you

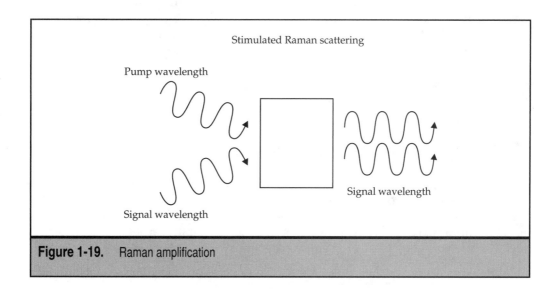

Figure 1-19.   Raman amplification

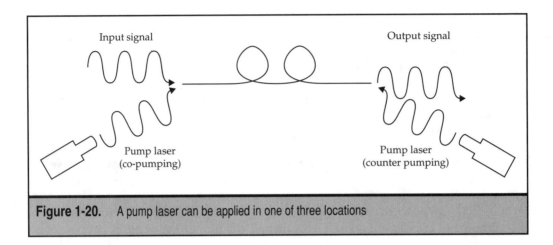

Figure 1-20. A pump laser can be applied in one of three locations

add a pump laser, which will amplify the signal along the fiber's run until the pump signal ultimately fades away.

You can apply a pump laser in different locations to generate different kinds of Raman amplification. This is illustrated in Figure 1-20 above.

▼ Applying the pump at the beginning of the fiber is called *co-pumping*.

■ Applying the pump at the end of the fiber is called *counter-pumping*. This placement generally yields better results than co-pumping.

▲ Pumps can be applied at both ends, in what is called *co-counter pumping*.

A pump laser emitting a single wavelength is useful for transmissions sent across single-mode fiber. However, if you are using a wavelength division multiplexing (WDM) system, several different pump wavelengths will need to be generated and used together to amplify every wavelength.

NOTE: We'll explain WDM in more depth in Chapter 3.

OPTICAL NETWORKING OBSTACLES

Even though optical networks are fast, robust, and error-free, there are still chinks in the optical networking armor. Optical networking faces a number of challenges that prevent it from being a perfect medium. Such factors as attenuation and dispersion can cause signal loss within an optical network. Let's take a closer look at the causes of these obstacles and discuss some ways these problems can be mitigated.

Attenuation

Plain old glass, we told you earlier, is crummy when it comes to sending information across an optical network. The light is blocked by impurities and, as a result, doesn't come across at the receiving end. But even in very pure silica glass fiber, light *attenuates*. Attenuation means that light is lost within the fiber. Attenuation is due to several factors:

▼ *Absorption* of light to atoms within the fiber

■ *Rayleigh scattering*, scattering caused by miniscule changes in the core's refractive index

▲ *Mie scattering*, a result of the core not being a perfect cylinder

The primary causes of attenuation are the length of the fiber and the wavelength of the light. Figure 1-21 shows the loss in decibels per kilometer (dB/km) by wavelength from Rayleigh scattering, absorption, and total attenuation from all causes.

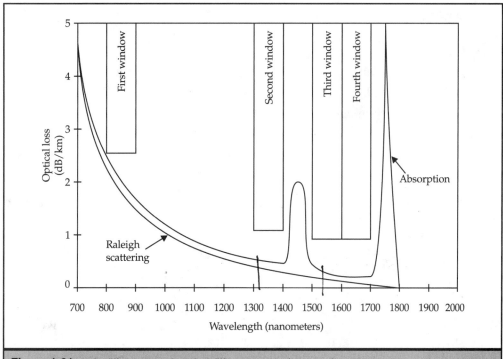

Figure 1-21.   At different wavelengths, different types of attenuation can occur

The best way to fight attenuation is through amplification. Amplification keeps the photonic emissions strong and prevents them from falling into such pitfalls as attenuation.

Dispersion

When a pulse of light is traveling along a fiber, the signal is not only susceptible to attenuation but can also be distorted. This distortion within fiber is called *dispersion*. Dispersion can happen in several different ways and produce different results.

- ▼ *Chromatic dispersion* is caused by different wavelengths of light traveling at different speeds. Optical signals cannot be completely pure wavelengths. They must contain a range within the wavelength, so they smear as they travel through the fiber.

- ▲ *Polarization mode dispersion (PMD)* is another way light signals travel at different speeds through fiber. This arises because the fiber material is slightly denser along one side than the other, and it is more difficult to predict and correct than chromatic dispersion.

In single-mode fiber, chromatic dispersion has two components: material dispersion and waveguide dispersion.

- ▼ *Material dispersion* happens when wavelengths of light travel at different speeds through the fiber. Light sources, no matter how narrow, emit a number of wavelengths within a range. When this range of wavelengths travels through a medium, each individual wavelength arrives at a different time.

- ▲ *Waveguide dispersion* happens because of the different refractive indices of the fiber's core and cladding.

This result of the phenomenon of waveguide dispersion is a propagation delay in one or more of the wavelengths relative to others. Because fiber shows losses at particular wavelengths, this tells us that fiber has specific wavelengths at which it prefers to transmit data (why fight the current? Go with the flow). Optical networks transmit at wavelengths at or around 1550 nm. This is the point of minimum loss in standard optical fiber, and the reason 1550 nm transmissions are so popular.

Take a look back at Figure 1-21. In addition to highlighting where attenuation occurs, the figure also shows where the best wavelengths for optical networking exist.

Nonlinear Effects

Sir Isaac Newton's third law of motion makes this interesting observation: For every action, there is an equal and opposite reaction. In a linear system, an optical network's output is directly proportional to the input. Think of it this way: if you love pizza, every slice of pizza you eat steadily increases your joy.

That's all fine, good, and predictable with linear systems, but what happens in a non-linear system? Unfortunately, a nonlinear system becomes more and more difficult to predict. Comparing linear and nonlinear effects (as shown in Figure 1-22), we can see how the two diverge as the nonlinear effects curve away from linear effects. Let's carry the pizza example a little further. Let's say that you love Mario's cheese pizzas. With every slice you eat, your joy consistently increases (this is represented as a linear effect). However, you go to a buddy's house, but there isn't a Mario's in his neighborhood. Instead, he only has a Luigi's and on top of that, he orders pineapple and Canadian bacon. This time, with each slice you eat, your pleasure doesn't double, instead, your pleasure (*output* in a nonlinear system) is less than double. This is represented in Figure 1-22 by the nonlinear effect sketch.

Charting your joy relative to different slices of pizza is certainly fascinating, but what does that have to do with optical networking? This phenomenon applies to optical networking, because nonlinear effects are becoming more evident with the introduction of WDM systems and ever-increasing bit rates. Linear effects (such as attenuation and dispersion) can be compensated for, but nonlinear effects accumulate. They are the fundamental limiting mechanisms to the amount of data that can be transmitted in optical fiber. Because of these factors, the amount of optical power within fiber is increasing; and with high optical powers, nonlinear effects become noticeable. In low-bit-rate systems, they are largely invisible.

There are two types of nonlinear effects: Kerr effects and scattering effects.

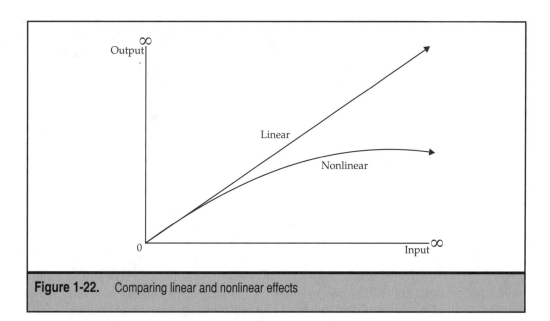

Figure 1-22. Comparing linear and nonlinear effects

Kerr Effects

Kerr effects consist of three different phenomena. In an optical fiber, the core has a specific refractive index that determines how light travels through it. Depending on how intense is the light traveling through the core, this index can change. This intensity-dependence, known as the Kerr effect, can cause the following issues:

  ▼ **Self phase modulation**   This occurs when a wavelength can spread into adjacent wavelengths on its own.

  ■ **Cross phase modulation**   This occurs when several different wavelengths in a WDM system can cause each other to spread out.

  ▲ **Four wave mixing**   This occurs when two or more wavelengths can interact to create an entirely new wavelength.

Scattering Effects

There are two types of nonlinear *scattering effects* to be aware of in optical networks.

  ▼ **Stimulated Raman scattering**   This occurs when light loses energy to molecules in the fiber and is reemitted at a longer wavelength. This is due to the loss of energy.

  ▲ **Stimulated Brillouin scattering**   This occurs when light within the fiber creates acoustic waves. This can scatter the light into different wavelengths and disrupt the signal.

Because of nonlinear effects, like scattering and Kerr effects, data can be lost or corrupted. However, these effects are not total thorns in our side. After all, a similar phenomenon occurs to make Raman amplification possible. So, if you prefer, you can look at this with a glass-half-full point of view.

Limitations

Beyond the very specific technical obstacles we discussed previously, there are other barriers to optical networking. These obstacles tend to revolve around one of the classic obstacles to anything—money. Not only are optical networks more expensive than traditional electronic networks, but also there are other cost considerations that must be dealt with. Though the issues listed in the sections to follow are current obstacles, efforts are underway to ameliorate them and make optical networking easier and less expensive to develop.

Provisioning

Optical networking equipment is great in that it provides high bandwidth and high speed. But ISPs that are switching over to all-fiber systems have a bit of a problem. It's not a technical problem so much as it is an organizational issue. In order to make money from their investment in optical equipment, ISPs need service-provisioning hardware and software that allows them to manage their networks, automatically allocating capacity, tracking usage, and providing statistics for billing purposes.

The big hurdle right now is that there's no agreement on just how optical provisioning should be implemented. Currently, vendors are using proprietary solutions. Many are using solutions based on multiprotocol label switching (MPLS) for optical networks. An effort is underway to develop MPLS for this task, but the completed version is a long way off.

NOTE: MPLS is a way to forward packets through an internetwork. Routers, situated on the edge of a network, apply simple labels to packets. Then, routers, switches, or other network devices within the network can switch packets according to the labels.

Furthermore, there is considerable disagreement in the industry as to whether MPLS is the best way to provision optical networks. Problems include ISPs with legacy equipment that cannot handle MPLS, all the way down to the physical layout of a city itself.

The Last Mile

"The Last Mile" sounds like it should be one of those football movies from the 1970s where Burt Reynolds played a quarterback with some fatal illness. His final act before dying bravely was to carry the pigskin across the goal line, with his archrival from Denver breathing down his neck.

In reality, however, the Last Mile is the gap in the all-fiber optic network between end-user buildings and the main fiber optic networks that circle around and through cities. The Last Mile is typically where high-speed networks break down, because the space between the phone company's equipment and a building (hence, "The Last Mile") is typically old, slow twisted copper wire. Bridging this gap has been a major obstacle to the fast and cost-effective deployment of broadband service. If you've ever tried to get digital subscriber line service to your home or business, you'll understand exactly what an albatross this Last Mile business can be.

So why not replace all the old, crusty copper wire with fresh, fast, fiber? It's all about expense. In order to replace that wiring, streets would need to be ripped up and replaced. One company that seems to have a workaround for this problem is CityNet. They are deploying last-mile fiber through a city's sewer pipes using a computer-controlled robot. It might be a while before a robot is stringing fiber through the sewers in your neighborhood, however, so the Last Mile problem is still something to take into consideration.

Expense

One of the biggest obstacles that can cause an immediate halt to any fiber project is the cost. Once a discussion of cost comes up, that's when you'll have to swim or get out of the pool. Fiber optic networks are more expensive than copper. On an average, fiber optic switch ports and adapter cards cost about 50 percent more than similar copper components.

But though this is an obstacle, the good news is that the climate is improving. When you factor in the cost savings associated with fiber (fewer repeaters and switches are needed in LAN installations, for instance), the overall cost drops to only about 20 percent more than a copper setup. In the past, fiber's big price tag had little to do with the equipment itself. The majority of the expense came from having to lay in transceivers and connectors. Thanks to new products in this area, optical networks are becoming more and more prevalent.

Optical networking is just like anything else in life. You have to take the good with the bad, the bitter with the sweet, and the lighting-fast bit rates with the Brillouin scattering. If you are willing to deal with some headaches, you should be able to reap the rewards of a high-speed, high-capacity network that will keep your data flowing at the speed of light.

SUMMARY

What makes the topic of optical networking so complex is also what makes it such a useful technology. The marriage of optics and networking creates unique capabilities, but it also creates unique challenges.

Optical networking allows for fantastic speeds in the transmission of voice and data. Conventionally speaking, electrical WANs make use of T-1 (1.544 Mbps) and T-3 (45 Mbps) connections. In a LAN environment, speeds are peppier, clocking in at 100 Mbps and even 1 Gbps. Most optical networks are enjoying WAN speeds of 10 Gbps, though many can go as fast at 40 Gbps. In the labs, speeds of 1.6 Tbps are being fine-tuned.

Optical networks use two different technologies to transmit data across the miles. First, there must be some way to turn data in electrical form into light. This is accomplished by a laser or an LED. Once converted into light, the data is transmitted across a silken fiber smaller than a human hair. The fiber is made out of extremely pure glass, which allows the light to traverse vast distances.

As much an improvement as fiber is over copper wire, it is not without its own roadblocks. Attenuation and dispersion are the two main culprits that can keep your optical network from achieving the long hauls of a metropolitan area network (MAN) or a WAN. However, using an amplifier can help resolve some of these problems.

It's also important to recognize that optical networking is not a panacea. Optical networking can work just great inside an Internet service provider or as part of the Internet's backbone, for example. That functionality, however, hits a huge speed bump when it encounters the Last Mile problem. Additionally, though costs are coming down, the expense involved in an optical network means that one can't just build one on a whim.

CHAPTER 2

History of Optical Networking

If we wanted to be quite literal, the roots of optical networking (that is, communication via light signals) could be traced back to our cave-dwelling ancestors. For instance, as we see in Figure 2-1, whenever Grog starts a fire outside the communal cave, the rest of the tribe sees the light of the fire and knows that he's just run down an antelope and is preparing dinner. Of course, this example takes the notion of optical networking to an extreme, but the roots of optical networking are spread across dozens of small and large accomplishments throughout human history.

One might think that optical networking is a relatively new endeavor, made possible by the exponential growth of the Internet. In reality, optical networking (the basics of it at least) goes back hundreds of years. True, the ancient Egyptians didn't possess computer networks with 10 Gbps speeds (unless you subscribe to the teachings of Erich Von Daniken, in which case you know that the ancient Egyptians, in conjunction with extraterrestrial engineers, had more technological power 3000 years ago than we do today—but that's a discussion for another time). No, the Egyptians didn't have computer networks, but they did know about how to spin glass into fine threads.

With simple beginnings and the study and research of a number of scholars and inventors, optical networking has developed into the technological marvel it is today. In this chapter, we take a closer look at the roots of fiber optics and find out how we got from there to here.

The history of fiber optics and its evolution is a long and complex story owing much to inventors, scientists, and businessmen in a number of loosely related fields. We couldn't possibly tell the entire story in the space available, but a look at some of the high points (and low points) should give you an appreciation of how fiber optics have progressed.

OPTICAL NETWORKING THROUGH TIME

As with so many modern marvels, the basics of optical networking emerge from discoveries and research spanning centuries. If it wasn't for Benjamin Franklin's kite flying fetish, we wouldn't know about electricity. Likewise, optical networking owes much to the observations and discoveries of many researchers and laypeople.

In this section, we examine the foundations on which optical fiber is built. We look at the science behind fiber optics; the construction and evolution of optical fiber; and the earliest kinds of networks.

Discoveries and Innovation

In developing modern optical networking gear, no one at AT&T stood up and shouted, "Eureka! Let's stretch glass into fine threads and transmit information across it!" Rather, the notion of using light to carry sound from one point to another had already been steadily growing over the years. The idea of using glass as a transport medium was recognized better than a hundred years ago. But to develop fiber optics into a viable technology, it is necessary to understand how glass could be formed into threads and how light would travel through those threads.

Figure 2-1.   Grog the caveman's tribe knows when dinner's ready by the glow of the campfire

In this section, we take a closer look at when man first began pulling glass into fibers—for ornamental reasons first, and then realizing their scientific value years later. Then, we'll follow the tracks of time and talk about the men who discovered how light could be bent, and who introduced us to the principles on which fiber optics are based.

Ancient Designs

At the beginning of this chapter, we had a little fun with the notion of Grog the caveman's "optical network," which used the light of his fire to tell the tribe that dinner was ready. Though this illustrates a basic concept (sending messages with light), the physical and scientific roots of optical networking appeared 4500 years ago.

In Egypt and Mesopotamia, craftsmen were just starting to understand how to make glass. One thousand years later, they had honed their craft to mold sculptures out of glass. As man's knowledge and mastery of glass craftsmanship developed over the succeeding years, glassmakers were able to turn glass into ornaments and chandeliers that seemed to shine from within. They may not have known it at the time, but they were using internal reflection to get that shine.

By medieval times, scientists were studying how total internal reflection worked, but its mysteries wouldn't reveal themselves until the law of refraction was developed in the seventeenth century. Two hundred years later, the newest and most exciting subjects in physics didn't involve glass anymore. By the nineteenth century, glass was in window frames, in doors, and on kitchen tables everywhere. It had turned from a magical force that inspired the Egyptians three millennia earlier, to a common household item.

Semaphore Towers

With all due respect to Grog the caveman, the first optical network truly dates back to the 1790s. French engineer Claude Chappe developed an optical telegraph system consisting of a series of semaphores that were mounted on tall towers. Human operators would convey messages from one tower to the next until the message had reached its destination.

Operators inside the towers would gaze through telescopes to a neighboring tower, waiting for a message to come through. As Figure 2-2 illustrates, when a message was transmitted, they would relay that message by pulling ropes that would operate the semaphore. In turn, this would be observed by an operator in the next tower, who would repeat the message, and so forth.

Optical telegraphs were far from perfect, however. Because each tower had to be manned, they were labor intensive and expensive to operate. Further, the network couldn't be used in foul weather or at night, because of the lack of visibility. By the mid-nineteenth century the electric telegraph replaced the semaphore towers.

Fountains

Swiss physicist Daniel Colladon and French physicist Jacques Babinet discovered one of the first methods of bending light in the early 1840s. Coincidentally, both men discovered this phenomenon at about the same time, but in two different European cities.

Aquatic Optics   Colladon was a professor at the University of Geneva who was trying to demonstrate the properties of flowing water to his students. The students in the back of the classroom, however, couldn't see the water, so he used an arc lamp, focusing the light through a lens and into a water tank. As the rays of light in the water tank hit the edge of the jet at a glancing angle, total internal reflection kicked in, and the rays of light stayed within the stream of water. This effect is shown in Figure 2-3.

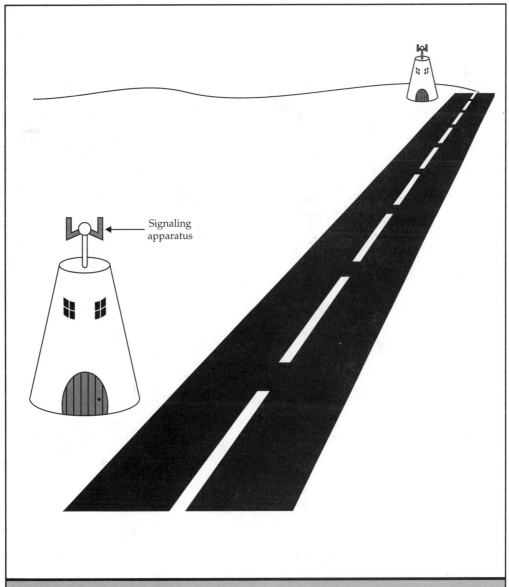

Figure 2-2.   Optical telegraphs used a network of semaphore stations that would relay a message across the countryside

Meanwhile, in Paris, Professor Babinet had rigged a somewhat similar device for his own demonstrations. Rather than using the system of pumping light into a water tank, Babinet focused candlelight under a glass bottle as he poured water from the top. As with Colladon's fountain, the rays of light hit the edge of the water stream and total internal reflection guided the light through the stream.

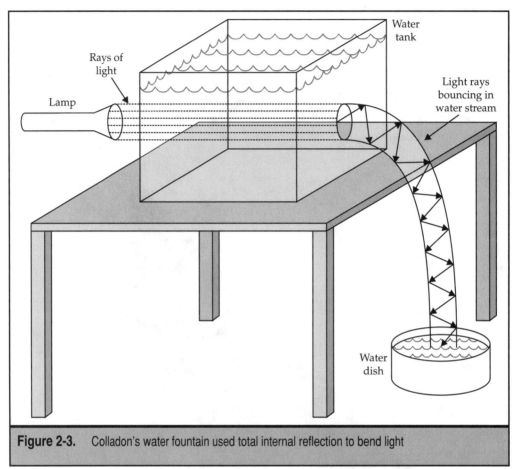

Figure 2-3.   Colladon's water fountain used total internal reflection to bend light

But where Colladon developed his light fountain into a big production with specially designed tanks and by routing light into the water tank, Babinet's contribution took a much more interesting scientific twist. He observed that light would travel through bent streams of water and also glass rods.

Public Displays   Colladon and Babinet's discovery wasn't immediately useful for anything, so it remained just an interesting phenomenon until 1884, when fountains were constructed at the International Health Exhibition in London. The Prince of Wales had encouraged the city's water companies to show the city's clean, pure water. In response, Sir Francis Bolton—the city's water examiner—designed an illuminated fountain.

To generate the magnitude of light necessary to illuminate the water streams, Bolton used the raw electrical power of arc lights. These lights were located at the base of the fountain and shone through glass plates on the water jets. Multicolored filters were also used to change the color of the water streams.

From the spectator's point of view, the fountains were a glorious sight to behold—especially in Victorian England, where gas lamps and candlelight were still the most prevalent ways to turn night into day.

From the International Health Exhibition, the popularity of illuminated fountains grew and grew, with bigger and bigger fountains built for different events. Each fountain became more ambitious than the one before it, utilizing different techniques to send colored light through jets of water.

Photophone

An interesting precursor to today's optical networks was an invention patented by Alexander Graham Bell in 1880. Bell's optical telephone, which he named the Photophone, used sunlight to transmit calls. Sunlight was focused on the surface of a mirror that vibrated when sound waves struck it. On the receiving end, a selenium cell would be modulated by the vibrating sunlight and the voice would be reproduced.

In the end, however, the Photophone suffered from the same shortcomings that the semaphore networks endured. If it was dark out, the device wouldn't work, and it was only useful over short distances. Ultimately, Bell's earlier invention—the telephone—won the long-distance communications race.

So we can see that in the nineteenth century physicists and inventors started to tinker with light and its capabilities, but these men were just slightly ahead of their time. It would take another century until these discoveries and inventions could be brought together in the application we now know as optical networking.

Illuminated Rods

Even though scientists weren't as much in love with light as they had been in centuries past, that didn't mean that the study of light was completely abandoned. In the late nineteenth century, inventors tried to develop a system to deliver light to hard-to-reach places. With gas or oil lamps, this was difficult because too much heat was generated along with the light. This was dangerous when the light source (burning quietly in the corner and giving off soot) was too close to expensive or fragile objects.

Illuminating a room wasn't the only function of light. Surgeons and dentists also needed a way to see what they were doing, but without roasting a patient's organs. To address this concern, in 1888 two Viennese inventors attached an electric lamp to one end of a glass rod, then pressed the rod against the patient's throat. The glass rod carried the light (but not the heat) to the patient's skin, where the larynx could be examined.

Ten years later in Indianapolis, a man patented a "dental illuminator" that used a curved glass rod to deliver light into the mouth. A lamp was placed on one end of the rod and the light would shine through the rod, bending at the curve, and be projected into the patient's mouth. In the 1930s, DuPont developed a plastic that replaced glass for these applications. This new plastic was lighter, cheaper, and easier to bend.

Spinning Threads of Glass

The core of fiber optics (pun intended) is an extremely thin strand of glass. To be of use in optical networking, not just any kind of glass can be used, and it must be manufactured to precise specifications for diameter, strength, composition, and density. This isn't something you made during your spare time in shop class when the instructor was yelling at a kid for not wearing safety goggles.

In the last section, we discussed how inventors and scientists learned how to manipulate light. But for that light to be useful, it must traverse ultra-thin glass wires. In this section, we take a look at how glass was first spun into silken threads and how it was continually developed, year after year, into a form that was usable for optical networking.

Fiber Through the Years

Like a slew of other fiber optic basics, the fabrication of glass into fibers has its roots in ancient cultures. Let's take a quick look at glass fibers through the ages:

▼ Around 1600 BC, the Egyptians made rough fibers of glass that were used as ornamentation on pottery.

■ During the Renaissance, Venetian glassmakers decorated vessels with thin strands of glass.

■ In the eighteenth century, French industrialist René de Réaumur developed "spun glass" when he was trying to make artificial heron feathers. His technique involved dipping a spinning wheel into molten glass. Unfortunately, his fibers were very short and rather brittle.

■ The manufacture of glass threads was improved by the early nineteenth century, when glassmakers had developed techniques to make glass fibers longer and stronger. They were spun from molten glass that—as the glass cooled—was wrapped around a reel. Using this technique, glass fibers could get up to three meters in length, but were quite fragile.

▲ Glass fibers were being made into threads as fine as silk by the late nineteenth century. These threads were woven into fabrics or used to make fake bird feathers. But making fibers this small proved to be tiresome because the sheer size of the threads made their manufacture and handling difficult.

Even as techniques in the creation of glass fibers continued to advance, no one was able to make long lengths of glass fiber that were durable and a consistent thickness. Further, it wasn't until Victorian times that anyone had considered sending light through the glass.

Charles Vernon Boys

One of the pioneers of glass fiber development was London physics instructor Charles Vernon Boys. Because of his interest in his own research (and subsequent lack of interest in his teaching duties), he was unpopular with his students.

NOTE: Boys's employer, the Royal College of Science, was located near the fountains from the Health Exhibition in London's South Kensington district just three years earlier.

In 1887, Boys was experimenting with the effects of delicate forces on various materials. In order to record those measurements, Boys had to suspend various items from a thread. The threads, however, had to be strong, thin, and elastic. Threads of silk were too weak, and threads of metal were not elastic enough. Boys tested glass fibers that were a quarter of a millimeter thick, but he decided they were useless because, like the steel threads, the glass threads were inelastic.

NOTE: One of Boys's students was author and visionary H.G. Wells.

Boys decided to develop his own threads of glass for his experiments. He built a tiny crossbow and fabricated tiny arrows by attaching a needle to a piece of straw. The arrow was attached to a length of glass rod with wax, then the glass was heated to the point of melting and fired through an open doorway between two rooms. As the arrow flew across the room, a tiny, silken thread of glass hung in the air before wafting gracefully to the floor. The resulting thread was about 30 meters long and $1/10,000^{th}$ of an inch in diameter. The thread was so uniform, said Boys, that one end was just one-sixth greater in diameter than the other end.

Boys tried his technique with a number of other types of materials. He tried using different blends of glass, using glass from different sources (glasses, plates, windows, and so forth), and even using rubies and sapphires. Ultimately, he applied his technique to quartz. The resulting threads were as strong as steel threads.

Boys's work in developing thin threads of glass and quartz was critical in the progress of glass threads that were durable, of a uniform thickness, and several meters in length. His advances were critical in the evolution of glass fiber.

Glass Fabrics—Scientific Marketing at Its Finest

As scientists and inventors made progressively finer strands of glass, a logical development was to weave the glass fibers into cloth.

Herman Hammesfahr, a German immigrant in America, patented his own version of glass fiber. His patent caught the eye of the Libbey Glass Company, who wanted to show off something at the 1892 Chicago World's Fair. Weaving in threads of satin, Hammesfahr was able to make a dress using glass threads. As eye-catching as the fabrics were, they were rather impractical. The fibers were itchy, and the wearer couldn't sit down or the glass would shatter.

Glass dresses were largely unusable, but that was fine. The fabric was used as a means to show off fine glass fibers and their capabilities. Even though you didn't want a pair of undershorts made from glass fibers, industry wanted the threads because they could be woven into a mesh and used for such applications as a filter in corrosive liquids.

In spite of this flash point of glass fiber expediency, the first three decades of the twentieth century didn't see much development in the field of glass fibers. It wasn't until late 1931 that the Owens-Illinois Glass Company of Newark, Ohio, mass-produced glass fibers. By blowing air into molten glass, threads of glass were lofted into the air, where they quickly cooled, producing a soft, billowy cloud of glass fibers. Meanwhile, the Corning Glass Works was also developing its own glass fabric that—unlike Herr Hammesfahr's invention—could be folded without shattering the fibers. Thus was born the fiberglass industry that lives on today.

Spanning the Distance

When we think of the word "network" today, our minds tend to wander to such things as our computer network, a cellular telephone network, and even a broadcast television network. These networks are all constructs of the latter half of the twentieth century and were the stuff of fantasy and fiction a century and a half ago.

Though no one was able to have a wireless chat with a friend on another continent from his or her horse-drawn carriage, some forward-thinking individuals were ruminating about viewing things from far away. Remote viewing, as we describe in the next section, is one of the the earliest pursuits of television. After looking at remote viewing, we'll take a look at the first widespread network and the basis from which today's optical networks have progressed.

Remote Viewing

In this day and age, we take for granted our ability to be on the Senate floor in Washington, D.C.; to study the congregational habits of wildebeest in Africa; and to get a missile's-eye view of a soon-to-be-decimated Iraqi bunker. We can be in all these places with the press of a button on a remote control.

Though a video camera on every corner is commonplace today, such a notion was just starting to be pursued in the early 1900s. Scientists had theorized that if light could be channeled through glass rods (much as they had done with the illuminated fountains), then these rods could convey special shapes of light—namely, images.

The idea is sound. In fact, it is the basic way television, computer imaging, and printing work. The picture on your television, monitor, or newspaper page is made up of thousands or millions of tiny little dots.

When a television broadcast occurs, the television camera doesn't really send you the true image. Rather, the camera scans the scene, from top to bottom, recording individual dots of light. It sends those dots through the air, where your antenna picks them up and reproduces them on your television screen. This process is shown in Figure 2-4.

Such was the basis of remote viewing. If an image could be transmitted through a series of glass rods, it could be reassembled at the far end, thus conveying an image across great distances. The image is transmitted point-by-point, as shown in Figure 2-5, and the point of light must be viewed at the same location as it was picked up or the image will not be recognizable.

Computer images are generated pixel-by-pixel on a computer screen. If you look closely enough, you'll see that computer images are made up of thousands of dots of light. Newspaper and magazine photographs are reproduced the same way. Look closely at a newspaper or magazine page, and you'll see those images are composed of tiny dots.

During the Victorian Era, the quest to transmit images across great distances was known as *remote viewing*. But, since you probably can't recall a great many Victorian Era

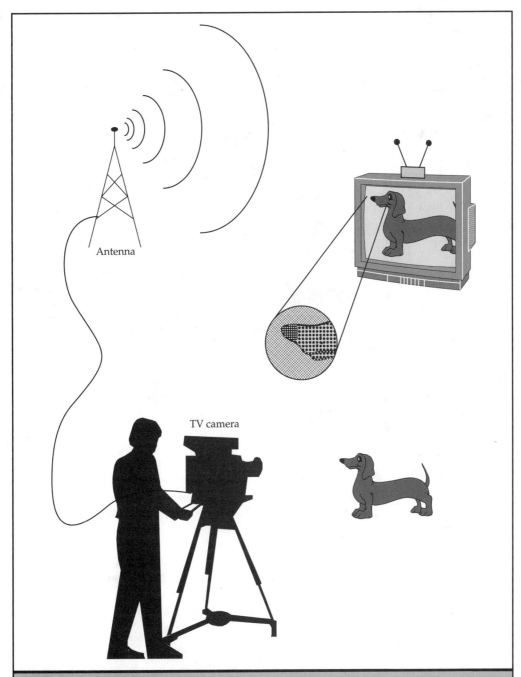

Figure 2-4.   Television broadcasts are made up of millions of tiny dots of light that are reassembled by your television set

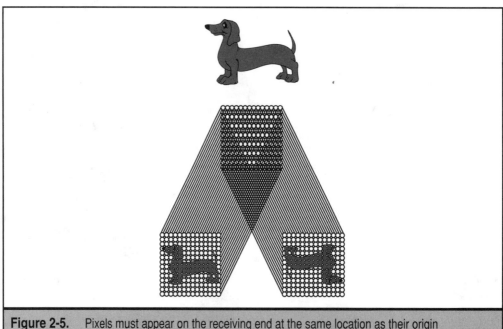

Figure 2-5.   Pixels must appear on the receiving end at the same location as their origin

television programs, you're probably already ahead of us when we say they couldn't get it to work. Problems stemmed from the size of the glass rods and image quality. These problems were so clearly insurmountable that the project's development was scrapped altogether.

Telephone Networks

No matter how enraged you get when your telephone bill arrives, if you used the telephone network when it was first developed, you'd have a new appreciation for what we can do. Sure, there were no telemarketers to interrupt your dinner, but the system itself was not the user-friendliest system around.

Today, telephone networks are one of the chief users of optical networking (they were the key developers, in fact). We'll talk about how the telephone companies moved from electrical to optical transmissions later in this chapter, but for now let's take a closer look at how the telephone network began.

Switching   If you've ever watched an episode of *The Andy Griffith Show*, then you'll probably remember Andy picking up the phone and asking Mabelle or Shirley to connect him to the Studebaker dealer in Mt. Pilot. When he made that call, he was using a system that employed a switchboard—the low-tech precursor to today's modern electronic switches.

Now, when you punch a telephone number into the keypad on your phone, the telephone company uses an electronic switch to direct your call. However, Andy, Opie, et al. relied on an operator sitting behind a board in a central office in Mayberry, where she would have to physically connect one line to another for a call to be placed, as shown in Figure 2-6. Central offices were connected to each phone in the town. As cities and telephone demand grew, so too did the need for extra offices and more operators.

As the system expanded, so did the realization that there should be a mechanical means to connect calls. A rotating switch was introduced that moved the switchboard out of the system. When a dial was rotated on the customer's telephone, that series of "clicks" was transmitted to the switching station, where the rotating switch routed the calls.

Progress and demand being what they are, however, the telephone system was outgrowing the rotating switch's capacity and the hunt was on for the next trend in switching—electronic switches. The advent of the transistor made electronic switching possible, thus making the telephone infrastructure smaller and more efficient than in the days of Mabelle switching a call to Mt. Pilot, or the clickety-clack of a rotating switch.

Infrastructure   Switching solved the "logical" problems inherent in a telephone network. It is easy to think about switches as a bus depot—as the buses come into the station, passengers get off one bus and onto another one. Using this example, if a switch is the depot, what are the roads?

The roads leading into the depot are the wires connecting station to station. As more telephone calls were made, there was a demand for more wires. It is akin to a small town experiencing a population boom. Even through a one-lane dirt road was enough to access

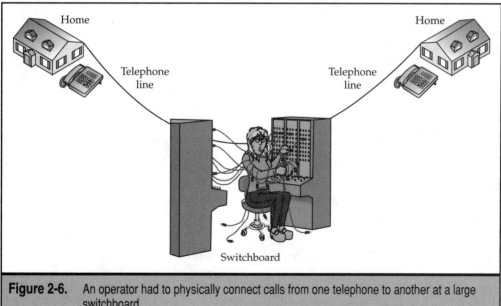

Figure 2-6.   An operator had to physically connect calls from one telephone to another at a large switchboard

the town, as it grows in size, soon that road is widened and paved. Such was the case for telephone lines.

Since long-distance communications began, we have been continually trying to beef up capacity. In the earliest telegraph networks, only one dot or one dash could be on the line at a time. Capacity has grown so that, now, thousands of telephone calls can be simultaneously carried across one strand of optical fiber.

FOUNDATIONS IN SCIENCE

In the previous section, we talked about some of the people and events that were the precursors to fiber optic technology. In this section, we'll talk about how fiber optics was becoming more of a reality, and we'll introduce the individuals and organizations interested in developing the finest fiber and the most powerful lasers.

We'll talk about how the pursuit of glass fiber changed from something to make fake bird feathers to a product that was extremely clear and would keep light within it. Also, since optical networking involves not only fiber, but also light, we'll talk about how the laser was developed and how it was tweaked to accommodate optical transmissions.

Starting in the 1960s, the race was on to develop fiber optics as a viable transportation medium for telephone traffic. Researchers for such American telecommunications companies as AT&T and GTE, British telephone companies Standard Telecommunications Laboratories and British Post Office, along with American glassworks Corning, were all striving to develop the clearest fibers and a continuous, coherent beam of laser light. At the end of this section, we'll talk more about that race and which developments nudged the world closer to high-capacity optical communications.

The Birth of Fiber

To use light as a means of communication, you have to actually *see* the light. Since light tends to travel naturally in a straight line, those communicating had to be in direct view of each other to see the light. But if that's not feasible, how can light be directed to its destination? In this section, we'll talk about one of the pioneers of directing light through a series of "light pipes."

Also, in our earlier examinations of glass fiber, the stuff was used for cosmetic purposes. In the early part of the twentieth century, researchers had figured out how to spin rather fine strands of soft glass that were good insulators and suitable for industrial purposes, but for light to be transmitted across the fiber, glass had to be much clearer and keep the light within its core.

Light Pipes

A few pages ago, we talked about the professors and inventors who used water as a means to bend light. This was a cute parlor trick and made for impressive illuminated fountains, but there was really no useful purpose, beyond demonstrating the interesting physical phenomenon and the ability to illuminate a fountain at night. Certainly, modern fiber optics owes to illuminated fountains what Ferrari owes to Grog the caveman for inventing the wheel.

Our last look back at the precursor of modern-day fiber optics takes us to a man who figured out how to direct reflected light to a specific point. A 1880s American inventor, William Wheeler, developed a way to channel light directly to the location where it was needed. Wheeler's light pipes could direct light to many different points. The pipes were constructed of hollow glass, were coated with silver on the outside, and used tilted panes of clear glass within the pipes. The pipes did not use total internal reflection; rather, light bounced off the tilted panes of glass at a glancing angle.

NOTE: The effect is similar to driving down the road and having someone pull in behind you, blinding you with sunlight reflected off of their rear windshield.

As Figure 2-7 shows, light pipes use a series of tilted panes of clear glass to transmit light from one end of the pipe to the other. Like so many other inventions, Wheeler's light pipes never became a household name, but he did figure out how to direct light to a specific location.

Cladding

As you remember from our earlier discussion about the components of fiber optic cabling, a second layer of glass encases the core. This layer, called the cladding, is made from a less-dense type of glass than the core. When photons strike the barrier where core and cladding meet, they are reflected back into the core. This keeps the light within the fiber so that it can bounce all the way to the end of the optical fiber.

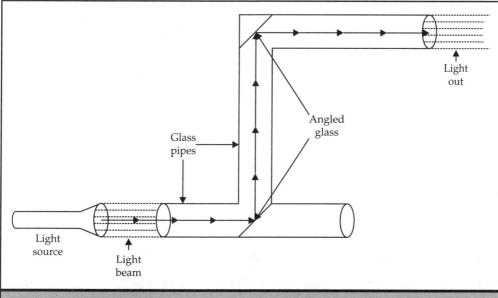

Figure 2-7.   Light pipes used tilted pieces of glass to pass on the beams of light, rather than bouncing light off the sides of the pipes

But, you might be thinking, if we want to reflect light back into the core, why not just wrap the core with something really shiny, like a mirror? The reason is that even though mirrors appear to reflect everything back from their surface, in actuality they absorb quite a bit of light. In fact, they absorb about 10 percent of the light that strikes their surface. As we see in Figure 2-8, if a piece of optical cabling used a mirror instead of cladding, a bit of light would be lost each time it bounced off the wall of the fiber. After a few bounces, there would be no light left to convey the message.

In 1951, Abraham Cornelis Sebastian van Heel, president of the International Commission for Optics and a professor at the Technical University of Delft in the Netherlands, was the man who finally figured out that a glass cladding was the key to keeping light within fiber.

Earlier fibers were single strands of glass, which achieved total internal reflection using air as the cladding. Van Heel covered a single strand of glass or plastic fiber with a transparent cladding that had a lower refractive index. This step solved many problems that researchers had run into while trying to develop optical fibers for such uses as image transmission or endoscopics. Adding the glass cladding made the following improvements:

▼ The total reflection surface was protected from contamination.

▲ When glass fibers were set side-by-side, the cladding prevented cross talk resulting from the tendency of unclad fibers to bleed light into one another.

Glass-clad fibers were continually refined over the decade, and by 1960 glass-clad fibers were achieving attenuation rates of about one decibel (dB) per meter. This rate was fine for endoscopics, but it still wasn't good enough for communications.

Pure Silica Glass

In Chapter 1, we told you that fiber optics couldn't use just plain, everyday glass. Even though it looks perfectly clear, it is filled with microscopic impurities, and the light wouldn't even go a few meters before it was totally absorbed. Obviously, when we need light to travel thousands of miles, we need something that can go the distance.

The ultimate solution—pure silica glass—was almost crossed off a short list of alternatives before it was chosen. In 1966, Charles Kao, a researcher at Standard Telecommunications Laboratories in London, was convinced that silica glass was the only type of

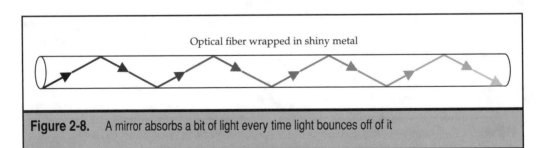

Figure 2-8. A mirror absorbs a bit of light every time light bounces off of it

glass that could deliver with a line loss of just 20 dB/km. Previous efforts gave a best line loss at more than 1000 dB/km, but for communications systems to work across them, the line loss had to be lowered.

> **NOTE:** Twenty dB/km was the line loss goal because many researchers believed that was the threshold to cross, which would enable optical transmissions.

The problem with silica is that it has an extremely high melting point (1600 degrees Centigrade) and the lowest refractive index of all common glasses. In order for a cladding to be applied to the exterior of the silica glass, a layer of glass with an even lower refractive index must be applied. Though scientists at a number of different communications companies tried to find the purest glass, the goal of 20 dB/km was finally achieved by researchers at the Corning Glass Works (now known as Corning Inc.).

Three researchers at the glass works started by making cylindrical forms by adding purified materials and adding dopants to make the refractive index of the core slightly higher than that of the cladding. By fall 1970, they announced that they had made single-mode fibers that were below the 20 dB/km goal.

Lasers

In an optical networking capacity, optical fibers by themselves are like peanut butter without jelly. In order for an optical network to function, there must be light traversing the optical fibers. Scientists not only needed a strong light source, but they also needed something that would emit light at a specific wavelength. The laser was the answer to their strength and wavelength requirements.

First Generation

The laser is such a well-known and widely used device, that its origins are just as blurry as the invention of Kleenex tissues or Coca Cola. Today, lasers are everywhere. In fact, on the computer I'm using to write this, there are two lasers—one for the CD-ROM burner and one for the DVD player. These—and all the other applications that lasers are used for—were barely a twinkle in an inventor's eye in 1960 when the first laser was invented.

Though the groundwork for lasers was laid a decade earlier with the MASER (Microwave Amplification by the Stimulated Emission of Radiation), the first laser was realized in 1960 by Theodore Maiman. He fired brief pulses from a ruby cylinder at the Hughes Research Laboratories in Malibu, California.

The laser was useful because, as physicists realized, it was the first practical source of *coherent* light. If you look at a light bulb, a candle, the sun, or most any other light source, the light crosses much of the spectrum. A laser, on the other hand, produces light that is very focused and generates a signal at a specific wavelength, rather than the sloppy way other light sources radiate their beams.

Though Maiman's accomplishment was a scientific marvel, the use of ruby was not ideal for lasers. It fired only pulses and converted just a fraction of the input energy into laser light. In order for the laser to be useful for communications (and other applications), the laser had to be able to emit a continuous beam of light.

Six months later, in December 1960, Ali Javan, a physicist at Bell Labs, achieved a laser that could sustain a continuous beam of light. Javan's laser beam was generated by passing an electrical current through a gas. Javan used two types of gas for his laser:

▼ **Helium**, which would capture energy passing through the gas

▲ **Neon**, which took energy from the helium and converted it into light

Javan's laser became the first to emit a continuous (albeit invisible) beam of coherent light—at 1.15 micrometers—and became the standard for laboratory lasers. It remains the most prevalent kind of gas laser today.

Semiconductor Lasers

As monumental an achievement as Javan's laser was, it was still largely impractical for use in optical communications. It was around the time of the advent of the silica glass fiber and the laser (both, coincidentally, in 1960) that a "you got chocolate in my peanut butter/you got peanut butter on my chocolate" moment occurred. Lasers weren't good for transmitting information through the air—they needed a medium to guide them from point A to point B. Optical fibers needed a light source at a specific wavelength that could traverse their microscopic channel.

Since both lasers and usable fiber had been developed and were ready to go, the two needed to be coupled together. Unfortunately, the bulky gas laser was not the ideal candidate for the job. The chosen device to enable optical transmissions was a semiconductor laser. This type of laser was selected for three reasons:

▼ Solid-state devices were all the rage in the late 1960s, so they were a popular choice for the laser's construction.

■ Semiconductor lasers were easy to control and manage.

▲ Probably the most important factor was the sheer size of a semiconductor laser. Where Javan's gas laser needed to be transported around in a small truck, a semiconductor laser was no larger than a grain of sand.

Figure 2-9 shows how a semiconductor laser works.

You'll notice that the tiny piece of semiconductor material is composed of slices of *n*-type and *p*-type materials. In the first semiconductor lasers, these materials consisted of gallium arsenide. *N*-type materials are so called because they are a negative carrier, and *p*-type materials are so called because they are a positive carrier. When these two materials are sandwiched together, they become a *diode.*

NOTE: The way energy is expressed from the semiconductor material depends on the type of material. In some semiconductor materials, like silicon, energy is released as heat. Materials like gallium arsenide and indium phosphide release the energy as light.

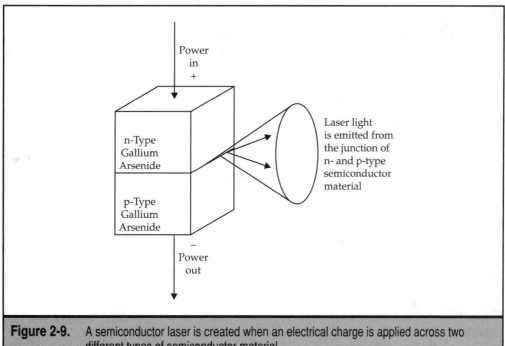

Figure 2-9.   A semiconductor laser is created when an electrical charge is applied across two different types of semiconductor material

When a current is applied across the diode, the junction where the two types of material meet generates light. This is how a light emitting diode (LED) works and is the basis for semiconductor lasers.

The first semiconductor laser wasn't the be-all and end-all of solid-state lasing. First, the lasers would only operate at the temperature of liquid nitrogen: −196 degrees centigrade. Second, they burned out rather quickly and the warmer they got, the more current was required to make them emit light. This, of course, was a vicious circle, because the more current was applied to a semiconductor laser, the more quickly it burned out.

It wasn't until spring 1970 that two independent groups designed the first room temperature semiconductor laser. In a scene reminiscent of Colladon and Babinet's near-simultaneous discovery of total internal reflection within a stream of water, in May a group from the Ioffe Physical Institute in Leningrad preceded the discovery by Bell Labs scientists in June.

Rather than two semiconductor materials sandwiched together, the Soviet group, led by physicist Zhores Alferov, used several types of semiconductor material in a "hoagie" sandwich of semiconductor material.

> *NOTE:* Who was actually first is still a matter of speculation. At the height of the Cold War, the Soviets were not especially forthcoming about details of their laser design. Further, their discovery was only printed in a Russian-language publication. However, because Alferov submitted his report on May 6—a month before the Bell scientists—Alferov is widely recognized as the first.

OPTICAL NETWORK SERVICE

Over the past several pages, we talked about the roots of optical networking. We looked back in time to people who hadn't the faintest idea of what their physical observations and inventions would produce. All these technologies have evolved to the point we are at today.

In this section, we'll take a closer look at the final form of these different technologies. We'll look at what makes up today's fiber optical networks, and how modern networks connect countries, cities, and even the computers and telephones on your desktop. We'll also tell the story of how fiber optics was finally rolled out on a large scale, who was the first to use this ultra-fast technology, and why it still isn't perfected.

Development

Up until the mid-1970s, researchers spent time trying to find the best laser that could be shot across the best fiber. But once those achievements were accomplished, what then? All it took was a lighting bolt to strike (literally) for inspiration.

In 1975, the police department in Dorset, England, suffered a severe communications blow when their radio antenna was struck by lightening. The power surge took out the department's communications system, and in order to maintain communications, a constable was sent up a hill to act as a relay.

Because he did not want to rely on a system that could be taken out by a power surge again, the chief constable called on Standard Telephones and Cables to connect his police department with fiber optics. Since fiber optics doesn't use electrons coursing through copper wire, it is immune to lighting strikes and power surges. Within a few weeks of the chief constable's request, Dorset became the first organization using fiber optics for network communications.

Tests and Trials

As encouraging (and revolutionary) as was the Dorset police department's new communications system, phone companies weren't ready to invest millions of dollars on optical technology, based solely on the success of a police department in southern England. Before the investment was going to be made in this new technology, more tests were needed to evaluate and prove fiber optics.

Atlanta   AT&T decided that a field trial was in order, and in January 1976, the company set out to see if fiber optics was the next big thing. In Atlanta, Georgia, engineers threaded 650 meters of fiber optic cabling through a duct under a parking lot and placed another length of fiber in an environmentally controlled duct so that the effects of weathering could be tested and evaluated.

When the power was turned on and the tests began, there was good news and bad news. The bad news was that a high amount of the lasers burnt out. However, that was somewhat expected and not a deal-breaker, because newer and more reliable lasers were continually being developed. The good news was that line loss was much lower than expected, and of the 144 fibers that were placed, only six failed (researchers had hoped they wouldn't lose more than 44 fibers).

Chicago   Following the success in Atlanta, AT&T's next step was to see how the delicate fibers would hold up in an urban setting. In many cases, telephone cabling was strung through sewer lines that were filled with water, muck, and rats. AT&T chose to connect three buildings in downtown Chicago. After the cable was carefully threaded through the ducts, not a single fiber broke. Using fiber and lasers that were slightly improved over the Atlanta tests, AT&T was ready to start regular digitized phone service beginning May 11, 1977.

The Winner   AT&T was ready to take its slaps on the back for being the first to offer optical telephone service. Unfortunately for them, they were a few days too late. While AT&T conducted its field trials, GTE Laboratories had quietly conducted its own tests in a 10 km stretch between Long Beach and Artesia, California.

GTE's system operated with LEDs instead of lasers and carried 6.3 megabits per second (Mbps), in contrast to AT&T's laser-based system that carried 45 Mbps. However, GTE's optical system was able to carry telephone traffic by April 22—three weeks ahead of AT&T.

Connecting the Continents

Despite a minor disagreement in the late eighteenth century, America and England have been good friends—and good friends like to stay in touch. To facilitate communications with our friends across the pond, a number of cables have stretched from North America to England. The very first cable was laid in 1858 between Newfoundland and Ireland and operated until about 1920.

It wasn't until more than a century later that American and British telephone companies got serious about connecting the continents. In 1953, TAT-1 was the first transatlantic telephone cable. TAT-1 was a pair of coaxial cables beefed up with 51 vacuum tube repeaters that could carry 36 telephone circuits. The venture was a joint project of AT&T and the British Post Office. Despite its reasonably low capacity and reliance on vacuum tubes, the cable was still in use up until 1979. Gradually, more TATs were stretched between North America and England. Capacity was reached with TAT-7, placed in 1983, which topped out at 4000 telephone circuits.

NOTE: TAT-7 was a duplicate version of TAT-6, which was placed in 1976. So, technically, the limit of coaxial cable was reached in 1976. Because fiber wasn't an option yet, however, the best that could be done to add telephone circuits was to add a second cable with the same capabilities.

With the development of optical cabling, it was only a matter of time before their capacity and reliability were exploited and they were sunk into the briny deep. In 1980, AT&T announced that TAT-7 would be the last coaxial transatlantic cable. The next cable to connect North America with Europe would be the fiber-based TAT-8. The cable—which would connect Tuckerton, New Jersey, with England and France—was capable of carrying 40,000 telephone circuits. The cable would start in New Jersey, then traverse the Atlantic seabed to a point off the coast of Europe, where it would split in two. One end would connect to England; the other would connect to France. AT&T won the contract to connect America across the Atlantic; Standard Telephones and Cables would connect England to the splitting point, and French Submarcom would connect France to the splitting point. In 1988, the cable was completed and open to carry the most telephone traffic ever contained on one cable. Once TAT-8 was in place, the face of international telecommunications changed, and soon the 40,000-channel TAT-8 was filled to capacity. It was followed by TATs -9 through -11.

All the action seems to have been occurring in the Atlantic, but there are also a number of transpacific fiber cables and dozens of shorter runs of fiber cable connecting coastal cities and islands.

From Washington to Boston

Optical networks were getting the job done in metropolitan areas, but microwaves were still accomplishing long-distance communications. Given an open space, microwaves did an excellent job transmitting long-distance calls. However, one of the most important stretches—between Washington, D.C., and Boston—was not the best for microwave communications.

The link between Washington, D.C., and Boston—also known as the Northeast Corridor—is an especially important piece of the telephone network. The link carries important governmental and industrial telephone traffic. However, the terrain and city placement along the Northeast Corridor did not make microwave communications a viable solution. In January 1980, AT&T decided that its first placement of a long-distance optical network would be along the Northeast Corridor.

The system would have been a great achievement; however, disputes over the system design, the capacity, and which companies would install varying portions of the Northeast Corridor system made the project a major hassle, further complicated by the division of the Bell System into AT&T and the seven baby bells. Add to that the competing long-distance companies that were sending 400 Mbps (as compared to AT&T's 270 Mbps). By the time the project was completed, it was already obsolete.

Introducing Data to Optical Networks

Optical networks are fantastically suited for computer networking. A voice telephone call must be converted from an analog signal into an electrical signal, then again to an optical signal before it traverses an optical network. Data, on the other hand, must undergo only one conversion—from electrical to optical.

Though optical networking is now at a cost level that an organization (given proper budgeting) can implement for its own high-speed data or Voice over IP (VoIP) needs, the first organizations to use optical communications were the technology's developers—telecommunications companies.

But since the late 1980s, the optical networks have started taking on an increasing amount of data traffic. As the Internet starting gaining popularity, tier-one Internet service providers (ISPs) have moved to optical networking to keep high levels of data flowing through their channels.

As the Internet has expanded and evolved, the need to keep data flowing through its channels is more important than ever. Enabling that high speed across the main trunk of the Internet—its so-called backbone—are optical networks.

The largest American Internet backbone providers include AT&T, Cable & Wireless, GTE, Sprint, Teleglobe, and UUNet (the first ISP, which started operations in 1987). On an international scale, the large U.S. backbone providers, as well as firms such as British Telecommunications and France Telecom, provide global backbone services.

The Last Mile

One of the greatest hurdles to the world of optical networking doesn't come when information has to stretch from a city on one coast to a city at the opposite end of the continent. It doesn't come when the stream of information has to span the continents on submarine cable. The biggest obstacle occurs between your front step and the nearest telephone substation.

The Last Mile is one of the last great obstacles to complete optical networking (the other obstacle being economics). In this section, we examine why the Last Mile is such a problem and what efforts (all failures) have been made to ameliorate it.

Throughout the telephone network, links are connected with fiber optic cable and other high-speed connections, as illustrated in Figure 2-10. However, you'll notice that once the links reach homes and businesses, the connections become small, slow-speed wires.

So what keeps the phone company from coming out and rewiring everyone's home with a high-speed connection? Mainly, it's a matter of expense. As we'll see later in this section, other attempts at high-speed Last Mile connections were too expensive to continue.

First, however, let's look back more than four decades, to when city planners foresaw the need for high-speed Last Mile connections.

Television Versus Quality Versus the Last Mile

Two of the most prevalent connections to any home (if you don't count utilities like gas or electrical service) are telephone and cable television.

In the early 1960s, television was taking heat (as it so often does) for providing awful programming. The solution, some thought, was to make television interactive so that one could do more with the television than stare blindly at it for hours on end. The solution, many thought, was a *wired city*—one that was able to connect homes with schools and businesses and provide two-way communications.

The obvious solution seemed to be developing the wired city with a network of coaxial cables. This was a good enough idea; however, coaxial cable networks were an

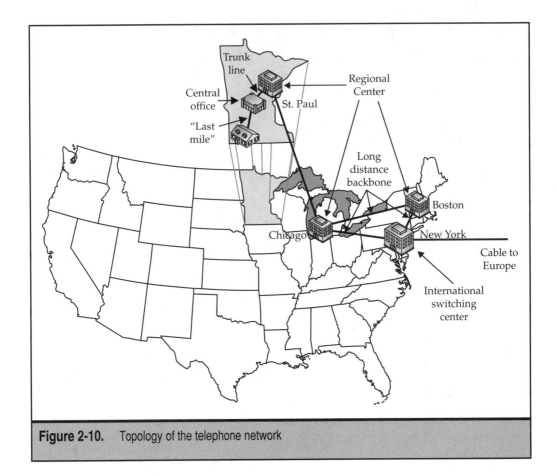

Figure 2-10. Topology of the telephone network

imperfect solution. The problem is that coaxial cable networks did not have the ability to switch, delivering specific content to specific homes—they were only good for broadcasting. Conversely, telephone lines are small connections with excellent switching capabilities. Ultimately the idea was scrapped, and the high-capacity links between homes, schools, and businesses never materialized.

High-Speed Cities

There have been a number of implementations of high-speed links to ameliorate the Last Mile problem. Unfortunately, they all succumbed to the great leveler—price. Two of the most impressively expensive failures took place in Japan and Canada.

Hi-OVIS   In Japan, during the early 1970s, the Ministry for International Trade and Industry began testing a service called Highly Interactive Optical Visual Information System (Hi-OVIS). It used fiber optics at a time when American and British companies were testing it for large-capacity rollouts. In Japan, fiber would connect the homes of 158 people and 10 public institutions.

The system would allow residents to join in on discussions using their own video camera and receivers, plus they could access computer files, including such information as weather and news. Further, a video-on-demand service was available from the Hi-OVIS programming center.

The only hitch to this system was that it cost roughly 10 billion yen, which is about $US80 million. That worked out to about $US500,000 per household and proved to be far too expensive.

Elie   In 1981, the Canadian government tried its own high-speed Last Mile experiment in the city of Elie, 50 km west of Winnipeg. The government was trying to keep young people from fleeing the farm country for the city, and one way was to beef up the telecommunications system.

The network was given a budget of $US7.5 million to serve 150 homes (about $US50,000 per home). The network was a hit with the residents of Elie. They were finally able to have private phone lines, and the television service was outstanding—especially during the frostbitten Canadian nights. They were also able to take advantage of a computer network that would allow them to get news and other information.

However, there was still the issue of price. After adding up the pros and cons, the powers that be decided to pull the plug on the expensive high-speed network.

Making Strides

As prohibitive as the Last Mile can be for fiber optic implementations, several efforts are underway to apply fiber for long-haul applications.

Global Crossing is one such company that provides communications platforms to global corporations. The company's network already spans oceans and continents, crossing the Atlantic and the Pacific and emerging at landing stations along the coasts in North and South America, Europe, and Asia. These connect to terrestrial wires, linking major cities around the world. Global Crossing is in the process of laying an intricate optical network that, when complete, will span more than 100,000 miles, reaching 27 countries and more than 200 major cities.

All-optical networks are not pie-in-the-sky ideas, either. For example, Broadwing is an ISP for medium-sized and large businesses that is the first provider with a fully deployed, all-optical network.

The Future

As you saw in the preceding examples, it wasn't the technology that failed or faltered; rather, it was the sheer price tag associated with these rollouts. So does that mean certain doom for any other implementations of Last Mile fiber? Not necessarily.

Remember, these examples occurred two and three decades ago, and to be sure the face of telecommunications has changed. Since the Hi-OVIS test, fiber has become more refined and less expensive. Also, one of the biggest costs associated with the Hi-OVIS system was manning the programming center at the heart of the system.

Other burgeoning technologies, like Passive Optical Networks, are expected to bring costs down. PONs save on laser transmitters by splitting optical signals between 8 to 16 homes. Additionally, data compression techniques could mean the capability to send more information across the line.

Furthermore, the demand to bridge the Last Mile is greater than ever with more and more people using the Internet. During the times of Hi-OVIS and Elie, the Internet was a little-known network called ARPANET and was used as a backup system for the Department of Defense.

The final chapter on the history of optical networking is yet to come. In fact, now is a great time to be witness to this ever changing, ever improving technology.

CHAPTER 3

Optical Architectures

N ow that you know the basics of optical networking, understand the physics, and have perused a thumbnail sketch of optical networking history, we'll take a closer look at how fiber optics are rolled out into a network. In this chapter, we'll talk about the two main optical networking architectures in use today: the Synchronous Optical Network (SONET) and wavelength division multiplexing (WDM). In addition to these widely used architectures, we'll also talk about an emerging architecture that was developed by networking giant, Cisco Systems.

Before we delve into the nuts and bolts of optical network architectures, we'll talk a bit about multiplexing, which is a means of combining several optical signals into one, conjoined, signal. Multiplexing is an effective tool because it reduces the cost of fiber rollouts, because it uses just one strand of fiber.

MULTIPLEXING

By definition, a network is a conjunction of numerous devices, combined into an interconnected unit. By forming a network, devices can share each other's resources for the betterment of everyone who uses that network. That's all nice and good within a local area network (LAN), where devices can talk to each other easily. But what happens when two—or more—devices (*nodes* in internetworking parlance) want to communicate across a great distance? If one node at a time is allowed to use the wide area network (WAN) or metropolitan area network (MAN) link, then there will be a horrible lag and rampant lack of productivity while workers sit around twiddling their thumbs. The way to allow several people to use a lone link is by *multiplexing*.

In this section, we'll examine the basics of multiplexing—especially how they apply to optical networking.

Fundamentals

Optical networks can send signals from a number of different sources across the same stretch of fiber. But for this to happen, those signals must be combined together. This is accomplished with a device called a *multiplexer* ("mux" for short). A mux takes optical wavelengths from multiple fibers and melds them into one light source for transmission across a lone stretch of optical fiber.

On the receiving end, the system must be able to separate those wavelengths so that they can be transported to their respective destinations. This is accomplished with a *demultiplexer* ("demux"), which separates the beam into its wavelength components and directs them to their individual fibers.

NOTE: Demultiplexing must be accomplished *before* the light is detected, because photodetectors are broadband devices that cannot isolate a single wavelength.

There are two types of muxes and demuxes:

▼   **Passive**, which are based on prisms, diffraction gratings, and filters

▲   **Active**, which combine passive devices with tunable lasers

The key challenge in a passive system is to minimize crosstalk and maximize channel separation. Crosstalk is a way to gauge how well channels are separated, and channel separation refers to the equipment's ability to distinguish each wavelength.

There are two types of mux/demux configurations. The first, as shown in Figure 3-1, is a unidirectional muxing/demuxing system that allows wavelengths to flow one way across the fiber. When multiple wavelengths enter the mux, they are converged into one signal, then transmitted across the network, ultimately ending at the demux, where the wavelengths are separated and routed.

For this configuration, the needed pieces of equipment are a mux and a demux.

In Figure 3-2, we see an example of a bidirectional muxing/demuxing system. This means that wavelengths can travel simultaneously both ways across the fiber. At each end are devices called *multiplexers/demultiplexers* (mux/demux) that do both jobs of combining and separating wavelengths.

Types of Multiplexing

There are three popular ways to multiplex a signal. Two are used for both electrical and optical networks; a third is unique to optical networking. Multiplexing might be a function of the transmitter, independent of the transmitter, or facilitated by the transmitter, though logically separate. There are three ways that multiplexing occurs within an optical network. The following sections explain the three ways of multiplexing a signal in an optical network.

Time Division Multiplexing

Time division multiplexing (TDM) systems send multiple signals across a path by intertwining the bits from the separate data streams. This type of multiplexing occurs independent of the transmitter, but it may also be incorporated into the transmitter package.

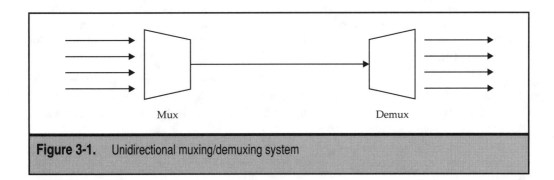

Figure 3-1.   Unidirectional muxing/demuxing system

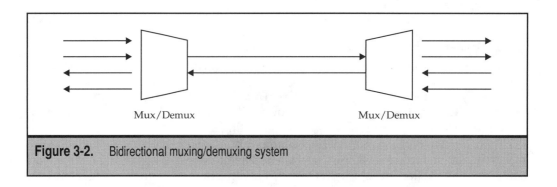

Figure 3-2. Bidirectional muxing/demuxing system

In a TDM system, the information is discrete in time; therefore, a transmission scheme can provide rest periods between transmissions.

In a telephone network, for instance, a pulse code modulation transmission scheme transmits six bits every sampling period. If these six binary digits can be sent in short pulses, additional time remains in the channel when other signals can be sent. The time allocated to one sample of one message is called a *time slot*.

Frequency Division Multiplexing

Frequency division multiplexing (FDM) combines multiple analog signals by placing them at different frequencies in a broadband analog signal. You encounter this whenever you turn on a television set connected to cable service. Television channels in a cable television system use FDM. By using this type of multiplexing, cable carriers can put dozens of channels on one cable.

Wavelength Division Multiplexing

TDM and FDM are types of multiplexing that apply to both electrical and optical networking. Wavelength division multiplexing (WDM), however, is unique to optical networking and is the optical equivalent of FDM to electrical signaling.

WDM is quite similar to FDM, but whereas FDM operates using electrical signals, WDM uses optical signals. WDM transmits on two or more different wavelengths. The signals are generated by two different light sources within the same transmitter, then are combined for transport across the fiber. On the receiving end, they are separated back into their respective channels. For example, a single fiber could carry a signal at 1300 nanometers (nm) and another at 1550 nm.

NOTE: WDM is an important way to multiplex signals and is the core of optical multiplexing. We talk about WDM, and its popular successor dense WDM (DWDM), in greater detail later in this chapter.

Optical Demultiplexing

Once a signal is muxed and sent across the fiber, it is time for the next step, demuxing. Though the process of muxing is reasonably straightforward, demuxing is much more difficult in an optical system. The following are all methods employed to demux an optical signal.

Prismatic

You may not be aware of it, but back in seventh grade science class when you shot a beam of light through a prism, you were demuxing the light. As Figure 3-3 shows, as light enters the prism and is refracted from the other side, it has been split into a rainbow. In essence, the prism has demultiplexed a polychromatic light source into specific wavelengths.

If you beamed the rainbow through a lens and focused each wavelength on a strand of optical fiber, then you would have been able to demultiplex the light source and deliver the separated wavelengths into destination fiber.

Diffraction Grating

Another way to demultiplex a polychromatic light source is to aim the beam of light at a piece of diffraction grating, as shown in Figure 3-4. A diffraction grating is an etched array of very fine lines that reflects (and blocks) light at different wavelengths. Each wavelength is diffracted at a different angle, then sent to a different point. By using a lens, these split wavelengths can be focused on individual fibers.

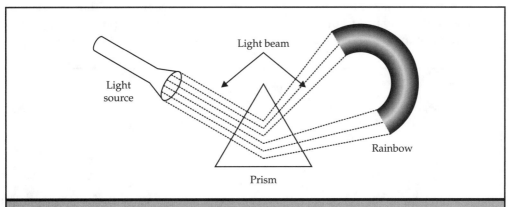

Figure 3-3.   A prism breaks polychromatic light into component wavelengths

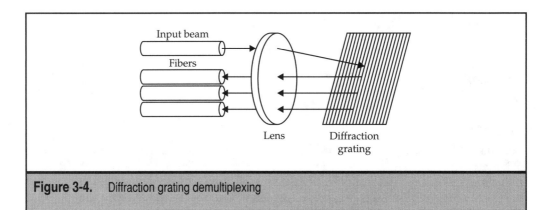

Figure 3-4. Diffraction grating demultiplexing

NOTE: You can see this optical phenomenon first hand (pun intended) by holding your index and middle fingers close together, so that there is a thin space between them. Face a light source and open and close your fingers slightly until you see fine black lines appear. This occurs because wavelengths of the visible light spectrum are being blocked by the gap in the same way that a diffraction grating prevents unwanted wavelengths from entering the transmission system.

Arrayed Waveguide Grating

Also based on diffraction are arrayed waveguide gratings (AWGs). Often called an *optical waveguide router* or *waveguide grating router,* an AWG device consists of an array of curved-channel waveguides. As shown in Figure 3-5, when light enters the input cavity, it is diffracted and then enters the waveguide array. The waveguides within the array are curved and therefore have a different length. This difference in length introduces phase delays in the output cavity, where an array of destination fibers are connected.

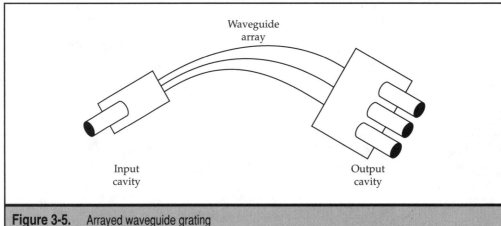

Figure 3-5. Arrayed waveguide grating

As a result of this process, different wavelengths experience maximal interference at different points, corresponding to the output ports.

Film Filters

The last type of demultiplexer uses thin film filters in multilayer interference filters. By situating these thin, film filters within the optical path, specific wavelengths can be sorted out. The filters are designed to transmit one wavelength, while reflecting other wavelengths.

As Figure 3-6 shows, by cascading these devices off one another, a number of wavelengths can be demultiplexed.

Given these different techniques, AWG and interference filters are the most popular. This is because filters are quite stable and offer good isolation between channels. However, filters can be inefficient.

AWGs are popular because they can both mux or demux at the same time. Additionally, they are best for environments where large channel counts are prevalent, and where the use of cascaded thin film filters is impractical. One concern is that they are sensitive to extreme temperatures and not suited for all environments.

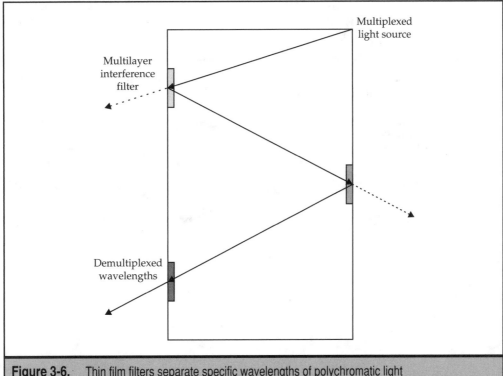

Figure 3-6.   Thin film filters separate specific wavelengths of polychromatic light

Add/drop Multiplexing

Between the time a signal was multiplexed and when it was demultiplexed, as shown in Figure 3-7, multiple wavelengths share the same fiber. However, there are often times when it would be necessary to add or remove a wavelength from the fiber before the main signal is terminated.

For instance, let's say a run of fiber stretches between New York and Los Angeles. The fiber is routed through Chicago and Las Vegas. If a signal runs between New York and Los Angeles, it would be a tremendous waste of infrastructure if the system couldn't add or remove signals in Chicago and Las Vegas (as well as any other points in between).

This can be accomplished with an add/drop multiplexer (ADM). Rather than combining or unraveling all wavelengths, the ADM can add or remove specific signals while allowing others to pass through.

SONET ADM

In the next section, we talk about SONET, the most prevalent optical networking architecture in use today. First, though, let's take a moment to discuss add/drop multiplexing and how it is specific to SONET.

SONET does not require manufacturers to offer ADMs that operate at specific levels. Therefore, one vendor might have one ADM with access at DS-1 levels, while another might offer access at both DS-1 and DS-3 levels.

NOTE: DS-*x* is a transmission rate used in North American telephone systems. DS-1 is equivalent to a T-1, at about 1.5 Mbps. DS-3 is about 45 Mbps.

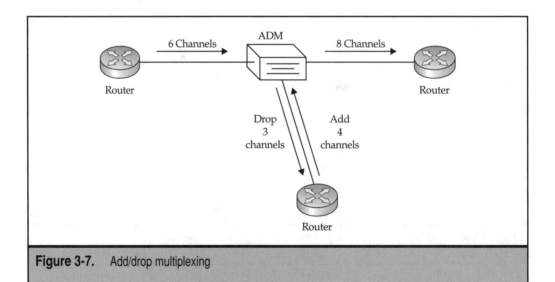

Figure 3-7. Add/drop multiplexing

Furthermore, in a rural environment, an ADM can be installed at a terminal site or a transitional location for use consolidating traffic from geographically dispersed areas. The ADM serves as an interface between the various network signals and SONET signals.

In single-stage multiplexing, an ADM can multiplex/demultiplex several tributary DS-1 signals into or from an STS-N signal (we'll explain STS in more detail a few pages from now). They can be used at terminal locations, at intermediate locations, or in hub configurations. At an intermediate location, an ADM can drop lower-rate signals for transport on different facilities. An ADM can also add lower-rate signals into a higher-rate STS-N signal. The rest of the traffic simply continues straight through.

Optical ADM

Optical ADM (OADM) is an all-optical version of ADM and is a key component in the movement toward all-optical networks. OADMs are similar in many respects to SONET ADM, except that only optical wavelengths are added and dropped, and no conversion of the signal from optical to electrical takes place.

There are different types of OADMs that fall into two functional categories:

▼ **First-generation OADMs** are fixed devices that are configured to drop specific wavelengths while adding others.

▲ **Second-generation OADMs** are reconfigurable and capable of dynamically selecting which wavelengths are added and dropped.

In current MANs using dense wavelength division multiplexing (DWDM), thin film filters have emerged as the popular OADM technology. This is due to their low cost and stability. Second-generation OADMs are emerging and are using such technologies as tunable fiber gratings.

SONET

The most basic and popular architecture for an optical network is the Synchronous Optical Network (SONET).

SONET is a standard for optical telecommunications transport developed by the Exchange Carriers Standards Association (ECSA) for the American National Standards Institute (ANSI), the body that sets industry standards in the U.S. for telecommunications and other industries. The comprehensive SONET standard is expected to provide the transport infrastructure for worldwide telecommunications for at least the next two or three decades.

NOTE: In Europe, SONET is known by another acronym, SDH, which is short for Synchronous Digital Hierarchy. We'll talk about the specifics of SDH later in this section.

SONET is so speedy that you could transmit an entire 650MB CD-ROM from New York to Seattle in less than one second. Not only is SONET fast, but it's also rather versatile. Voice calls from one office to another can be multiplexed along with data and fired out across the same fiber. Further, because of the generous bandwidth SONET affords, compression and encapsulation into Internet Protocol (IP) packets is unnecessary. For comparison's sake, a single OC-3 connection can carry more than 2000 simultaneous voice calls. Further, all types of data can be multiplexed alongside the calls.

NOTE: Don't confuse SONET with a sonnet. Whereas SONET is a type of optical network, a sonnet is a poem of fixed verse of Italian origin consisting of 14 lines that are typically five-foot iambics rhyming according to a prearranged scheme.

SONET offers a top-end bandwidth of OC-192 (9.952 Gbps) and can carry a diverse range of information. In addition to high speeds, SONET features bit-error rates of one error in 10 billion bits. Compare this with copper transmission methods that have bit-error rates of one error in 1 million bits.

Evolution

Prior to the advent of SONET, optical networks in the public telephone network developed their own individual systems to carry information, optically. They used proprietary architectures, equipment, multiplexing formats, and maintenance procedures, thus making the process of interconnecting with other telephone companies difficult. These organizations—regional Bells and interchange carriers in the United States, Canada, Korea, Taiwan, and Hong Kong—needed standards so that they could use equipment from different vendors and make their networks as compatible as possible.

Bellcore first conceived SONET in 1984. The goal was to produce a common standard for fiber optic transmission systems that would provide the operators with a common, simple, economical, and flexible transmission network. In 1988, work by standards committees had resulted in the publication of a national standard for SONET.

The publication of a standard allowed vendors to build equipment to transport information point-to-point, but they did not spell out the nature of the messages or commands that conduct performance monitoring or control, or allow equipment from different vendors to function together. This would come later in three different phases:

▼ **Phase One**   This phase, approved by ANSI in 1988, defined transmission rates and characteristics, formats, and optical interfaces.

■ **Phase Two**   This phase defined such things as synchronization, adjustments for wander and jitter, embedded operations channels, and central office electrical interfaces.

▲ **Phase Three**   This phase completed the development of SONET and included additional network management, performance monitoring, and control functions.

SONET established 51.84 Mbps as the base signal for the new system. This is also known as OC-1. (As you remember from our earlier discussions of speed, OC-1 has long since been left in the dust.)

Overview

SONET increases configuration flexibility and bandwidth availability over older tele-communications systems. Some advantages are:

▼ Equipment requirements are reduced.

■ Network reliability is increased.

■ SONET provides a synchronous multiplexing format for carrying low-level digital signals and a structure simplifying the interface to digital switches and add/drop multiplexers.

■ SONET standards allow interconnection of products from different vendors.

■ SONET defines a flexible architecture that can accommodate future applications and transmission rates.

■ SONET defines optical carrier (OC) levels and electrically equivalent synchronous transport signals (STSs) for the fiber optic–based transmission hierarchy.

■ SONET standards are based on the principle of direct synchronous multiplexing, which is key to cost-effective and flexible networking. Basically, tributary signals can be multiplexed directly into a higher rate of SONET signal without intermediate stages of multiplexing.

■ SONET provides a high level of network management and maintenance functions.

▲ SONET signals can transport all the tributary signals in use today. This means that SONET can be deployed as an overlay network to an existing network and provide enhanced flexibility.

One of the chief benefits of SONET is its capability for use in the three traditional tele-communications application areas: long-haul networks (network backbones); local networks (access networks); and loop carriers. It can also be used on a local CATV network. Its versatility makes it extremely popular.

Rings

SONET networks are deployed in dual ring configurations, as shown in Figure 3-8. All the nodes in the network are connected to dual, counter-rotating optical rings. One ring serves as the primary path; the other, as a backup.

Quite often, the network elements on the ring are ADMs that can add or remove payload easily from any point along the ring. They are connected to both rings, and in the

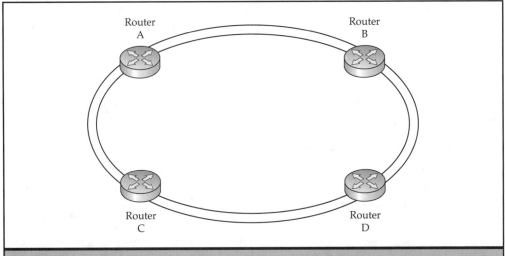

Figure 3-8. SONET is configured as a large ring, passing packets from node to node

event the primary ring fails, the devices on the failed path will detect the failure and "wrap," sealing the ring off within 50 ms, preventing a failure of the network. This capability, known as automatic protection switching (APS), is a key benefit to ring architectures. Ring architectures are used in major networks to eliminate the possibility of total failure of the network.

Ring architectures fall into two categories:

▼ **Unidirectional Path-Switched Rings (UPSR)** This is a two-fiber architecture. One fiber is used as the primary path; the other is the backup. Most information is sent across the primary path, but *keepalive* messages are sent across the backup fiber to ensure that it still functions. Whereas the primary ring flows information in one direction, the backup fiber flows information in the opposite direction.

▲ **Bidirectional Line Switched Rings (BLSR)** This is a four-fiber transmission architecture in which each pair of fibers serves as a separate bidirectional system.

Should the primary path in a UPSR configuration fail, the muxes on either side of the failure will become aware of the failure immediately because of the instant loss of the signal. At that point, the system switches over to the backup path.

However, this is more difficult in a situation where the fiber is cut between nodes A and B (please refer back to Figure 3-8). When the fiber is cut, the transmission switches to the backup ring. Now, the only way A can transmit to B is by going backward through nodes D and C. As a result, timing and synchronization issues can arise. For geographically small networks, this is not a problem, but if the nodes are situated cities apart, this can be a significant problem, especially if an application is expecting an answer at a certain time—this can throw the timing off considerably.

One way to avoid those synch problems is by using an architecture like BLSR, which is the most common architecture in North America. BLSR rings send data in both directions, so that if there is a switchover to the backup fiber, there won't be problems with synchronization. If all four fibers between nodes A and B are cut, for instance, they all instantly wrap to ensure the integrity of the ring. Furthermore, often the four fibers of a BLSR are placed along different routes, thus providing even more protection against a crazed backhoe driver.

Another type of ring is picking up steam as an alternative to four-fiber BLSR. Two-fiber BLSR transmits signals on both rings simultaneously. Each node on the ring is configured to glean its primary signal from the fiber of one ring or the other. Further, each run between nodes carries capacity for both the active and protected traffic. This ensures that bandwidth will be available in the event of a ring failure.

Structure

Like its conventional electrical cousins, SONET transmits data across the network in frames. *Frames* are a way to encapsulate and transport data in a way that it can be read by receiving nodes.

SONET signals are talked about in two ways:

▼ **Synchronous transport signal (STS)** refers to the electrical portion.

▲ **Optical carrier (OC)** is used to discuss the optical portion.

We're talking about optical networking here, you're probably thinking. What does an electrical portion—STS—have to do with anything? The main reason is that when SONET was first developed, there was still a need for an electrical component because optical switches weren't available, thus making an electrical equivalent necessary. STS is used for very short distances, like those within a switch cabinet.

Since it is accomplished electrically, STS-*x* is used to describe the *frame generation* within a switch. OC-*x* is used to describe the signal transmission from point to point.

As we mentioned in Chapter 1, bandwidth ranges from 51.84 Mbps at OC-1 to 9.953 Gbps at OC-192. Some vendors are able to handle rates at OC-786 (which is the same power to transmit seven CD-ROMs in just one second).

NOTE: An important consideration when you're purchasing optical equipment is to make sure the equipment is compatible with your local exchange carrier (LEC). Even though SONET is a standard, there are subtle differences in the way some bytes are used in the overhead of various vendors. It's best to match your equipment with the LECs.

Framing SONET

As data enters a SONET switch, it is placed into an STS frame. As Figure 3-9 shows, an STS-1 frame is a 9 × 90 byte matrix. All bytes are transmitted in order, starting at the first bit in the upper left and proceeding from left to right, ending at the frame in the lower right. This format was chosen because it would be too cumbersome to display the data as a straight line of 810 bytes.

The STS-1 payload has the capacity to transport up to the following:

▼ 28 DS-1s

■ 1 DS-3

■ 21 2.048 Mbps signals

▲ Combinations of each

Let's take a closer look at what makes up an STS frame. It is divided into two sections:

▼ Transport overhead (TOH)

▲ Synchronous payload envelope (SPE)

These sections can be compared to the header and payload sections of a conventional data frame.

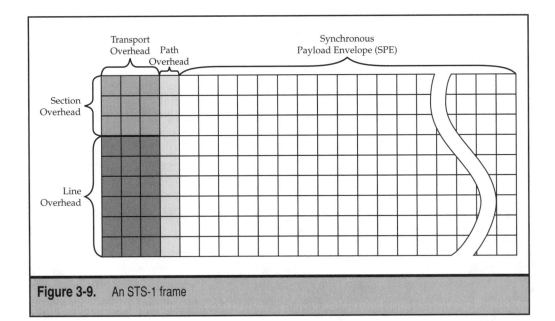

Figure 3-9. An STS-1 frame

TOH The TOH provides data crucial to the construction of an STS frame. The TOH is further subdivided into two more portions:

▼ **Section overhead (SOH)** The SOH uses a 3 × 3 byte block of the frame. It is the lowest level, just above the physical layer, and controls how the frame is transmitted from one regenerator to the next.

▲ **Line overhead (LOH)** The LOH uses a 6 × 3 byte block of the TOH and handles the SPE's placement within the frame. It also provides instructions to the ADMs about extracting the SPE.

In the next section, we'll take a closer look at what each individual byte within the TOH is responsible for.

SPE The second component of the STS frame is the SPE, which contains the meat of the frame. The SPE contains one nine-byte column called the path overhead (POH) and 86 columns of payload data. The POH contains information about the payload data and its position within the SPE.

As we mentioned earlier, the basic signal of SONET is the STS-1. The STS frame format is composed of nine rows of 90 columns of eight-bit bytes, or 810 bytes. At a rate of 8000 frames per second, that works out to a rate of 51.840 Mbps. This is known as the STS-1 signal rate—the electrical rate used primarily for transport within a specific piece of hardware. The optical equivalent of STS-1, known as OC-1, is used to talk about transmission across the fiber.

The SPE consists of 783 bytes and can be illustrated as an 87-column × 9-row matrix. The first column contains 9 bytes and contains the STS POH. Columns 30 and 59 are not used for payload but rather contain fixed data. The remaining 756 bytes in 84 columns are designated as the STS-1 payload capacity.

Depending on what type of data is contained within the frame, the SPE's payload can vary. For instance, if information at DS-3 rates is to be sent across the line, it can be mapped to the frame directly into the SPE payload. However, if a sub-DS-3 service is being transmitted, a revised container must be defined.

The STS-1 SPE can start anywhere within the STS-1 envelope, as shown in Figure 3-10. Most often, it starts in one STS-1 frame and extends into another. To keep track of the payload's starting point, a pointer contained in the TOH designates the location of the byte where STS-1 SPE begins.

The STS POH precedes each payload and is used to communicate various items of information from the point where a payload is mapped into the STS-1 SPE to where it is delivered. Take another look at Figure 3-10. Starting at byte J1, the data is written, from left to right, from top to bottom, even if the POH and SPE must cross two frames.

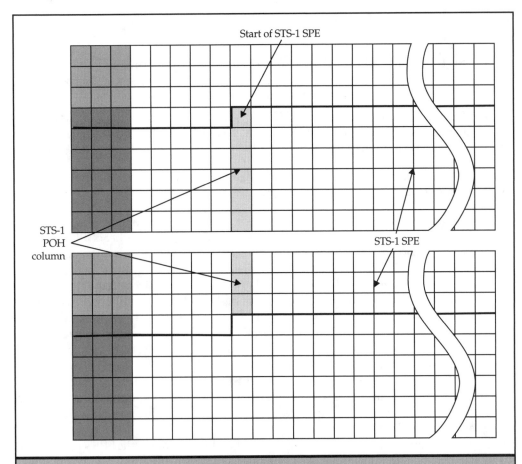

STS-1 POH column

Start of STS-1 SPE

STS-1 SPE

Figure 3-10.   The payload can begin anywhere within the envelope; usually it uses two frames

The VTs

In addition to the basic format of an STS frame, SONET also defines synchronous formats at sub-STS-1 levels. In order to fit smaller payloads within an STS frame, the STS payload may be subdivided into *virtual tributaries (VT),* which are synchronous signals used to transport lower-speed transmissions.

In SONET, four VT types exist, as shown in Table 3-1. Each VT type carries a different bandwidth, thus requiring a different amount of space within the payload.

Because of the varying sizes of VTs within a payload, SONET smoothes over the rough edges by defining a VT group (VTG). There are seven VTGs within a single STS-1

Virtual Tributary Type	Payload Type	Bandwidth	Size (in columns)
VT1.5	DS-1	1.728 Mbps	3
VT2	E-1	2.304 Mbps	4
VT3	DS-1C	3.456 Mbps	6
VT6	DS-2	6.912 Mbps	12

Table 3-1.   Types of Virtual Tributaries (VTs)

frame. Each VTG occupies 12 columns of the payload. To keep things organized, VTs are matched and placed into a VTG containing identical services. A single VTG can contain:

▼   Four VT1.5s

■   Three VT2s

■   Two VT3s

▲   One VT6

A pointer is created and defines the type of service that a single VTG is carrying. Before all seven VTGs are placed into the payload, they are interleaved, leaving columns 33 and 62 empty. This sorting and grouping allows SONET to sort out each channel from the others.

Overhead Bytes

In order to deliver easier multiplexing and more functionality, SONET uses a good deal of overhead information. This amount of overhead also provides for expanded operations, administration, maintenance, and provisioning (OAM&P) capabilities. SONET's overhead information comes in three layers, which are shown in Figure 3-11.

▼   **Path overhead** is carried across the entire length of the network, from end to end.

■   **Line overhead** is used for the STS-N signal between muxes.

▲   **Section overhead** is used for communicating between adjacent network devices, such as regenerators.

The following sections take a closer look at what is contained within each type of overhead. Figure 3-12 gives an overview of the overhead bytes, and Table 3-2 explains the duties of those bytes.

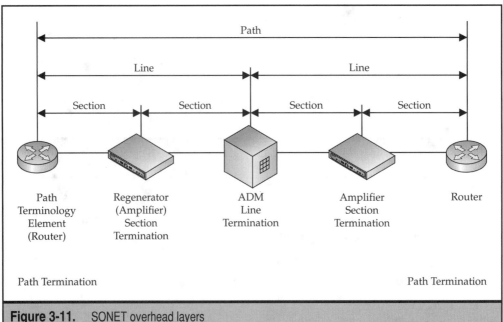

Figure 3-11. SONET overhead layers

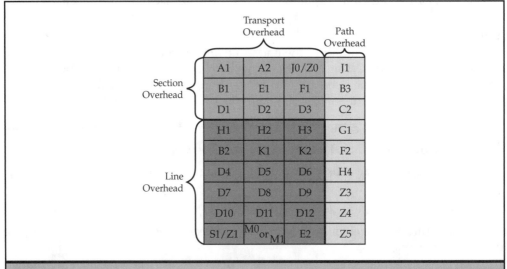

Figure 3-12. STS's overhead bytes

Byte	Overhead Type	Function
A1–A2	Section	*Framing*—These bytes indicate the beginning of an STS-1 frame.
B1	Section	*SOH bit-interleaved parity (BIP) code*—This byte is a parity code byte used to check for transmission errors over a regenerator section. This byte is defined only for STS-1 number 1 of an STS-*N* signal.
B2	Line	*LOH BIP*—This parity code byte is used to establish if a transmission error has occurred on the line. It is even parity and is calculated from all the bits of the line overhead and SPE of the previous STS-1 frame before scrambling. This byte is provided in all STS-1 signals in an STS-*N* signal.
B3	Path	*POH BIP*—This parity code bit is used to determine if a transmission error has occurred over a path. Its value is calculated from all the bits of the previous SPE before scrambling.
C2	Path	*Signal label identifying payload*—This byte is used to indicate the content of the SPE, including the payload status.
D1–D3	Section	*SOH data communications channel*—These three bytes form a 192 Kbps message channel for operations, administration, maintenance, and provisioning (OAM&P) between section-terminating equipment. The channel is used from a central location for alarms, control, monitoring, administration, and other communication needs. It is available for internally generated, externally generated, or manufacturer-specific messages.
D4–D12	Line	*LOH data communications channel*—These nine bytes form a 576 Kbps message channel from a central location for OAM&P information between line entities. A protocol analyzer is required to access the information.
E1	Section	*SOH orderwire*—This byte is used as a local orderwire channel for voice communication between regenerators, hubs, and terminals.

Table 3-2.   The Roles of Bytes Within an STS Frame

Byte	Overhead Type	Function
E2	Line	*LOH orderwire*—This byte provides a 64 Kbps channel between line entities for an express orderwire. Used by technicians as a voice channel, it is ignored as it passes through regenerators.
F1–F2	Section	*User channels (F1)*—These two bytes are set aside for users' purposes. They end at all section-terminating equipment. They can be read and written to at each section terminal in that line. *User path channel byte (F2)*—This byte is used for user communication between path elements.
G1	Path	*Path status*—This byte is used to carry path-terminating status and performance information to the originating path terminal. The entire duplex path can be monitored from either end or from any point along the path. Bits 1 through 4 are allocated for an REI function. Bits 5, 6, and 7 are allocated for an RDI-P signal. Bit 8 is currently undefined.
H1–H2	Line	*SPE location pointer*—These two bytes are allocated to a pointer indicating an offset in bytes between the pointer and the first byte of the SPE. The pointer bytes are used in all STS-1s within an STS-*N* to align the STS-1 transport overhead. Also, these bytes indicate concatenation and detect STS path alarm indication signals (AIS-P).
H3	Line	*Pointer action byte*—This byte is allocated for SPE frequency justification. It is used in all STS-1s within an STS-*N* to carry the extra SPE byte in the event of a negative pointer adjustment. This byte is not defined when it is not used to carry the SPE byte.
H4	Path	*Multiframe indicator*—This byte provides a multiframe indicator for payload containers. It is used only for tributary unit payloads.
J0/Z0	Section	*Section trace (J0)/section growth (Z0)*—This byte was refined from an earlier byte and is now either the section trace byte (in the first STS-1 of the STS-*N*) or a section growth byte (in the second through *N*th STS-1s).

Table 3-2.   The Roles of Bytes Within an STS Frame *(continued)*

Byte	Overhead Type	Function
J1	Path	*STS Path trace byte*—This byte is user-programmable and repetitively transmits a 64- or 16-byte E.164 format string. The receiving terminal in a path can verify its continued connection to the intended transmitting terminal.
K1–K2	Line	*Automatic protection switching channel*—These two bytes are used for protection signaling between line-terminating entities for bidirectional automatic protection switching and for detecting AIS-L and remote defect indication (RDI) signals.
M0 or M1/Z2	Line	*Line Far End Block Error (FEBE)*—The M0 byte is defined for STS-1 in an OC-1 or STS-1 electrical signal. Bits 5 through 8 are allocated for line remote error indication. The M1 byte is located in the third STS-1 in an STS-*N* and is used for REI-L functions. The Z2 byte is located in the first and second STS-1s of an STS-3 and the first, second, and fourth through *N*th STS-1s of an STS-*N*. These bytes are designated for future growth. OC-1 and STS-1 electrical signals do not contain the Z2 byte.
S1/Z1	Line	*Synchronization status*—This byte is located in the first STS-1 of an STS-*N*. Bits 5 through 8 of that byte convey the network element's synchronization status. The Z1 byte is located in the second through *N*th STS-1s of an STS-*N*. It is designated for future growth. OC-1 and STS-1 electrical signals do not contain the Z1 byte.
Z3–Z4	Path	*Future growth*—This byte is unassigned.
Z5	Path	*Network provider information*—This byte is used only by the network provider.

Table 3-2.   The Roles of Bytes Within an STS Frame *(continued)*

Section Overhead   Section overhead (SOH) contains nine bytes of the transport overhead. This overhead is accessed and generated by section-terminating equipment, like regenerators. This overhead supports functions such as:

- ▼ Performance monitoring (STS-N signal)
- ■ Local orderwire
- ■ Data communication channels to carry information for OAM&P
- ▲ Framing

SOH occupies the first three rows of columns 1 to 9.

Line Overhead   Line overhead (LOH) contains 18 bytes of overhead, which is accessed and generated by line-terminating equipment, such as an ADM. This overhead supports such functions as:

- ▼ Locating the SPE in the frame
- ■ Multiplexing or concatenating signals
- ■ Performance monitoring
- ■ Automatic protection switching
- ▲ Line maintenance

Line overhead is found in rows 4 to 9 of columns 1 to 9.

Path Overhead   Path overhead (POH) is the nine-byte column preceding the STS SPE. The POH contains nine bytes per 125 microseconds starting at the first byte of the STS SPE. POH facilitates communication between an SPE's creation point and its termination point. This overhead supports functions including:

- ▼ Performance monitoring of the STS SPE
- ■ Signal label (the content of the STS SPE, including status of mapped payloads)
- ■ Path status
- ▲ Path trace

The POH is found in rows 1 to 9 of the first column of the STS-1 SPE.

VT Overhead   There is another type of POH that is introduced whenever a VT occurs. A VT POH contains four POH bytes per VT SPE, starting at the first byte of the VT SPE. The VT POH is used for communication between the VT SPE's creation point and its termination point.

A VT POH allocates four bytes:

- ▼ V5
- ■ J2

- ■ Z6
- ▲ Z7

V5 is the first byte of a VT SPE, while the remaining bytes occupy the corresponding locations in the subsequent 125-microsecond frames of the VT superframe. The V5 byte provides the same functions for VT paths that the B3, C2, and G1 bytes provide for STS paths—specifically, error checking, signal label, and path status.

STS to the Nth Degree

Since SONET has been around for better than 15 years, there must have been some speed enhancements. But based on the STS-1 frame, how can we send data at higher rates? By using an STS-N frame.

SONET scales nicely because to beef up data transmission rates, several STS-1 frames can be *interleaved* into a larger STS frame. For instance, if three frames were interleaved, you would have an STS-3 frame. Twelve interleaved frames would produce an STS-12 frame, and so forth.

NOTE: STS-x follows the OC-x numbering convention. For instance, after STS-3 comes STS-12, STS-48, STS-96, and STS-192.

To make this work, the TOHs of the individual STS-1 frames are aligned before interleaving, but the SPEs are not required to be aligned, because each STS-1 frame has a payload pointer, indicating the location of the SPE.

To illustrate just how this works, let's use STS-3 as an example. STS-3 comes in two flavors: STS-3 and STS-3c (it sounds like buying a new model car and having to choose between the less expensive model and the one with leather seats and the 12-CD changer).

STS-3   As you can see in Figure 3-13, an STS-3 frame just looks like the steroid-pumped brother of an STS-1 frame. This is because an STS-3 frame is simply three STS-1 frames that have been interleaved. SONET gear recognizes STS-3 by seeing three sets of framing information bundled together. These bytes are A1 and A2 (refer back to Table 3-2 and Figure 3-12 for this location).

It all comes down to timing. For these three sets to work as one, the STS-1 frames must be in perfect synch; otherwise, the data would be scrambled and the switch couldn't tell what type of frame it is. For perfect synch, the second and third frames must be offset to match the first frame. Once the TOHs are adjusted, the offset is placed in a pointer, which is used to locate the SPE. The three SPEs are interleaved and placed into the SPE of the STS-3 frame.

STS-3c   Like the new car model that comes complete with the gas pedal warmer and the built-in entertainment system, STS-3c is the deluxe version of STS-3. The STS-3c frame is able to handle higher data rates than DS-3, like those from an ATM or FDDI network.

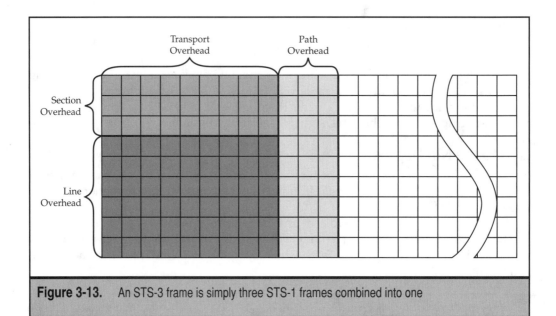

Figure 3-13. An STS-3 frame is simply three STS-1 frames combined into one

NOTE: The "c" in STS-3c stands for *concatenated*.

The difference between STS-3 and STS-3c is the lack of two columns of POH in the STS-3c frame. If those columns can be so easily dropped, you might be saying, why even have them in the first place? It is possible to drop two POH columns because the STS-3c frame is made up of data flowing at a higher rate than STS-1. It normally fills the entire SPE and only needs one POH column. Further, there are two bytes that can be dropped from the TOH because, unlike the STS-3 frame, STS-3c is not a combination of smaller STS frames.

Since STS-3 frames are interleaved to create larger frames, ADMs have an easy time pulling individual VTs out of an STS-3 frame. SONET ADM makes it unnecessary to demux the entire frame at each switch to extract a DS-1 transmission, for instance. Because the bytes are interleaved, the switch knows exactly where the DS-1 portion resides, and it can extract those bytes. It could even insert other bytes as the frame makes its way through the network.

SDH

We've told you that SDH and SONET are largely synonymous. That's true, but just to a point. In the United States and Japan, we use SONET. In Europe, however, the standard is

SDH. The two systems operate in basically the same manner; the functional difference is that a few of the bytes are assigned differently.

The most noticeable difference between the two formats is the terminology. Think of it as like the subtle language differences between America and England. In America, we have elevators; the British have lifts. In America, we eat French fries; the Brits eat chips. Americans have the synchronous transport signal (STS); the British (and the rest of Europe) have the synchronous transport module (STM). They're the same thing, just called something a little different.

But the differences aren't just superficial. The first level of STM is STM-1. However, it cannot be directly mapped to STS speeds. In reality, STM-1 is equivalent to STS-3. The other differences go down to the bytes within the frame. As we see in Figure 3-14, using the same size as an STS-3 frame, STM-1 is built a bit differently.

▼ The regenerator section overhead (RSOH) occupies the first nine bytes of the top three rows.

■ The administrative unit (AU) pointer is located in the fourth row of nine bytes. This operates similarly to bytes H1 and H2 (refer back to Figure 3-11 and Table 3-2).

▲ The multiplex section overhead (MSOH) occupies nine bytes of rows 5–9 and is similar to LOH.

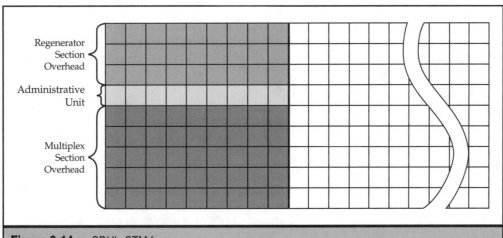

Figure 3-14. SDH's STM frame

Virtual Tributary Type	Payload Type	Bandwidth
TU-11	DS-1	1.728 Mbps
TU-12	E-1	2.304 Mbps
TU-2	DS-2	6.912 Mbps
TU-3	DS-3	49.152 Mbps

Table 3-3.   SDH's TUs

Furthermore, whereas SONET uses VTs, SDH offers four *virtual containers,* which are known as *tributary units (TUs).* TUs are designed to transport the various payload types found in countries that rely on STM. Table 3-3 shows this.

DWDM

In its beginning, SONET delivered bandwidth that was previously unimaginable. At the time, delivering OC-3 levels (155.52 Mbps) provided more bandwidth than anyone knew what to do with. Of course, those were in the mid-1980s, a decade before the Internet and high-bandwidth applications. Technology kept delivering faster and faster optical carriers. After OC-3, there were OC-12, OC-48, and beyond.

OC-48 (2.5 Gbps) is a popular speed for SONET; however, the next level, OC-192 (10 Gbps) is about the best SONET will be able to deliver. Sure, ten years ago no one knew what a gigabit was, but now we do and we can't get enough of them. The problem is that 10 Gbps is about the limit of TDM, the multiplexing technique used in SONET. The solution is to jump to WDM. WDM (as we discussed earlier) is to optical networks what FDM is to electrical networks. Besides the obvious photons versus electrons difference, the primary divergence is that WDM works on very high frequencies.

Most WDM systems operate in the C Band (the third window, at 1550 nm), which allows for close placement of channels and the use of erbium-doped fiber amplifiers (EDFAs) to improve signal strength. Older systems that spaced channels 1.6 nm (200 GHz) apart were called WDM systems. Because newer systems can pack even more channels into a wavelength, they are referred to as dense WDM (DWDM). Systems can place forty 10 Gpbs channels across a single strand of fiber for a total bit rate of 400 Gbps.

Spectral Specifics

Figure 3-15 shows, more or less, the optical spectrum. On the left half of the figure are the ultraviolet region (which is beyond human vision) and the visible spectrum. The visible spectrum contains all the wavelengths of light that the human eye can detect. In optical

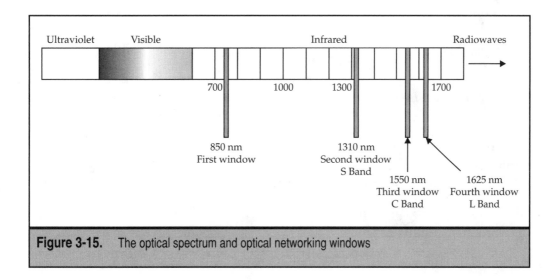

Figure 3-15. The optical spectrum and optical networking windows

networking, however, all the action takes place on the right-hand side of the spectrum, notably between 700 and 1700 nm (which is also beyond our vision).

Within that region of the spectrum are certain areas where attenuation is low. These regions, called *windows*, are little islands in an ocean of high absorption.

The first optical networks used lasers and LEDs that used a precise wavelength. Specifically, they used 850 nanometers (nm). This wavelength was ideal because it was the first window open in silica-based optical fibers. After 850 nm, other wavelengths started gaining in use. They are:

▼   The second window at 1310 nm (also known as the S Band) soon became popular, because it had even lower attenuation than the first window.

■   The third window is open at 1550 nm (also known as the C Band) with even lower loss.

▲   The fourth window is open around 1625 nm (also known as the L Band) and is currently the focus of study and development.

These windows and wavelengths are important to know because they are the wavelengths at which optical networking occurs, plus they are key components in DWDM.

DWDM Development

WDM has evolved from a system that multiplexed two channels to a system that can multiplex 160 channels for transmission across a lone strand of fiber. The following sections describe the evolution from WDM to DWDM.

WWDM

The earliest WDM systems were formed in the late 1980s and used two widely spaced wavelengths—either 1310 nm and 1550 nm or 850 nm and 1310 nm. This was often called *wideband WDM (WWDM)*. Figure 3-16 shows how this early form of WWDM was deployed.

Notice that one fiber of the pair is used to transmit and one is used to receive. This design is the most efficient arrangement and still the one found in most DWDM systems.

NWDM

By the early 1990s, a second generation of WDM had developed, called narrowband WDM (NWDM). With this design, two to eight channels could be used. But now, rather than using channels in two different windows, these channels were spaced about 400 GHz apart in the 1550 nm window.

NOTE: In optical networking parlance, you'll hear channels referred to as *lambdas* and represented by "λ." No, that's not Prince's last name, it's the Greek symbol for lambda.

DWDM

Optical networking progress didn't slow with NWDM. By the mid-1990s, DWDM architectures were on the rise. DWDM systems provided quite a boost to fiber capacity with their ability to carry 16 to 40 channels, which were spaced from 100 to 200 GHz apart in the 1550 nm window.

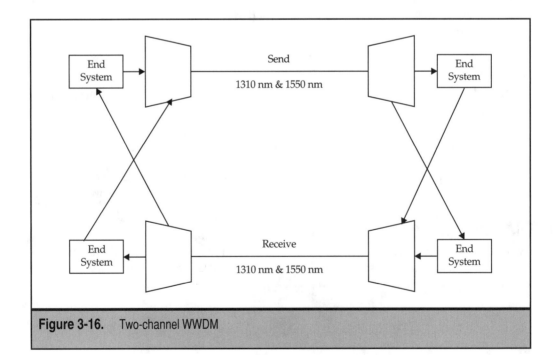

Figure 3-16.   Two-channel WWDM

Even though DWDM's early rates were impressive, by the late 1990s, DWDM had become so refined that systems could handle 64 to 160 channels, spaced just 50 or 25 GHz apart. In addition to increasing bandwidth capacity, systems had also made considerable improvements in their configuration flexibility, add/drop functions, and management.

CWDM

Even though one can squeeze 160 lambdas out of a strand of fiber, it is not ideal for long-haul applications. Squeezing so many channels together can be deleterious in a distance environment. However, channels can still be multiplexed to save on infrastructure costs. Coarse WDM (CWDM) uses a lower channel count without the cost, challenge, and complexity of amplification and tight lambda spacing.

How DWDM Works

DWDM uses a small number of physical-layer functions. In Figure 3-17, we see a schematic for a four-channel DWDM transmission. In this example, each channel occupies its own, unique wavelength. At different points in the network, different actions occur:

1. **Signal generation** A solid-state laser for each channel provides stable light within a specific bandwidth that carries the digital data, modulated as an analog signal.

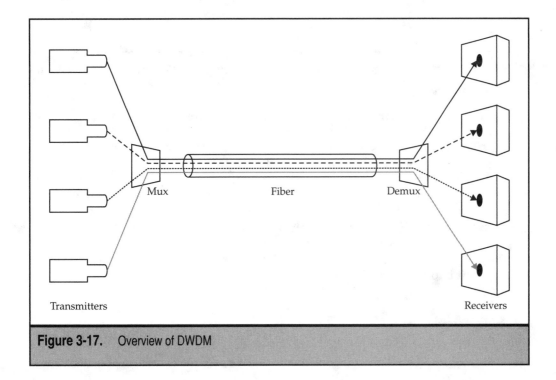

Figure 3-17. Overview of DWDM

2. **Signal combination**   The signals from several lasers are routed to a multiplexer, where they are combined for transmission. Whenever a signal is muxed or demuxed, there is a certain amount of loss. The amount of loss depends on the number of channels being combined and can be largely ameliorated with optical amplifiers.

3. **Signal transmission**   As the multiplexed signal is sent across the fiber, the risk of such problems as crosstalk and signal degradation must be considered. These problems can be minimized by controlling channel spacing, wavelength tolerance, and laser power levels. It is during the signal transmission portion that the optical signal might need to be optically amplified.

4. **Signal separation**   Once the signal arrives at the destination point, it must be broken apart into its individual lambdas.

5. **Signal receipt**   Once demultiplexed, the signal is received by a photodetector, then converted into an electronic form and sent to other network devices.

The lambdas are separated by 100 GHz to avoid fiber nonlinearities, or even closer if the fiber can support a 50 GHz gap. Each lambda is individually modulated, and the signal strengths (for best results) should be close to one another.

A challenge to DWDM network administrators comes in the form of equipment maintenance. In our preceding example, we are using four lasers. However, DWDM allows for dozens of lambdas on each run of fiber. So let's say a service provider is using 24 lasers, one for each lambda. That would mean that the provider would have to have 24 spare lasers in case of laser failure. Obviously, this is a costly proposition.

NOTE: There is an effort to develop tunable lasers that can be tuned to any output wavelength. This would reduce the number of spares that a network administrator would have to keep on hand.

The most popular form of tunable light source is the external cavity tunable laser (ECTL). Figure 3-18 shows a diagram of how this type of laser works.

The signal is sent through a laser diode, which emits a range of wavelengths that must be tuned to a much more precise wavelength. To accomplish this, the light is bounced off a piece of diffraction grating (which, as we mentioned earlier, is an etched array of very fine lines). These fine lines are etched onto a segment of fiber using ultraviolet light. Then, the grating can be tuned by rotating the diffraction grating so that a certain wavelength of light is reflected back into a cavity in the laser (as shown in Figure 3-18). Other wavelengths bounce harmlessly away from the laser.

The grating reflects just the desired wavelength back into the laser, where it is amplified and sent into the fiber.

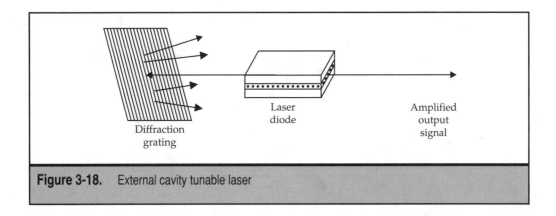

Figure 3-18. External cavity tunable laser

Optical Amplification and DWDM

As you remember from Chapter 1, as optical signals traverse a fiber optic network, the signal fades because of attenuation and dispersion. In long-haul networks, the signal must be regenerated periodically.

For instance, in a SONET optical network, each fiber carrying a signal (generally 2.5 Gbps) requires an electrical regenerator every 60 to 100 kilometers. As more fiber is added to a network, more regenerators are necessary. This adds cost to the network, not only in the price of the regenerator hardware, but also in the facilities to house and power them.

DWDM networks not only provide more capacity on each fiber optic line, but they also reduce the total cost of long-haul networks. As Figure 3-19 shows, whereas a nonmultiplexed network would require several regenerators for each piece of fiber, a DWDM network requires just one run of fiber and one set of amplifiers.

A single optical amplifier is able to boost the power of all the channels on a DWDM fiber without the need to demultiplex, process, and remultiplex the signals individually. An optical amplifier simply amplifies the signals; it does not reshape, retime, or retransmit them as a regenerator does. Although signals on a DWDM network may need to be reshaped, retimed, or retransmitted, this must be done only about once every 1000 km.

Accordingly, a 32-channel DWDM system would require just one optical amplifier, as opposed to the 32 separate regenerators on a nonmultiplexed system. In fact, the optical amplifiers would replace even more regenerators on longer spans, because more regenerators would be required than amplifiers.

NOTE: A word of clarification is in order. SONET uses regenerators (most often ADMs), where the optical signal is converted into electrical signals, amplified, then converted back into an optical signal and sent on its way. DWDM uses optical amplifiers, which require no conversion to an electrical signal.

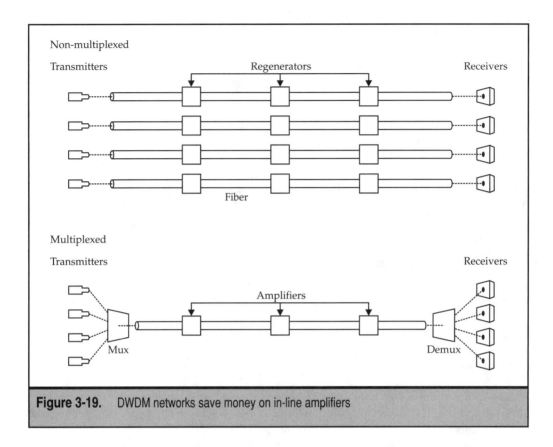

Figure 3-19. DWDM networks save money on in-line amplifiers

Furthermore, the use of optical amplifiers in DWDM systems makes the process of adding more channels much easier. For instance, if you wanted to add 10 more channels, you wouldn't have to lay 10 more strands of fiber and add the corresponding number of regenerators. Rather, all you'd need to do is install additional transponders in the DWDM systems at either end of the WDM links. The optical amplifiers that are already in place would amplify the new channels along with the others.

Typically, the cost savings more than make up for the cost of new DWDM systems. Most long-haul network operators are deploying DWDM systems, and fiber upstarts that are laying large amount of fiber are generally using DWDM to provide even more capacity.

SONET Versus DWDM

Depending on which expert you talk to, WDM is either on its way out and SONET will remain the top dog, or SONET will lose its lead to WDM. That doesn't even take into consideration DWDM or any other architecture. So what's really going to happen?

While sales of SONET systems continue to grow, WDM is picking up steam as a competing technology. According to Probe Research, the SONET market will grow from $US15.7 billion in 1999 to $US33.7 billion by 2005. At the same time, the WDM market will climb from $US4.5 billion in 1999 to $US38.2 billion by 2005.

Researchers at RHK present a closer look at North American figures. North American SONET business is expected to more than double from $US7.3 billion in 1999 to $US17.2 billion in 2003. DWDM, they project, will leap from $US3.4 billion to $US15.2 billion during the same time frame. Even though WDM is gaining, don't look for it to completely supplant SONET. Because switching from SONET to other technologies is expensive—and largely unnecessary—we will still see both architectures in wide use.

DYNAMIC PACKET TRANSPORT

SONET and DWDM are all technologies that are widely used and have technical specifications that have been developed and/or approved by the Institute of Electrical and Electronics Engineers (IEEE) or the Internet Engineering Task Force (IETF). This makes them standardized so that a range of vendors can use them.

Cisco Systems, of San Jose, California, has introduced its own way to transport information around an optical network. Cisco's Dynamic Packet Transport (DPT) is being positioned as a challenger to SONET. Though DPT is not a standard, Cisco has been pushing the IEEE and the IETF to set up study groups to develop standards for the underlying technology, known as the Spatial Reuse Protocol (SRP).

DPT Overview

DPT is an optical ring technology, which, unlike SONET, allows the full fiber ring bandwidth to be utilized. DPT provides the potential evolution from multilayered infrastructure equipment to intelligent network services based on Open Systems Interconnection (OSI) layer-3 (Internet Protocol [IP]/multi protocol label switching [MPLS]) service and the optical transport layer.

NOTE: We'll talk about the layers of the IP stack in more detail in Chapter 4.

DPT technology employs a new media access control (MAC) layer protocol called the SRP, which supports scalable and optimized IP packet aggregation and transport in LANs, MANs, and WANs. The SRP ensures fiber usage fairness by using a fairness algorithm and destination packet removal. In doing so, the SRP can scale a number of nodes, while still ensuring a high delivery of high-priority IP packets.

DPT uses a bidirectional ring, which is composed of two symmetric, counter-rotating fiber rings. Each of these rings can be used simultaneously to pass data and control packets. Figure 3-20 shows the DPT ring architecture along with data and control packet flow.

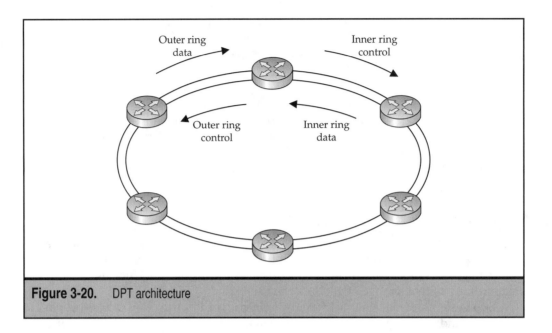

Figure 3-20.   DPT architecture

The differentiation between the two rings is that one ring is called the *inner* ring and the other is called the *outer* ring. DPT sends data packets along the fiber in one direction (upstream) while sending control packets in the other direction (downstream). By doing so, DPT is able to use both fibers simultaneously, maximizing bandwidth.

Spatial Reuse

To maximize the amount of available bandwidth, DPT employs the SRP. The SRP (which we will explain in more depth later in this section) is used to increase the overall amount of bandwidth. This is accomplished by using *destination stripping*. The destination node strips the packets from the ring, opening up bandwidth.

In contrast, such data ring technologies as FDDI or Token Ring did *source stripping*. With source stripping, packets moved around the entire ring before the sender removed them. This left the packets on the ring, even after they had been received at their destination, wasting bandwidth.

Figure 3-21 demonstrates how DPT's spatial reuse works. In this example, Router 2 is sending packets to both Routers 6 and 4. Meanwhile, Router 7 is sending traffic to Router 1. In each case, the fact that the destination router strips off the unicast data from the ring frees bandwidth. In our example, this means that the conversation between Routers 7 and 1 need not be delayed because of the excess traffic generated by the other routers.

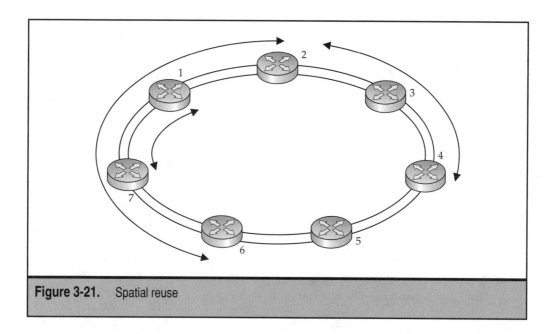

Figure 3-21. Spatial reuse

Fairness

DPT also ensures a level of fairness in its network. To ensure that each node on the DPT ring is able to transmit and receive data, the DPT ring uses an algorithm called the SRP fairness algorithm (SRP-fa). This algorithm is employed to guarantee the following:

▼ **Global fairness**   SRP-fa ensures each node a fair share of the ring's bandwidth by controlling the rates at which packets are forwarded into the ring. This ensures that no single node can hog all the bandwidth and cause extreme lags.

▲ **Local optimization**   In spite of the fairness issue, local optimization allows bandwidth-hungry applications from one node to be able to use ring bandwidth that other nodes might not need at the moment. The bandwidth-hungry node can use more that its fair share of resources, as long as no other nodes are negatively impacted.

Not only is it important to ensure that enough bandwidth is available (thanks to spatial reuse), but for a network to be speedy and efficient, all nodes on that network must be able to have an equal shot at getting their packets on the ring.

The Spatial Reuse Protocol (SRP)

The core technology of DPT is the Spatial Reuse Protocol (SRP). On a DPT ring, each node uses a distributed copy of the SRP-fa in its MAC layer. In order to ensure that space on the ring is being used efficiently, it is necessary to have a set of rules that govern what nodes can and cannot place on the ring at any one time.

SRP Operations   The SRP takes care of the following functions within a DTP network:

▼   **Receive operations**   Packets entering a node are copied to a receive buffer if the destination address (DA) matches the node's address. If the packet is also designated as a unicast packet, then the packet is stripped and sent to the appropriate higher-layer processes. The packet is queued up in the node's transmit buffer (TB) for forwarding to the next node if any of the following conditions exist:

■   If the DA of the packet does not match the node's address

■   If the packet is a multicast and the packet's source address (SA) does not match the node's address

■   If the packet passes time-to-live and cyclic redundancy check (CRC) tests

▲   **Transmit operations**   A packet sent from the node is a packet that either has been forwarded or has originated from the node via the TB. Packets are prioritized, and the higher-priority packets are sent first. As long as the low-priority buffer is empty, the high-priority queue will be transmitted. However, if there are packets in the low-priority queue, then it will be sent in accordance with SRP-fa rules.

By regulating how the nodes transmit information, the SRP ensures that bandwidth is used economically and efficiently.

SRP-fa   When a node in a DPT network experiences congestion, it will send a message (called an advertisement) to upstream nodes via the opposite ring. The advertisement relays the value of the node's transmit usage counter. Next, upstream nodes adjust their transmit rates not to exceed the values sent by the congested node. In addition to adjusting their own transmit rates, the nodes will send the advertisement to their immediate upstream neighbors. In the event a congested node receives an advertisement from another node, it will transmit its minimum level of traffic, along with speed advisories. A node's congestion is detected when the depth of the low-priority transmit buffer reaches a preset threshold.

In the event nodes are not transmitting data, *usage packets* are occasionally sent out to carry advertised values and act as *keepalives* to inform upstream nodes that a data link is still present.

The SRP-fa does not bother itself with nodes that are not actively transmitting. The SRP-fa concerns itself only with low-priority packets. High-priority packets do not have to follow SRP-fa rules, because they can be transmitted any time as long as there is enough space in the buffer.

High-priority packets can, however, be limited if need be by using a feature like the committed access rate (CAR) before it is sent to the DPT ring.

DPT Versus SONET

As we said earlier: DPT is an emerging technology. How far it emerges is largely dependent on how many networks are built with Cisco devices using DPT and if it is blessed by
the IEEE or the IETF.

SONET still reigns as the popular optical architecture, and there are a few factors that
are likely to keep SONET on top.

So far, DPT has been implemented only on Cisco's routers. What's more, these aren't
cheap models either—they're big and they require a dump truck full of money to buy. For
example, a fully loaded Cisco GSR 12000 router can cost $US200,000—about three times
more than a small SONET router.

Even though DPT uses both rings for such things as self-healing and redundancy, it still
doesn't match the speeds of the latest SONET routers. Currently, each DPT ring operates at
OC-12. SONET is, inherently, less efficient than DPT, because it uses only one of its rings,
whereas DPT uses both. However, current SONET routers support OC-192 speeds—which
(on just one ring) is eight times faster than DPT.

On the other hand, DPT has its own features that SONET can't touch. The big benefit
is that DPT supports multicasting. SONET supports multicasting in theory, but it would
require operators to install SONET cross-connects, which are more costly than routers.

DPT also makes optical networking an easier pursuit. Because of its "plug-and-play"
capabilities, it is easier to install DPT devices, thus enabling operators to automate service
provisioning.

As optical networking is a new technology (as compared to conventional electrical
networks), there are only a few ways to share data between network elements. Even
though optical networking doesn't have as many transport methods as conventional
electrical networks, the optical architectures provide a means to transmit large amounts
of data from point to point.

One way to achieve these high bit rates is through multiplexing and demultiplexing.
The ability to combine several channels into one and transmit it across a lone strand of fiber increases capacity as much as 160-fold.

The first and most widely used optical architecture was SONET. Established as a standard in the mid-1980s, SONET is the most widely used architecture today. Despite its
prevalence and availability, SONET is not perfect. As its speeds top out at OC-192, increasing demand for bandwidth is bringing other technologies into the fray.

Multiplexing is the basis of DWDM, which uses various wavelengths within the four
optical windows to converge many channels into one. Because it combines many channels, it can transmit far more data than SONET.

Finally, an emerging optical networking architecture is Cisco's DPT. Based largely on
the ring technology of SONET, it uses infrastructure resources much more efficiently
than SONET. Unfortunately, it is not as fast as SONET and is still a proprietary technology of Cisco Systems.

PART II

Optical Networking Tools, Applications, and Vendors

CHAPTER 4

Optical Networking Design

The process of designing a network can be a challenge in and of itself. When optical considerations are added, the process becomes even more complex. Both electrical- and optical-based networks share some common ground in the realm of network design. In this chapter, we examine the specifics of networking design in general and optical networking design in particular.

NETWORKING BASICS

In order for you to design your own network—or update an existing one—it's important to understand how networks function. Networks are not only a conglomeration of devices and cabling, but also a conjunction of technologies and techniques.

For networks—and internetworks—to function properly, devices on the network must speak a common language. On the Internet, devices must also know how to locate each other in a vast sea of computers and other devices. In this section, we'll talk about those issues and examine the OSI reference model, protocols, IP addressing, and specific considerations of optical networking design.

OSI Reference Model

One of the key technologies behind network design comes from a standard established in the late 1970s. The Open Systems Interconnect (OSI) Reference Model was established to provide the standard by which computers could communicate with each other.

The OSI Reference Model has seven functional layers. Each defines a function performed when data is transferred between applications across a network, as illustrated in Figure 4-1. Each protocol communicates with a peer that is an equivalent implementation of the same protocol on a remote system.

For example, the Simple Mail Transfer Protocol (SMTP) is an application layer protocol that communicates with peer e-mail applications on remote systems. The e-mail applications do not care whether or not the physical layer is optical fiber or a twisted-pair Ethernet connection. They are concerned only with functions within SMTP.

▼ **Layer 1**   The *physical layer* deals with the actual transport medium that is being used. It defines the electrical and mechanical characteristics of the medium carrying the data signal. Some examples include coaxial cable, fiber optics, twisted-pair cabling, and serial lines.

■ **Layer 2**   The *data link layer* governs access to the network and reliable transfer of packets across the network. It controls synchronization of packets transmitted as well as error checking and flow control of transmissions. Token-passing or collision-based techniques like Ethernet work at this layer.

■ **Layer 3**   The *network layer* is concerned with moving data between different networks or subnetworks. It's responsible for finding the destination device for

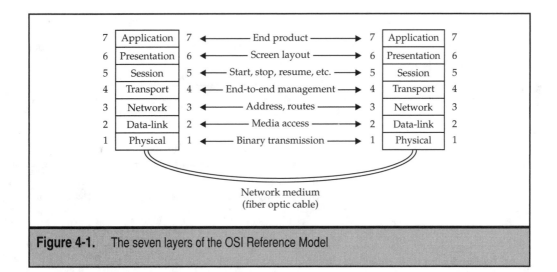

Figure 4-1.   The seven layers of the OSI Reference Model

which the data is sent. IP together with IP routing is a function of Layer 3 of the OSI model.

■ **Layer 4**   The *transport layer* takes care of data transfer, ensuring that data reaches its destination intact and in the proper order. The Transmission Control Protocol (TCP) and User Datagram Protocol (UDP) operate at this layer.

■ **Layer 5**   The *session layer* establishes and terminates connections and arranges sessions between two computers. The Lightweight Directory Access Protocol (LDAP) and Remote Procedure Call (RPC) provide some functions at this layer.

■ **Layer 6**   The *presentation layer* is involved in formatting data for the purpose of display or printing. Data encryption and character set translation such as ASCII to EBCDIC are also performed by protocols at this layer. BIOS and file storage methods work on this level.

▲ **Layer 7**   The *application layer* defines the protocols to be used between the application programs. Examples of protocols at this layer are SMTP, HTTP, and FTP.

Datalink Protocols

One might think that getting computers to share information is simple: just plug one into the other and watch the data flow. If only it were that easy. In order for the information to pass back and forth between computers, it's necessary to have protocols in place to act as an intermediary or a messenger service.

Ethernet

The most popular network technology is *Ethernet,* which carries data at a rate of 10, 100, or 1000 megabits per second (Mbps).

> **NOTE:**   You'll often hear 100 Mbps Ethernet referred to as *Fast* Ethernet and 1000 Mbps Ethernet referred to as Gigabit Ethernet.

Ethernet operates by contention. Devices sharing an Ethernet local area network (LAN) segment listen for traffic being carried over the wire and defer transmitting a message until the medium is clear. If two stations send at about the same time and their packets collide, both transmissions are aborted and the stations back off and wait a random period of time before retransmitting.

Ethernet is inherently less expensive than other technologies, thanks to the random nature of its architecture. In other words, the electronics needed to run Ethernet are easier to manufacture because Ethernet doesn't try to control everything on the LAN.

The obvious disadvantage of Ethernet is that a lot of raw bandwidth is sacrificed to aborted transmissions as a result of collisions. Theoretical maximum effective bandwidth from Ethernet is estimated at only 37 percent of raw wire speed. However, the equipment is so inexpensive that Ethernet has always been, on balance, the cheapest form of effective bandwidth.

ATM

Asynchronous Transfer Mode (ATM) transmits 53-byte cells instead of the packets used by other protocols. A *cell* is a fixed-length message unit. Like packets, cells are pieces of a message, but the fixed-length format leads to certain characteristics:

- ▼ **Virtual circuit orientation**   Cell-based networks run better in point-to-point mode, where the receiving station is ready to actively receive and process the cells.

- ■ **Speed**   The hardware knows exactly where the header ends and the data starts in every cell, thereby speeding processing operations. ATM networks run at speeds of up to 622 Mbps.

- ▲ **Quality of Service (QoS)**   Predictable throughput rates and virtual circuits enable cell-based networks to better guarantee service levels to types of traffic that are high-priority.

As with token-passing architectures, ATM's deterministic design yields high effective bandwidth from raw wire speeds.

If ATM is so much better than other network protocols, why aren't all networks running it? The answer lies in the fact that most traffic is not sensitive to transmission latency. The added expense and complexity of ATM can be hard to justify in the absence of a lot of multimedia traffic, because there is sufficient time to repackage messages at the receiving end. Figure 4-2 shows examples of both types of traffic.

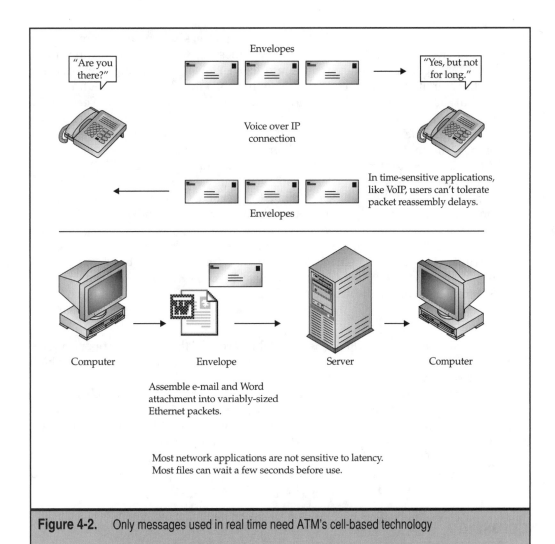

Figure 4-2.   Only messages used in real time need ATM's cell-based technology

An even more important consideration that keeps ATM off the world's desktops is a simple matter of finances. ATM is far more expensive to implement than comparable technologies. In a LAN setting, it is too costly to deploy ATM. However, in the network core, the technology and its cost can be easier to justify.

Normal messages aren't particularly sensitive to intermittent delays or the sequence of delivery. For example, an e-mail message with a document attached might be 20KB. The user doesn't care about the order in which various chunks of the message are received and wouldn't even be aware of any delays. Therefore, the network can deliver the message as it sees fit.

Compared to the tiny size of ATM cells, Ethernet packet size can range from 64 bytes to over 1500 bytes—up to about 25 times larger per message unit. By being so much more granular, ATM becomes that much more controllable. However, there is a downside as a result of that granularity. Attached to the beginning and end of each cell is routing information about each cell. This is known as the *cell tax*. Though the granularity of each cell is beneficial, the cell tax takes its toll because bytes are sucked up thanks to the extra overhead. An Ethernet packet, for example, that is 1500 bytes needs only one header, whereas sending the same amount of information over ATM requires about 25 headers.

ATM is designed to run over fiber optic cable operating the SONET. As with token-passing architectures, ATM's deterministic design yields high effective bandwidth from its raw wire speed. Most ATM backbone LANs run OC-3 or OC-12. Most intercity links run OC-12, although major Internet backbone providers are now wiring OC-48 to meet ever-increasing bandwidth demands.

Most intercity Internet trunks are OC-12 running ATM, with OC-48 taking over the heavier trunks. For example, UUNET—one of the largest Internet backbone providers—uses 622 Mbps fiber optic cabling to connect Chicago with Atlanta, and 2.5 Gbps OC-48 to link New York with Washington, D.C.

FDDI

Fiber Distributed Data Interface (FDDI) is a 100 Mbps protocol that runs over fiber optic cable media. FDDI uses a token-passing architecture to control media access, yielding high effective bandwidth from its 100 Mbps wire speed.

FDDI's architecture made it attractive for use in backbone LANs, especially for office campuses and other large-area applications. FDDI has started to fade from the scene, because ATM and Gigabit Ethernet are usurping it as the backbone technology of choice.

FDDI uses dual rings to provide additional reliability because of their redundant paths. The secondary ring goes into action when the primary ring fails. As Figure 4-3 shows, FDDI isolates the damaged station by wrapping around to the secondary ring and looping back in the other direction, thus keeping the ring intact.

IP Addressing

The Internet is a big, big place, holding billions of Web pages—and getting bigger every day. Designers had to come up with a way for you to easily find what you want. To that end, IP addresses were developed. These numbers, which you've probably seen here and there, are four sets of digits—or octets—separated by decimal points, like 220.151.102.0, for example.

IP Addressing Basics

IP addressing solves the problems of Internet organization, and computers can easily keep track of these addresses. We forgetful human beings have problems, however, keeping track of really long strings of numbers like 220.151.102.0. So, to make the process easier for us, we use Uniform Resource Locators (URLs), which are then translated back into IP addresses.

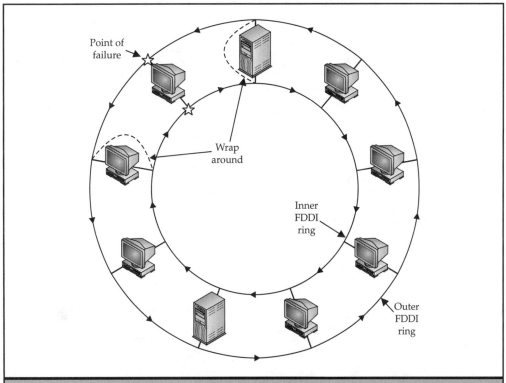

Figure 4-3. FDDI was the backbone of choice for years because of its speed and redundancy

URLs only exist to make surfing the Internet easier; they aren't true IP addresses. In other words, if you type the URL "www.velte.com" into your browser, a query is sent to the nearest Domain Name System (DNS) server to translate the URL to an IP address, as shown in Figure 4-4.

Translation to IP addresses is necessary because the routers and switches that run the Internet don't recognize domain names. Indeed, an IP address must be used just for your query to get as far as the DNS server.

All Internet addresses are IP addresses, issued by the Internet Assigned Numbers Authority (IANA). Domain names are issued by an organization called InterNIC (for Internet Information Center). The primary responsibility of these organizations is to assure that all IP addresses and domain names are unique. For example, www.velte.com was issued by InterNIC; and its IP address, 64.66.150.248, was issued by the ISP, which for its part was issued the IP address from the IANA.

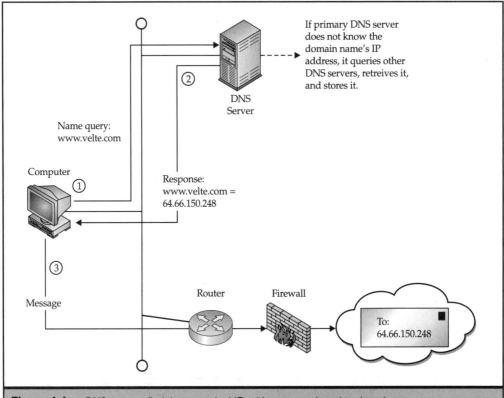

If primary DNS server does not know the domain name's IP address, it queries other DNS servers, retreives it, and stores it.

DNS Server

Name query:
www.velte.com

Computer

Response:
www.velte.com =
64.66.150.248

Message

Router   Firewall

To:
64.66.150.248

Figure 4-4.   DNS servers find the numerical IP addresses assigned to domain names

NOTE: A new organization called the Internet Corporation for Assigned Names and Numbers (ICANN) was started in early 1999 to take over assignment duties.

The IP Address Format

Every node on the Internet must have a unique IP address. This includes hosts as well as networks. There's no getting around this rule, because IP addressing is what ties the Internet together. Even stations connected to a LAN with its own addressing system (AppleTalk, for example) must translate to IP in order to enter the Internet.

It's somewhat ironic that, despite the requirement that every IP address be unique to the world, at the same time they all must be in the same format. IP addresses are 32 bits long and divided into four sections, each 8 bits long.

Routers use IP addresses to forward messages through the Internet. Put simply, as the packet hops from router to router, it works its way from left to right across the IP address until it finally reaches the router to which the destination address is attached.

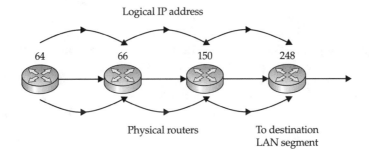

Logical IP address

64   66   150   248

Physical routers   To destination
                          LAN segment

Of course, sometimes a message will go through several router hops before moving closer to its destination. More frequently, messages skip over entire octets and move to the destination LAN segment in just one or two hops.

Protocols, IP addressing, and the OSI Reference Model are common attributes shared between electrical and optical networks. These items help tell networking devices how to communicate with one another, and they provide a framework for connectivity. Another issue in ensuring effective connectivity is ensuring there is enough power in a network connecting one device to another. In the next section, we look at specific issues that challenge the design of optical LANs and how you can plan ahead for those challenges.

Optical LAN Considerations

By virtue of the somewhat tricky nature of optical fiber and photon loss, it is impractical just to buy a spool of optical fiber, string it through your building, and plug it in to connectors, expecting it to work. Connecting optical fiber requires an element of planning to ensure that you have a system with the correct capabilities.

Budgets

The first task in designing a fiber optic network is power budgeting. That means that you have to subtract all the system's optical losses from the power delivered by the transmitter and ensure that there is still enough power to drive the receiver at the desired bit-error rate or signal-to-noise ratio. You should also add some padding above the receiver's minimum requirements to allow for unexpected sources of loss, such as system degradation or splicing.

NOTE: When talking about power, it's important to know what power you're talking about. Manufacturers like to speak in terms of peak power (that is, the most their product generates). Peak power tends to be about twice as much as the average power. If you are mindful of your terms—peak or average power—you shouldn't run into any problems.

Loss

Even though fiber optic cabling is made with "pure" silica glass, there are still enough impurities within the core to impede a certain level of photon flow. The simplest way to approximate how much loss will occur within a strand of fiber is to multiply the attenuation (measured in dB per km) by the transmission distance. Further, light emitting diodes (LEDs) with large emitting areas excite high-order modes that leak out through the cladding as they travel. This loss (which winds up being a maximum of about 1.5 dB) occurs in the first few hundred meters of the fiber. This means that in multimode fibers, the first few hundred feet have a higher amount of loss than the rest of the run. Once your fiber exceeds a full kilometer or so, then the actual loss and the calculated loss are about equal.

Losses in an optical network come from such sources as:

▼ Loss transferring light from the source to the fiber

■ Connector loss

■ Splice loss

■ Coupler loss

■ Fiber loss

▲ Fiber-to-receiver coupler loss

As we've noted, attenuation in an optical network is measured in decibels. Decibels are a logarithmic unit measuring the ratio of output power to input power. Loss in decibels is often expressed as:

$$dB \text{ LOSS} = -10 \times \log_{10} (\text{POWER IN}/\text{POWER OUT})$$

Therefore, if the output power is 0.001 of input power, the signal has experienced a 30 dB loss.

Decibels can be a confusing subject. They aren't a simple, linear measurement. Rather, they are logarithmic and multiply by a factor of 10 as they progress. For example, 20 dB is not twice as much as 10 dB. Rather, it 100 times as much as 10 dB (10×10). Thirty dB is 1000 times more than 10 dB ($10 \times 10 \times 10$), and so forth.

NOTE: An increase of 5 dB is an increase by a factor of the square root of 10.

Managing loss in an optical network is an extremely important job. Let's take a closer look at some common sources of loss.

NOTE: Decibels are actually tenths of the unit *Bel* named for Alexander Graham Bell.

Light   One of the largest light losses comes when light is being transferred from the source into the fiber. The problem is lining up the light source with the optical core (which, as you recall, is only about 62 micrometers in diameter). This is an even greater problem in systems with LEDs that are larger than the fiber core, as shown in Figure 4-5.

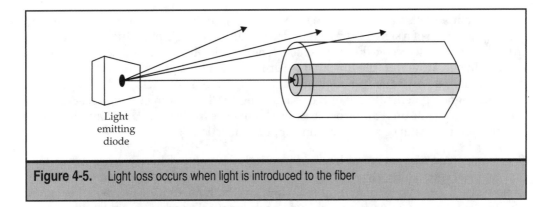

Figure 4-5. Light loss occurs when light is introduced to the fiber

Four things can happen to the light in systems where the emitting area is larger than the core:

▼ Some of the light is lost in the cladding and dissipated

■ Some light rays are emitted at angles outside the fiber's acceptance angle

■ Some light might miss the fiber entirely

▲ Some light makes it successfully into the core—but not the full power of the light emitting diode (LED).

These losses can take a hefty toll on power output. An LED generating 1 mW can have that amount cut to 50 microwatts (µW), which is a 13 dB loss.

Lasers, on the other hand, typically introduce a full milliwatt into the fiber, because they are very specific and focused. However, there are several good reasons why LEDs exist—price and convenience. LEDs are considerably cheaper than lasers, and they aren't a chore to keep cool and tuned. Finally, LEDs last longer than lasers.

Receivers   It's important to work a balancing act with the power budget of your optical network. The sensitivity of your receivers must be weighed against the power in your network. If, for instance, your network is consuming too much of your fiber's power, then there won't be enough for the receiver to decipher. The problem is exacerbated as bit rates increase. As the bit rate accelerates, the receiver needs more input power to operate within defined bit-error rates. Conversely, if the data rate is held constant, but the power is lowered, expect bit-error rates to ramp up sharply. For example, a 1 dB drop in power can increase your bit-error rate 1000 times. A good technique—especially at the outer limits of your network's reach—is to lower the bit rate.

NOTE: So what's the problem? Just jack up the power, right? Wrong. A higher power level can overload your detector and introduce its own bit errors.

For example, let's say you've got a LAN with hosts at the far corners of your building. If the light source of a signal is traveling through the building's fiber, the hosts closest to the light source will receive the best signal strength and will be able to send and receive at optimal levels. However, the host that is furthest from the light source may encounter errors because there just isn't enough power to carry the bits so quickly. Rather than try to boost the signal (potentially out of the usable range of the equipment), it is best to lower the transmission rate until the errors cease. Naturally, the furthest host will have the lowest bit rate, but it will still be speedier than copper connections.

Connectors   A major source of loss in an optical network is where splices, connectors, and couplers enter your network. Manufacturers of connectors generally provide a rating of how much loss they will account for. They give both maximum and average values. For instance, let's say in your network you use six optical connectors, each with a maximum loss of 1 dB and an average of .5 dB. You could be safe with your calculations and just expect a 6 dB loss, thanks to the connectors. On the other hand, it would be more realistic to assume that you are running in the average range with a total loss of 3 dB. It's safer to assume the worst (especially for power budgeting), but remember that too much power can overload your receivers.

Fiber

Your choice in fiber is another factor to consider in your network. With multimode fibers, increasing the fiber's core diameter or the numerical aperture increases the amount of light collected by the fiber.

Single-mode fibers also will do better with a wider core. For instance, if you use a strand of fiber with a 10 µm core you'll see a huge loss (more than 19 dB) as compared with a core that is 50 µm in diameter.

One way to lessen this problem is by using tiny lenses that focus the light into the fiber core. You will still experience hefty losses, but they will be much less than the previous examples illustrated.

Example

Now that we've thrown some of the variables your way, let's take a look at a very simple optical LAN. In our design, we have an office building and two computers, which are on opposite ends of the building (as Figure 4-6 illustrates). We are using an LED transmitter, and because of the distance between the computers, we need several optical connectors. Table 4-1 outlines each component of our connection and shows how much loss there will be as a result of each item.

In this scenario, you can see that the two largest sources of loss are the LED and the connectors. We could improve the overall loss budget of this scenario by getting an LED and fiber that are closer in size to each other. Also, we could buy connectors that have less loss.

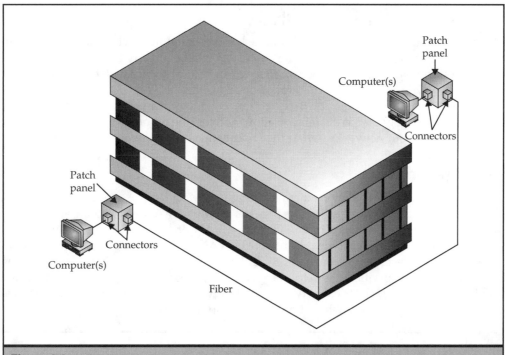

Figure 4-6. Example of loss budgeting

NOTE: Notice also that we included a 6 dB *margin*. This is the "padding" that you'd ideally like to work into your network (but without overloading your receiver). By leaving some additional wiggle room in your network, you can splice accidental cuts or additional growth that you wouldn't be aware of at the time of the network's design. Typical margins generally range from 3 to 10 dB.

Source of Loss	Loss (dB)
LED transmitter	–16 dB
Fiber loss (200 m @ 2.5 dB/km)	–0.5 dB
Connectors (6 @ .5 dB)	–3 dB
Margin	–6 dB
Total (needed receiver sensitivity)	–25.5 dB

Table 4-1. Example of Loss Budgeting

PHYSICAL CONSIDERATIONS

When designing a network, an important task is understanding where individual components will physically reside. In some cases, this will be already decided for you (employee desktops, an equipment room, and so forth), but in other cases, you may be able to decide where you can locate devices for optimal results.

In this section, we talk about where networking devices can be located and how they can be connected together. We'll tell you about networking topology basics and then how you can design your networks so that they maintain a high level of reliability.

Network Topology

The layout of a network is referred to as its *topology*. Most devices—computers, servers, add-drop multiplexers, and other components on the network—are connected to other networks through either hubs or switches on a LAN or switches, routers, and optical cross-connects (OXCs) on a wide area network (WAN). These tools give network administrators more choices in both the physical and logical network topologies. Before talking about optical fiber specifics, it is helpful to understand some design philosophies that are used in conventional, electrical networks. Not only are these designs used in electrical networks, but they are also design types used in optical networking.

NOTE: We'll explain what OXCs are a little later in this chapter.

When you design an optical network, efficiency is critical. Efficiency in design and, ultimately, management will mean lower costs for layout and construction, seamless migration and operation, and a lower optical loss. Last but not least, an efficient design will mean cost savings when bringing fiber to the desk.

Depending on your organization's layout, setup, and functions, your optimal network layout will vary. In this section, we take a closer look at the four prevalent network topologies in optical networks. Each of the four network types has advantages and disadvantages, depending largely on the application.

Bus

In a bus network, all the nodes are connected in a single line. This topology is especially useful in manufacturing or assembly line environments where a product starts on one end of the factory and is finished at the far end. The nodes are laid out in a linear array alongside the factory machinery. Because the equipment requires such overhead clearances, there is normally more than enough room to string cable through the workroom.

> **NOTE:**   The nodes are in a single line as it relates to the bus line. The line may bend and connect a couple floors or bend around wall. If the bus goes around a corner, it doesn't cease being a bus line.

In a conventional network, nodes can be easily tapped into the bus in parallel with a direct connection or by using an attenuating tap. Attenuating taps are nice because they allow for speedier connections, but they can be a pain to connect.

Fiber optics, on the other hand, aren't so easily connected. You can't simply splice into the fiber and run a cable down to a terminal. Instead, tapping must be done with a modem. The intermediate modems in the bus (except for the modems at either end of the string) are repeaters that connect with the other nodes, passing the optical signal to all the modems on the bus. Figure 4-7 shows what a fiber optic bus network looks like.

Ring

Nodes in a ring topology are connected in a circular fashion. Each node is a repeater, and all nodes operate at the same speed under the same protocol. In theory, a simple ring handles complex processes, but in practice, relatively few processes lend themselves to a ring layout. A ring network can, however, be advantageous in high-reliability applications, because it can be installed in a modified *self-healing* configuration.

A ring topology attaches hosts in a logical ring. We use *logical* to describe a ring topology because the LAN, WAN, or MAN segment behaves like a ring by passing signals in a round-robin fashion as if the devices were actually attached to a looped cable. Physically, though, ring topologies may be configured however the physical environment demands. This fact is shown in Figure 4-8.

As you recall from Chapter 3, the ring topology is the topology for such architectures as SONET and Cisco's Dynamic Packet Transport (DPT) and provides for self-healing services.

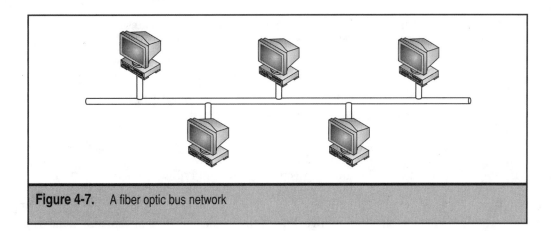

Figure 4-7.   A fiber optic bus network

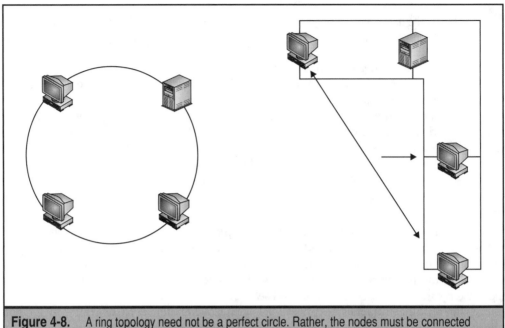

Figure 4-8.   A ring topology need not be a perfect circle. Rather, the nodes must be connected in a logical ring

Collapsed Backbone

There are a number of different kinds of cabling stretching through office buildings around the world. Such cabling as broadband, baseband, and fiber cables are the three main types that one is likely to encounter when looking into a piece of cabling conduit:

▼   **Baseband** is the popular Ethernet cable used to connect nodes electrically. It's the "base" in such cable identifications as 10baseT.

■   **Broadband** is the same type coaxial cabling used by cable television companies and can carry a number of channels simultaneously.

▲   **Fiber**, as we've described earlier in this chapter, is glass cabling that allows light signals to be transmitted between nodes.

A *collapsed backbone* brings all the interbuilding LAN connections into one location. This allows for easier management and lessens the chance that a cable plant problem will affect multiple buildings. The interconnection equipment typically resides in a building protected with a controlled environment and backup power. This topology is shown in Figure 4-9.

Routine management of the network is improved when the backbone is collapsed into a central location. Using a collapsed backbone, network problems can be isolated to a

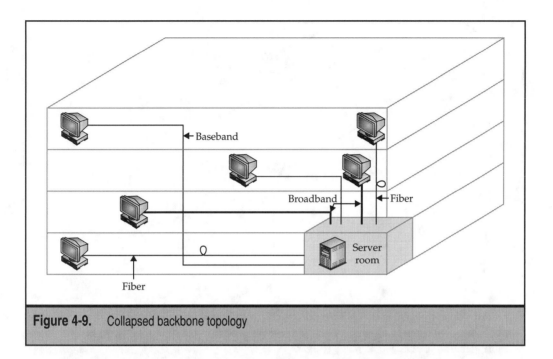

Figure 4-9.   Collapsed backbone topology

lone building. However, as networks evolve, the collapsed environment of the TCP/IP topology will be entirely routed, immeasurably improving performance for end users.

Star

The preferred topology used by network designers is the *star topology*, which breaks the network into easier-to-manage segments, rather than one overtaxed bus. Breaking things into smaller LAN segments makes it easier to meet current needs and still leave room for future change and growth. Network segmentation also improves network performance by isolating traffic. Users within a work group or department are most likely to send messages to one another, so putting them on their own LAN segment means others won't get caught in their traffic.

In a star topology, reliability is enhanced because what happens on one LAN segment doesn't affect the overall network; the fault is isolated within the segment where the trouble started. Also, the modularity of hierarchical networks naturally enhances security and manageability because devices can be grouped in ways that best fit management needs. Figure 4-10 shows common variations on the basic star topology.

The topology of a network is, of course, most closely tied to the organization's geography: who's on what floor, which server sits where, and so on. But other considerations also come into play. Table 4-2 lists network design factors and how they affect decisions about what to do when designing a network.

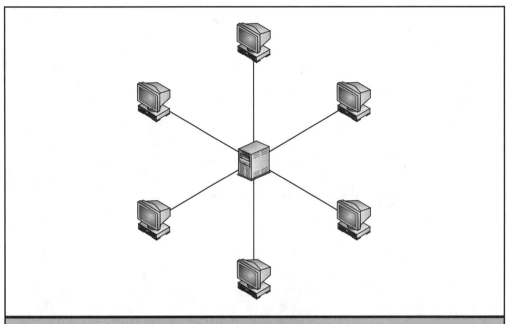

Figure 4-10. The star topology is the network's basic building block

Factor	Network Design Consideration
Preexisting cable plant	To save time and money, network designers frequently try to run networks over wiring already installed in the walls and ceiling spaces of a building. Sometimes they have no choice, and the type of network devices that can be used is dictated by preexisting cabling.
Performance goals	Projected network traffic loads and end-user "need for speed" can influence the class of network devices and cabling plant used.
Platforms	The installed base of network operating systems and computer platforms frequently dictates network design decisions.
Security	Topology layout is often used as a way to help enforce security.

Table 4-2. Topology Design Factors (Besides Geography)

Expansion Considerations

Networks are works in progress. Even though your network design will likely reflect your organization's current needs (and more than likely look ahead to include wiggle room for future expansion), there will come a time when expansion will exceed your design's capacity.

Each of the topologies we just discussed comes with its own pros and cons for network expansion. The following traits should be considered when designing your network:

▼   Bus networks add nodes to one end or the other. Expansion is easy if the growth continues from either end. However, if you have to add nodes between the ends, expansion can be difficult.

■   Star networks are expanded by adding new arms with separated nodes and connecting cables. Expansion is possible as long as the central device has enough capacity to handle the extra nodes. Further, the star topology allows additions to be made while the network is up and running.

▲   Ring networks are rather difficult to expand, because growth will require a disruption to the ring. Expansion cannot be done while the network is in operation without disrupting the ring.

Expansion is something that every network designer must be cognizant of, whether the network is electrical or optical in nature. It is important to balance the mission of your network against future expandability to ensure simpler growth.

Design

There are key systems in a network that absolutely, positively cannot fail. Hundreds of users (if not more) would be unable to work, resulting in a deleterious impact on revenues. Customers would become irritated and lose faith in your company. Typically, these systems are servers providing a database or Web presence for many users and have significant network traffic associated with them. Since hardware (and software) components fail over time, the solution has been to create redundant systems.

Reliability

In a fiber optic network, 80 percent of outages can be attributed to cable damage. This can happen in an office building if someone unwittingly trips over a length of cable, or even in an industrial environment, where a backhoe slices through underground fiber.

In a bus or ring topology, the entire network goes down if the cable is damaged. In these topologies, the nodes aren't able to operate as isolated units.

However, as you remember from our discussion of SONET and DPT, both architectures are *self-healing ring* networks. The ring is designed to send signals clockwise and counter-clockwise by adding another ring of fiber and transmitters/receivers at each node. Both cables can be collocated in the same conduit, because even if both cables are cut, the network will go on functioning. Similarly, if a node goes offline, the rest of the ring will continue following a switchover that will go unnoticed by users.

Using a modular fiber optic design can reduce the cost of a ring topology. Rather than duplicating the modem, you only need to add a transmitter/receiver module and a self-healing ring module to each modem.

In a bus topology, if modems are already present, the network can be given self-healing attributes by connecting the two ends and inserting additional modules, essentially creating a ring topology. Because you would be adding modules, rather than modems, installation time and costs are reduced.

Different applications with varying reliability needs can use different network topologies. For extremely critical environments, nodes can be arranged in a self-healing ring. Less critical environments can use a bus, star, collapsed backbone, or hybrid topology.

Hybrids

Although the basic network topologies we discussed earlier in this section cover many networking scenarios, cases sometimes arise when a variant or a combination of two types of topology is needed. Hybrid variations on the basic network topologies tend to incorporate the star topology. This is because of its high degree of reliability. In the star topology, if a line is damaged or a node goes offline, then the entire network does not suffer. On the other hand, in the event the *star node* (or the center node) fails, all connected devices lose connectivity.

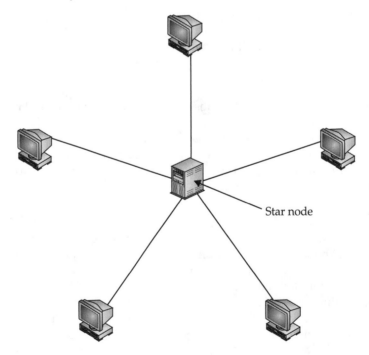

Star node

Let's take a closer look at some hybrids that might suit your network design.

Bus-Star Layout   The *bus-star* topology is used commonly in industrial settings. For instance, let's consider a cosmetics factory. Along the bottling line, nodes are connected on a linear bus. However, the portion of the factory where the cosmetics are prepared prior to bottling has several control points that radiate from a central star. In the event of damage to the bus cable, the star can continue functioning.

Star-Bus Hybrid   The *star-bus hybrid* configuration is most often used in applications that stretch out for great distances, like oil production, for instance. Each computer-regulated device, such as an oil well, storage tank, or valve controller, is regulated by a node on a local bus. Several of these buses converge to form a giant star. If a cable or node fails on any of the buses, the other buses are not affected by the outage.

Ring-Bus and Ring-Star   *Ring-bus* and *ring-star* configurations are, as the names suggest, the convergence of ring and star or ring and bus topologies. For example, a node on the ring can also be part of a bus. Alternatively, it can be the star node. The ring is designed to be self-healing for the most critical processes, while the less critical processes are connected in a bus or a star.

Quadruple-Hybrid   The final hybrid is a combination of all four network topologies. *Quadruple-hybrid* combinations combine bus, star, ring, and collapsed backbone into a ring-bus-star–collapsed backbone topology. As in the conventional ring network or the ring hybrids we mentioned earlier, the most important processes are connected as part of a self-healing ring. The other nodes are configured in bus, star, or collapsed backbone, as the location and application demand.

Redundancy

Even the best-planned topologies are susceptible to failure. There can always be a rogue backhoe or a slowwitted worker who, despite your best efforts, will find a way to crash your system. Sometimes, bums living under a bridge can start a fire and torch your cabling.

So what happens if your devilishly well designed network comes crashing down? A good way to ensure reliability is through redundancy. It's the main reason why SONET and DPT architectures use dual rings—in the event one ring fails, it is easy enough to switch over to the sister ring.

NOTE: As you likely remember, DPT uses the capacity of both rings for day-to-day operations; however, the system will still work in the event one of those rings is damaged. Flip back to Chapter 3 for more information about DPT.

For optimal reliability, it is a good idea to have a redundant system in place in the event of failure. Redundant systems, as backups, need not be mirror images of the primary system. For instance, if your primary system uses fiber, your backup could be electrical, using copper wire.

For long-distance environments, merely duplicating the cabling can be problematic. To send the signal down two separate cables, each modem needs an optical splitter and a combiner. The use of a splitter introduces a 3–6 decibel (dB) signal loss to the network. This much signal loss can create distortion unless the distance is not too great.

In a star topology, if the star node is especially vulnerable, you can simply duplicate just that node. You need not bother duplicating the individual nodes on the star, because the rest of the network will still continue to operate even if a node on a lone arm fails.

Replacing the star node may seem simple and straightforward; however, it can still be a costly endeavor. Since the star node has to be powerful and complex, it is likely to be rather expensive. When locating a star node, it is a good idea to locate the backup in a different location than the primary star node. Naturally, this adds more dollar signs to the price of the project, but it also adds more reliability. For instance, if you locate the primary and backup star nodes on different floors of the building and a fire sprinkler goes off, shorting out the primary node, the backup node won't be gargling alongside its brother.

The ring topology provides its own level of reliability through redundancy, simply by virtue of the way it operates. In the event a cable is cut, mutilated, or otherwise damaged, the backup cable will handle the traffic. Even if both the primary and secondary cables are cut, traffic can still flow.

For even better reliability, however, it is best to locate the second ring in a different location and with a different route than the primary ring.

WIDE AREA NETWORKS

As packets course through a WAN, they wind their way through different levels. First, they start at access points—one could be a business's or individual's ISP. From there, they make it to edge networking devices before moving into the network's core, aggregate, and backbone. Once they reach the other side of the network, they follow this process in reverse. They leave the network core, enter the edge devices, and then are transmitted to access points.

In this section, we look at the different layers of a WAN and how optical designs can improve performance in these areas. Specifically, we will discuss access (including more on the Last Mile problem), edge, aggregate, core, and backbone systems.

Access

The Last Mile problem (which we discussed in earlier chapters) is a great speed bump in optical networking. With the exception of the cream of the Fortune 500 crop (which happen to have the resources to be part of a SONET ring), fiber is not readily available to every business, organization, or individual. Even though there is a million-lane-wide highway out in the core of the public network, the entrance ramp is a single, metered lane.

It's because of this abrupt bottleneck that such applications as VPNs, video on demand, and other high-bandwidth gobblers aren't a part of everyone's life. Some industry observers even doubt whether such new (and somewhat unavailable) technologies as broadband and digital subscriber lines (DSL) will be able to keep up with bandwidth demands.

PONs

One solution to the access problem is via fiber. Passive optical networks (PONs) place optical couplers on a length of fiber. In essence, these couplers act a lot like the "Y" connector to which you hook your garden hose. When water courses through the hose and hits that connector, half of the water goes one way, half goes the other way. With optically coupled fiber, when light hits the coupler, half goes one way, half goes the other.

Thanks to such technologies as WDM, once a piece of fiber is in place, it doesn't need to be removed if more capacity is needed. Rather, additional wavelengths of light can be added. At least this is the case for the foreseeable future.

Fiber offers ISPs a number of benefits over copper counterparts. For instance:

▼   Fiber has a low infrastructure cost.

■   Fiber can be used for a number of service offerings.

■   Fiber is a scalable resource.

▲   A fiber network doesn't have the distance problems and service limitations of other access solutions.

PONs are also able to provision a single wavelength so that it can be shared among several customers. The protocol that enables this, called dynamic wavelength slicing (DWS), divides the wavelength into segments. The segments need not be the same size, so each customer sharing a wavelength can pay for a certain amount of the bandwidth size. What's better is that the amount of the wavelength used can be increased or decreased instantly using management software at the ISP. DWS is an excellent tool because not many lone organizations will have much use for their own OC-192 connection. As such, DWS allows a service provider to divide the wavelength and save money in the process.

Recently, the Federal Communications Commission (FCC) ruled that incumbent local exchange carriers (ILEC) were required to unbundle dark fiber assets and allow competitive local exchange carriers (CLECs) to have access. On the surface, this may seem like a great way to get more competition into the optical networking market. In reality, however, ILECs haven't been hurrying to deploy fiber into neighborhoods and industrial parks because another company would be able to use that fiber. However, the FCC went back and clarified by saying if ILECs deploy advanced packet- or cell-based infrastructure, the fiber would not be subject to unbundling.

NOTE: Dark fiber is optical fiber that has already been placed but is not yet in use. When deploying a fiber optic solution, the most expensive part is not the cost of the fiber itself; rather, it is the cost to dig up the street. To reduce this cost, rights-of-way owners may take the initiative and bury fiber when a road is torn up. Alternatively, when planting lit fiber, it makes good financial sense to include a few unused (dark) fibers.

OCDMA

A challenger to dense wavelength division multiplexing (DWDM) in metro applications is a technology called optical code-division multiple access (OCDMA).

In terms of cost, OCDMA is expected to be comparable to metro DWDM; however, maintenance and provisioning costs are much lower. Furthermore, OCDMA is compatible with DWDM in that one system can link to the other (such as where a metro network links to the long-haul network).

OCDMA is an optical variation on the technology used to boost cellular phone system capacities. Each channel is assigned a unique code, which allows multiple channels to be overlaid in the same bandwidth space. For this to happen, an OCDMA system requires a broadband light source, filters to apply the code, and a modulator to add the signal to the coded channel. Because all the channels occupy the same bandwidth, one light source can carry all the channels. DWDM, as you recall, requires a high-precision laser for each channel. On the detection end, filters decode the channel and extract the data. Along the network, installing an optical tap and drawing a little power from the fiber can add intermediate points.

But DWDM isn't dead yet. In spring 2001, start-up CodeStream burned through $50 million trying to get OCDMA off the ground and wound up crashing and burning, filing for bankruptcy, and firing 40 employees.

The Edge

Edge devices work at the border of a network. Essentially, they serve as concentration points for traffic and load balancing against available resources, policy enforcement, and protocol internetworking in heterogeneous networks. Edge devices are shown in Figure 4-11.

Edge devices are typically the origination point for IP services and provide less than 20 gigabits per second (Gbps) along their backplane.

Backbone and core devices, on the other hand, are responsible for the high-speed packet flows to their destinations. These devices respond to directives from the edge and ensure that resources are available across the WAN. In the core and backbone, devices are more robust and have 20 Gbps or more on their backplane.

As bandwidth becomes a hotter and hotter property, look for these core and edge devices to grow in vast numbers. By 2003, estimates researchers RHK, the edge switch and router market will exceed $21 billion. At the same time, the core switch and router market will top $16 billion.

Backbone

In the past, adding an additional fiber to SONET scaled Internet backbones. While this helped to increase the capacity of the backbone, it wasn't until the introduction of DWDM that service providers were able to make some impressive capacity improvements.

An important consideration of backbone management is ensuring its scalability. Like so many other networking environments, backbones are works in progress and

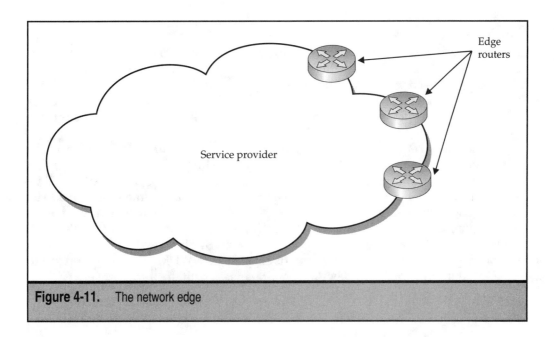

Figure 4-11.   The network edge

constantly evolving. Scalability means more than just ensuring available bandwidth. It also includes:

▼   Rapid provisioning to ensure capacity is accessible quickly. This means that provisioning times are a matter of hours, rather than a matter of weeks or months

■   Simple management, which allows the network to be more readily configured for a more streamlined topology

▲   Invisible upgrades that won't upset or inconvenience existing customers

In the past, backbone ISPs scaled bandwidth using ATM switches. This combined the bandwidth from several routers into one. This layer was necessary because routers reached capacity at OC-3 and could not carry a full SONET load. By using an ATM switch, the signals could be combined into a SONET OC-12 or OC-48. This was a good way to increase capacity and it could scale seamlessly, but it was not simple to manage, it was not a quick provisioner, and it added additional points of failure.

The next generation of core networking equipment allows bandwidth to be scaled much more easily and smoothly. It removes the ATM layer, consolidating the network into a scalable, two-tier architecture. A DWDM network with OXCs allows terabits of bandwidth to be available to the routing layer. Adding bandwidth is a matter of installing a card on an optical switch, which makes a lambda in the DWDM system available as a SONET port.

Design

Internet backbones are built in mesh topologies, as shown in Figure 4-12. As we mentioned earlier, this is a preferable topology because it provides the most efficient way to deliver any-to-any connectivity. In this topology, the optical switch provides the lambdas that are the same speed as the router's I/O ports. These lambdas can be connected through the DWDM network to provide the router with full or partial mesh connectivity to its peers.

As efficient and effective as a mesh is, this topology also requires the most port usage of any topology. Because of the sheer number of ports required, mesh backbones tend to be reasonably small in size, consisting of tens of nodes.

Also, that there are so many nodes in a backbone means that a terabit router has to be configured with hundreds of interfaces. The port problem is only worsened if a pair of nodes requires multiple paths because of bandwidth demand.

Once DWDM is introduced into an optical backbone, the bandwidth of a single port is multiplied and the required number of ports is lessened. DWDM ports could be used to connect routers and optical switches or connect devices with the transport network.

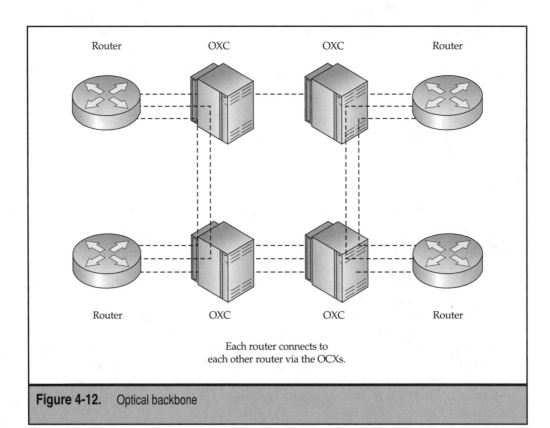

Figure 4-12. Optical backbone

Electrical Usefulness

Though OEO is the biggest hindrance to an all-optical network, it will be many years (some observers say as much as a decade) before electrical components are completely removed from the optical equation.

If one can figure out how to tame the electrical beast, its impact can be lessened. In an optical backbone, a great increase in bandwidth and performance comes by integrating electrical and optical functions. This reduces the number of OEO conversions that must take place.

As shown in Figure 4-13, there are three OEO conversions that take place when routers and switches handle packets. These occur when a packet:

1. Enters an optical switch

2. Passes through the router

3. Exits the switch

By combining the optical switch and terabit routing functions, there is just one OEO conversion. Not only does this improve system efficiency and reliability, but it also reduces the cost of a combined system.

Furthermore, this conjunction couples the electrical and optical switch fabrics closely together, reducing overhead and improving efficiency. Also, you save power and space in your equipment rooms.

As more bandwidth is made available by DWDM, backbones must be designed much more tightly. Networks that are able to increase their density and reduce network complexity by integrating optical switching and electrical routing will pave the way for systems that can handle hundreds of terabits.

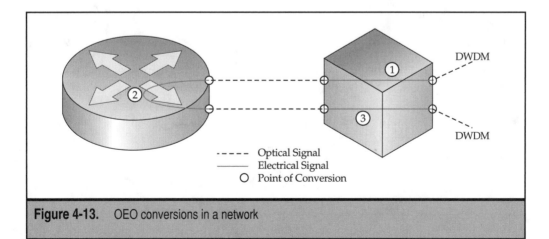

Figure 4-13.   OEO conversions in a network

Long Haul

An optical core and an optical backbone are largely synonymous. They both are the "highway" in "information superhighway." The only real distinction lies in their respective sizes. As we mentioned earlier, a backbone tends to be a couple dozen nodes in size. However, a core may be the same size, or made of several backbones.

Composition

Long-distance optical cores are made up of mostly SONET rings. As Figure 4-14 shows, a cross-country system employs multiple interconnected rings. To establish a circuit from New York to Los Angeles (in our example), ADMs are connected back-to-back in Chicago and Las Vegas. The device making the connection is usually a patch panel or an OXC.

Though this seems easy and straightforward on paper (doesn't it always?), in practice, there are a number of hurdles to be aware of. For a long-haul network to function, an end-to-end circuit between New York and Los Angeles must be established on each of the component SONET rings. For instance, the same time slot must be available on the rings connecting both cities. Circuits may have already been provisioned, so this can be difficult as circuits are shifted from one time slot to another.

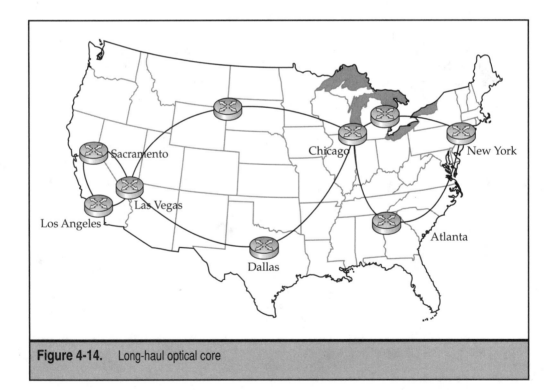

Figure 4-14. Long-haul optical core

To make this process smoother, the highest-bandwidth rings are deployed to give more combinations of time slots. This is the very motivation for upgrading from OC-48 to OC-192. This improvement gives four times as much bandwidth and therefore four times as many time slots. In the event a circuit still cannot be located, the circuit must be dropped at an intermediate node and added to a different time slot, adding yet another step in the connection.

Once the resources are allocated and the design phase is over, a technician must physically visit each intermediate point and connect the output of one ADM to the next. Naturally, this provides a number of opportunities for human error. It is not uncommon for a cross-country circuit to require six months for provisioning.

SONET Versus DWDM: Round II

This discussion again raises the comparison between SONET and DWDM. Unlike with SONET, which requires a technician to visit each intermediate point, with DWDM a technician on one end and a technician on the other end install new transmitters and receivers, and the bandwidth can be provisioned in a matter of hours. Further, SONET ADMs tend to be rather inefficient. In long-haul capacities, ADMs tend to use four-fiber, bidirectional line switched rings (BLSRs). As you remember, in a SONET configuration, there are two rings—one in a primary capacity for carrying data, the other as a backup. Unfortunately, this means that half the network's infrastructure is dark. What's worse, if one runs into the design difficulties we mentioned in the last section, another 20 percent of the bandwidth may suffer. In essence, the network would have only 30 percent of its capacity available to it.

NOTE: Of course, this can depend on your point of view. If you consider only a single ring as "full capacity," then the bandwidth loss just described would gobble up just 40 percent of your available bandwidth.

Conversely, DWDM can add 160 lambdas to those rings. This isn't entirely realistic, however, because the patch panel to connect the ADMs and the space required to house 160 ADMs per fiber (remember the BLSR would have four fibers—two transmitting, two receiving— bringing the total of ADMs to 320) would be absurd.

FABRICS

In this section, we take a closer look at optical fabrics. If you remember Chapter 2, you may remember discussion about inventors and businessmen who wove optical fibers into fabric, which were used to make dresses and other specialty garments.

In this discussion, the term *fabric* doesn't have anything to do with a piece of cloth. Rather, fabrics are a series of switches within a network. A fabric refers to the way switches in a network are interconnected.

In this section, we touch briefly on the topic of optical switching (which we will talk about in greater depth in Chapter 5), the attributes that make a good fabric, fabric sizes, and overlays that give your fabrics extra functionality and power, such as Multiprotocol Label Switching (MPLS) VPNs.

Switching

For a truly optical network (delivering both high capacity and speed), carriers and providers will have to make a move to all-optical switches. These switches steer light pulses between different spans of fiber without having to convert them into electrical signals at any point.

The promise of all-optical switching is appealing. These switches promise to eliminate capacity bottlenecks, reduce costs, and improve future technology deployments. The only problem with this is that the current generation of all-optical switches aren't, really, all-optical. There is still some electrical functionality involved that acts as a bottleneck.

At present, vendors are experimenting with a number of Star Trek–sounding technologies to facilitate all-optical switching. Some of the technologies include:

▼ Liquid crystals

■ Bubbles

■ Holograms

▲ Thermo- and acousto-optics

As compelling as some of these technologies sound, none of them are ready for wide release. Some observers are theorizing that there won't be one übertechnology that will handle everything for optical fabrics. Rather, these technologies are expected to be used in a broad range of applications. As such, some will likely be popular in large-scale OXCs, while others will be best suited for optical add-drop multiplexers.

NOTE: We'll give more attention to these technologies in Chapter 5.

One technology that has picked up steam in recent months is micro-electro-mechanical systems (MEMS). As Figure 4-15 shows, MEMS are arrays of miniature tilting mirrors. This technology is found in the latest "all-optical" switches. Though a popular component of optical switches, MEMS are still electronically based.

Currently, optical switches from Ciena Corporation, Tellium, Inc., and Sycamore Networks, Inc., for example, use electrical cores. This means that as the light pulses enter the switch, they are converted back into electrical signals so that their passage through the switch can be handled by conventional application specific integrated circuits (ASICs).

Though, ideally, the goal is an all-optical switch, the use of electrical processing allows the switches some benefits, such as handling smaller bandwidths than entire wavelengths, which is more appropriate for current market needs. Further, the electrical cores make network management simpler, thanks to existing standards for electrical switching. Conversely, optical equivalents are not in place as of yet.

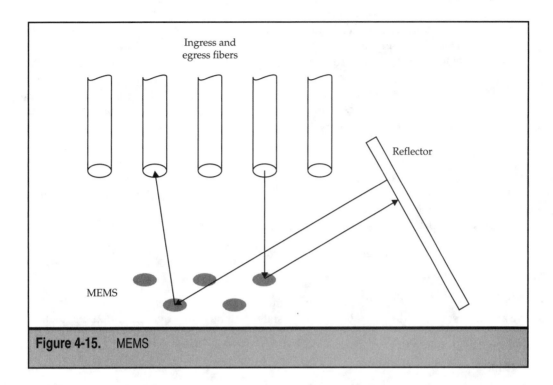

Ingress and
egress fibers

Reflector

MEMS

Figure 4-15.   MEMS

So does that mean networks should always be behind the eight ball when it comes to technology? Of course not. Electrical cores may not be able to keep up with the number of wavelengths that will be thrown at them, especially as DWDM becomes more prevalent. The fastest ASIC technology won't support anything beefier than a 512 × 512 port electrical core.

Metrics

As mentioned earlier, a range of technologies are vying for optical switching supremacy. It's more likely that these technologies will be used for specific applications. What would be the best switching fabric in one situation may be completely wrong in another.

Vendors are working on more than one switching fabric, but not in an effort to cover their bases. Rather, they are betting that each technology will find its own home. The following are some of the ways that optical fabrics can be measured.

Matrix Size

The sentiment "size matters" seems to be the mantra for optical fabrics. Vendors have been developing optical switches with 1000 × 1000 ports (or more) in an effort to tame the thousands of wavelengths that DWDM systems are generating. In reality, however, the need for these kinds of behemoth switches is a couple years away.

Furthermore, it's likely that carriers will buy several small switches, rather than a few big ones. This might be impractical for a carrier who would have to install two of the behemoths (one for live traffic and the other as a standby). In this configuration, the carrier would also have to buy 1000 1 × 2 switches to switch incoming traffic from one giant switch to the other. Then, another set of 1000 1 × 2 switches would be needed to get the traffic back on its original track. Instead, optical switching fabric developers are giving more attention to 8-, 16-, 32-, and 64-port switches that can be used in OADMs and metro equipment.

Attenuation

A threat to any optical network is attenuation. The addition of switches adds a greater amount of attenuation to optical designs and will adversely affect your optical power budget. Optical switches have two main sources of attenuation:

▼ The coupling between the fiber and the switch

▲ The switch material

Liquid crystal and MEMS have the best attenuation rates, of between 1 and 2 deci-bels (dB). Conversely, lithium niobate and solid-state switches have demonstrated attenuation of 4 dB.

Scaling

The ability to add on to a network (in networking parlance this is called *scaling*) is another important consideration. Some technologies and vendors are better than others in this field. For instance, some may be able to develop useful 8 × 8 or 64 × 64 port optical fabrics. However, they cannot scale into the hundreds or thousands that would be needed. Some fabrics make fine OXCs but aren't scalable enough to work in the network core.

Speed

Photons coursing through a fiber optic network certainly connote an image of speed. After all, photons are moving at the speed of light and can make it to their destination as fast as anything possibly can.

In optical fabrics, however, there are two important speeds to keep in mind:

▼ Switching light in a few milliseconds (ms) is fast enough for rerouting traffic around problems. SONET, as you recall, can switch the direction of its traffic in just 50 ms. In that amount of time, it can recover any dropped packets and the users and applications remain oblivious to any of the network's problems.

▲ Switching light in a few nanoseconds (ns) is fast enough so that individual packets can be forwarded to different destinations.

Furthermore, the *switching frequency* can be a determining factor in the choice of switching fabric. For example, in protection switching the switch is rarely used. In that case, maintaining state is its main functional requirement.

If your fabrics are going to be very active, it is important to be aware of their rise and fall times. The rise and fall times in active fabrics should be as close to equal as possible, to avoid switches going out of phase during periods of high activity.

Granularity

In some configurations, optical fabrics do little more than act as patch panels, sending the wavelengths from one fiber to another. In *protection switching,* that's all the switch needs to do—unless there is a failure, in which case the switch will reroute the wavelengths around the problem.

However, fabrics can become more complex if single wavelengths must be stripped from an aggregate and routed to another fiber, as in the case of an ADM. In this case, some technologies are better suited for the task than others.

Applications

In conventional networking, switches in LANs are used to connect servers to clients, printers, and other networking devices. But they can be used for other applications, as well. Similarly, optical switches can serve a number of functions, not the least of which is improving response times and adding redundancy.

The following are some of the applications for which optical fabrics can be used:

▼ **Automatic protection switching** If a strand of fiber is cut by a distracted backhoe driver or burned by bums under a bridge, it is a switch that reroutes traffic to its destination, avoiding the hobo barbecue. Traffic can get back on track in these cases by using a 1×2 optical switch.

■ **Network monitoring** An optical network can be monitored by connecting a $1 \times N$ switch to an optical time-domain reflectometer (OTDR). The switch can also be used to drop a signal or add a network analyzer to monitor the network without disrupting traffic.

■ **Component testing** Switches can be used to test components, cables, and subsystems. Testing components in real-world applications is greatly improved by using optical switches. This is because many tested components can be monitored on a specific switch channel.

■ **OADM** OADMs are used to separate and add wavelengths from aggregate signals without having to demux the entire wavelength. OADMs are used most often in metro deployments because of the high amount of traffic. Many OADMs use 2×2 switches to switch wavelength channels from a DWDM stream. Carriers who use optical switches in conjunction with their OADMs can choose which wavelengths to drop by using the appropriate software, instead of using fixed OADMs that use specified wavelengths. An OADM can use several 2×2 switches or a single, larger switch fabric, like 16×16 in the metro or 64×64 in a long-haul network.

> ▲ **Optical cross-connect** An OXC is a large-matrix optical switch that sits at a high-traffic intersection and performs any-to-any switching, whether the traffic is bands, wavelengths, or fibers. Optical cross-connects do several tasks, from network restoration to network management.

Fabric Size

DWDM has ameliorated many of the problems facing optical networking. Because of its ability to combine many lambdas on a single fiber, capacity has increased while costs have been kept down, because there is no need to lay additional fiber. As blessed as DWDM seems, however, we are far from a perfect, harmonious optical network.

The problem arises when optical data enters a fabric. When optical signals enter a fabric, they hit a bottleneck when they must be converted from optical to electrical signals, then back to optical (in shorthand, this process is known as OEO).

Optical Cross-Connects

OXCs are used to switch wavelengths between input and output fiber while adding and dropping local traffic. In the coming years, several carriers expect to need nodes capable of switching thousands of input and output wavelengths. For instance, let's say the carrier has 32 fibers and each fiber carries 160 wavelengths. That means the carrier must have a 5120 × 5120 OXC.

The most flexible architecture for this type of fabric is the opaque, wavelength interchange cross-connect (WIXC), which is shown in Figure 4-16. WIXCs receive and transmit wavelengths by transponders at each port. With this architecture, a wavelength can be switched to any other fiber through a process called *transponder wavelength conversion*.

NOTE: The term *opaque* means that the router knows of its presence. *Transparent*, on the other hand, means that the router does not know of its presence.

The downside to this type of architecture, however, is the price. The price for an OC-192 receiver pair is about $US5000. In a 5120 × 5120 node, 5120 ports at $5000 comes out to $US25.6 million, just for transmitters and receivers. When you add all the other components, labor, and equipment, this can top $US125 million. That amount doesn't include the optical switch fabric, transceivers, mux/demuxes, and sundry other components. Very large service providers might need 100 of these nodes would bring the total to $US12.5 billion. If you want to design a system using OC-798 levels, you're looking at an amount 2.2 times more than OC-192.

Big or Small

Given the cost implications of the previous section, a better alternative is the wavelength selective cross-connect (WSXC). This can be built using a single, large fabric or with multiple, smaller fabrics (as shown in Figure 4-17).

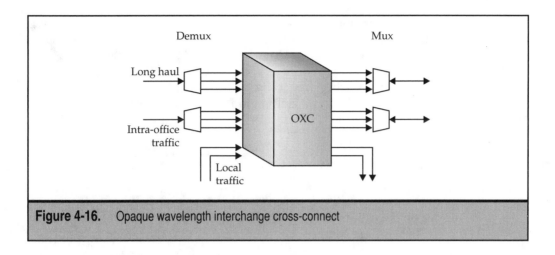

Figure 4-16. Opaque wavelength interchange cross-connect

The WSXC divides the aggregate wavelength into its component wavelengths. Because these wavelengths are at different spectra, it is easy to think of them as colors. The WSXC switches all the "blue" wavelengths between fibers on one plane, the "red" wavelengths

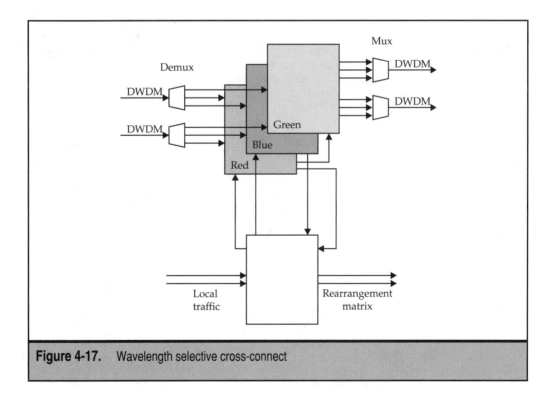

Figure 4-17. Wavelength selective cross-connect

between fibers on a separate plane, the "green" wavelengths on yet another plane, and so forth. Using our previous example, if a node has 32 fibers, each carrying 160 wavelengths per fiber, this will require a single 5120 × 5120 switch or 160 32 × 32 switches. Though the single, large switch will allow local traffic to be added or dropped, if the designer were to allow extra ports for adding and dropping traffic, then the ideal solution is to use several smaller fabrics, rather than a single large one. There are several reasons why numerous small fabrics are preferable to a single, large one:

▼ Reliability

■ Ease of serviceability

▲ Lower cost of ownership

Not only is cost an issue, but also there are a number of reasons why several smaller fabrics are preferable to a large fabric:

▼ A second fabric must be maintained in the event of a failure. With several small fabrics, a few can be kept on hand and deployed when needed, rather than a giant, expensive one.

■ As the size of your fabric increases, so does its complexity.

▲ The time to repair a single, large fabric will mean more downtime in the event of failure.

If, for example, an entire 32 × 32 small fabric went down, at most, 32 channels would be lost. Because of its size, the other channels would still be operable and it would be much simpler to swap in a new fabric for the failed one.

Fabric Overlays

One of the critical architectural decisions that must be made before protocols can be established is the nature of the interface between the optical core and the service delivery platforms at the optical edge. In an electrical overlay model, data networks (using IP, ATM, and so forth) have no topological visibility to the underlying transmission infrastructure. For example, if an IP router has three T1 links to another IP router, it has no involvement in how the transmission infrastructure provides connectivity. Advantages of the overlay model include:

▼ Simplicity

■ Functionality separation

■ The ability to change technologies in the transmission layer independently of the service layer

▲ Hierarchical network management

MPLS

Speeding packets through a network is what good network design is all about. One method of enabling that speed and efficiency is via an overlay model called Multiprotocol Label Switching (MPLS). Routers, situated on the edge of a network, apply simple labels to packets. Then, routers, switches, or other network devices within the network can switch packets according to the labels. This process is ideal, because it requires minimal lookup overhead.

How It Works

Conventional Layer 3 IP routing is based on the exchange of network availability information. As a packet winds its way through a network, each router makes decisions about where the packet will be sent next. This information is based on information in Layer 3 of the header. This information is used as an index for a routing table lookup to determine the packet's next hop. This process is repeated at each router in the network. At each hop, the router has to resolve the next destination for the packet. This series of hops within an MPLS network is known as a label switched path (LSP).

The downside of this process is that the information within the IP packets—information about precedence, for example—is not considered when forwarding packets. For best performance, only the destination address is considered. But because other fields within the packet could be relevant, an in-depth header analysis must take place at each router along the packet's path.

MPLS streamlines this process by attaching a *label* on each packet. Think of conventional IP routing as like addressing a letter. It tells the post office where to send the letter. MPLS takes addressing to another level by adding extra instructions—like writing "Perishable" or "Do Not Bend" on the envelope.

The label includes important information about the packet:

▼ Destination

■ Precedence

■ A specific route for the packet, if one is needed

■ Virtual Private Network (VPN) membership

▲ Quality of service (QoS) information

MPLS causes the Layer 3 header analysis to be performed only twice—at the edge label switch router (LSR) as it enters and exits an internetwork. At the LSR, the Layer 3 header is mapped into a fixed-length label and applied to the packet. Figure 4-18 shows how a label is applied to a packet.

The 32-bit MPLS header contains the following fields:

▼ The label field (20 bits) carries the actual value of the MPLS label.

■ The Class of Service (CoS) field (3 bits) can affect the queuing and discard algorithms applied to the packet as it is transmitted through the network.

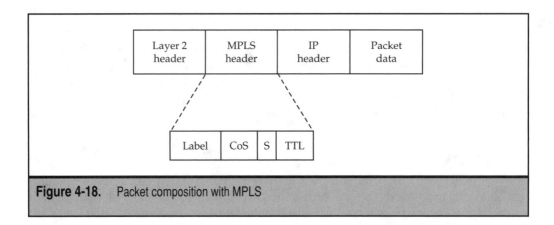

Figure 4-18.   Packet composition with MPLS

- ■ The Stack (S) field (1 bit) supports a hierarchical label stack.
- ▲ The TTL (time-to-live) field (8 bits) provides conventional IP TTL functionality.

Next, as the packet crosses the routers in an internetwork, only the label needs to be read. Once it reaches the other end of the network, another edge LSR removes the label, replacing it with the appropriate header data linked to that label.

A key result of this arrangement is that forwarding decisions based on some or all of these different sources of information can be achieved by means of a single table lookup from a fixed-length label. Label switching is the merger of switching and routing functions—it combines the speed of switches and the traffic engineering of routers.

Benefits

MPLS offers many advantages over traditional IP over ATM routing protocols. Label switching and hardware switching work together to deliver high degrees of performance. For multiservice networks, MPLS allows a switch to provide ATM, Frame Relay, and IP service on a single platform. This is ideal, because supporting all these services on a single platform is not only cost-effective, but it also simplifies provisioning for multiservice providers.

The following benefits highlight some of the usefulness of MPLS:

- ▼ **Integration**   MPLS combines IP and ATM functionality, making the ATM infrastructure visible to IP routing and eliminating the need for mappings between IP and ATM features.

- ■ **VPN performance**   With an MPLS backbone, VPN information need only be processed where packets enter and exit the network. Additionally, the Border Gateway Protocol (BGP) is used to deal with VPN information. The use of both MPLS and BGP makes MPLS-based VPN services easier to manage and much more scalable. We'll talk about MPLS-based VPNs in more detail later in this chapter.

■ **Reduction of burden on core services**   Because MPLS examines packets when they enter and exit a network, internal transit routers and switches need only process the connectivity with the provider's edge routers. This prevents the core devices from becoming overwhelmed with the routing volume exchanged in the Internet.

▲ **Traffic engineering capabilities**   MPLS's traffic engineering capabilities enable network administrators to shift the traffic load from overburdened sections to underused sections of the network, according to traffic destination, type, load, and time of day.

MPLS Network Structure

An MPLS network has three basic components. They are:

▼ **Edge label switch routers**   Edge LSRs are situated at the physical and logical boundary of a network. These devices are usually routers but can also be multilayer LANs or proxy devices.

■ **Label switches**   These devices switch packets according to the labels. In addition, label switches may also support Layer 3 routing or Layer 2 switching.

▲ **Label Distribution Protocol**   The Label Distribution Protocol (LDP) is used alongside network layer routing protocols and distributes label information between MPLS network devices.

MPLS provides internetworks with an unprecedented level of control over traffic, resulting in a network that is more efficient, supports more predictable service, and can offer the flexibility required to meet constantly changing networking situations.

Synergy with Optical Networking

Given the functionality of MPLS, you may notice a similarity between an MPLS LSR and an OXC; and between an MPLS LSP and an optical channel trail. Just as an LSR switches labels, an OXC switches on lambdas (which brings the new acronym *lambda*-switched router (LSR)) from the input to the output ports. Establishing an LSP requires each intermediate LSR to map to a particular input label and port. Likewise, establishing an optical channel trail requires each intermediate OXC to map a specific input lambda and port to an output lambda and port.

An OXC—like an LSR—needs routing protocols like Open Shortest Path First (OSPF) to share link-state topology and other optical resource information for path calculation. They also need signaling protocols like RSVP and LDP to automate the process of configuring the OXCs to create optical channels trails.

Figure 4-19 illustrates a typical core network of OXCs with its perimeter of edge devices. These establish optical trails through the core. A large, complex backbone with numerous OXCs would have a number of optical trails through the network. At any edge device in the network, the device would act as the ingress device and would be the origination point of multiple optical trails between the same egress devices.

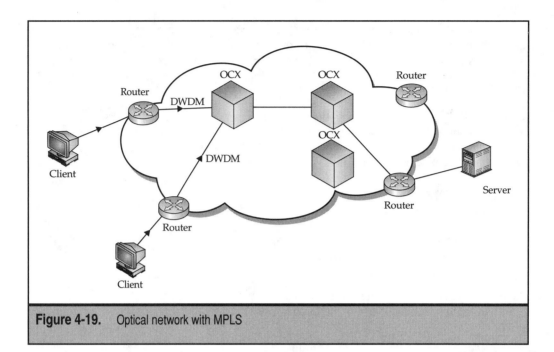

Figure 4-19. Optical network with MPLS

MPLS VPN

One application for MPLS that shows the most benefit is support for virtual private network (VPN) services. Using MPLS with VPNs is more beneficial than using ATM or Frame Relay permanent virtual circuits (PVCs) or other forms of tunneling to connect routers.

To better understand VPNs using MPLS, it's helpful to take a closer look at what, exactly, a VPN is.

What Is a VPN?   As so often happens in the computer business, marketing hype can muddle an otherwise clear term. In the case of VPNs, some confusion exists over what's *virtual* in a VPN—the privacy or the network? Here's the two-part definition of a virtual private network:

▼ VPN topology runs mostly over *shared* network infrastructure, usually the Internet, and has at least one private LAN segment at each end point.

▲ VPN sessions run through an encrypted connection.

To operate through encrypted connections across the Internet, the network segments at each end of a VPN must be under the administrative control of the organization (or organizations) running the virtual network. In practical terms, this means that the end point routers must be under a common security and operational regimen. Above all, the end point routers in a VPN must operate a common encryption scheme.

Traditionally, long-distance connectivity to an internetwork relied on a WAN with a leased line. Further, a leased line is simply not an option for an individual who is traveling and cannot be in one place long enough for a leased line to be justified. The following are some reasons why VPNs are making an impact on the leased line market:

▼   **Lower costs**   Leased lines require expensive transport bandwidth and backbone equipment. Additionally, VPNs don't need in-house terminal equipment and access modems.

■   **Network agility**   Relatively speaking, VPN links are easy and inexpensive to set up, change, and remove. Because of this, an organization's communications infrastructure won't be traumatized when a VPN is installed, reconfigured, or removed. Further, the availability of the Internet ensures that you can connect your VPN nearly anywhere.

▲   **Access**   Because of its availability, subscribers anywhere on the VPN have the same level of access and view of central services (e-mail, internal and external Web sites, security, and so forth).

The Overlay   Using MPLS for VPN services provides a number of advantages over the PVC-based model:

▼   Customers can choose their own addressing plans. They don't necessarily have to overlap those of other customers or the service provider.

■   Each customer can be assured that the data will not be delivered anywhere but to sites within the customer's own VPN.

■   Encryption is not needed.

■   The model scales very well.

■   MPLS VPN supports an *any-to-any* communications model among sites in a VPN without having to install a full mesh of PVCs.

▲   Each customer using MPLS VPN appears to provide a private IP backbone over which the customer can access his or her own resources, but not those of another customer.

As far as the customer is concerned, the chief advantage of the MPLS VPN model is that routing is simplified over the PVC model. Instead of managing the routing over a complex virtual backbone of numerous PVCs, an MPLS VPN customer can use the service provider backbone as the default route to the company's sites.

As Figure 4-20 illustrates, a service provider is using an MPLS VPN for two customers. The provider does not have to allocate resources to either of the customers. For instance, you'll notice that Customer 1 and Customer 2 can connect to the same provider edge (PE)

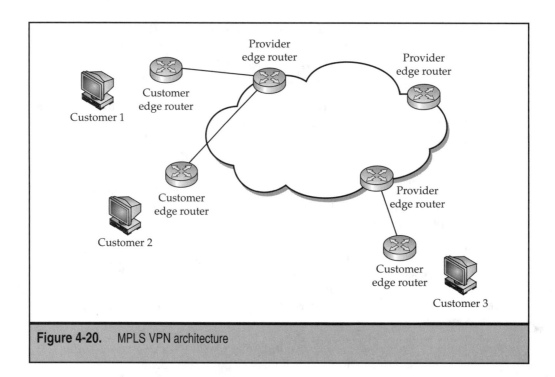

Figure 4-20. MPLS VPN architecture

router. Customer edge (CE) routers peer with other provider PEs and exchange routing information using one of three protocols:

▼ Routing Information Protocol (RIP)

■ Border Gateway Protocol (BGP)

▲ Static routes

Packets traveling from one customer to the destination site are sent as unlabeled IP packets. These stop at the PE router, which applies labels based on the incoming interface and the destination.

Next, the routers use MPLS to carry the packets across the provider backbone. That the system uses labels and not IP addresses allows the network to handle overlapping IP addresses. Since the incoming interface determines which labels to apply and accepts only unlabeled packets, customers aren't allowed to "spoof" their way into a VPN.

Components of an MPLS VPN A provider does not have to maintain a one-to-one relationship between customer sites and VPNs. A site can have multiple VPNs, but a site can associate with only one VPN routing/forwarding (VRF) instance. A customer-site VRF contains all the paths to the site from its member VPNs.

There are three components to an MPLS VPN network:

▼ **VPN route target communities** This is a list of all other VPN community members. VPN route targets must be configured for each VPN community member.

■ **Multiprotocol BGP (MP-BGP) peering of VPN PE routers** MP-BGP propagates VRF contact data to the members of a VPN community. MP-BGP peering must be configured in all PE routers of a community.

▲ **MPLS forwarding** MPLS transports traffic between community members via a VPN service-provider network.

With these pieces in place, an MPLS VPN will allow secure, private links to be established between secure nodes.

All-Optical Mesh Net

It's no secret that the Internet is getting bigger and beefier each and every day. As more and more streaming audio, video, and large files are transferred across the Internet, bandwidth is being gobbled up on both electronic and optical networks. Currently, data traffic accounts for more than half of the traffic on the public network. That number is expected to rise to 26 times the amount of voice traffic by the end of 2003.

Point-to-point networks, unfortunately, do not allow the scalability, low cost, or provisioning speed that the next generation of Internet traffic will demand. The best response to this demand for bandwidth is an all-optical mesh network.

Optical mesh networks allow operators to scale their networks to accommodate terabit capacities, support point-and-click service provisioning, support existing IP routers, and reduce costs by decreasing electronics at regeneration stations.

As we pointed out earlier, SONET is a good architecture for today's needs but tops off at OC-192. Further, SONET's ring-based architecture is still a network of point-to-point connections that requires redundant connections and equipment to ensure reliability. Also, SONET requires that half of the network's capacity is held in reserve for restoration and protection.

A solution to SONET's rings is an all-optical mesh architecture. As Figure 4-21 shows, this topology allows multipoint-to-multipoint connections for Internet traffic. Since the mesh connects several devices, it also reduces the amount of equipment needed to transport traffic, while still increasing network capacity.

Configuring a mesh allows the network operator to design around a number of different variables, granting support for a number of types of traffic as well as protection against device failure. In the event the fiber was cut, for example, and since multiple routes are available, the network device need only reroute to an alternate path.

Eliminating Electronics   Another advantage to the all-optical mesh topology is the elimination of electronics from the core. Further, in long-haul applications, electronic regeneration is not necessary, which means a five- to eight-fold increase in the distance a signal

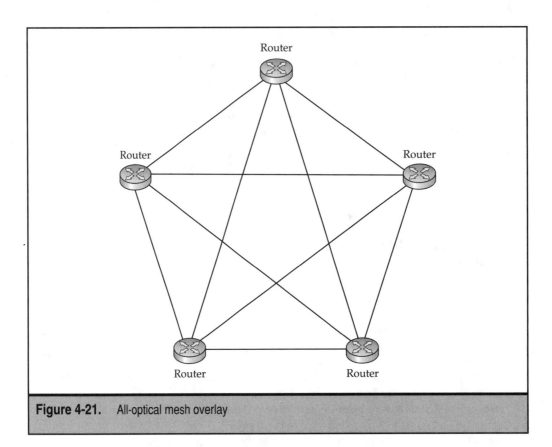

Figure 4-21.   All-optical mesh overlay

can travel before having to be amplified or regenerated. Also, optical switches and OADMs can route wavelengths straight through a network, eliminating the overlay of electrical switches in the network core where many fibers intersect or at drop sites. By reducing the number of network devices, there is also a heightened level of network reliability.

Technique   It isn't just a beefy all-optical mesh that makes a robust network. Ensuring that an integrated network management system is included will make an immeasurable difference. Traditionally speaking, optical network improvements have required technicians to visit each regeneration site along the circuit.

     With an optical mesh, on the other hand, new traffic routes can be assigned remotely with network management applications. Traffic can be redirected to new paths by installing a transmitter-receiver pair at the origination and endpoint of the transmission path without any adjustment to the equipment along the route. Not only does this simplify the process of provisioning resources, but it also speeds up the process by months.

     All-optical mesh networks provide long-haul, all-optical, high-capacity, reliable networks. Incorporating an all-optical design into a network's design will allow it to keep pace with the demands of the bandwidth-hungry nature of the Internet and other networking applications.

The process of designing an optical network is not an easy one. It isn't a simple matter of stringing fiber optic cable between a few floors, then plugging in routers, switches, and computers. To do an effective, efficient job, it is necessary to consider a multitude of variables, from your organization's structure to the individual components you'll be using.

Once you understand the variables involved, you can start constructing your network.

CHAPTER 5

Optical Switching
and Routing

Without routers and switches, networking and internetworking simply could not happen. These two network devices—along with specific routing and switching designs and protocols—keep packets flowing across an internetwork. Routers, which are "intelligent" devices, are able to discern the best path for a packet through the network. Switches forward packets to specific destinations designated in the packet's header.

In this chapter, we discuss the general functionality of routers and switches. This is the type of functionality that one would find in either an electrical network or an optical one. Then we look specifically at optical routers and switches, along with the issues that they raise.

ROUTING AND SWITCHING BASICS

Routers and switches are used in both electrical and optical networks. But no matter what type of network in which they are used, their basic functionality remains the same. Routers in optical networks route packets as they would in an electrical network; and switches in an electrical network perform the same functions as they would in an optical network.

In this section, we give an overview of router and switch function. We'll talk about how they are used in a network's deployment, where they are placed in a network topology, and how they can be used for optimal networking functionality. Finally, though switches and routers perform the same essential functions in both electrical and optical networks, there are specific issues that affect optical deployments.

Routers

In a nutshell, routers do exactly what their name says: they route data from a LAN to another router, then another router, and so on until data is received at its destination. Routers also act as traffic cops, allowing only authorized machines to transmit data into the local network so that private information can remain secure. In addition to supporting these dial-in and leased connections, routers also handle errors, keep network usage statistics, and handle security issues.

Routing for Efficiency

When you send an e-mail message to your Aunt Sadie on the other side of the country, it's routing technology that ensures she alone, and not every computer hooked up to the Internet, gets the message. Routers direct the flow of traffic between, rather than within, networks. For instance, let's consider how routers can be used within a LAN to keep information flowing.

Design-O-Rama, as shown in Figure 5-1, is a computer graphics company. The company's LAN is divvied into two smaller LANs—one for the animators and one for the administration and support staff. The two subdivisions are connected with a router. Design-O-Rama employs eight people: four animators and four other staffers. When one animator sends a file to another, the large file will use a great deal of the network's capacity. This results in performance problems for the others on the network.

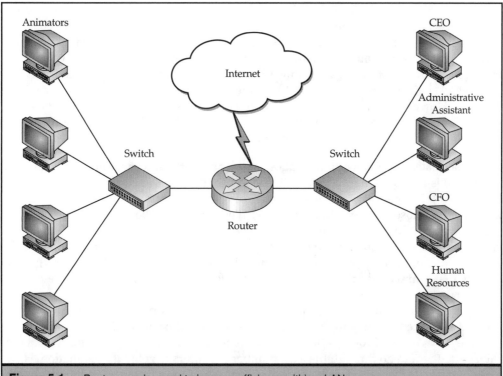

Figure 5-1. Routers can be used to improve efficiency within a LAN

NOTE: Remember how Ethernet works. A single user can have such a dramatic impact on the network because each information packet sent by one computer is received by all the other computers on the Ethernet LAN. Then each computer examines the packet and decides if it was meant for itself.

To keep the animators from constantly slowing down the network, the network was divided into two—one for the animators and one for everybody else. A router links the two networks and connects them both to the Internet. The router is the only device on the network that sees every message sent by any computer on either network. When an animator sends a file to a colleague, the router looks at the recipient's address and keeps that piece of traffic isolated on that LAN. On the other hand, if the animator wants to query the human relations department about vacation time, the router knows to let that piece of traffic through to the HR department.

Routers and the Internet

In our previous example, we examined how a router could be used locally. Now, let's broaden the scope of what routers do to include their functionality across the entire Internet.

For the sake of comparison, let's first talk about how a telephone call is routed across the country. Say it's Aunt Sadie's birthday and rather than send an e-mail message, you want to call her. When you make a long-distance call, the telephone system establishes a stable circuit between your telephone and Aunt Sadie's. The circuit may involve hopping through a number of steps, including fiber optics, copper wires, and satellites. This end-to-end chain ensures that the quality of the line between you and Aunt Sadie will be constant. However, if the satellite goes offline or work crews cut the fiber optic cable, your conversation with Aunt Sadie will be cut short. The Internet avoids this problem by making its "calls" in an entirely different way.

Packets and Paths   Whatever information is sent across the Internet (e-mail, Web pages, and so on) is first broken into 1500-byte packets (or smaller), as directed by the Internet Protocol (IP). The packets are transmitted across a number of routers, each one forwarding the packet closer to the destination device. The packets will be transmitted via the best available route. This type of network is called a *packet-switched* network. Each packet could take the same route, or none of the packets could take the same route. Once the packets show up at the destination computer, they are reassembled. This process goes so quickly that you wouldn't even know that the file was chopped into 1500-byte packets and then reassembled.

Figure 5-2 illustrates how a packet-switched network operates. The routers in the Internet are linked together in a web. The packets follow the path of least resistance to ensure they arrive at their destination in a reasonable amount of time. It seems logical that each packet would go through the least number of routers to get to its destination. However, sometimes that isn't feasible, because congestion may be clogging the ideal path. Routers send the traffic around the congested portions of the Internet for increased speed and efficiency.

This may seem like a very complicated system—as compared to the process followed when placing a telephone call—but the system works for two important reasons:

▼ The network can balance the load across different pieces of equipment on a millisecond-by-millisecond basis.

▲ If there is a problem with one piece of equipment in the network while a message is being transmitted, packets can be routed around the problem to ensure that the entire message is received.

The routers that make up the main backbone of the Internet can reconfigure the paths that packets take because they look at all the information surrounding each data packet, and they tell each other about line conditions and problems sending and receiving data on various parts of the Internet.

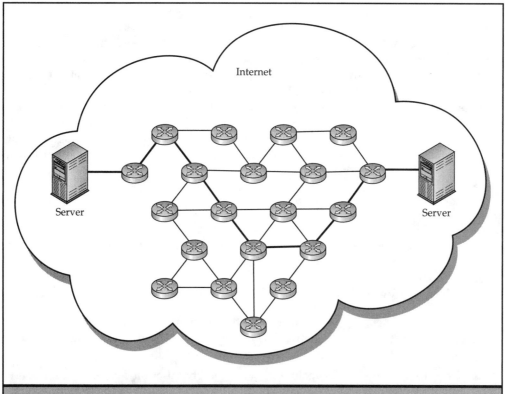

Figure 5-2.   Routers send packets across the path of least resistance

All Shapes and Sizes   Not every router is responsible for the fate of packets whizzing across the Internet. Routers come in different sizes and do more or less, depending on how big and sophisticated they are. For instance:

▼   If you have enabled Internet Connection Sharing between two Windows XP–based computers, the computer that is connected to the Internet is acting as a simple router. This router does very little—it just looks at data to see which computer it's meant for.

■   Routers that are used to connect small offices to the Internet do more. They enforce rules about security for the office LAN, and they generally handle enough traffic that they tend to be stand-alone devices.

▲   The biggest routers (the ones used to handle data at the major traffic points on the Internet) handle a lot of information—millions of packets each second. These are stand-alone devices that look more like Maytag made them than a network device company.

Let's consider the medium-sized router—it's probably something humming away in a small room at your business. This router has only two networks to deal with—your LAN and the Internet. The office LAN connects to the router via an Ethernet connection. The router might also have two connections to your company's ISP—a T3 and an ISDN connection. For the most part, your traffic comes and goes via the T3 line. However, the ISDN line is used in the event something goes awry with the T3 line. In fact, the router is configured to send data across the ISDN line, because the configuration table has been programmed to switch over in case of an emergency.

This router is also tasked with another function—it's a layer of security against outside attacks. Although firewalls are routinely used to prevent attacks, the router is also configured to keep the bad people out.

Switches

It's no exaggeration to say that switched network technology is revolutionizing how internetworks are designed and what they can do for users. Over the past decade, switches have begun pushing internetworks to size scales and service levels many considered unfeasible not long ago.

But what exactly are switched networks? How do they work?

▼ They run at very high speeds because they operate at the data-link layer (layer 2) instead of at the network layer (layer 3), where routers operate. This enables switches to process traffic quickly, without creating bottlenecks.

▲ They have many of the capabilities of a router, but they sit between the host and the backbone, instead of between backbones as routers do. Switches can take control over traffic at or near its source, whereas the router usually doesn't take over until the message is ready to begin its trek to a remote LAN. Taking control at the source takes much of the randomness out of network operations.

How an Individual Switch Works

Almost all computer advances in one way or another come down to miniaturization and speed, and the network switch is no different. The predecessor of the switch was a *hub*. A hub would broadcast incoming data indiscriminately to all its ports. Switches, on the other hand, are smart and fast enough to read both the source port and the destination port of each frame and "switch" messages between the two (thus the name). This difference is shown in Figure 5-3.

NOTE: The use of *port* here denotes a physical connection to the switch, not a virtual, layer-4 port normally associated with an application.

Much like routers, switches examine destination and source addresses as messages pass through. Switches differ from routers in that they're looking at layer-2 media access control (MAC) addresses instead of layer-3 IP addresses.

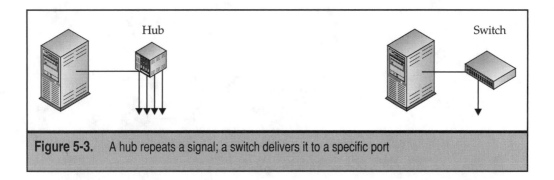

Figure 5-3.   A hub repeats a signal; a switch delivers it to a specific port

The switch, like the hub, provides a shared media LAN into which hosts can connect. But the switch is, at the same time, able to assume router-like duties, for two reasons:

▼ Switches have more powerful electronics than hubs (they have more transistors crammed onto their printed circuit boards).

▲ They operate at the data-link layer (layer 2), which means they don't have to dig as deep into packets as layer-3 routers.

Beefed-up electronics make the switch a speed reader. But while switches are smart, they're not nearly as smart as routers. The switch is, in effect, assigned a lighter reading assignment than routers because it handles traffic at layer 2.

To illustrate this, Figure 5-4 traces a message through a hypothetical switched network. The first step takes place between the host sending the message and its switch port. To do this, the switch reads the incoming message's destination MAC address and instantly moves it to the outbound port it associates with that destination MAC.

Because the message is switched to a targeted outbound port instead of being replicated to all ports (as in a hub), it encounters no collisions. This makes more bandwidth available and moves messages at faster throughput speeds.

The same process holds for the message's second step. As the message pours out of the outbound port on Switch 1, it has dedicated bandwidth (no collisions) over the cable connecting it to the port in Switch 2. The switching process again repeats itself through the third step all the way out to the destination host.

When a switch receives a message seeking an address it doesn't know, instead of dropping the message, the switch broadcasts the message to all its ports. This process is called *flooding*, which is necessary for discovery-type messages. For example, a host uses Dynamic Host Configuration Protocol (DHCP) when it boots up to locate nearby services such as network printers. Without flooding, switches could not support broadcast messages sent by DHCP and other utilities.

Switched Networking Basics

How is it possible to have dedicated bandwidth all the way through a multiple-device network connecting hundreds of hosts? The answer is that switched networks balance intelligence with raw power.

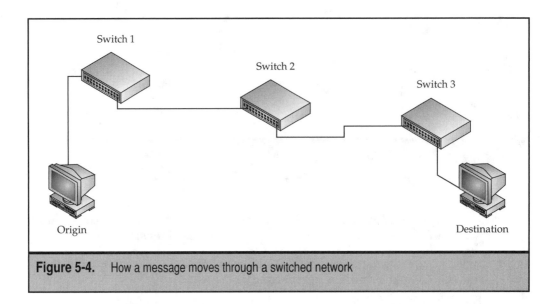

Figure 5-4. How a message moves through a switched network

In simplified terms, routers move messages through an internetwork to their destinations by working from left to right across the destination's IP address. As the message hops between routers, the router checks the routing table maintained in each new router, trying to match the next part of the destination IP address. When the router finds a more complete match, the message physically moves through the internetwork to the router whose location is represented by that matched IP address information. Sooner or later, all the IP address parts are matched, and the message arrives at the router serving as the gateway to the destination host.

In sharp contrast, a message must find its way through a switched network without the luxury of hierarchical IP addresses. Switched networks operate using MAC addresses, which are considered to be flat in topology. A MAC address—also called a physical address—is a sort of network serial number assigned to a host's network interface card (NIC). The first half of every MAC address is a vendor code signifying the manufacturer of the NIC; the second half is the serial number of the actual device. If you move a device to the other side of the world, its MAC address remains unchanged. Switched networks are completely flat in that because they rely solely on MAC addresses, they in effect think all devices and hosts are attached to the same cable. Beyond the friendly confines of the home LAN, a MAC address is a small clue. How, then, do switched networks manage to deliver messages?

When a switch is turned on, it begins building a dynamic address table. It does so by examining the source MAC address of each incoming frame and associating it with the port through which it came. In this way, the switch figures out what hosts are attached to each of its ports.

As Figure 5-5 shows, MAC addresses are passed back through a chain of cooperating switches until they reach the switch building its dynamic address table.

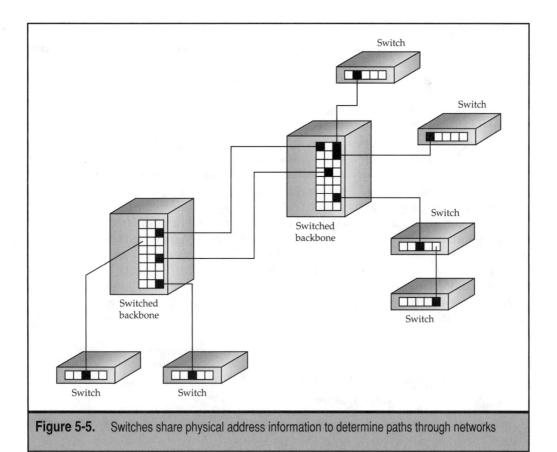

Figure 5-5.   Switches share physical address information to determine paths through networks

Theoretically, a switch could eventually compile a list containing the MAC addresses of every switch in the world. To prevent that from happening, switches drop unused MACs after a default period of five minutes. The dynamic address table isn't as smart as routing tables, which use all types of costing algorithms to choose optimal paths. A switch simply places the most frequently used MACs toward the top of its dynamic address table. Together, these two procedures guarantee that the switch's network path-finding intelligence is at least fresh and more likely to be reliable.

Designing Switched Internetworks   Even if a switch's dynamic address table could identify a path through a very large switched internetwork, if that path required hundreds or even just dozens of hops, it would be too slow. Two technologies have been developed to solve this problem:

▼   Switched backbones

▲   Multilayer switching

Switched Backbones   *Switched backbones* are high-end switches used to aggregate bandwidth from other switches. The idea of a switched backbone is for it to have the biggest dynamic address table of all. Switched backbones are frequently configured with multiple high-end switches, both for purposes of redundancy and in order to attain blazingly fast throughput rates.

It'd be neat to tell you that switched backbones are fat, high-tech cables strung atop towering pylons in electrical utility power grids, or that they're meshed networks of very fast and expensive T3 high-speed phone circuits. But they're not. Even the biggest of the big switched backbones is an unglamorous collection of refrigerator-like boxes cabled together, quietly humming away in a computer room somewhere.

A switched backbone's job is to concentrate what would otherwise be many hops into a single hop through a single backbone LAN. This is what's meant by *bandwidth aggregation.* Switched backbones pack large amounts of memory and throughput into a single configuration. Not all switched backbones are behemoths. A switched backbone might be a device about the size of a pizza box sitting in a rack in a data closet. Remember, a backbone is simply a relatively fast LAN interconnecting other LANs.

While switched backbones aren't absolutely necessary in smaller networks, they probably are in very large ones. You might remember when AOL's network collapsed. After the headlines faded, gurus lambasted AOL for having stuck with its mostly router-based topology too long.

Switched backbones are implemented using any of four technologies:

▼ ATM (Asynchronous Transfer Mode)

■ Fast Ethernet or Gigabit Ethernet

■ FDDI

▲ Token Ring

Many large internetworks inevitably have subnets implementing a variety of technologies. For this reason, many vendors' switches feature any-to-any switching between ATM, Gigabit Ethernet, Fast Ethernet, Token Ring, and FDDI.

Aggregating bandwidth, of course, means rolling up messages from a large number of subsidiary switches. Because switched networks deal only in MAC addresses, hierarchical routing cannot do this. The workaround is to create levels of switches through uplink ports. Figure 5-6 depicts how this configuration funnels the traffic from many hosts through the host switch out to the backbone switch.

This configuration technique enables designers to create a power hierarchy in lieu of a logical hierarchy. Switched networks aggregate traffic into the bandwidth of a single switch to help the message find its way. Described in basic terms, this is accomplished by a switched backbone machine having more switches connected directly to it and thus building a much larger dynamic address table.

Each switch's ability to aggregate bandwidth into a high-speed intelligent backbone relies on most or all of the advanced switching technologies introduced in Table 5-1.

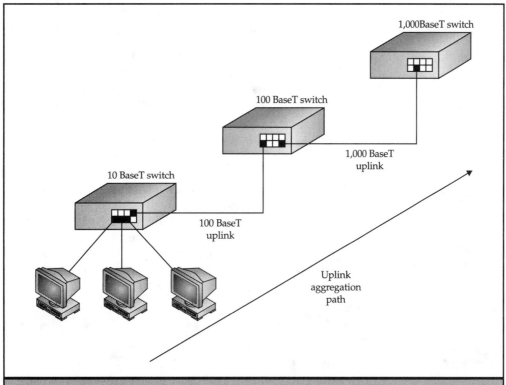

Figure 5-6. Uplink ports aggregate traffic into the switched backbone

Technology	Description
Address Cache	Also called MAC cache—the maximum number of MAC addresses a switch can maintain in its dynamic address table, which is a function of a combination of factors, including DRAM and CPU capacity.
Wirespeed	Also called forwarding rate—the rate at which a switch can pick up a stream of packets from an incoming cable, usually expressed in packets per second (pps).

Table 5-1. Key Switching Technologies

Technology	Description
Backplane (Switch Fabric)	The data rate of the switch's bus, which services CPU, memory, and I/O controllers, expressed in megabits per second (Mbps), gigabits per second (Gbps), or terabits per second (Tbps).
IP Multicast	Certain message types tend to be multicast, where, for example, one copy of a message is sent to 1000 hosts instead of 1000 copies being sent. Doing this through a switched network requires a switch with sufficient processing power, memory capacity, bus speed, and software to handle such large MAC addressing transactions. IP Multicast is becoming an important switch technology as the world moves to the type of traffic lending itself to multicast messaging, such as video conferencing.

Table 5-1.   Key Switching Technologies *(continued)*

Multilayer Switching   *Multilayer switching* is a hybrid of routing and switching technologies. Even the best-designed switched networks must still use routers at some level. The hierarchical topology of layer-3 IP addressing has much better "aim" than do switched network schemes, given that routers use hierarchical addresses instead of flat MAC addresses. This is why smart network designers are using multilayer switches to augment switched networks with the capabilities of a router to identify optimal paths to destinations. Depending on the manufacturer, multilayer switching is also called *IP switching*, *layer-3 switching*, *shortcut routing*, and *high-speed routing*.

Operators of very large internetworks—mainly organizations running big intranets—are offering services where users can click a hyperlink in one place and suddenly create a message demanding information or services from a faraway server. As users increasingly move about an internetwork to use its remote services, the capacity of its routers is strained. Properly implemented, multilayer switching can deliver tenfold throughput improvements at heavily traveled connection points, although it's a relatively new and immature technology.

Multilayer switching works by first determining the best route or routes through an internetwork using layer-3 protocols and storing what it finds for later reference. Users who come along later wanting to travel that route do so via switches, bypassing the router (and the bottleneck it would cause).

Even if multilayer-switching technology is not integrated into a switched network, some routing should still be used to provide some form of hierarchical topology to the network. This is necessary not only to maintain networkwide performance, but also to enhance security. Switches will not displace routers from internetworks in the foreseeable future. However, multilayer switching could be the industry's first step toward melding what are now two technologies into one—much as the bridge was subsumed by the router five to ten years ago.

Optical Considerations

The preceding section gave a general, overall view of how routers and switches work. Naturally, however, when optical functionality is figured into the mix, there are some unique traits that must be explained. One of the most important attributes of optical routing and switching is that there is no "pure" optical routing or switching at this point.

In this section, we'll talk about what's keeping networking stuck in electrical networks and discuss the ramifications of this hurdle.

The "All-Optical" Myth

In spite of the fact that vendors are advertising their wares as "all-optical," the truth of the matter is that they are not, in fact, all-optical.

As we mentioned in Chapter 4, all-optical networks must currently endure some sort of conversion from optical to electrical, then back to optical. This process is called an optical-electrical-optical (OEO) conversion. It is at this point that a bottleneck occurs and speeds diminish. Even if the conversion, itself, took no time, there would still be a delay. If the conversion could be eliminated, then data rates could be pushed, theoretically, somewhere between 25 and 75 terabits per second.

But in addition to the OEO conversion problem, there are two other issues that must be addressed before all-optical networks can become a reality: routing and buffering.

Routing   Optical devices operate in point-to-point or ring topologies. *Point-to-point* means that light moves from Node A to Node B. If the fiber is cut, then the packet doesn't go anywhere. *Ring* topologies, on the other hand, offer more protection. In the event the ring is cut, then the ring can wrap around itself, and the packet will still make it to its destination.

If a more complex topology is required, like a mesh, then routing must be introduced. Currently, there is no physical-layer routing protocol to enable this. Let's say that we have a network, like the one shown in Figure 5-7, with nodes in St. Paul, Chicago, and St. Louis. If I'm in St. Paul and decide to send a packet to St. Louis, how does the network know which route to take? Does it go directly to St. Louis or can it go through Chicago? What if the link between St. Paul and St. Louis is down? These questions are answered by routing protocols. In a conventional network—with routing protocols in place at layer 3—the network knows to avoid the downed link and forward the packet through Chicago.

In an all-optical network, the network wouldn't know how to get around the damaged link, because there is no routing protocol at the physical layer.

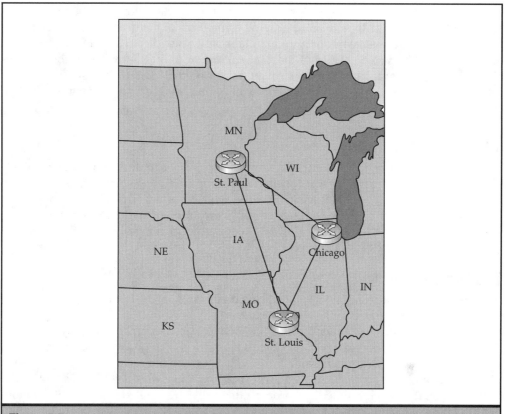

Figure 5-7. Routing protocols are needed to reroute packets in the event of a downed link

Buffering The second obstacle to all-optical networking is devising a means to buffer light. In conventional networks, electrical packets can be stored briefly while their destination is determined.

The ability to buffer light is important because if packet header information needs to be read or there is a node with congestion, the packets won't be lost. Further, think about an optical node with two lambdas arriving at the same time. One of the lambdas will be lost, because the node will be unable to handle two incoming signals.

There exists a technique called a *fiber-delay link,* which is essentially a long spool of fiber, and which works like a very short holding pattern for airplanes. But given the speed the wavelength is moving, and the number of bits that would have to be stored, the fiber "spool" could be hundreds of miles long. Additionally, signal loss will occur as the transmission goes through all that fiber. Further, if another packet arrives immediately after the first, you need a second delay loop.

Vendors continue to research and develop new and innovative ways to deal with optical networking technology. However, estimates range between 10 and 50 years before truly all-optical switching and routing technology will be available.

OEO Conversion

The routers and switches used in optical networking are still electrically based and are not pure optical platforms. This means that the optical signals must undergo a conversion before the packets can be examined and redirected. An OEO conversion is done for a number of reasons, including:

▼   In switches and routers, the signal has to be converted so that the packet headers can be studied. In regenerators, the signal can be beefed up only if the signal is in electrical form.

NOTE: Don't confuse regeneration with amplification. Amplification does not require an OEO conversion and can take place right on the optical fibers. Furthermore, regenerators also retime the signal, whereas amplifiers don't provide this function.

▲   On a long-haul network, an OEO conversion may take place every 600 kilometers (km) for regeneration. Newer regenerators, in conjunction with postamps, line amps, and preamps, on the other hand, are expanding that distance to 4000 km.

Though packets are still able to traverse an optical network at extremely fast rates (even with the OEO process), the process is inefficient and a source of bottlenecks. Optical networking vendors are struggling to come up with truly all-optical networking devices. Ideally, an optical network would require no conversions from beginning to end. The speed and capacity of such a network would be practically limitless.

While the truly all-optical network is many years away, many vendors are optimistic that they will be the ones to break the OEO barrier.

OPTICAL SWITCHING

Though all-optical switching is still a fantasy, optical switches now in use are providing what functionality they can for optical networks. These switches use some incredible technology to send lambdas from one device to another. Additionally, there are other technologies vying for inclusion in optical switches.

In this section, we'll examine the technology used for optical switches. Depending on size, capacity, speed, and cost, one technology may prove superior to another, at least for specific switching needs. Finally, we'll look at optical cross-connects (OXCs), which are, though technically not switches, providing this functionality in their own, hardwired way.

Basics

Over the years, the pipes that carried Internet and organizational network traffic have been forced to grow. The plumbing that was the Internet's infrastructure worked just fine, just as long as the network grew at a manageable pace. During this time, the service provided by electronic routers and switches was measured in megabits. As the Internet and bulkier applications have taken their toll on network infrastructure, carriers have been forced to add capacity, and managing all that bandwidth with electrical devices has become a chore.

The main way to accomplish optical switching is by using a sophisticated digital cross-connect. When data networking was still a fledgling industry, facilities were created by manually patching the ends of circuits into a patch panel. In the early 1980s, digital cross-connects took over this role, taking the expensive, time-consuming, and error-prone patch panel out of the equation.

For optical networking, this process works all right, assuming you don't mind an OEO conversion. Because of this conversion, vendors strove for an all-optical solution, finally developing the OXC. The first OXC, the LambdaRouter by Lucent Technologies, used a micro-electrical-mechanical system (MEMS) as its core technology.

The MEMS (which we will expand upon later in this section) is still, technically, an electrical system (electronics move the tiny mirrors of the MEMS), but it was a good step toward all-optical technology.

Switching Technologies

In Chapter 4, we touched briefly on some of the optical switching technologies under development by vendors. In this section, we take a closer look at these technologies and how they stack up against each other. The basic philosophy behind many of these technologies was originally developed for use in industries other than optical networking. Now, however, they are being modified for use in optical environments.

This conversion isn't a simple process, because optical switching, of course, has its own quirks and unique requirements that necessitate adjustments to the technology. This is also uncharted territory for carriers and telecoms that would invest thousands (if not millions) of dollars on untested, unproven technology. At this stage, some of this technology is still largely developmental, whereas vendors are actively deploying other technology. For example, the most popular new technology for optical switching follows Lucent's example and uses MEMS.

An issue to be cognizant of while reading about these architectures is that a system that is useful in one environment may not be as useful in another. Largely, the determining factor on which of these technologies will be the most popular comes down to market factors and how well vendors are able to develop them.

MEMS

As we described in Chapter 4, MEMS is a technology that uses an array of tiny mirrors to redirect wavelengths from one fiber to another. The mirrors are made from semiconductor materials, like silicon, and are already popular components in other industries. These so-called "micromachines" are prevalent in automotive, aerospace, and electronics industries.

MEMS are constructed similarly to integrated circuits. With MEMS, the etching process produces not only electrical and optical pathways, but also miniscule structural elements. Further, the use of silicon rather than metal has two benefits:

▼ Existing silicon fabrication techniques can be used.

▲ Silicon mirrors are more stable than metallic mirrors when temperatures are elevated and electrical fields are applied.

To understand the size of a MEMS system, a 256 × 256 MEMS array uses mirrors that are one-half millimeter in diameter. These mirrors are positioned one millimeter apart, and the entire array sits on a silicon wafer that is 2.5 centimeters on each side. For sake of comparison, this array is about 32 times denser than an electrical switch matrix. Furthermore, because the optical switch won't need to convert 256 wavelengths into electrical signals, the switch consumes only about one-hundredth the power of traditional optical cross-connects.

There are two types of MEMS, as Figure 5-8 illustrates. They are:

▼ **Two-dimensional (2-D)**   In a 2-D array, the mirrors operate in just two dimensions. The mirrors flip up and down and serve as simple redirectors. When the mirror is switched down, the wavelengths simply pass over them. When the mirrors are switched up, the wavelengths are redirected to a different output port.

▲ **Three-dimensional (3-D)**   In a 3-D array, mirrors can be angled in any direction, not just up and down. The arrays are configured in pairs at 90 degree angles to each other. As wavelengths enter the switch from the input ports, they are deflected off a mirror in the first array onto a mirror in the second array. In turn, the wavelength is redirected to the designated output port. Because the mirrors are aiming the wavelengths at very small targets, it is important that the mirrors are properly calibrated and tuned. The accuracy must be to the millionth of a degree. These 3-D MEMS arrays are good for large OXCs, especially if groups of wavelengths can be switched together from one fiber to another.

Software in the MEMS switch processor decides which fiber will be selected as the output fiber. The control software sends a signal to an electrode, which creates an electromagnetic field, tilting the mirror to its desired angle. Because the design, construction, and usage of 2-D mirrors are at a more advanced stage than 3-D arrays, they are likely to be the technology used in first-generation all-optical switches.

The 2-D arrays can generally handle 32 × 32 ports. For larger switching needs, however, several arrays can be connected to create cores up to 512 × 512. The 3-D arrays, on the other hand, can handle thousands of ports, but a switch that size has not been created, yet.

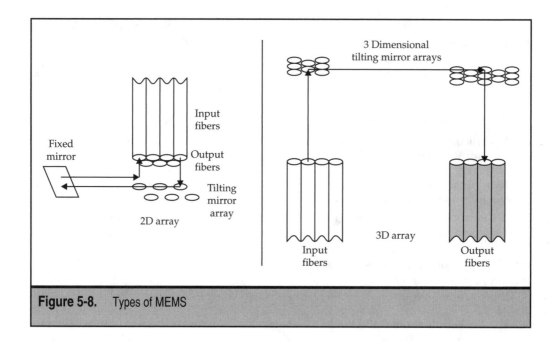

Figure 5-8. Types of MEMS

Liquid Crystal

Liquid crystals are the same technology behind laptop computer screens and digital watches. Liquid crystals are molecular chains with a long, thin, and nearly one-dimensional shape. When an electrical field is applied to liquid crystals, they line up and turn opaque. This same technology that puts images on a laptop computer screen or numbers on a digital watch face can be used in optical switching.

Liquid crystal switches operate when an electrical charge is applied to them, changing the polarization of the light. Because liquid crystals are long and thin, they let only light with a certain orientation through.

Liquid crystal switches depend on the polarization of the light for operation and switch in several stages:

1. First, a filter determines the polarization of the incoming light.

2. The light is directed to the liquid crystal, which alters its polarization.

3. Finally, the light strikes a passive optical device, which changes the light's path, depending on its polarization.

Liquid crystal switches use two components for their functionality:

▼ **Cell** The cell is formed when two pieces of glass sandwich liquid crystal material. The glass is coated with a transparent oxide material that conducts electricity. The cell reorients the polarized light as it enters the switch.

▲ **Displacer**   This is a composite crystal that redirects light as it leaves the cell. Light polarized in one direction is sent to one output waveguide by the displacer, while light polarized at a 90-degree angle is sent to a second output waveguide.

Figure 5-9 shows the cell and displacer in action. Both the cell and the displacer have a default setting, and when no power is applied, the wavelengths are automatically guided across the default path. When a voltage is applied, however, a new path is created, as indicated by the dashed lines.

Vendors are finding that liquid crystals are better suited for optical attenuators than for switches. This is because liquid crystals can throttle the amount of light passing through, rather than just deflecting it. However, in terms of switch construction, this type of technology is well suited for small, wavelength-selective switches.

Bubbles

A very popular technology used in printers is also at the core of an optical switching technology. In a bubble jet printer, the print head contains a number of tiny holes, which are used to shoot out ink onto the page. Blowing ink out of selected holes forms letters and images.

The core of a bubble optical switch is constructed in two layers:

▼ **Silica**   The silica layer is the bottommost layer where optical signals travel. On this layer, a series of parallel waveguides (which are microscopic trenches) are

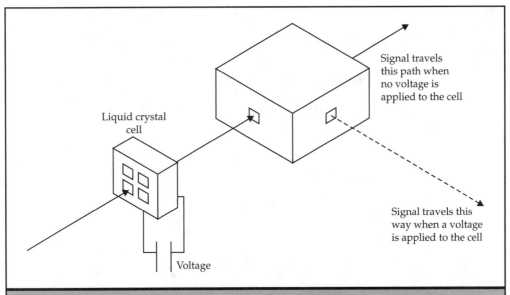

Figure 5-9.   The cell and the displacer are at the core of the liquid crystal switching system

etched into the silica and intersect another series of parallel trenches at 120-degree angles.

▲ **Silicon** The next layer sits atop the silica and contains the bubble technology. As light traverses the optical trenches in the silica, a bubble will form at a trench junction, which causes the light to glance off the bubble and take a new route.

Light traversing the silica trenches can continue along its default path and emerge on an output port. However, if the switch decides that the wavelength must be rerouted, small electrodes in the silicon layer create the bubble, as shown in Figure 5-10. As with a bubble-jet printer, the electrodes heat up the liquid to create a gas, in turn causing a bubble to be formed.

In the leftmost portion of Figure 5-10, we see how light proceeds through the layers in its default mode. With nothing to block its path, it continues directly across the established route. In the lower portion of the figure, however, we see what happens when the signal needs to be sent to a different output port. In this case, as the light travels across a silica trench, the switch decides that the wavelength must be rerouted, so a bubble swells to block the path. The wavelength glances off the bubble and continues along the new path.

The bubble technology is used by Agilent Technologies, Inc., in add/drop multiplexers. The switch package has 128 fiber jumpers—32 for input, 32 for output, and 64 for channel adding and dropping. This technology is also useful for scalable switches, as chips can be connected together to form a larger architecture.

Holograms

The same technology that let Luke Skywalker know Princess Leia was in trouble with the Galactic Empire is in use in some optical switches. Hologram-based optical switches employ an electrically charged diffraction grating to create a hologram inside a crystal.

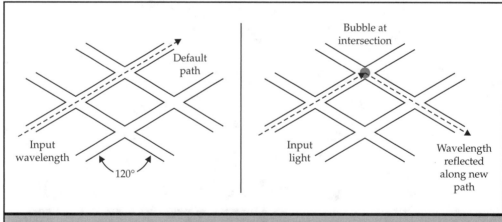

Figure 5-10. Bubble technology is used to reflect a wavelength and send it along a different path

As we mentioned in Chapter 3, a diffraction grating is a small piece of film with a series of tiny, parallel stripes etched on it, and these stripes reflect specific wavelengths. When a voltage is applied to the grating, the wavelength is deflected to an output port. As with the other technologies we have discussed, with no voltage, the wavelength simply passes directly through.

For purposes of switching, each input fiber requires its own row of crystals, one for each wavelength on the fiber.

Holographic switches scale very well, but they are best suited for switching individual wavelengths, rather than groups of wavelengths. These types of switches are extremely fast, switching in nanoseconds. This means that this type of switch could be used for switching packets in an optical router.

Thermo-Optical Waveguides

Waveguides are paths on an integrated circuit that have the same properties as optical fiber. In fact, they can be manufactured using the same process used to manufacture integrated circuits. In essence, the waveguides are part of the integrated circuit. But although the waveguides are built using integrated circuit technology, the waveguides still contain a core and a cladding, just like normal fiber.

A thermo-optical waveguide uses a change in temperature to alter the phase of the wavelength traversing the waveguide. As a result of the phase change, the wavelength can take a different path through the waveguide.

As Figure 5-11 shows, a thermo-optical switching element has an input waveguide and two output waveguides. Between the input and the output are two short, internal waveguides that split the input light.

Next, the light is sent across two paths—one normal and the other heated by a small resistor with an electrical charge applied to it. The change in temperature heats one of the waveguides, which causes the waveguide to physically lengthen. This lengthening changes the phase of the wavelength. When the wavelengths are brought back together, the phase difference pushes the light wave onto the second output waveguide.

In the event no heat is applied to the split wavelength, when the two are recoupled, they then proceed on the default path.

NOTE: Since the splitting and coupling occur in such a tiny space, there is hardly any loss to the wavelength.

Thermo-optical technology is used, primarily, for making small optical switches—generally 1 × 1, 1 × 2, and 2 × 2. Because it is a planar technology, larger switches can be constructed by combining 1 × 2 components on the same wafer.

The simplest type of thermo-optical switch is a 1 × 2 (also known as a Y-splitter). When heat is applied to one arm of the Y, its refractive index changes, blocking the light from traveling down that arm.

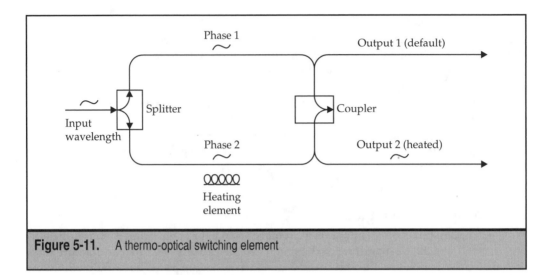

Figure 5-11.   A thermo-optical switching element

Thermo-optical switches come in two flavors:

▼ **Digital optical switch (DOS)**   These switches use a step-like response. If more heat is generated from the heater than necessary, the switch remains in the same state, whether it is on or off. DOSs can be made from silica or polymer. Polymer DOSs draw 100 times less power but cause higher optical losses.

▲ **Interferometric switch**   These switches are more compact, but they are rather wavelength sensitive. Because of this, they require exact temperature controls. Incoming light is split and sent across two different waveguides. Next, they are recombined and split one last time. One of the waveguides is heated, thus changing its optical path length. If the paths are the same length, then light chooses one exit. If they are different lengths, they choose the other.

Only one internal waveguide needs to be heated, which eliminates an additional expense. Further, since waveguides are constructed in a fashion similar to integrated circuits, they can be built en masse and cheaply.

Further, the wafer substrate is the same material used for integrated circuit lasers and detectors, which makes it possible for a number of components to be integrated onto a single wafer.

S-Bugs

The final technology we'll examine is a cross between two other types of switches—liquid crystal and holographic. The company that makes this type of switch, Digilens Inc., has trademarked the name as Electrically Switchable Bragg Gratings (ESBGs). That acronym is shortened even further to "S-Bugs."

S-Bugs are based on diffraction gratings. However, with the application of liquid crystals, the gratings can be built up or eliminated entirely with the application of an electric voltage. This occurs by using tiny drops of liquid crystals suspended in a layer of polymer, then positioned on top of a silica waveguide. When no voltage is applied to the grating, a specific wavelength is reflected. When voltage is applied, the grating disappears and the light passes directly though the waveguide.

This means that S-Bugs can do two different things at the same time. They can single out a certain wavelength, and they can switch the wavelengths. This is beneficial because this eliminates the need for a second (costly) device. S-Bugs have great potential for ADMs, because of their capability to switch out a specific wavelength from an aggregate.

Comparison

The last few sections have introduced a number of compelling switching technologies. As you noticed, some of the technologies were fast, others were slow. Some were able to handle a large number of inputs and outputs, while others were best with just a couple of each. As a result, none of these technologies is best for all purposes (though MEMS seems to be the golden boy of optical switching for the time being).

Table 5-2 compares the attributes of the technologies just described and can give you an idea of a certain technology's benefits and liabilities.

Optical Cross-Connects

In Chapter 4 we touched, just briefly, on OXCs. OXCs are often confused with switching devices (and it doesn't help that we're discussing them here in a section dedicated to switching). Even though they serve a somewhat similar function, OXCs are functionally different.

The core difference is that OXCs redirect wavelengths on a physical level—they are permanently hardwired via manual configuration to send traffic along predetermined paths. Switches, on the other hand, can send traffic according to the network's dynamic needs.

In this section, we take a closer look at the cousin of the optical switch—the OXC. Optical switches, in practice, are really just beefed up OXCs. The shuffling of wavelengths done in an OXC is done by configuration, not by reading packet headers.

Function

In an electrical system, there is no need for a cross-connect. Because electricity likes to follow the path of least resistance, it's easy enough to connect the appropriate wires and make data go where you want. That's not so simple on an optical network, however. Without having to force an OEO conversion, OXCs manage the task of switching wavelengths to predetermined fiber.

For the sake of illustration, let's say we've got four input fibers and four output fibers as shown in Figure 5-12. Each fiber is carrying four multiplexed wavelengths. As these lambdas enter the OXC, the OXC will rearrange the 16 lambdas onto the OXC's respective

Technology	Speed	Reliability	Loss	Power Consumption	Scalability
MEMS	Slow. Gets slower the larger the fabric becomes: 10 milliseconds (ms) for 8 × 8, 20 ms for 16 × 16.	Questionable. So many moving parts means it's a matter of time before the MEMS fails. Also, MEMS are susceptible to the effects of shock and vibration, which can result in losing the signal.	A 4 × 4 switch can experience 3 dB loss, 16 × 16 can experience 7 dB loss. Expect more loss if multiple modules are linked together.	Higher than other optical switch technologies, lower than electrical switches.	2-D systems can be built to 32 × 32. However, multiple modules can be linked together, producing 512 × 512. 3-D systems can support thousands × thousands—in theory.
Liquid crystals	Slow, largely due to the viscosity of the liquid crystals. Some vendors are heating the crystals to make them react faster.	Good—no moving parts to conk out.	Can be problematic, because the different beams of polarized light must follow unique paths before being recombined. If one path is shorter or longer than the others, loss will occur when the signal is recombined.	Low for *bistable* crystals. These crystals switch from one state to another. Power consumption is slightly higher for crystals that have only one stable state and must have a constant current applied to them.	Good, but vendors aren't building systems larger than 80 ports.

Table 5-2.   Comparison of Optical Switching Technologies

Technology	Speed	Reliability	Loss	Power Consumption	Scalability
Bubble	10 ms.	Good. No moving parts, but the bubble must be sustained. Existing bubble jet printer technology has worked out manufacturing issues.	4.5 dB per 32 × 32 switch.	Unknown.	32 × 32, but they can be linked together into larger switches. Beware of loss as more and more devices are interconnected.
Holograms	Very fast—nanoseconds.	Good. No moving parts.	4 dB loss for a 240 × 240 switch.	Moderate. High voltages are required.	High. Can be used in switches with thousands of ports.
Thermo-optical waveguides	Polymer designs switch in just a few ms; silica is slower—between 6–8 ms. Some vendors are toying with designs claiming 2 ms.	Good. No moving parts, but the constant warming and cooling of the waveguides might have an adverse effect on the equipment.	Silica has low loss, and polymers have a high loss. However, there is movement in polymer development, resulting in lower loss.	Polymer switches have low power consumption —about 5 milliwatts (mw). Silica has higher power consumption —about 500 mw.	A 16 × 16 port switch can be built on a single silica wafer. Size is not limited by optical loss, but rather by the heat generated by these devices.
S-Bugs	100 microseconds. This is 100 times faster than MEMS or bubbles and 10 times faster than thermo-optics. However, it is not as fast as holograms.	Good. No moving parts.	Low—1 dB.	50mw.	Small.

Table 5-2. Comparison of Optical Switching Technologies (continued)

output fibers. The first issue of concern is that some of the wavelengths on the different fibers may have the same wavelength. It will be impossible for two lambdas with a similar wavelength to be combined and sent to the same output port. To avoid this problem, a *transponder* within the OXC will shift one of the wavelengths to an available channel.

The only problem with the use of transponders is that they have been, conventionally speaking, electrical devices. Because they are electrical, this brings an OEO conversion, which can slow down the OXC. Recently, however, optical transponders have been introduced, eliminating the need for an OEO conversion. Optical transponders are far from perfected, however. They are still relatively new, and the bugs are still being shaken out. Furthermore, they are expensive and inefficient. From a monetary point of view, it still makes more sense to suffer the OEO conversion.

Earlier we mentioned that OXCs differed from switches in that OXCs send lambdas to predetermined output ports. Switching takes place by examining headers on packets, then determining which port the packet should be sent to. OXCs don't do anything of the sort. Looking back to our example in Figure 5-13, if this were an optical switch, all the lambdas could be sent to a single output port. However, because it is an OXC, the lambdas are reconfigured and sent to their predetermined output ports. Also, there is nothing to say that a lambda must be cross-connected to another fiber. If need be, it can continue along its original path.

Lambdas are cross-connected based on the configuration of a cross-connect table. A cross-connect table is shown as Table 5-3; it explains, in tabular form, how the lambdas are connected in Figure 5-12. This type of table is similar to switching tables used in ATM switches and helps to ensure that no port is overbooked or left out completely.

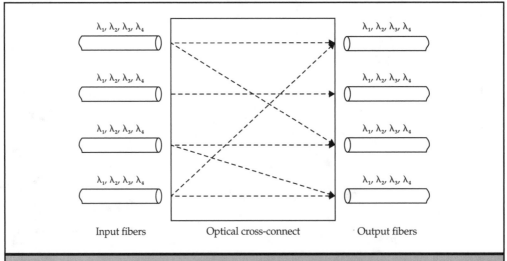

Figure 5-12.   Optical cross-connects send lambdas along predetermined routes

Input Port	Input Wavelength	Output Port	Output Wavelength
1	λ_1	3	λ_1
1	λ_2	3	λ_2
1	λ_3	1	λ_1
1	λ_4	1	λ_2
2	λ_1	2	λ_1
2	λ_2	2	λ_2
2	λ_3	2	λ_3
2	λ_4	2	λ_4
3	λ_1	3	λ_3
3	λ_2	3	λ_4
3	λ_3	4	λ_1
3	λ_4	4	λ_2
4	λ_1	1	λ_4
4	λ_2	1	λ_3
4	λ_3	4	λ_3
4	λ_4	4	λ_4

Table 5-3.   Optical Cross-Connect Table

OXC Element

To ensure optical networking's high speed, the key to OXCs is ensuring that all the traffic streams are cross-connected entirely in the optical domain. The component that allows this to occur is the *optical cross-connection element* or *fiber switching junction*.

In order to transfer lambdas from one path to another, optical channels are created on a silicon chip. The "fiber cores" are arranged on the chip so that the cores actually come in contact with each other for about three millimeters. This is shown in Figure 5-13.

Even though the photons coursing through the cores are optical, electromagnetic forces can still affect them. When a voltage is applied (or withdrawn from) the junction where the cores touch, the electromagnetic force causes the photons to move from one core to the other. As Figure 5-13 shows, λ_A enters the element across Input Fiber 1. Meanwhile, λ_B enters the element on Input Fiber 2. When the two lambdas reach the section where the cores touch, a voltage is applied, and the lambdas change place. Now, λ_A is heading to Output Fiber 2, while λ_B is heading to Output Fiber 1.

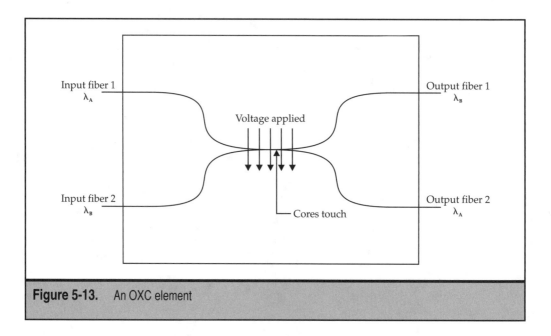

Figure 5-13. An OXC element

A series of OXC elements can be meshed together to build a larger OXC. Figure 5-14 shows how this looks.

In this example, four lambdas (A, B, C, and D) are entering the OXC. By applying a voltage across all the OXC elements, we see how their final paths are determined. For simplicity's sake, we'll follow λ_A along its path, which is shown in a darker line. It is useful to note that in this particular architecture, the only two lambdas that were redirected to new output fibers were λ_A and λ_D. To keep the action easy to follow, we're showing you a very basic configuration. In a larger system with multiplexed signals, there would be a more complex system of cores and transponders that would allow all input ports to mesh with all output ports.

Though unable to provide the dynamic functionality of a switch, OXCs are useful tools at junction points where lambdas on one path must be shifted to another. Because of their optical design, they are also able to provide this service at high speeds.

OPTICAL ROUTING

Because of the router's importance in the development and functionality of the Internet (routers are used to connect networks together), as capacity and bandwidth increase, so will the importance and duties of the router. First, current terabit routers will provide the necessary beefiness until, ultimately, a truly all-optical router is developed.

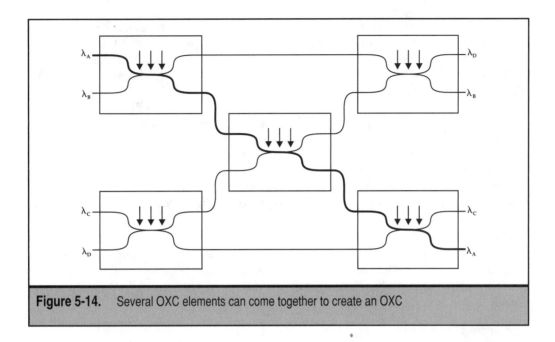

Figure 5-14.   Several OXC elements can come together to create an OXC

In this section, we take a closer look at the basics of optical routing; the design of an all-optical router; how optical routers can increase overall network performance; and how optical and terabit routers can be used to change the functional face of the Internet.

Basics

Throughout this book, we've been banging the drum of optical networking's speed and capacity, and it's true: fiber optics provides a capacity that is unequaled. But with all that bandwidth and speed, the current internetwork bottlenecks are going to be faced with some extreme challenges.

For example, as Gigabit Ethernet frames with ever-increasing IP packet counts start traversing an internetwork, there must be a way to handle so many large frames coming so quickly. Will an electrical IP router be able to handle 2000 packets per second? And that's just per channel. What happens when dense wavelength division multiplexing (DWDM) combines ten similar-sized channels? Will an IP router be able to handle 20,000 packets per second on each link?

Luckily, terabit IP routers (also known as *carrier class* routers) are in existence. These are beefier than backbone routers and the routers used in an enterprise environment. These routers can support up to 60 Gbps (some vendors claim upward of 150 Gbps) per port for a total of 1 terabit per second (Tbps). Further, these behemoths can be linked together in *clusters* to make one large router with a capacity of about 19 Tbps. In this configuration, carrier-class routers can be situated in the same room, or they can be 15 km apart.

These routers, however, are still aimed at the SONET/SDH market, supporting rates between OC-3 and OC-192. In their own defense, they can still handle 16 OC-192 ports at 10 Gbps each, which is far from slouching off. Some believe that SONET/SDH will eventually be squeezed out of this market to make room for Gigabit Ethernet and DWDM. Whether that will come to pass is largely up to the marketplace.

As we've noted in the switching section, the optical bottleneck will be alleviated only when truly all-optical routing and switching are developed. As it stands, optical data can course through networking devices, but unless the packet headers are read and the correct path chosen without an OEO conversion, the bottleneck will still remain.

Not only do optical routers need to be able to decipher packet headers, but they must also be intelligent. They must be able to communicate with one another to devise the best router-to-router path for packets to follow to get to their final destination.

Types

Optical routers are useful and provide different functions in singular locations of a network. Different tasks will be asked of optical routers positioned at the edge, where services are created, and in the core, where scaling will demand new architectures. Let's take a look at the new types of optical routers.

Edge/Aggregation Routers   Edge/aggregation routers are optimized around packet forwarding. These optical routers will likely use MPLS along with other advanced network processors and ASICs (application-specific integrated circuits) for processing packets toward both the core and the customer. Because of this capability, these optical routers will support more than simply packet forwarding to the core, providing carriers with an IP services infrastructure.

Core Routers   Core routers are used to get packets across backbones as quickly as possible. Optical routers in the core will likely use traffic management capabilities with MPLS, increasing their capacities up to OC-192 levels. Further, because next-generation optical network designs are likely to combine smaller bandwidths at the network edge (more on that later in this section) into a larger DWDM transmission, the core routers will have to manage terabit- and petabit-level rates of transmission.

Design

Though the all-optical router is still a fantasy, routers do exist that manage wavelengths. These routers still involve an electrical conversion, but until the bugs can be worked out of the all-optical router, this is what we have to work with. Figure 5-15 shows how an optical router works.

NOTE: In the next section, we'll gaze into our crystal ball and show what might be on the horizon in terms of all-optical router design.

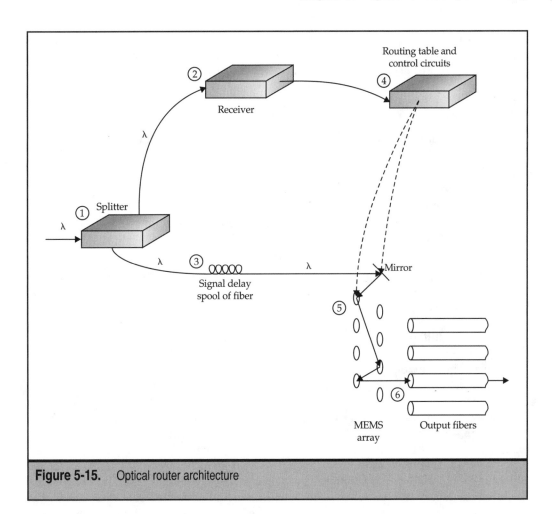

Figure 5-15.   Optical router architecture

In this design, only the headers from the packets need to be stripped off and deciphered, electronically. Let's take a closer look at what happens when wavelengths enter the router:

1. A wavelength enters the router. If a packet header is found in the stream, the wavelength is split in two and sent across different paths. One path will mean conversion to an electrical signal; the other path will remain optical and never be converted.

2. The wavelength will be converted to an electrical signal using an optical receiver. Only the header information needs to be stripped off and studied. By removing just the header, time is saved because the entire packet need not be analyzed.

3. While its doppelgänger is converted into electricity and studied, the pure wavelength is sent through a delay loop. Because it takes time to study the headers and decide where to send the packet, the light is passed through this loop as a delaying measure. Since there is no way to store data optically as there is electronically, the optical signal must be sent across a longer path to delay it.

4. The header information, now converted to an electrical signal, is studied by the router, which looks up destination information on its routing table. The router maintains the routing table (like any other router) by communicating information with its neighbors. But in addition to sharing routing table information with electrical signals, optical routers can send the information optically.

5. When the output information has been determined, a MEMS array is adjusted (again, electronically) so that the emerging optical packet is fired into the correct output fiber.

6. Finally, the wavelength is guided into the output fiber and proceeds on to its destination.

Since we're talking about terabits per second, this process occurs in the blink of an eye. Obviously, this system presents a number of inefficiencies. First, the OEO conversion takes time. Second, sending the optical wavelength through the loop to delay causes, well, delay and provides an opportunity for signal loss.

For a truly all-optical router or switch, there will have to be a major advancement in computer technology, one that will bring an optical computer into service. This advancement is a ways off, but in the meantime, scaling terabit routers may have to be enough.

Though terabit routers seem to be the next best move for carriers and service providers, the demand hasn't been there. In April 2001, industry big dog Cisco discontinued its ONS 15900 Wavelength Router. The technology was acquired through Cisco's purchase of Richardson, Texas–based Monterey Networks, Inc., in 1999. Cisco attributed the discontinuation to a lack of service providers willing to deploy the technology as quickly as Cisco had anticipated. They further attributed the lack of interest for the router to a slowdown in capital spending by service providers.

Speed and Scaling

One of the chief demands of optical networking is faster connectivity and wider pipes. In the past, service providers could meet this bandwidth demand by adding more routers and increasing port speeds. However, the ceiling on that capability has been reached: adding multiple routers creates operational issues. Further, adding more routers causes more ports to be consumed for router-to-router connections. A better way to add routing capabilities is to add capacity and speed to the existing infrastructure.

High-speed routers, based on optical fiber interconnects rather than electronics, provide that higher level of throughput and capacity. The interconnect (or *backplane*) at the core of networking infrastructure equipment is an important consideration in establishing the speed and scalability capabilities of the router. Terabit routers will allow carriers to expand the Internet infrastructure in a smooth, economical way.

Terabit routers using an optical backplane provide thousands of high-speed ports in a single router. To ensure the continued rowth capacity for such a device, the router's intrasystem backplane must support the connection of hundreds or even thousands of line interface cards, as well as multiple chassis, thus creating a large, single-router system. Additionally, the backplane must also be scalable both in speed and capacity so that it will be compatible with future expansion.

Interconnect Technologies

As the need for greater speed and capacity has increased, so have advances in backplane technologies. Bit rates and speeds have continued to increase as electronic devices have evolved. Unfortunately, copper connections have resided at the heart of these nodes. Overall, as helpful as this advancement has been, backward compatibility has suffered. Advances in speed and bit rates have also meant that old devices and infrastructure have had to be replaced with bigger, faster devices.

The step to fiber optics supports very high data rates, and fiber can operate in a broader range of frequencies than copper. Additionally, fiber is quite scalable and can handle yet higher data rates without having to be replaced, as one would have to do with new types of copper-based systems.

At the core of many optical backplane designs are parallel optics devices that use parallel ribbon fibers. As shown here, ribbon fibers are made up of a dozen individual fibers, bound together to make a single unit. The fiber can be either single-mode or multimode (depending on the network architecture), and the distance can be as far as 100 meters, which is usually adequate for an optical backplane:

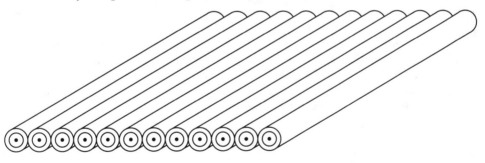

NOTE: Using specialized fiber, this distance can be expanded to one kilometer.

Data comes across an optical link into the router via the line interface card. It is converted to an electrical signal and sent to a framer and packet-processing device. The packet processor establishes how the packet should be handled, and the packet is sent into the switching fabric.

An incoming OC-192 link, for instance, is traveling at 10 Gbps. On an electrical system, the backplane would have to be 50 bits wide and running at 200 Mbs. When confined to a single printed circuit board, incoming data won't have any problem interconnecting, thanks to the connection's simplicity and proximity. But when faster, complex signals are transmitted across an entire system, the system gets tighter.

When copper is eliminated from the equation, the data can once again flow smoothly. Data can be multiplexed into numerous high-speed connections coursing through the optical ribbon fiber. A low-cost interconnection can be built by using arrays of vertical cavity surface emitting lasers (VCSELs) connected to optical ribbon fiber. This system can act as the foundation for the interconnection of cards and chassis.

Size Shouldn't Matter

In electrical networks, topologies have been constrained by distance considerations. As a matter of course, electrical components work better when placed closer to each other.

NOTE: Typically, a velocity of 1 ft/nanosecond is the accepted speed of propagation for electrical signals. It was this physical limitation that gave rise to the unique physical design and circuit pack interconnectivity of the first Cray computer in order to minimize this propagation delay time.

Oftentimes, routers and other nodes do not have the luxury of proximity. A packet coming to a specific router could be redirected to any port. The connecting nodes may be positioned within a few meters of each other; they may be positioned across the continent. As carriers expand their infrastructure, they are likely to discover space becoming a premium. If a router cannot be located in the server room with the rest of the equipment, it might wind up on another floor. In this case, transferring packets between ports will be more complex than redirecting them across a card or a patch cable. Instead, they have to traverse a few hundred feet of cabling.

Fiber optics eliminate the space issue. Because optical devices operate at the speed of light, distance and proximity aren't the concern that they are for electrical networks. With bandwidth demand and high-speed access on the increase, network designers should be keeping an eye on scalability.

Scalable routers that use optical interconnects can provide thousands of high-speed ports. When those ports are linked together as a single router, they also provide a scalable, inexpensive device.

Routers Shape the Next-Generation Internet

It goes without saying that the Internet infrastructure in place today was built with electrical, IP routers in varying levels of size, complexity, and capacity. However, as fiber optics adds to the overall bandwidth needs of the Internet, it will be inefficient simply to throw bigger, beefier routers at the problem.

To be sure, a major player in the next-generation internetwork will be the terabit router or—when created—the all-optical router. But just swapping out an old router with a new one eliminates the opportunity to take advantage of optical networking's capabilities. In conjunction with a terabit router will be a new node configuration.

The core of today's optical network architecture consists of four layers:

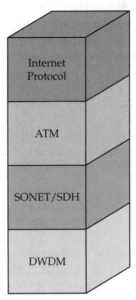

▼ **IP** and other sources of content

■ **ATM** for traffic engineering

■ **SONET/SDH** for network transport

▲ **DWDM** for fiber capacity

Whereas this has been a functional deployment, it is out of date and is too slow to scale to optical networking needs.

Scaling

In the four-layer core just described, establishing a connection between routers is difficult. Even more arduous is provisioning bandwidth across the SONET/SDH layer, which can take months of manual labor to accomplish. This is because of SONET/SDH's ring architecture. As separate rings interconnect to provide connectivity between remote nodes, that capacity must be established across each ring along the connection route. At locations where the rings meet, they must be physically connected.

For example, let's consider the case of a company that wants to establish an OC-192 connection between New York and San Francisco. In order to enable that connection, there must be simultaneous availability of one OC-192 time slot on each ring. If a particular ring simply does not have the available time slot, then time slots on the other rings must be reserved until a new ring can be built. At this point, SONET/SDH ADMs are installed in a full loop around several cities.

Next, if DWDM capacity is not available around the loop, then new DWDM equipment must be installed. Again, if the bandwidth is not available on other rings, then the project must be delayed until bandwidth has been provisioned across the entire route.

Even if the stars are in alignment and the SONET/SDH path is actually provisioned across the country, there can still be a bump in the road if the ATM layer doesn't have the capacity to support the connection. Ultimately, the speed of scaling along with the "weakest link" factor means that the four-layer architecture needs to be improved.

Too Many Protocols

Not only are the networks becoming convoluted, but the functionality of these layers is also waning.

▼ Advances in IP-friendly protocols—like multiprotocol label switching (MPLS)—allow traffic engineering to be split between the IP layer and the optical layer.

■ ATM has made itself useful in IP networks by forming virtual connections between routers. These virtual connections make it easier to build router networks because they give the routers the appearance of being just a single hop apart, when in actuality the virtual path may have to connect several routers. As network capacity grows, that virtual path becomes equivalent to a single wavelength. In the optical core, ATM will be a dinosaur.

▲ SONET/SDH has been useful in voice and leased-line networks, but in the future, routers will be able to handle packets at the OC-192 and OC-768 levels.

The most egregious problem involving the four-layer stack concerns all the "middlemen" in the equation. Let's examine what happens to a packet when it enters a network with the four-layer stack:

1. A stream of data enters an ingress router, where it is divided into smaller packets. Each piece is given a header containing information about the packet's source and destination. Though this is a big header, it is largely ignorable because IP packets are very large to begin with.

2. Next, the IP packets are sent to the ATM layer. At this point, they are further segmented into 48-octet pieces. Each of these pieces is given a five-byte header, and becomes an ATM cell. At this point, the overhead that has been added is about 10 percent of the size of the cell.

3. The cells are then sent to the SONET/SDH layer, where they are packaged into frames for transport across the optical network. About five percent of the frame is overhead.

It should be obvious that there is more going on with the four-layer protocol stack than in a room full of bored bureaucrats. The tax that SONET/SDH, IP, and ATM take is enormous. Furthermore, ATM is a tough technology in and of itself. It is expensive, not especially good for video or audio, and no better for data than other technologies.

Collapsing the Four-Layer Stack

One means to streamline the protocol stack is to collapse it into two layers, eliminating the ATM and SONET/SDH layers entirely. Moving their tasks to the IP and DWDM layers, respectively, would do away with them while still enabling their functionality. For instance, Quality of Service (QoS), which is provided by ATM, would be moved to the IP layer, Meanwhile, survivability, provided by SONET/SDH's self-healing rings, would be moved to the DWDM layer.

How to Get Rid of a Protocol   To collapse the ATM layer into the IP layer, one of two things must occur:

▼ IP must become capable of managing and carrying out QoS without having ATM's adaptation layer to rely on. This could be accomplished by using the type of service bits in concert with the differentiated services protocol to create and enforce QoS levels. For this to work, however, a universal implementation of DiffServ/Type of Service (TOS) would be required.

NOTE: A TOS bit tells the network how the packet should be handled. For instance, it would describe what kind of precedence the packet should receive.

▲ MPLS could be deployed at a layer between 2 and 3, as we illustrated in Chapter 4.

DWDM is a way to combine multiple channels of information on one fiber. DWDM is fast, but dumb. Current capacity allows up to 160 wavelengths to be combined for simultaneous transmission. However, if the fiber is cut, all 160 transmissions are lost.

SONET/SDH, on the other hand, is slow, but smart. It can handle just one wavelength per fiber, yet because of its ring architecture and self-healing capabilities, a cut fiber or disabled router is circumvented within 50 ms, causing no network delay.

A way to combine the best of both technologies is called a *digital wrapper*. The digital wrapper encloses each wavelength's traffic in a low-overhead frame containing additional data, which enables DWDM to detect and correct errors, perform optical-layer performance monitoring, and provide ring protection on a lambda-by-lambda basis. Because this technology will allow SONET/SDH functionality to be applied to DWDM in a ring topology, no third protocol is necessary. Thus, SONET/SDH can be eliminated.

Bigger, Badder Routers at Work   As a result of the stack being collapsed, functions that are normally performed in the network core can be achieved at the network's edge in customer-provided equipment. Those tasks include:

▼ Aggregation

■ Concentration

■ QoS

▲ Policy enforcement

When these tasks are migrated to the network edge, a high-speed router becomes needed to handle these functions. This is where terabit routing comes into play.

NOTE: So what's left to do in the core? Just very high speed data transport.

A terabit or optical router would serve nicely as the foundation of this new layer. To build and scale these networks, terabit routers can connect backbone routers through optical paths. This provides reliable wavelength transmission and traffic engineering.

By eliminating SONET/SDH and ATM devices, network simplicity is also ensured. Because these devices will be removed, only a terabit router and an IP router are necessary in a long-haul environment with DWDM terminals.

Here's how the two-layer stack will process packets in its architecture:

1. The IP router will groom packets from DS-1, DS-3, OC-3, and OC-12 streams into larger OC-48c or OC-192c streams.

2. The terabit router will map these streams to lambdas for transport across the network.

3. As traffic increases, more lambdas are added. They are matched between appropriate router pairs: for instance, data, voice, and video.

Necessary for this network's functionality is an optical routing protocol, Cisco's Wavelength Routing Protocol (WaRP), for instance.

The routing protocol views the network's complete bandwidth pool, providing auto-provisioning of end-to-end wavelength paths in a matter of moments. Further, the routing protocol can allocate and provide bandwidth according to a number of QoS principles.

It's simple—the Internet simply would not exist without such devices at routers and switches. As computer technology has become so critical to our lives, so has the functionality that routers and switches provide.

Unfortunately, true optical routing and switching are not yet fully realized. Though they are still on a few drawing boards in a few vendors' offices, their role will be critical when they are finally created. Not only will they be important to carry the heavy levels of bandwidth that optical networking provides, but they will also be important to reshape the building blocks of the Internet.

CHAPTER 6

Vendors and Their Wares

Though the number of vendors offering optical networking gear is nowhere close to the number offering conventional, electrical gear, there is still a respectable number of vendors and optical equipment from which to choose.

This chapter examines just a few of the vendors out there. As you will see, some vendors (like Cisco) offer a comprehensive line of optical products, from kicked-up core routers to high-capacity transmission systems. Meanwhile, others (like Tellium) focus on a few products, maybe just offering a couple versions of a switch. No matter what your optical networking need, this chapter is meant as a quick overview of some of the big names out there and is by no means a complete listing. In fact, such a list would be nearly impossible, as new vendors make their presence known daily.

Further, the issue of price is not examined in this chapter. This is because vendors tend not to give their prices unless you're buying something. Suffice it to say that all of the products included in this section cost tens of thousands of dollars. Furthermore, your price will depend heavily on how much you buy and from whom. We'll leave the bargain hunting up to you. This chapter will look at the offerings current at the time of publication from (in no particular order) Cisco Systems, Inc.; Tellium, Inc.; Nortel Networks, Inc.; Juniper Networks, Inc.; CIENA Corporation; Sycamore Networks, Inc.; Lucent Technologies, Inc.; and Foundry Networks, Inc.; in the context of overviews of these companies' roles in the optical marketplace.

CISCO SYSTEMS, INC.

Even if you have just a passing familiarity with networking (be it optical or electrical), Cisco Systems, Inc., should not be a new name to you. A couple years ago, Cisco faced no rivals—its stock was as high as any company, and when someone mentioned competing companies, you could hear the word "competing" being put in oral quotation marks.

A lot has happened since then. Cisco stock has fallen back closer to earth, and now it can be said that there are competing vendors out there. Cisco may have been nudged from its lofty perch, but it is still wildly popular and comes with a score of devices for any size network.

Overview

Cisco incorporated in December 1984 and now finds its IP-based networking solutions installed at corporations, public institutions, telecommunication companies, and commercial enterprises of all sizes. Cisco provides a broad line of solutions for transporting data, voice, and video within buildings, across campuses, or around the world. The company's solutions are designed to allow both public and private networks to operate with flexibility, security, and performance.

Cisco's products offer a range of end-to-end networking hardware, software, and services. Generally, the products are purchased in combination (although they can be purchased separately) to connect internetworks. Because Cisco offers so many products, it is easy for them to reach a vast audience, no matter what the internetworking or networking need. Further, buyers can acquire additional equipment to further scale their organization as it grows. The Cisco product portfolio offers a broad range of end-to-end networking hardware, software, and services. Products are used individually or in combination to connect computing devices to networks or computer networks with each other. The company's breadth of product offerings enables it to offer a wide range of solutions to meet customer requirements. Many of the company's products are easily upgraded or expanded, offering customers the ability to extend their networks as their needs grow, while protecting their investments. Cisco also provides products and services that allow customers to transform their various data networks to a single multiservice data, voice, and video network.

Cisco provides optical networking solutions through its Cisco ONS 15000 series optical networking systems. The Cisco ONS 15000 series enables multiservice networking and bandwidth management for scalable, data-optimized networks using dense wave division multiplexing (DWDM) and SONET technology for metropolitan networks.

Transport Systems

Transport systems are the devices used to transmit optical information from one location to another. Cisco offers a number of transmission systems that are generally employed by large telecoms and carriers. These devices are rather large and expensive. Transport systems tend to be high capacity—and they have to be. They send billions (sometimes trillions) of bits per second to their destinations.

ONS 15800 DWDM Platform

For long-haul connections, Cisco offers the ONS 15800 DWDM platform. It offers 64 wavelengths, at 10 gigabits per second (Gbps): 32 in the C-band, and 32 in the L-band. This is achieved by amplifying the L band of the fiber to utilize 1565 nanometers (nm) to 1605 nm wavelengths, and by utilizing out-of-band forward error correction (FEC). FEC helps alleviate bit errors introduced by dispersion and attenuation.

Out-of-band FEC uses seven percent of the payload in a 10 Gbps channel to correct errors in a signal. By decreasing the number of bit errors in a transmission, FEC also helps increase span lengths and channel counts. The FEC algorithm used in the ONS 15800 adds redundancy to the transmitted bits, thus enabling the network to identify and correct corrupted bits within a data sequence.

This platform accommodates signals of OC-12/STM-4, OC-48/STM-16, and OC-192/STM-64. Multiplexed wavelengths can be transmitted up to 500 km through the use of distributed optical amplifiers along the optical route.

Ideally, the ONS 15800 operates in distances between 600 km and 1600 km, which is where the best results are achieved. Cisco says it has acquired 25 customers for the ONS 15800 since 1998, including Cogent Communications, Cambrian Communications, Telecom New Zealand, and Velocita, an emerging carrier in which Cisco has about a half-billion dollar stake.

ONS 15540 Extended Services Platform

The Cisco ONS 15540 Extended Services Platform (ESP) is designed for enterprise and service provider networks. Organizations want high-capacity storage networking and cost-effective expansion of Gigabit Ethernet traffic into the metropolitan area. At the same time, service providers need to be able to rapidly provision new services across wavelengths for increased revenues and service level agreement guarantees on those services.

The ONS 15540 supports multiple network and storage protocols, including:

▼ Gigabit Ethernet

■ Enterprise Systems Connection

■ Fibre Connection (FICON)

■ Fibre Channel

■ SONET

■ ATM

▲ Token Ring

Initially, these will all run transparently. In future releases of the hardware, these will be supported in switched mode, in which a wavelength can be combined with as much traffic of the same type as possible.

An ONS 15540 system can be configured to operate in point-to-point, hub-ring, and mesh-ring networks. Optical add/drop multiplexer (ADM) modules are optional and can add or drop four, eight, or 16 lambdas at a time.

The wavelengths operate between 1310 nm and 1550 nm and provide up to 32 channels per fiber, 64 in a fiber pair. Each transponder in the unit operates between 16 Mbps and 2.5 Gbps. Four transponders can be installed in each unit.

ONS 15454 and 15327 Optical Transport Platforms

The Cisco ONS 15454 is one of the most popular metro optical platforms. Cisco boasts over 600 customers and 30,000 systems using the ONS 15454. The transport's smaller brother, the ONS 15327, is a metro edge optical transport platform that is based on the ONS 15454.

Both the ONS 15454 and the ONS 15327 assume the functions of multiple network elements. They combine SONET/SDH transport, integrated optical networking, and multiservice interfaces, including:

▼ Ethernet

■ Fast Ethernet

■ DS1

■ DS3

▲ SONET OCN

Both devices are scalable to OC-192/STM-64 and can be managed under the Cisco Transport Manager. The devices both maintain a small footprint, low power consumption, and easy provisioning across networks.

A common design in high-rise buildings is to deploy the ONS 15327 to cover a certain number of floors. Then, multiple ONS 15327s are aggregated into an ONS 15454 system in a telecom closet. Another way to deploy the system would be in a campus environment where the ONS 15327s would each cover a specific geographic region, then all the signals would be aggregated at the ONS 15454.

The service densities of both the ONS 15454 and the ONS 15327 are listed in Table 6-1.

ONS 15200 Series Metropolitan DWDM Systems

The Cisco ONS 15200 series Metropolitan DWDM systems are billed as the first wavelength to the building metro system—that is, they bring metro wavelengths directly to a customer's premises, rather than having to first go through a provider. The ONS 15200 delivers instant wavelengths to the customer, interoperates with existing products (like the aforementioned ONS 15454 and ONS 15327), and offers a high service density and low cost per wavelength. The big attraction to service providers is that it is simple and inexpensive.

The ONS 15200 drops channels in single wavelength increments, aggregates wavelength and subwavelength services, and supports a range of topologies, including:

▼   Metro ring

■   Star

▲   Point-to-point

The Cisco ONS 15200 Metro DWDM solution includes the ONS 15252, 15201, and 15216 devices. The ONS 15252 is a multichannel unit, while the ONS 15201 is a single-channel unit; these combine to provide such wavelength services as Gigabit Ethernet and OC-48 Packet over SONET (PoS) in a one rack unit platform.

	Cisco ONS 15327	Cisco ONS 15454
DS1	28	112
DS3	3	96
OC-3	4	20
OC-12	1	5
10/100 Ethernet	8	120
Gigabit Ethernet	4	20

Table 6-1.   Capacities for the ONS 15327 and the ONS 15454

The Cisco ONS 15216 platform provides:

▼ Optical filtering for combined wavelengths launched by the Cisco ONS 15454 and ONS 15327

■ Optical ADM to exchange wavelengths on SONET/SDH spans between the 15252 or 15201, the 15454, and the 15327

▲ Optical performance monitoring and amplification in stretches up to 400 km.

The Cisco ONS 15252 and 15201 have no practical limitations aside from the optical power budget for the number of channels that can be carried on a single fiber pair.

ONS 15190 IP Transport Concentrator

The Cisco ONS 15190 series is an IP transport management platform aimed at ISPs, specifically for the metro and metro access. It is designed to support OC-12/STM-4 and OC-48/STM-16 levels.

The ONS 15190 complements Cisco's Dynamic Packet Transport (DPT) line and can be used to create logical rings over star-based fiber topologies. Further, the ONS 15190 can be reordered, inserted, or removed without disrupting the system.

The ONS 15190 supports Cisco's single ring recovery (SRR) protocol. In PoS mesh topologies, the ONS 15190 offers APS redundancy. Further, it minimizes network troubleshooting time by monitoring the quality of the optical signal, SONET/SDH frames, and alarms.

The ONS 15190 offers the following features:

▼ Establishment of logical rings over star topologies at speeds ranging from OC-12c/STM-4 to OC-192c/STM-64

■ Maximizes bandwidth usage of existing fiber infrastructures both at the physical level (by utilizing WDM technology) and at the transmission level (supporting Spatial Reuse Protocol)

■ Offers a centralized network management and monitoring system

■ Supports up to 8 SRP rings simultaneously or 16 PoS connections

■ Reduces network exposure to human error

■ Reduces overhead costs

■ Improves network scalability and serviceability

▲ Provides SONET/SDH and PoS alarms and error reporting

ONS 15104 Bidirectional Regenerator

ONS 15104 is a bidirectional OC-48/STM-16 regenerator that supports single-mode optical fiber transmission when connected to an OC-48 PoS card or DPT in a Cisco 12000 GSR.

The ONS 15104 provides OC-48 line extensions in increments of up to 80 km. This product is the first regenerator that works with Cisco's IOS operating system. That means that customers can add this regenerator to their existing Cisco components and use the same command line interface across the network.

The ONS 15104 provides a SONET/SDH interface that allows it to be used in environments that may be migrating from SONET to IP. The regenerator uses optical-to-electrical-to-optical regeneration with a delay of 20 microseconds (µs).

In terms of functionality, the ONS 15104 regenerates the Synchronous Payload Envelope (SPE) and line-layer overhead, and it terminates and generates the section-layer overhead. The regenerator also monitors the insertion of the B1 and C1 bytes (for more information on the function of these and other SONET bytes, flip back to Chapter 3).

Metro 1500 series

The Cisco Metro 1500 series DWDM, with the introduction of the new four-port Enterprise System Connection (ESCON) TDM functionality, supports up to 128 ESCON channels over 32 wavelengths using a single IP address.

This WDM channel module allows the 1500 to quadruple its ESCON channels, while reducing per-port costs. The 1500 is able to reach such a high density by multiplexing four 200 Mbps ESCON channels into a single Gigabit Ethernet–like frame, then mapping that aggregate signal onto an International Telecommunications Union (ITU) grid wavelength.

The 1500 offers a number of WDM channel modules that support rates between 10 Mbps and 2.5 Gbps. The different modules ensure that both low-speed and high-speed services can be accommodated. Further, each module is able to support single-mode and multimode fibers.

The following list some of the features of the Metro 1500:

▼ Data rate: 4 × 200 Mbps (ESCON)

■ Transmitter wavelength range: 1280–1360 nm

■ Receiver wavelength range: 1280–1570 nm

■ Fiber type: Multimode

▲ Link distance: 0.2 km on multimode fiber

Switches

We talked extensively about switches in Chapter 5. These devices operate predominantly at layer 2 and direct traffic to specific devices. Not only must these devices know where to send traffic, but they must be able to direct different types of traffic (ATM, SONET/SDH, and so forth) across an optical medium. This section takes a closer look at Cisco's offerings in the realm of optical switching.

MGX 8850

Cisco's MGX 8850 IP+ATM Multiservice Switch enables the delivery of a range of services while scaling from DS0 to OC-48c/STM-16 speeds. The switch is aimed at edge and backbone needs.

By using the PXM-1 switching card, providers can deploy a complete set of narrowband services with 1.2 Gbps of nonblocking switching. Upgrading to the PXM-45 card can deliver 45 Gbps of nonblocking switching.

The MGX8850 offers the following features:

▼ IP virtual private networks (VPNs) using Cisco IOS software-based Multiprotocol Label Switching (MPLS)

■ Digital subscriber line (DSL) aggregation

■ Wireless aggregation

■ Optical service integration

■ Multiservice access (for instance, the ability to provide IP, ATM, and Ethernet access)

■ Full suite of voice-over-IP and voice-over-ATM capabilities with full interworking

■ Frame Relay capabilities, with QoS

■ High-density Point-to-Point Protocol (PPP) for Internet access and aggregation

■ Full-featured narrowband ATM for managed data, voice, and video services

▲ High-density broadband ATM for wholesale ATM services

Table 6-2 compares the MGX8850 with both the PXM-1 and PXM-45 cards.

	MGX 8850 with PXM-1 Card	MGX 8850 with PXM-45 Card
Switching capacity	1.2 Gbps	45 Gbps
T3/E3 ports	2	192
OC-3c/STM-1	4	192
OC-12c/STM-4	1	48
OC-48c/STM-15	n/a	12
Connections	12,000	40,000

Table 6-2. Comparison of the MGX 8850 with XM-1 and PXM-45 Cards

BPX 8600

The BPX 8600 family of switches sits at the network edge, the location where service creation and differentiation have the most impact on a network. The switches are standards-based ATM switches with IP and ATM capabilities. They provide the application-layer visibility of IP and the Quality of Service (QoS) features of ATM.

There are three switches in the BPX 8600 family:

▼ **BPX 8620** for broadband ATM services

■ **BPX 8650 IP +ATM Switch**, which supports broadband and MPLS for IP services

▲ **BPX 8680 Universal Service Node**, which offers broadband, narrowband, and MPLS services

The BPX 8600 family allows services to be customized for specific needs. The BPX 8600 family offers a range of user interfaces and speeds up to OC-12/STM-4, enabling an organization to deliver data, video, Internet, LAN, VPN, and Systems Network Architecture (SNA) services. The BPX 8600 series can also support broadband, narrowband, and IP services.

Further, the Cisco BPX 8600 family helps service providers with their service-level guarantees for any type of traffic or application. A sophisticated queuing architecture, QoS capabilities, and connection admission control features work together to meet service level agreements (which we discuss in more depth in Chapter 9).

Table 6-3 compares some of the characteristics of each switch in the BPX 8600 family.

Mechanical design	2 slots for redundant control/switch modules 1 slot for alarm status module 12 general-purpose slots for interface modules
Switch fabric	Peak switching capacity of 19.2 Gbps 12 800/1600 Mbps switch ports that support up to OC-12/STM-4 rates
Network interfaces	T3/DS3 E3 OC-3/STM-1 OC-12/STM-4

Table 6-3.   Comparison of the BPX 8600 Family Features

Network interface features	16 queues for class-based queuing
	Queues programmable for:
	  Maximum queue depth
	  Minimum service bandwidth
	  Maximum service bandwidth
	  Cell loss priority (CLP) thresholds
	  Explicit Forward Congestion Indication
	  (EFCI) thresholds
	  ForeSight closed-loop, rate-based congestion
	  management

Table 6-3. Comparison of the BPX 8600 Family Features *(continued)*

Routers

In the previous section, we talked about Cisco's switches. The devices that really make the Internet and internetworking possible are routers. Routers operate at layer 3 and tell networks where each other is in the larger scheme of internetworking.

Routers are complex devices, and are even more complex when optical functionality is added to them. The following illustrates what Cisco offers for optical routers.

12000 Series Gigabit Switch Routers

Cisco's 12000 series Gigabit Switch Routers (GSRs) were designed for service providers and enterprise IP backbones. The Cisco 12000 GSR family includes:

▼ **Cisco 12008** This GSR has eight slots, with seven used for traffic that can support:

■ 84 DS3

■ 28 OC-3c/STM-1c

■ 28 OC-12c/STM-4c

■ 7 OC-48c/STM-16c

■ **Cisco 12012** This GSR has 12 slots, with 11 used for traffic that can support:

■ 132 DS3

■ 44 OC-3c/STM-1c

■ 44 OC-12c/STM-4c

■ 11 OC-48c/STM-16c

- **Cisco 12016** This GSR has 16 slots, with 15 used for traffic that can support:
  - 180 DS3
  - 60 OC-3c/STM-1c
  - 60 OC-12c/STM-4c
  - 15 OC-48c/STM16c
- ▲ With support for 15 OC-192c/STM-64c interfaces in the future

The 12000 family of GSRs was designed to meet bandwidth, performance, service, and reliability needs inherent in today's core backbones. A modular, multigigabit crossbar switching fabric allows bandwidth to be scaled in the following increments:

- ▼ 40 Gbps for the Cisco 12008
- ■ 60 Gbps for the Cisco 12012
- ▲ 80 Gbps for the Cisco 12016

The routing functions are performed in the gigabit route processor (GRP), which is responsible for running the routing protocols and building the routing tables from the network topology. This information is then used to build the forwarding tables distributed to the line cards. In addition, the GRP is also responsible for the system control and administrative functions.

The line cards also handle packet-forwarding functions. A copy of the forwarding tables (computed by the GRP) is distributed to each of the line cards, which then performs a lookup of each destination address for the datagrams. The datagrams are switched across a crossbar switch fabric to the destination line card.

Table 6-4 compares some of the features of each member of the Cisco 12000 GSR family.

	Cisco 12008	Cisco 12012	Cisco 12016
System bandwidth	40 Gbps	60 Gbps	80 Gbps
Chassis slots	GRP, line cards: 8 slots Switch fabric: 5 slots	GRP, line cards: 12 slots Switch fabric: 5 slots	GRP, line cards: 15 slot Switch fabric: 5 slots
GRP	Processor: 200 MHz Memory: 64–256MB EDO 20MB flash	Processor: 200 MHz Memory: 64–256MB EDO 20MB flash	Processor: 200 MHz Memory: 64–256MB EDO 20MB flash

Table 6-4.   Comparison of the Cisco 12000 GSR Family of Routers

7400 Series

The Cisco 7400 Application Specific Router (ASR) is compact, uses a stackable architecture, and is designed for application-specific routing in service provider and enterprise networks.

The Cisco 7400 router uses the Parallel eXpress Forwarding (PXF) technology patented by Cisco Systems and utilizes a "pay-as-you-grow" granularity with a small, stackable form. It has the highest density and performance for a single rack unit device in the industry and has a high level of flexibility and versatility with more than 40 modular interfaces to help customize the device.

Cisco markets three versions of the 7400 to unique target markets:

▼ **Cisco 7401 ASR-BB**   Broadband subscriber aggregation including xDSL, ISDN, Fiber to the Curb (FTTC), and wireless. Its features include:

- Point-to-Point (PPP) over ATM, PPP over Ethernet, and PPP over virtual LAN (VLAN)

- Routed bridge encapsulation (RBE) for RFC 1483 permanent virtual circuits

- Virtual routing for high-density circuit termination

- Password Authentication Protocol (PAP)/Challenge Handshake Authentication Protocol (CHAP), Remote Authentication Dial-In User Service (RADIUS), and Terminal Access Controller Access Control System (TACACS) authentication

- Intelligent Layer 2 Tunneling Protocol (L2TP) support

- Differentiated, value-added services with hardware-accelerated PXF services along with flexible modular interfaces for traffic aggregation, including OC-3, DS-3, Fast Ethernet and Gigabit Ethernet, and PoS

- Ideal for low- and medium-density aggregation for network operators, competitive local exchange carriers (CLECs), and Internet service providers (ISPs)

- MPLS VPN and full L2TP to MPLS support

■ **Cisco 7401 ASR-CP**   Managed service (customer premises equipment and customer leased equipment) and full MPLS provider edge and MPLS VPN services. Its features include:

- ATM, Frame, Dynamic Packet Transport (DPT), PoS, channelized, and serial interfaces from 64 kilobits per second (Kbps) to OC3/STM-1

- The full range of traditional Cisco routing protocols including Routing Information Protocol (RIP), RIP version 2, Interior Gateway Routing Protocol (IGRP), Enhanced IGRP (EIGRP), Intermediate System–to–Intermediate System (IS-IS), and Border Gateway Protocol (BGP)

- Virtual routing for high-density circuit termination with increased security, flexibility, and scalability

- Ideal for low- and medium-density aggregation for network operators, CLECs, and ISPs

- MPLS VPN, MPLS provider edge, and full L2TP to MPLS support

- Stackability

- Differentiated, value-added services with hardware-accelerated PXF services along with flexible modular interfaces for traffic aggregation, including OC-3/STM-1, T3/E3, Fast Ethernet and Gigabit Ethernet, PoS, and more.

▲ **Cisco 7401 ASR-GW**   Network Service Gateway for QoS enforcement or hardware-accelerated service. Its features include:

- Network address translation (NAT)

- Access control list (ACL)

- Cisco Express Forwarding (CEF)

- NetFlow accounting and export

- Low-latency queue (LLQ)

- Class-based Weighted Fair Queuing (CBWFQ)

- Class-based Weighted Random Early Detection (CBWRED)

- Policing/CAR

The ability of the router to focus on application routing enables the Cisco 7400 products to deliver a rich suite of services and performance tailored for their specific market applications.

7600 Series

The Cisco 7600 series Internet router delivers optical WAN and MAN services. These new products deliver high-performance application combinations and services for enterprise and service provider customers and offer multiprotocol routing that scales to OC-48 speeds.

The Cisco 7600 is ideally positioned for deployment at the network edge—in both service provider and enterprise environments. As part of the Cisco 7000 family of routers, these new midrange routers reduce network complexity and cost of ownership by enabling consolidated delivery of multiple, simultaneous applications, such as voice over IP, VPN, and layer-7 content recognition and switching, on the same high-performance, extensible platform.

The Cisco 7600 series offers the following chassis options:

▼ Cisco 7603

■ Cisco 7606

▲ Cisco 7609

Each is specifically designed to fit different space requirements and applications.

The 7600 series offers a range of functionality, including:

▼ WAN interfaces ranging from DS0 to OC-48/STM-16

■ High-speed channelized optical connectivity (channelized OC-12 and channelized OC-48 to DS3)

▲ For service providers and high-end enterprise customers:

    ■ Highly scalable standards-based implementation

    ■ Layer-2 transport across layer-3 MPLS core

    ■ End-to-end IP QoS support

    ■ Support for layer-2 and layer-3 MPLS VPNs

    ■ MPLS-based traffic engineering support for Internet/metropolitan service providers

    ■ Basic MPLS switching support for ISP core

Table 6-5 compares the different characteristics of the 7600 series chassis.

Cisco offers a variety of Optical Service Modules (OSMs) for the Cisco 7600 series to meet interface scalability needs and allow for IP service applications. These OSMs provide connectivity at rates from OC-3 to OC-48. Each OSM has two PXF processors and provides up to six megapackets per second (Mpps) IP services performance.

NOTE: Mpps is a measure of how many packets are being processed by a device per second. It is similar to bits per second; however, packets contain many bits of information.

	Cisco 7603	Cisco 7606	Cisco 7609
Height	7 inches (four rack units [RU])	12.25 inches (7 RU)	33.5 inches (20 RU)
Bandwidth	32 Gbps	160 Gbps	256 Gbps
Switching performance	15 Mpps	30 Mpps	30 Mpps
Service performance	6 Mpps per optical service module (OSM)	6 Mpps per OSM	6 Mpps per OSM

Table 6-5.   Comparison of the Cisco 7600 Series of Routers

The following OSMs are supported:

▼ Packet over SONET
  - 8- or 16-port OC-3c/STM-1c with 4 ports of Gigabit Ethernet
  - 2- or 4-port OC-12c/STM-4c with 4 ports of Gigabit Ethernet
  - 1-port OC-48c/STM-16c with 4 ports of Gigabit Ethernet
- ATM
  - 2-port OC-12c/STM-4c with 4 ports of Gigabit Ethernet
  - Gigabit Ethernet
  - 4-port Gigabit Ethernet WAN
▲ Channelized
  - 4- or 8-port OC-12c/STM-4c (DS3) with 4 ports of Gigabit Ethernet
  - 2-port OC-48c/STM-16c (DS3) with 4 ports of Gigabit Ethernet

TELLIUM, INC.

Tellium, Inc., designs and develops high-speed, high-capacity optical switching systems that allow service providers to deliver high-speed services. Tellium's line of intelligent optical switches is designed to meet increasing capacity and service demands of providers. The company's products—based on hardware combined with feature-rich software—enables providers to grow and manage their networks quickly and efficiently.

Overview

Since early 1999, Tellium has turned its efforts to the development of optical switches. In September 1999, the company shipped its Aurora 32 Optical Switch and, in the third quarter of 2000, shipped its next generation Aurora Optical Switch.

Tellium was founded in May 1997 by former employees of Bell Communications Research (a.k.a. Bellcore, now Telcordia). Tellium's technical team holds more than 50 patents in the realm of optics and is led by former employees of AT&T, Ascend Communications, Bay Networks, Nortel Networks, Lucent Technologies, MCI, Cisco, Yurie, and Telcordia.

Switches

Tellium's optical switches intelligently route data traffic between network nodes and enable service providers to rapidly plan, provision, manage, and restore services. Tellium's optical switching products deliver SONET/SDH protocols, performance monitoring, fault location, and service restoration, while eliminating complex and expensive SONET/SDH equipment. Tellium's line of optical switches is used in a range of networks, including the metro, regional, and national networks.

Aurora 32

The first product in Tellium's lineup, the Aurora 32 switch, was introduced in 1999. Named "1999 Infovision Product of the Year" by the International Engineering Consortium (IEC), the Aurora 32 is compactly designed and ideal for cramped spaces. In addition to space concerns, the Aurora 32 also consumes less power than other switches.

The Aurora 32 is designed for service providers that require a small equipment footprint to maximize the efficiency of their central office floor space. This system switches 32 optical channels that vary in speed from 155 Mbps up to 2.5 Gbps. The Aurora 32 is designed to work either by itself or in conjunction with the rest of the Aurora family of optical switches.

The 32-port Aurora 32 provides up to 2.5 Gbps switching capacity for optical signals. However, it is able to handle a number of different rates, including OC-3, OC-12, and OC-48 levels.

Further, the switch combines the grooming and transport functionality of a SONET/SDH ADM with the bandwidth management of a nonblocking cross-connect. The end result is fewer elements to manage.

Ultimately, the audience for the Aurora 32 is the entry level. And because the Aurora family is modular, it is easy to add more switches to this model, providing smooth expansion.

Aurora 128

The next switch in Tellium's offerings is the Aurora 128. This switch was designed with voice, video, and data convergence in mind.

The Aurora 128 is similar to the Aurora 32 in that it provides a compact footprint; however, it is best suited for small and medium-sized businesses, or as a node in a large, space-constrained organization. Like the Aurora 32, it can serve as a stand-alone device, or part of a larger mesh.

The Aurora 128—an optical core switch for central office applications—supports up to 128 OC-48/STM-16 or 32 OC-192/STM-64 ports, up to a total of 320 Gbps of bidirectional traffic. The switch can be used in either SONET or SDH optical mesh network architectures.

The Aurora 128 combines the functionality of SONET/SDH ADMs and Optical Cross-Connects (OXCs) into a single element that can provide up to 2.5 Gbps grooming for high-speed IP routers, ATM switches, or other service-layer elements. The switch can scale from 80 Gbps to beyond 1.2 terabits per second (Tbps). Like Tellium's other offerings, the Aurora 128 uses Tellium's StarNet Software Suite for network management.

Aurora Optical Switch

The top line of Tellium's products is its Aurora Optical Switch. The Aurora Optical Switch is designed to provide automated service delivery and restoration of optical services in regional and national networks. Its initial capacity delivers 1.28 terabits of switching bandwidth or 512 optical channels at 2.5 Gbps. Each of the channels supports SONET/SDH signals. The Aurora Optical Switch operates at optical signal speeds up to 10 Gbps and is designed for service providers.

The 512-port Aurora Optical Switch brings 1.28 Tbps of scalable switching capacity to the network core. Carriers can use any combination of 2.5 Gbps to 10 Gbps up to the total capacity. In service growth can exceed 1.28 Tbps, which allows a layer of future-proofing.

Tellium boasts that the Aurora Optical Switch, when used in conjunction with the StarNet Operating System, can improve core network cost efficiency by up to 50 percent and lowers capital expenditures by 60 percent. Further, they claim a 99.999 percent reliability on the switch.

Like the other Aurora products, the Optical Switch has a small footprint, and low power consumption and lower operations and maintenance costs than traditional ADM/DCS networks. It is also managed via the StarNet Software Suite.

Integrating SONET/SDH Gateway functionality, including port-programmable SONET/SDH performance and fault management, are other feathers in Aurora Optical Switch's cap.

NORTEL NETWORKS, INC.

Like Cisco Systems, Nortel Networks is one of the big dogs in the field of optical networking. Nortel is a global supplier of networking solutions and services that support both the Internet and private data, voice, and video. Nortel is focused on building the infrastructure, service-enabling solutions, and applications for high-performance internetworking. Nortel operates in two segments—its service provider and carrier segment and its enterprise segment.

The company offers a broad portfolio of products to providers and carriers, including optical networking solutions, access and core solutions, wireless and professional systems.

For enterprises, Nortel offers products and solutions that run the gamut of customer needs, including products and services for large offices and products and services for small offices.

Switches

Nortel offers a variety of switches for optical networking needs. They serve SONET/SDH requirements and operate at high speeds. These switches can be found in carriers, backbone providers, and telcos.

OPTera Connect DX

The OPTera Connect DX switch offers cross-connect functionality while also providing aggregation services. Further, it is an ADM node and a hub. The OPTera Connect DX supports SONET/SDH standards on a single platform, so it can handle service requirements at 155 Mbps, 622 Mbps, 2.5 Gbps, and 10 Gbps, including Gigabit Ethernet.

The DX can also terminate multiple OC-48/STM-16 rings, allowing it to handle more management tasks, and it can groom data streams from STS-1 up to STS-192c.

Another feather in the DX's cap is its scalability. It can start handling hundreds of gigabits per second and scale up to multiple terabit levels. Using a parallel optical interface, the DX can interconnect with several other OPTera Connect DXs, for multiterabit capacities.

The DX's architecture allows it to use multiple optical interface cards, including 16 OC-3/STM-1 interfaces, 4 OC-12/STM-4 interfaces, and two Gigabit Ethernet and OC-192/STM-64 interfaces.

The following illustrates some of the highlights of the OPTera Connect DX:

▼   Built-in scalability to 320 Gbps

■   Flexible networking and service delivery capabilities

■   Small footprint, low power consumption, lower costs

▲   Network optimization and greater profitability via OPTera Smart OS

OPTera Connect HDX

The OPTera Connect HDX is a multiterabit switching platform that provides end-to-end service, as well as automatic provisioning and management of wavelengths. The HDX enables end-to-end service connectivity and grooming for subwavelengths (down to STS-1) up to 40 Gbps wavelengths and higher. The HDX is able to connect to the OPTera Long Haul transmission system by utilizing DWDM optics.

The HDX is highly scalable and allows the connection of hundreds of IP, ATM, and SONET/SDH interfaces. The HDX has a switching capacity of 384 OC-192 (or 73,728 STS-1 signals) per shelf. The total switching capacity for the HDX can be scaled from 960 Gbps to 3.84 Tbps. In the future, Nortel promises to expand that ability up to 40 Tbps.

Powered by Nortel's OPTera Smart OS, advanced signaling capabilities are utilized, based on the Automatically Switched Transport Network (ASTN) standard. This provides connectivity to enable automated provisioning, routing, and restoration of wavelength and subwavelength services.

The HDX is built on a dual-plane design and provides a fault-tolerant system. The following highlight some of the HDX's features:

▼   Future-ready platform, providing switch capacity of 7.68 Tbps per bay with scalability to 40 Tbps per system

■   OPTera Smart OS software enables full auto-discovery, network awareness, and dynamic connections from the metropolitan edge to the center of core networks. OPTera Smart OS control plane architecture is based on the ASTN standard

■   Ability to manage hundreds of 2.5/10/40 Gbps wavelengths

▲   Wavelength grooming capability down to the STS-1 level

OPTera Connect PX

The Nortel Networks OPTera Connect PX is a photonic switch that delivers more bandwidth than any other carrier-class, all-optical switch. It is designed with scalability in mind so that it can grow with a network's needs.

The PX is an all-optical switch that is based on 3-D Micro Electrical Mechanical System (MEMS) technology with 252 or 1008 duplex ports, scalable to 4000 ports. Within the system, there are no optical-to-electrical-to-optical (OEO) conversions (however, the MEMS are electrically driven, so don't be fooled into thinking this is a completely all-optical system, but it's darn close).

The PX is able to support bit rates ranging from OC-3 to OC-768. Additionally, the PX can work with the OPTera Connect HDX to make use of the HDX's sublambda grooming capabilities.

Like the other members of the OPTera family, the PX is powered by the OPTera Smart OS, which allows topology discovery and network awareness, real-time provisioning, and dynamic connections to respond to customer needs. Features of this model include:

▼ Multiterabit switching capacity

■ Future-proof qualities

■ Network optimization via OPTera Smart OS software intelligence

■ No OEOs in data path

■ Retention of transparency, bit rate independence

■ 3-D MEMS beam direction

■ Single-stage fully nonblocking organization

■ Wavelength transparent services

■ 252 × 252; 1008 × 1008 ports; scalable to 4000 ports

■ Single-lambda/port application beyond 40 Gbps

▲ Wave band/port application for further scaling

Transport

Nortel has a broad range of offerings for customers who need transport tools. Not only do the company's products serve the provider, but their metro transport line also offers several devices that are scalable and designed to be located on a customer's premises.

OPTera Long Haul 1600 Optical Line System

Nortel's OPTera Long Haul 1600 Optical Line System is a multiservice platform that provides end-to-end networking at several tributary rates. The 1600 is designed to scale into terabit capacity and features reliability and high performance. Services are offered at the following densities:

▼ 160 ports at 10 Gbps

■ 640 ports at 2.5 Gbps

■ 1280 ports at 1.25 Gbps

▲ 2560 ports at 622 Mbps

The 1600 features wavelength translators at 2.5 or 10 Gbps that provide open and transparent optical interfaces, allowing a range of services to be delivered directly from the optical layer.

It also features wavelength combiners that aggregate multiple 622 Mbps, 2.5 Gbps, or Gigabit Ethernet rates into a single 10 Gbps signal. It does this by using available wavelengths at 10 Gbps, rather than lower bit rates, thereby maximizing the per-fiber capacity.

Other features of the 1600 include:

▼ An optical protection ring module for self-healing

■ "Always on" per-channel protection against cable cuts and node failures

■ OPTera Long Haul 1600 optical amplifiers, which feature erbium-doped fiber amplifier (EDFA) technology and are designed for applications on all fiber types including dispersion-shifted fiber (DSF), non–dispersion shifted fiber (NDSF), or non–zero dispersion–shifted fiber (NZ-DSF).

■ A Multiwavelength Optical Repeater and an optical amplifier that can be configured as pre/post or line amplifiers supporting DWDM applications employing up to 32 wavelengths (320 Gbps bandwidth) over a single bidirectional optical fiber.

▲ An OADM permitting multiple wavelengths to be added or dropped at a midspan amplification point.

Nortel claims that, when combined with the FEC feature, the 1600 has a 1 in 10^{15} bit error rate (BER), thus allowing longer fiber spans and guaranteed levels of service.

OPTera Long Haul 4000 Optical Line System

Nortel's OPTera Long Haul 4000 Optical Line System is able to transmit 4000 km without the need for regeneration. The benefit to carriers is obvious—low-cost bandwidth that is easy to deploy. Further, this ability is ideal for high-speed data applications.

This span is accomplished using dispersion-shifted soliton transmission, distributed Raman amplification, and FEC.

NOTE: The theory behind solitons is that, since optical fiber is not precisely a linear waveguide, the nonlinearity—along with the fiber's linear dispersion—allows a specially shaped pulse to establish itself. This type of pulse is called a soliton. A major benefit of solitons is that they have stable propagation characteristics.

These features are part of the 4000's functionality:

▼ Wavelength translators at 10 Gbps provide open and transparent optical interfaces, allowing a range of services to be delivered directly from the optical layer.

■ Wavelength combiners aggregate multiple 2.5 Gbps rates into a single 10 Gbps signal. They do this by using available wavelengths at 10 Gbps, rather than lower bit rates, thereby maximizing the per-fiber capacity.

- ■ The 4000's optical amplifiers support DWDM ultra-long-reach applications and use up to 112 wavelengths at 10 Gbps per fiber pair with a total capacity of 1.12 Tbps.

- ■ The 4000 is designed for applications on all types of fiber, including DSF, NDSF, or NZ-DSF.

- ▲ An OADM permits multiple wavelengths to be added or dropped at a midspan amplification point.

OPTera Long Haul 5000 Optical Line System

Nortel's OPTera Long Haul 5000 Optical Line System features a high transmission capacity. Out of the box, it supports 40 Gbps of DWDM for backbone networks. However, that can be scaled to 80 Gbps. Some of the capabilities of the 5000 include:

- ▼ Transmitting one million simultaneous high-quality digital television or DVD signals

- ■ Carrying 100 million simultaneous Internet connections and 6 million simultaneous high-speed Internet access connections

- ▲ Delivering 640 and 2560 managed wavelength services at 10 Gbps and 2.5 Gbps, respectively

The 5000 can act as a stand-alone unit, or it can be coupled with the OPTera Connect HDX optical switch.

OPTera Metro Multiservice Platforms

Nortel offers a range of products that are well suited to the metro environment. Specifically, they offer the OPTera Metro 3000, 4000, and 5000 systems. Let's briefly look at each of these families of metro optical systems.

OPTera Metro 3000 Multiservice Platforms   Nortel's OPTera Metro 3000 Multiservice Platform offers options that reduce the capital investment and operational costs of building an optical network. The 3000 family is scalable enough to react to changes in the marketplace and serve applications in both customer premises and interoffice routes.
There are three platforms in the 3000 family:

- ▼ **OPTera Metro 3100 Multiservice Platform**   This compact shelf unit extends the services of the OPTera platform to customer premises with very low bandwidth requirements.

- ■ **OPTera Metro 3300/3400 Multiservice Platform**   The 3300/3400 platform is another compact shelf unit that is used in central office and customer premises. The Metro 3300/3400 offers expanded STS-1 termination capacity for high-bandwidth applications.

- ▲ **OPTera Metro 3500 Multiservice Platform**   This platform is scalable from OC-3 to OC-192 and offers DWDM with a variety of services, including TDM, ATM, and IP. This platform integrates with Nortel's entire optical portfolio.

OPTera Metro 4000 Multiservice Platforms   The OPTera Metro 4000 Multiservice Platforms are fully managed optical transport systems that handle with multirate, multiservice application needs in SDH-based metropolitan, regional, and access networks.

The OPTera 4100/4200 uses STM-4 optical aggregates to deliver a 622 Mbps payload or STM-16 aggregates to deliver a 2.5 Gbps payload with a high tributary port density, high scalability, and a small footprint. The system can provide access and support for mixed payloads and can be configured for:

▼ Terminal multiplexer

■ Hub

■ ADM

■ Regenerator

■ Cross-connect

▲ High port density shelf

Because of its compact size, the 4100 and 4200 are well suited for customer premises, street cabinets, and so forth.

OPTera Metro 5000 Multiservice Platforms   Nortel's OPTera Metro 5000 Multservice Platforms utilize DWDM to transparently deliver high-bandwidth network services across a scalable optical transport platform. The Metro 5000 optimizes the use of current fiber infrastructure in the metro, providing connectivity over a point-to-point or ring-based network.

There are three platforms in the OPTera Metro Multiservice family

▼ **OPTera Metro 5100 Multiservice Platform**   The OPTera Metro 5100 saves space, uses low power, and provides connectivity for smaller bandwidth requirements or for metro collocation.

■ **OPTera Metro 5200 Multiservice Platform**   The OPTera Metro 5200 uses the same cards and OS as the 5100 but provides four times the bandwidth for larger application needs.

▲ **OPTera Metro 5300 Multiservice Platform**   The OPTera Metro 5300 is a cabinet-sized device that sends up to 80 Gbps of DWDM service into enterprise and customer premises. It is a customizable platform that contains one or two 5200 shelves, which are preconfigured and ready to use.

JUNIPER NETWORKS, INC.

Juniper Networks, Inc., is a vendor whose routers are specifically designed and built for service provider networks and to accommodate the Internet. This is done because Juniper's products use an architecture that provides a separation between routing and packet forwarding functions. By separating these functions, Juniper is able to develop full-featured routing protocol and traffic engineering functionality through its JUNOS Internet software and wire-speed; and packet-forwarding performance through high-performance ASICs.

Overview

The company's next-generation backbone routers offer customers increased reliability, performance, scalability, interoperability, and flexibility.

Juniper's routers combine high-performance, ASIC-based packet-forwarding technology, its JUNOS software, and an Internet-optimized architecture.

The two main components of the M-series router architecture are:

▼ **Packet Forwarding Engine (PFE)** The PFE is responsible for packet forwarding performance and consists of Flexible PIC Concentrators (FPCs), physical interface cards (PICs), System and Switch Board (SSB), and state-of-the-art ASICs.

▲ **Routing Engine** The Routing Engine maintains the routing tables and controls the routing protocols. It consists of an Intel-based PCI platform running JUNOS software.

Control traffic is passed through a 100Mbps link and is prioritized and rate-limited to help protect against denial-of-service attacks. This architecture ensures IP service delivery by cleanly separating the forwarding performance from the routing performance. This separation ensures that stress experienced by one component does not adversely affect the performance of the other.

JUNOS is designed to meet the IP routing, operations, and control requirements of large service providers. Because of JUNOS' complexity and integration, Juniper's products can be located at critical points in a network.

The company's customers come in all shapes and sizes. They include end users, value-added resellers, and original equipment manufacturers (OEMs). In fact, WorldCom, Inc., accounted for about 18 percent of Juniper's revenues for 2000. The JUNOS software offers a full suite of Internet-scale and Internet-tested routing protocols. JUNOS uses all the major routing protocols, including:

▼ BGP4

■ DVMRP

■ PIM

■ IS-IS

▲ OSPF

JUNOS also provides a value-added layer of functionality with its implementation of MPLS. Featuring a modular design, JUNOS can run programs in protected memory space in conjunction with an independent operating system. This contrasts sharply to other OSes that are unprotected and prone to systemwide failure.

Routers

Juniper's routers are used worldwide by some of the largest service providers. The Juniper M-series Internet Backbone routers are built with IP networking in mind. Not only are these routers useful in core networks, but they are also used in access and mobile networks.

The M-series routers allow scaling to meet future bandwidth needs. Further, the M-series can deliver 40 Mbps forwarding performance per Internet Processor with an aggregate of up to 160 Gbps, depending on the model.

M5 and M10

The M5 and M10 Internet backbone routers are designed using the same architecture, ASICs, and JUNOS Internet software as the rest of the M-series family.

The M5 and M10 routers are designed for edge applications where dedicated access circuits must be aggregated. Because of their small footprint, they are also good for core applications in locations where space and power are at a premium. Scalability is ensured because there are a range of interfaces from T1 and E1 through OC-12c/STM-4 (on the M5 router) or OC-48c/STM-16 (on the M10 router). Additionally, these routers add such services as packet filtering and sampling.

The Internet Processor II ASIC forwards packets at a throughput rate of up to 5 Gbps (on the M5 router) and up to 10 Gbps (on the M10 router). The ASIC-based rate limiting, filtering, and sampling features enable you to scale IP services, providing the tools with which to manage larger networks at higher bandwidths.

The M5 router offers the following features:

▼ 6.4 Gbps throughput rate (3.2 Gbps full duplex)

■ 266 MHz CPU and supporting logic

■ Internet Processor II ASIC (40 Mpps forwarding performance)

■ One enhanced I/O Manager ASIC

  ■ Parsing, prioritizing, and queuing of packets

  ■ 2MB parity-protected SSRAM per I/O Manager ASIC

■ 8MB SSRAM for forwarding tables associated with ASICs

■ 200 milliseconds (ms) of delay-bandwidth buffering

■ Two 512KB boot flash EPROMs (programmable on the board)

▲ Two Distributed Buffer Manager ASICs for coordinating pooled, single-stage buffering

The M10 router offers the following features:

▼ 12.8 Gbps throughput rate (6.4 Gbps full duplex)

■ 266 MHz CPU and supporting logic

■ Internet Processor II ASIC (40 Mpps forwarding performance)

- Two Distributed Buffer Manager ASICs for coordinating pooled, single-stage buffering
- Two enhanced I/O Manager ASICs
  - Parsing, prioritizing, and queuing of packets
  - 2MB parity-protected SSRAM per I/O Manager ASIC
- 8MB SSRAM for forwarding tables associated with ASICs
- 200 ms of delay-bandwidth buffering
- ▲ Two 512KB boot flash EPROMs (programmable on the board)

M20

The next router in Juniper's M-series is the M20 Internet backbone router. This device is built for a variety of Internet applications, including dedicated access, public and private peering, hosting sites, and backbone core networks.

Like the M5 and M10 routers, the M20 uses ASIC technology to deliver such functionality as filtering, sampling, and rate limiting. The M20 also features a small footprint and includes the following features:

- ▼ Route lookup rates up to 40 Mpps
- 25.6 Gbps throughput rate (12.8 Gbps at full duplex)
- Performance-based packet filtering, rate limiting, and sampling with the Internet Processor II ASIC
- Redundant system and switch board and redundant routing engine
- Routing software with Internet-scale implementations of BGP4, IS-IS, OSPF, MPLS traffic engineering, class of service, and multicasting applications
- 512KB boot flash EPROM
- 333 MHz Intel Pentium II with 768MB DRAM
- 80MB flash drive for primary storage
- 6.4GB hard drive for secondary storage
- 110MB flash PC card for tertiary storage
- 10/100 Base-T auto-sensing RJ-45 Ethernet port for out-of-band management
- Two RS-232 (DB9 connector) asynchronous serial ports for console and remote management
- Enhanced I/O Manager ASIC
  - Parsing, prioritizing, and queuing of packets
  - 2MB parity-protected SSRAM per I/O Manager ASIC

■ 200 ms of delay-bandwidth buffering per FPC

■ Two Distributed Buffer Manager ASICs for coordinating pooled, single-stage buffering

■ PowerPC 603e processor running at 200 MHz for handling exception packets

▲ 33 MHz PCI bus, which connects the PowerPC 603e processor and the Internet Processor II ASIC

M40

The M40 Internet backbone router is designed with high-growth ISPs in mind. The M40 router provides bandwidth necessary to cost-efficiently grow networks to OC-48c/STM-16 speeds. Further, it offers the ability to perform such tasks as packet filtering, sampling, and MPLS traffic engineering.

The M40 Router offers the following features:

▼ One Internet Processor II ASIC for 40 Mpps packet lookup

■ 51.2 Gbps throughput rate (25.6 Gbps full duplex)

■ Two Distributed Buffer Manager ASICs for coordinating pooled, single-stage buffering

■ PowerPC603e processor running at 200 MHz for handling exception packets

■ 44 MHz PCI bus, which connects the PowerPC 603e processor and the Internet Processor II ASIC

■ 8MB SSRAM

■ 64MB DRAM

■ 512KB boot flash EPROM

■ 333 MHz Pentium II with 768MB DRAM

■ 80MB flash drive for primary storage

■ 6.4GB hard drive for secondary storage

■ 120MB LS-120 drive for tertiary storage

■ 10/100 Base-T auto-sensing RJ-45 Ethernet port for out-of-band management

■ Two RS-232 asynchronous serial ports for console and remote management

■ 3.2 Gbps full-duplex throughput per FPC

    ■ Enhanced I/O Manager ASIC

    ■ Parsing, prioritizing, and queuing of packets

■ 2MB parity-protected SSRAM per I/O Manager ASIC

▲ 200 ms of delay-bandwidth buffering per FPC

M160

The M160 Internet backbone router is Juniper's top end router and offers up to 8 OC-192c/STM-64 PICs per chassis (16 per rack) or up to 32 OC-48c/STM-16 PICs per chassis (64 per rack). The M160 ASICs translate optical bandwidth into new, differentiated IP services.

The M160 platform is aimed at large networks that need to be ensured of ongoing performance for feature-rich infrastructures. It is built specifically with large backbones in mind and with features enabled for future migration to the backbone edge.

The M160 router offers the following functionality:

▼   One Internet Processor II ASIC for 160 Mpps aggregate packet lookup (40 Mpps per SFM)

■   204.8 Gbps throughput rate (102.4 Gbps full duplex)

■   Two Distributed Buffer Manager ASICs for coordinating pooled, single-stage buffering

■   8MB of parity-protected SSRAM

■   Processor subsystem (One PowerPC 603e processor, 256KB of parity-protected Level 2 cache, and 64MB of parity-protected DRAM)

■   333 MHz mobile Pentium II with integrated 256KB level-2 cache

■   768MB SDRAM

■   80MB compact flash drive for primary storage

■   6.4GB IDE hard drive for secondary storage

■   110MB PC card for tertiary storage

■   10/100 Base-T auto-sensing RJ-45 Ethernet port for out-of-band management

■   Two RS-232 (DB9 connector) asynchronous serial ports for console and remote management

■   Optional redundancy

■   12.8 Gbps full-duplex aggregate throughput

■   Two Packet Director ASICs for dispersing and balancing packets across the I/O Manager ASICs

■   Four enhanced I/O Manager ASICs

   ■   Parsing, prioritizing, and queuing of packets

   ■   2MB parity-protected SSRAM per I/O Manager ASIC

▲   200 ms of delay-bandwidth buffering per FPC

CIENA CORPORATION

CIENA Corporation, incorporated in November 1992, makes products aimed at the intelligent optical networking market. CIENA's customers tend to be carriers of all sizes and include long-distance carriers, local exchange carriers, and Internet service providers. The core of CIENA's offerings are optical transport and intelligent optical switching systems. These systems allow carriers to provision and manage high-bandwidth services that their customers desire.

CIENA's products are targeted at three areas:

▼ Long-haul transport

■ Short-haul transport

▲ Intelligent switching

Later in this chapter, we will highlight each of CIENA's products serving these various markets.

Overview

CIENA incorporates an "open architecture" model, which allows its products to interoperate with other carriers' existing fiber optic transmission systems and networking gear. Specifically, that means it can connect with existing SONET gear, ATM switches, and IP routers. This architecture is known as CIENA LightWorks. The components of a LightWorks deployment can be sold separately or as part of a package. The idea behind the LightWorks architecture is to simplify a carrier's network by reducing the number of network elements.

To manage its optical offerings, CIENA's uses ON-Center, which is the company's integrated family of software-based tools for element-, network-, and service-layer management. Further, ON-Center is able to speed up the deployment of optical services.

In addition to offering its capital equipment products, CIENA is also designing equipment to offer revenue-generating optical-layer services. For instance, the LightWorks Toolkit is designed to allow carriers to offer dynamic, high-bandwidth services and handle real-time provisioning and prioritization.

Most of CIENA's product sales have been the long-distance optical transport gear, including (in 2000) the MultiWave CoreStream and MultiWave Sentry 4000.

Transport

CIENA's long-distance optical transport products include CoreStream, MultiWave Sentry 1600, and MultiWave 4000. Its short-distance offerings include the MultiWave Metro and MultiWave Metro One. CIENA's products use DWDM technology and enable carriers to cost-effectively add network bandwidth when and where they need it. As a result, service providers should be better able to scale their networks to meet demand.

CoreStream

CIENA's CoreStream is a DWDM optical transport system capable of 1.6 Tbps over a single fiber. The system is designed and aimed at service providers who need scalability and design flexibility. Because of the aforementioned open architecture, carriers can transport any type of traffic, including voice and data.

The CoreStream's scalability allows in-service capacity upgrades and a mix of wavelengths from 2.5 Gbps or 10 Gbps. Data rates at speeds down to OC-12 can be accommodated through multiplexers.

CoreStream uses a mix of tools to fit with existing service provider topologies, including:

▼ CoreStream optical ADMs

■ Raman preamplifiers and broadband optical amplifiers

▲ CoreStream terminals that interface with ATM, IP, and SONET/SDH equipment using DirectConnect short-reach interfaces

CIENA also claims high reliability through intelligent management using SmartSpan software that automates system operations. Reliability is also ensured because each CoreStream element contains specialized software intelligence. CIENA claims a bit error rate (BER) of 1 in 10^{15}. Further, CoreStream is equipped with intelligent data monitoring to help providers troubleshoot problems.

Other features of CoreStream include:

▼ 1.6 Tbps scalability

■ Design flexibility for a range of topologies

■ A range of interfaces including

    ■ OC-12/STM-4

    ■ OC-48/STM-16

    ■ OC-192/STM-64

■ Flexible optical add/drop options

■ Integrated performance monitoring

■ LightWorks ON-Center Optical Network Manager

▲ Out-of-Band FEC

MultiWave Sentry 1600

The MultiWave Sentry 1600 is another DWDM optical transport system. This delivers 40 Gbps on a single fiber. This system allows carriers to leverage existing technologies and use SONET/SDH, STM, IP, and asynchronous traffic on a single optical system. Not only can the Sentry 1600 provision SONET/SDH payloads, but it also allows the construction of ATM and IP networks without having to build an intermediary synchronous layer.

Because it uses inexpensive open interfaces, Sentry 1600 doesn't require long-reach optics in terminal equipment (as do SONET/SDH, ATMs, and cross-connects). Further, the system eliminates the need for SONET regenerators and uses the MultiWave Sentry OADM as a means to provide access bandwidth at midspan sites.

Like the CoreStream, the Sentry 1600 uses SmartSpan for network management along with the LightWorks ON-Center suite. Some of CIENA's MultiWave Sentry 1600's other features include:

▼ Scalability to 40 Gbps

■ 100 GHz channel spacing

■ Up to 16 OC-48/STM-16/OC-48c/STM-16c channels over a single fiber

■ Multiple channel rates:

   ■ SONET/SDH: 150 Mbps to 2.5 Gbps

   ■ Asynchronous (Plesiochronous Digital Hierarchy): 50 Mbps to 1.7 Gbps

■ Use of existing MultiWave Sentry Optical Line Amplifiers

■ Capability to add or drop four channels on a span

■ Span lengths of up to 800 km

■ Modulation, propagation, and demodulation within the optical transport system

▲ Modular architecture that permits incremental capacity upgrades

MultiWave Sentry 4000

The MultiWave Sentry 4000 is a DWDM optical transport system that more than doubles the rate of the Sentry 1600 with a throughput of 100 Gbps. It is aimed at long-haul applications and, like CIENA's other offerings, includes an open architecture allowing a blend of SONET/SDH, ATM, and IP on a common platform.

The Sentry 4000 supports up to 40 independent channels at speeds of OC-12/STM-4 or OC-48/STM-16. Both standard and concatenated rates are supported. From 1 to 40 channels can be added by the addition of channel modules to the span terminals.

Further, Sentry 4000 offers OADM capabilities to access bandwidth and midspan locations. Like its transport brothers, it is managed via SmartSpan and LightWorks ON-Center software.

Other features of the Sentry 4000 include:

▼ Scalability to 40 OC-12/STM-4 or OC-48/STM-16 channels on one fiber

■ Scalability to 100 Gbps of capacity on a single fiber pair

■ Ability to add or drop up to eight channels at an OADM site

■ 50 GHz channel spacing

■ Span lengths of up to 560 km

■ Fully transparent transport of SONET/SDH framed signals

▲ A modular architecture permitting incremental capacity upgrades

Throughput Comparisons

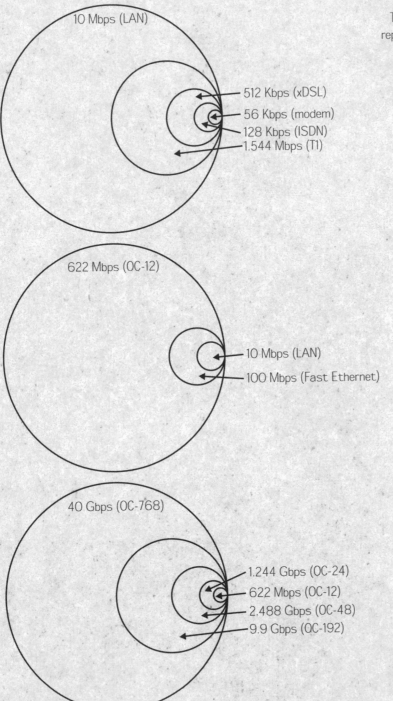

10 Mbps (LAN)

512 Kbps (xDSL)
56 Kbps (modem)
128 Kbps (ISDN)
1.544 Mbps (T1)

The area of each circle
represents the amount of
throughput each
technology provides

622 Mbps (OC-12)

10 Mbps (LAN)

100 Mbps (Fast Ethernet)

40 Gbps (OC-768)

1.244 Gbps (OC-24)
622 Mbps (OC-12)
2.488 Gbps (OC-48)
9.9 Gbps (OC-192)

Where Fiber Sits in a Network

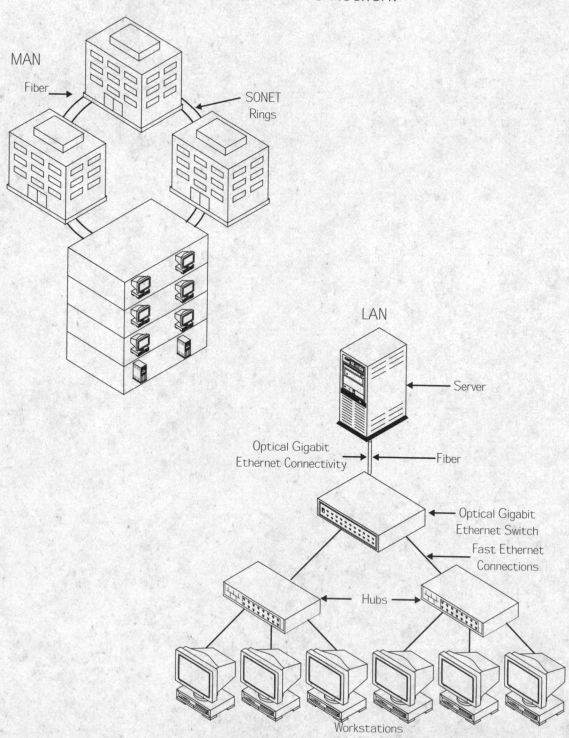

MAN

Fiber

SONET Rings

LAN

Server

Optical Gigabit Ethernet Connectivity

Fiber

Optical Gigabit Ethernet Switch

Fast Ethernet Connections

Hubs

Workstations

Where SANS Operate in a Network

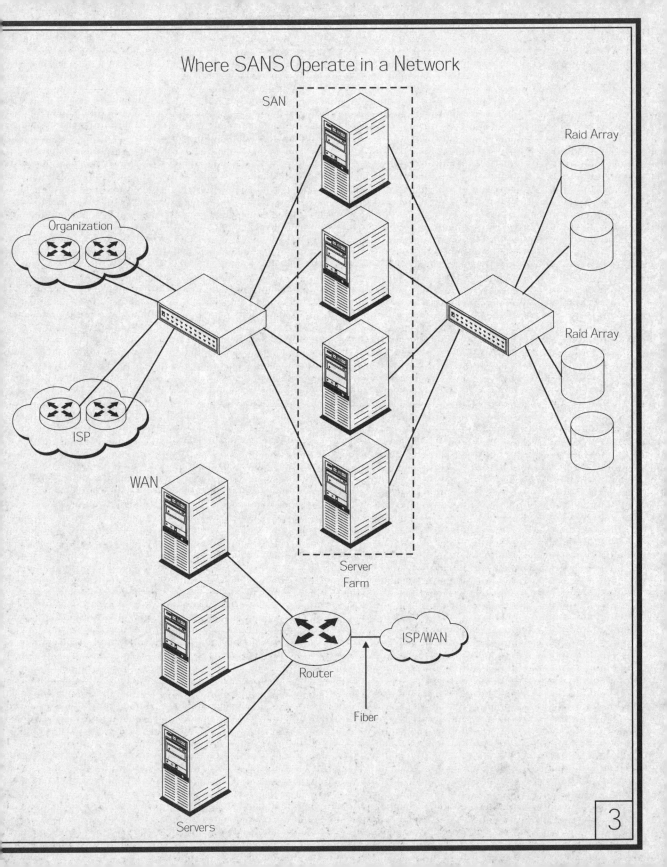

Fiberless Optics Design

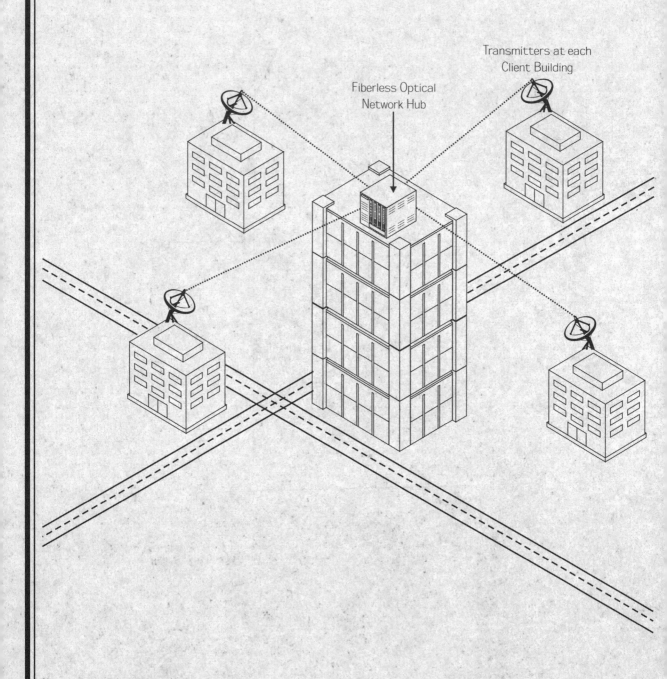

Transmitters at each
Client Building

Fiberless Optical
Network Hub

The Spectrum

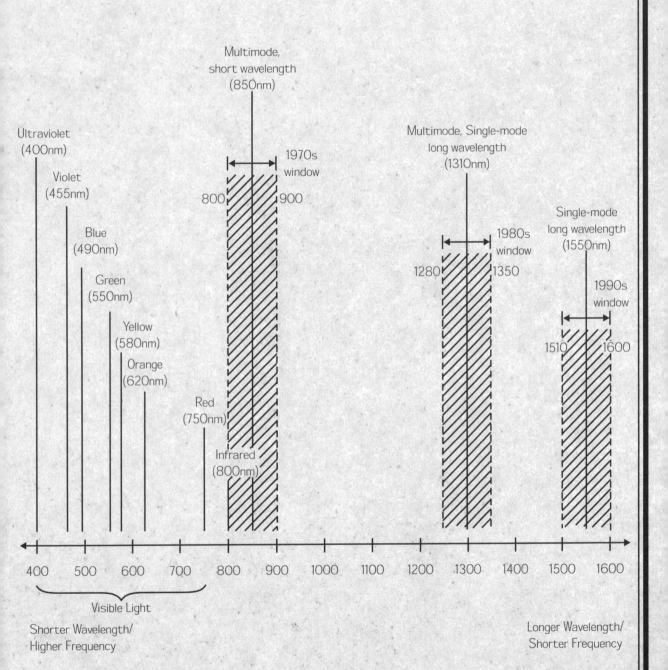

Visible Light

Shorter Wavelength/
Higher Frequency

Longer Wavelength/
Shorter Frequency

Electrical-Optical-Electrical Conversion

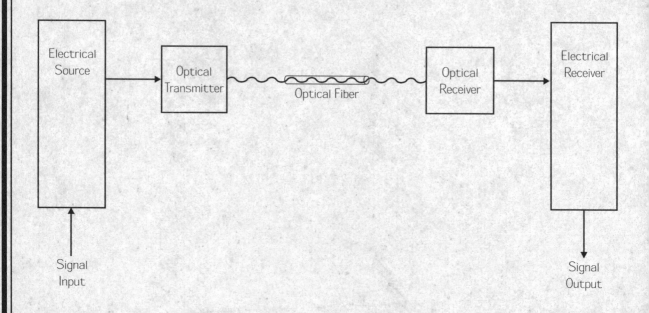

Network Topologies

Bus

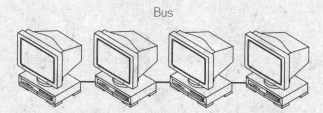

Mesh

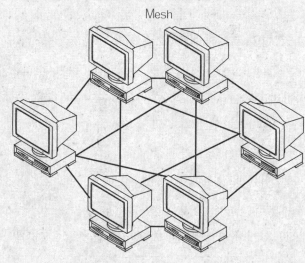

Point-to-Point

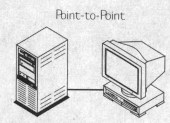

Star

Switch

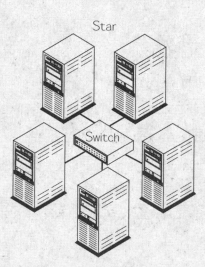

Ring

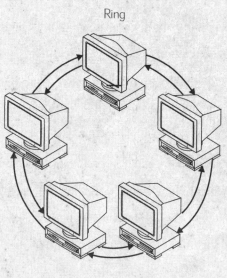

Multimode and Single-mode Fibers

Single-mode Fiber

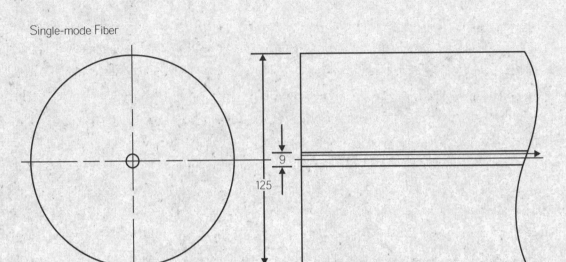

* Note: Measurements Are in Microns (MM)

Multimode Fiber

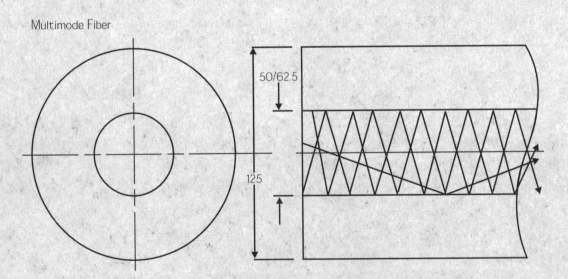

MultiWave Metro

The MultiWave Metro is a DWDM transport system that is designed for use in metro ring applications. The Metro system employs OADM nodes interconnected on a dual-fiber ring. It allows for up to 24 duplex channels across a single fiber pair, for a total of 240 Gbps with the Metro's 10 Gbps FEC transceivers.

The Metro supports a number of topologies, protocols, and protection schemes on the same fiber pair and in the same node. Because it is aimed at MANs, the Metro is an alternative to TDM rings when the total aggregate signal is greater than OC-12. Further, it is a good system to employ in new fiber builds when fiber exhaust is an issue.

The following highlight some of the Metro's other features:

▼ Simultaneous support of star, ring, and mesh applications

■ Optical-layer survivability

■ Allowance for networks to scale

■ 100 Mbps to 10 Gbps per wavelength

■ Integrated TDM multiplexing allowing up to 96 tributaries

■ Direct ATM, IP and SONET/SDH interconnection with long-haul and short-haul networks

■ Interoperability with Metro One

■ NEBS and ETSI compliance

▲ SONET/SDH performance monitoring

MultiWave Metro One

CIENA's MultiWave Metro One is a member of the MultiWave Metro family of DWDM transport systems. This device is intended for customer premises deployment. Metro One is an OADM node connected to other MultiWave Metro nodes on a dual-fiber ring.

Metro One supports a number of topologies, protocols, and protection schemes. When used with MultiWave Metro, its Arbitrary Connectivity feature allows it to simultaneously support these topologies:

▼ Point-to-point

■ Star

■ Ring

▲ Mesh

Because it, like other CIENA products, employs an open architecture, it is able to interface with SONET/SDH, ATM, IP, and most embedded management systems. Additionally, the open architecture allows providers to carry such technologies as:

▼ Gigabit Ethernet

■ ESCON

- FICON
- Digitized video
- ▲ Fibre Channel

Metro One is geared to the short-haul market and gives providers an option to optical rings when the aggregate is OC-12 or more. Further, Metro One is useful in new services that use existing fiber plants. A software design tool is included with the Metro One to aid in the planning of the DWDM ring.

Among other things, the Metro One:

- ▼ Provides optical-layer survivability
- Allows networks to scale in support of new high-bandwidth services
- Provides 100 Mbps to 10 Gbps per wavelength
- Allows integrated TDM multiplexing of up to four tributaries
- Allows ATM, IP, and SONET/SDH interconnection with both long-haul and short-haul networks
- Enables interoperability with MultiWave Metro
- Provides SONET/SDH performance monitoring
- Adheres to the ITU channel plan
- ▲ Operates over standard single-mode fiber

Switching

CIENA's intelligent optical core switches, CoreDirector, CoreDirector CI, and MetroDirector K2, enable carriers to manage bandwidth created by optical transport products. CIENA's switch line helps carriers solve issues of network scalability and growing operating costs by incorporating the functionality of multiple network elements into single elements with new switching capabilities and management.

CoreDirector

CoreDirector is CIENA's optical switch aimed at large central offices and is designed to deliver end-to-end optical capacity across the network. CoreDirector employs flexible protection options and is built for ease of use. CoreDirector utilizes the LightWorks Operating System to provide optical provisioning and management, along with a range of protection capabilities.

CoreDirector provides 640 Gbps of nonblocking, bidirectional switching in a single bay, and it provides the ability to upgrade to 38 Tbps in the future. It supports capacities of 256 OC-48/STM-16 or 64 OC-192/STM-64 interfaces, as well as OC-12/STM-4 and OC-3/STM-1 optical interfaces. In addition to switching duties, CoreDirector provides the functionality of SONET/SDH ADMs, digital cross-connects, and OXCs in one device.

CoreDirector supports a range of protection schemes, including Virtual Line-Switched Rings (VLSR), linear 1:N and 1:1 APS, and FastMesh. Other features include:

▼ Scalability from 640 Gbps bidirectional nonblocking switching in a single rack

■ Optical management for wavelengths down to STS-1s

■ Automated, real-time provisioning, and grooming using CIENA's LightWorks OS

▲ ON-Center integrated network and service management applications

CoreDirector CI

The CoreDirector CI is an optical backbone switch optimized for high-capacity optical switching in smaller backbone central offices (COs). The switch supports 64 optical interfaces. The CI is a switch that complements the 256-port CoreDirector, which is geared toward larger COs.

Though less expensive than the CoreDirector, it is still able to deliver the needs of a high-end backbone switch. Those capabilities include:

▼ SONET/SDH interfaces

■ Automated provisioning

▲ Mesh, ring, and 1:N restoration methods

Like other CIENA products, the CoreDirector CI also utilized the LightWorks OS, providing optical provisioning and management. Additionally, CI supports redundancy for critical modules, which can be hot-swapped.

The CI provides backbone switching and grooming services from STS-1 up to STS-768. Optical interfaces include:

▼ 64 OC-3/STM-1, OC-12/STM-4 or OC-48/STM-16

▲ 16 OC-192/STM-64

The system provides a nonblocking capacity of 160 Gbps and is expandable to 320 Gbps. The CI's ADM functionality allows it to support high-capacity trunks while adding or dropping lower-capacity tributaries. Other features of the CoreDirector CI include:

▼ Multifunction optical switching

■ Automated service provisioning

■ Multiple restoration schemes and fault-tolerant design

▲ Equipment commonality, which reduces operational and administrative expenses

MetroDirector K2

The MetroDirector K2 is a next-generation, multiservice access and switching platform aimed at service providers. It has been designed to fit into existing network environments.

The K2 is Telcordia (formerly BellCore) GR-63, Network Equipment Building Systems (NEBS), and Level 3 certified, as well as compliant with Operations Systems Modification of Intelligent Network Elements (OSMINE) standards.

The K2 is data-optimized and multiservice with integrated DWDM capabilities. It combines the functions of:

▼ Digital cross-connects

■ SONET/SDH ADMs

■ Multiservice data switches

▲ DWDM terminals

The K2 allows scalability from DS-1/E1 to multiple OC-192/STM-64s, as well as supporting Ethernet, Gigabit Ethernet, and ATM.

The K2 can support a variety of network topologies, including:

▼ Linear

■ Ring

■ Star

▲ Mesh

Because its chassis contains 12 slots, it can support multiple topologies, protocols, and rates. The K2 also offers the following features:

▼ Supports multiple services, including

    ■ TDM

    ■ Native data over SONET/SDH

    ■ 40-channel DWDM

■ Enables IP, ATM, 10/100 Ethernet, Gigabit Ethernet

■ Delivers scalability from 1.5 Mbps to 10 Gbps

■ Allows arbitrary concatenation for bandwidth optimization

■ Is designed to support linear, ring, star, and mesh applications simultaneously

▲ Provides point-and-click, end-to-end provisioning

Table 6-6 lists the number of ports allowed for each type of service.

Interface Cards	Port Density per Card
DS1	28
DS3	24
EC-1/DS3	24
DS3 Transmux	12
OC-3/STM-1	4 or 16
OC-3/STM1 or OC-12/STM-4	4 or 16
OC-48/STM-16	1
OC-192/STM-64	1
10/100 Ethernet	16
Gigabit Ethernet Tunneling	4
Gigabit Ethernet Bridging	4

Table 6-6.   Port Densities of the MetroDirector K2 Switch

SYCAMORE NETWORKS, INC.

Sycamore Networks, Inc., specializes in intelligent optical networking products aimed at telecommunications service providers. Sycamore's equipment allows a telecom to quickly and cost-effectively transform their optical network capacity into bandwidth for high-speed data services. Sycamore's software-based optical networking products are designed to allow service providers to use existing optical network infrastructure to deliver high-speed data applications.

Overview

While the rest of the industry is focusing on the metro, Sycamore Networks is turning its attention to long-haul and ultra-long-haul. For instance, in July 2001, Sycamore announced that KPNQwest plans to use the SN 10000 in a section of the provider's 20,000 km European network. The switch is being used in KPN's 4500 km Nordic ring and will carry about 100 terabits of capacity across six cities, including Stockholm and Helsinki.

Further, the ring will connect to KPNQwest's European network, which joins 44 cities. On this side of the Atlantic Ocean, it will also connect to 150 cities on Qwest Communications International's North American fiber ring.

Also, Sycamore has improved the process of ADM, by adding unlimited add/drop capabilities. This allows wavelengths to be dropped or added at any time, anywhere on the network. Other systems require expensive regeneration at each ADM site.

Sycamore's customer base includes up and coming carriers, existing carriers, CLECs, interexchange carriers, international competitive carriers, and ISP.

Switches

Sycamore's line of switches are aimed at services ranging from metro access and optical edge to the long-haul markets. Further, Sycamore switches can handle both SONET/SDH and DWDM technologies. The following highlights some of the features of Sycamore's switch offerings.

SN 16000

The top end in Sycamore's lineup is the SN 16000 optical switch. This provides for end-to-end wavelength switching and routing at the core of the optical network, integral for a meshed topology network. The SN 16000 is scalable and supports growth through its modular architecture, which has been designed to work with not only Sycamore's product line, but other vendors as well.

The switch can handle rates from STS-1 up to OC-192/STM-64 and support up to 512 OC-48 channels in both directions. Its processor hardware has enough power to support 1024 channels both in and out. The switch can also handle fewer links supporting higher speeds: 128 × 128 at OC-192. The SN 16000's processing power is meant to endear it to service providers, so they will be inclined to use the switch, which will allow for increased scalability.

SN 10000

Sycamore's SN 10000 is an intelligent optical transport product that provides high-speed services in long-distance and ultra-long-distance backbone networks. The SN 10000 has been designed to provide a complete stand-alone networking solution and to be capable of being configured in point-to-point, linear, ring, or mesh applications.

Recently, Sycamore has beefed up the SN 10000 by adding hardware and that can boost the distance an optical signal travels by up to 50 percent. This means the equipment can support 160 channels of OC-192/STM-64 for up to 2500 km. In ultra-long-haul applications, it can transport up to 80 channels for up to 4000 km—without regeneration.

Further, the SN 10000 offers a port density up to 64 wavelengths in a lone bay, and its built-in ADM features allow any wavelength to be added or dropped with no ill side effects. Automatic power balancing allows operators to use a point-and-click interface to add 160 wavelengths in about 15 minutes. The SN 10000 automatically balances power to optimize system performance.

As with the SN 8000, plug-and-play functionality allows just-in-time service delivery, tiered pricing schemes, and customer network management.

SN 8000

Sycamore's SN 8000 transport node uses DWDM and supports up to 120 wavelengths with any combination of OC-3, OC-12, and OC-48 services. It is able to extend transmission distances to 1600 kilometers without needing electrical regeneration.

Further, the SN 8000 was the first optical component to use a plug-and-play design, and its high-density OC-3 and OC-12 service modules allow as many as 16 OC-3 or 4 OC-12 services to share a single wavelength. Because of this functionality, the need for electro-optical network equipment—SONET/SDH ADMs and OXCs—is eliminated.

The SN 8000 provides ease of use, less space and power consumption, an increase in bandwidth distribution capability at lower costs, and increased equipment reliability and service availability.

SN 4000

Sycamore's SN 4000 is an optical edge switch that reduces head-end congestion and grooms high-volume traffic while still supporting SONET/SDH and protection schemes. The SN 4000, like the SN 3000, was designed to aggregate, groom, and switch optical data traffic in the metropolitan area network. Using Sycamore's wavelength management software, multiple services can be integrated onto a single wavelength, then switch to the access or metro designation in a network's topology.

The SN 4000's nonblocking switch fabric provides full SONET/SDH grooming at OC-48/ STM-16 to STS-1 levels. Meanwhile, its multiwavelength architecture supports dynamic, end-to-end service provisioning and management. The platform features a 480 Gbps, nonblocking switch fabric capable of supporting as many as 12 OC-192 ports or 48 OC-48 ports.

SN 3000

Sycamore's SN 3000 is an optical access switch designed for the metro access market to perform data stream aggregation, grooming, and switching functions. The SN 3000 is a redundant system, which is designed for central office deployments. Its compact footprint is meant to provide high port density and efficient space utilization.

The SN 3000 features an integrated subsystem for DWDM trunking and wavelength cross-connect. The SN 3000 platforms aggregate traffic from existing SONET/SDH rings or from subscribers, supporting a range of interfaces.

Further, the SN 3000 allows service to be customized, providing bandwidth on a just-in-time basis, and with a range of protection options (from fully protected to unprotected). Distributed switching and advanced signaling and routing software allow bandwidth flexibility and efficiency in a range of topologies, because they allow any-to-any connectivity.

Sycamore's WaveShare technology allows each wavelength to carry any combination of DS3, OC-3/STM-1, OC-12/STM-4, and Gigabit Ethernet traffic.

The SN 3000 also combines the functionality of SONET/SDH ADMs, DXCs, and DWDM into one element.

LUCENT TECHNOLOGIES, INC.

One of the biggest names in the world of networking, not to mention optical networking, is Lucent Technologies, Inc. The company incorporated in 1995 as a designer, developer, and manufacturer of communications systems, software, and products. Lucent supplies equipment and software to some of the world's biggest network operators and service providers.

Lucent's systems connect, route, manage, and store voice, data, and video in any combination, and they are used for wired access; local and long distance switching; intelligent network services and signaling; wireless communications, including both cellular and personal communications services (PCS); and high-speed, broadband multifunctional communications. The number of access lines that are services by Lucent switches is about 150 million lines.

Overview

Lucent's optical networking product family includes WaveStar OLS 1.6, WaveStar OLS Long Haul, WaveStar Bandwidth Manager and WaveStar Lambda Router Switches, SONET/SDH product lines, WaveStar 2.5G, WaveStar 10G, and WaveStar 40G Express.

Lucent's Bell Labs has garnered more than 2500 patents in optical technology alone. Lucent was first to market with a DWDM system in 1995 and has since shipped more DWDM systems than any other vendor. Lucent also was first to market with an all-optical switch.

Lucent Technologies, headquartered in Murray Hill, New Jersey, designs and delivers the systems, software, and services for next-generation communications networks for service providers and enterprises. Backed by the research and development of Bell Labs, Lucent focuses on high-growth areas such as broadband and mobile Internet infrastructure; communications software; Web-based enterprise solutions that link private and public networks; and professional network design and consulting services.

Transport

Lucent's line of transport equipment is quite popular and already in wide use by carriers and telcos worldwide. Lucent has named its premier family of transmission systems the WaveStar OLS, which comes in two different systems.

WaveStar OLS 1.6T

The WaveStar OLS 1.6T allows such capacity, says Lucent, that every man, woman, and child in the United States and Canada could simultaneously transmit a one-page e-mail message across the same network.

The WaveStar OLS 1.6T offers up to 160 10 Gbps wavelengths on one fiber. The system uses Lucent's "L-Band" optical amplifier, which allows network providers to transmit traffic through a fiber's largely unused wavelength band. Along with the OLS 1.6T and its amplifier, a network provider can double the number of wavelengths transmitted on the fiber from 80 to 160.

The WaveStar OLS 1.6T is an expansion of its already popular WaveStar OLS 800G. The OLS 800G uses DWDM to provide up to 320 2.5 Gbps wavelengths, or 80 10 Gbps wavelengths, for a total capacity of 800 Gbps (hence, OLS 800G). The OLS 800G is, itself, an expansion of the WaveStar 400G, which provided half the capacity of the 800G, or a quarter of the capacity of the 1.6T. For those providers already using the 800G, upgrading to the 1.6T can be done without service interruption, Lucent claims.

Lucent cut a deal with Time Warner Telecom in 2001 for $100 million in which the 800G OLS system will be installed in Time Warner Telecom's western region (Los Angeles, San Francisco, Oakland, Portland, Seattle, Boise, Idaho, Las Vegas, and Phoenix) with maximum stretches reaching 800 km. When more capacity is required, they will upgrade to the 1.6T system.

WaveStar OLS LongHaul Compact

The WaveStar OLS LongHaul (LH) Compact is based on the OLS 1.6T architecture. The system allows 160 Gbps across a single fiber (this is roughly equivalent to two million simultaneous telephone calls). Further, it allows a simultaneous mix of data channels, from 100 Mbps to 10 Gbps (from a variety of vendors) on one fiber.

The WaveStar OLS LH Compact is modular and helps networks expand as their services grow. For instance, they can increase from 2 to 15 OC-192/STM-64 channels up to 64 OC-48/STM-16 signals with the 10G muxing OTU (64 × 2.5 Gbps per fiber). The OLS compact also features ADM capabilities and FEC.

The WaveStar OLS LH Compact is designed to be as the name suggests—compact. That means it will fit in a single bay and also meets the size limitations set by the European Telephone Standards Institute.

Switches

Lucent is well known for its line of electrical switches, but it is also a provider of optical switches. Their switches serve many markets, from carriers to the core. The following highlights some of their high-speed optical switches.

GX 550

The GX 550 Multiservice WAN switch is a carrier-class core and service aggregation switch that supports ATM, frame relay, IP, and MPLS over a variety of SONET/SDH interfaces and IP/MPLS over Gigabit Ethernet.

A single switch supports up to 156 OC-3/STM-1 ports, 39 OC-12/STM-4 ports, or 9 OC-48/STM-16 ports, although most deployments utilize rich mixes of port types. The GX 550 provides layers 1, 2, and 3 protocol support over SONET/SDH interfaces. Long-range, intermediate-range, and short-range optics are supported.

QoS is delivered through both the GX 550 and other Lucent switches used in your network, a fact that is helpful in service management.

The GX 550 includes a quad-plane switching architecture, which delivers four QoS classes; traffic policing and shaping; flow control functions; connection admission control; permanent and switched virtual circuits and paths; high circuit setup rate; and high circuit capacities.

PoS and Frame over SONET (FoS) are supported by the GX 550. PoS and FoS interfaces allow high-speed, optical, standards-based IP, MPLS, and Frame Relay connections to other service providers and end users. Up to 39 Gigabit Ethernet interfaces are supported on the GX 550.

NX 64000

Lucent's NX 64000 multiterabit switch/router utilizes high-speed optics, while integrating key components. Like the GX 550, the NX64000 is a multiservice platform that can support IP, Frame Relay, MPLS, and ATM termination. It also boasts beefed up QoS functionality, with eight queues per port.

The NX 64000's terabit switch fabric supports up to 128 DS3, 128 OC-3c/STM-1, 64 OC-12c/STM-4, 128 Gigabit Ethernet, 64 OC-48c/STM-16, and 16 OC-192c/STM-64 ports per chassis.

Because it is a multiservice platform, the NX64000 allows providers to build off existing infrastructure and reduce the risks that come with future expansion and service mixes. Further, in-service routing and signaling software upgrades help providers make changes to the core without disturbing customers.

Other Products

Lucent offers other optical hardware in addition to its transport and switching gear. Multiplexing and OXCs are also pools in which Lucent has dipped its toe. Possibly the most notable device in this section is Lucent's WaveStar LambdaRouter, which has the distinction of being the first all-optical switch.

NOTE: Don't let the name Lambda*Router* confuse you; this device is actually a switch.

Mux/Demux

Some systems simply need to be able to combine several lambdas into a single wavelength. For those needs, Lucent offers two multiplexers: the WaveStar Time Division Multiplexer 2.5G and the 10G. As the names suggest, the 10G handles four times as much capacity as the 2.5G.

10G   The WaveStar Time Division Multiplexer (TDM) 10G supports high-capacity, self-healing transport at 10 Gbps. It also interconnects multiple 2.5G and 10G rings using a single network device. Further, it can support DS-3 up to OC-192 rates in a single bay.

In different networks, it can be used as an ADM, a terminal multiplexer, or a regenerator, which saves on floor space and costs. The 10G is also scalable and interworks with DWDM multiplexers and the WaveStar Bandwidth Manager (which we will discuss later in this chapter).

WaveStar TDM 2.5G   The WaveStar TDM 2.5G is the little brother of the 10G. It is a good starting point for SONET networks that expect to expand in the future.

Some of the WaveStar 2.5G's features include:

▼ Self-healing transport using bidirectional line switched ring (BLSR) and dual-ring internetworking

■ Integrated 2-fiber OC-48 BLSR

■ Multiple rings

■ Low-speed interfaces

■ 200 percent add/drop capacity (96 STS-1s)

▲ ANSI and BellCore standards compliance

The WaveStar 2.5G is compatible with other Lucent products, including the WaveStar 10G.

OXC

We talked about OXCs in Chapter 5, but let's cover their functionality again quickly. It's easy to think of OXCs as hard-wired switches. The lambdas are switched between input and output fibers, but the connections are hard-wired and cannot be changed to meet the current needs of the network, as with a switch. This is not to suggest that OXCs are useless—quite the contrary. There are deployments where an OXC is the best tool. However, they do not contain the intelligence that switches do. The following sections highlight two of Lucent's OXCs.

WaveStar Bandwidth Manager   The WaveStar Bandwidth Manager is an OXC that allows rate flexibility, bandwidth management, and quick provisioning of service capacity. The WaveStar Bandwidth Manager can handle interfaces from DS-3 to OC-192 with STS-1/STM-1 grooming granularity.

The bandwidth manager also supports a range of topologies, including 2- and 4-line BLSR and SONET/SDH. It features a capacity of 9216 1+1 SONET STS-1s and 3072 1+1 SDH STM-1s.

The StarWave Bandwidth Manager eliminates the need for multiple ADMs, as they can be configured on one device. Packets can be groomed so that low-speed traffic is placed in a faster channel (a measure that can be a revenue booster to a provider).

WaveStar LambdaRouter   A bit of a misnomer, the LambdaRouter is not really a router but an all-optical switch—in fact, it is the first all-optical switch. (Of course, the term "all optical" is not entirely true, because it still uses electrical MEMS to connect wavelengths on incoming fibers to outgoing fibers.)

It is a multiservice device, so SONET, SDH, ATM, and so forth can all be utilized and switched among any fibers. The LambdaRouter is 16 times faster than electronic switches used in communications networks and can switch billions of e-mail messages each second. At the heart of the LambdaRouter are two sets of 256 MEMS. Each set is embedded on a one-square-inch silicon base. With the aid of sophisticated software, the mirrors are tilted to reflect (and so direct) wavelengths from an incoming fiber to an outgoing fiber, thus eliminating the slow and power-consuming OEO conversion process.

The LambdaRouter features:

▼ Four bidirectional ports, each with one ingress connector and one egress connector

■ Power monitoring to detect losses, which can lead to switchover to an alternate fabric

■ Mesh restoration

▲ Upgrade capability to a larger optical switching fabric

FOUNDRY NETWORKS, INC.

Foundry Networks, Inc., designs, develops, and manufactures a broad range of end-to-end networking products for enterprises and service providers. Products cover needs from LANs to MANs to WANs. Because of their comprehensive list of products, Foundry can offer global end-to-end solutions for any location in a customer's networking infrastructure.

Overview

Foundry provides high-performance routing solutions from the Internet core to the edge of the ISP network with its network of Web and application servers. Foundry's Internet routers provide the performance needed to provide efficient core routing services. Its layer-2 and layer-3 switches provide intelligence and speed that bandwidth-intensive Internet applications require.

Foundry offers a broad range of networking devices aimed at Web-based enterprises and service providers. Its product line includes Internet core routers, Gigabit Ethernet edge switches, Gigabit core switches, and Gigabit Ethernet intelligent network service switches for server farms.

Foundry's network management solution, called IronView, is a comprehensive set of easy-to-use tools that simplify switch management. A command line interface is used to provide control of local and remote devices. IronView-utilized standard Simple Network Management Protocol (SNMP) and configuration applications are available on platforms supporting the protocol.

Routers

Foundry's optical routing offerings include NetIron400, NetIron800, and NetIron 1500. These Internet core routers provide high-performance switching capacity, scalability, and control. Interfaces range from 10 Mbps to 2.5 Gbps, and NetIron products are designed to meet the bandwidth and control requirements of service providers.

The key benefits of Foundry's product line includes reliability, switching capacity, Internet and LAN integration, compactness, long-haul links, and Gigabit Ethernet of up to 150 kilometers. The chassis-based Internet routers offer interfaces including OC-3c, OC-12c, and OC-48c PoS/SDH, OC-3 ATM, and Gigabit Ethernet.

The NetIron Internet Backbone Router family is designed for a range of service POP and Internet data center applications. Foundry's NetIron supports a variety of applications and capabilities, including:

▼ MPLS

■ BGP4

■ OSPF and multicast

■ Adaptive and fixed rate limiting

■ Gigabit Ethernet

■ ATM

▲ PoS

This functionality allows the NetIron router to meet the bandwidth and control requirements of service providers. NetIron's benefits include:

▼ Reliability

■ Switching capacity

■ Extensive LAN and WAN connectivity

■ Compactness

▲ Long-haul Gigabit Ethernet MAN links (up to 150 km)

NetIron can deliver up to 480 Gbps of nonblocking total switching capacity, and its modular chassis eliminates performance bottlenecks with wire-speed IP routing.

NetIron utilizes Foundry's IronCore architecture and IronWare software suite, delivering BGP4 and OSPF route processing, wire-speed regular or extended ACLs, and (at the top end router) up to 172 Mpps per chassis.

The NetIron router family offers a range of optical and electrical network interfaces, which are provided via high-density add-on modules. Rates include:

▼ 10/100/1000 Mbps Ethernet

■ ATM (OC-3c/STM-1)

■ SONET/SDH (OC-3c/STM-1)

■ OC12c/STM-4

■ OC-48c/STM-16

■ OC-192c/STM-64

▲ 10 Gigabit Ethernet

Differing distances can be spanned with the optical modules, including short distances (2 km), medium distances (15–20 km), and the long haul (20–150 km).

Management and routing modules are available and come with extended flash memory, two PCMCIA type II card slots, a PowerPC processor, and support for out-of-band network management. Further, device-level management is available through a CLI, a Web-based GUI, or SNMP-based network management systems.

Traffic can be filtered on the NetIron family through the use of hardware-based access control lists (ACLs). Up to 4000 ACLs can be configured to:

▼ Permit or deny packets by source IP address

▲ Permit or deny packets by source and destination IP address or other information including:

■ Source/destination host names

■ IP subnet and range

■ Source/destination TCP or UDP port/socket numbers

■ Well-known port numbers (0–1023)

Further, NetIron adds security features that protect the network against denial of service (DoS) conditions such as TCP SYN or smurf attacks.

NetIron also offers hardware-based multicasting support that allows the deployment of applications like video on demand. Also, they can forward copies of a transmission only to those ports that request it. This reduces overall traffic and improves performance.

Each member of the NetIron family offers a different level of power and is appropriate for different customers. The following sections outline the differences in the NetIron routers.

NetIron 400

Foundry's NetIron 400, the smallest of the NetIron family, features four slots and can process up to 41 Mpps. Further, its switching capacity is up to 128 Gbps.

NetIron 800

Foundry's NetIron 800 is an eight-slot device and can process up to 89 Mpps. Its switching capacity is up to 256 Gbps.

NetIron 1500

The NetIron 1500 is the largest member of the NetIron family, with a 15-slot chassis. It can process up to 172 Mpps and switches at a rate of 480 Gbps.

Switches

Foundry's optical switching offerings include the BigIron 4000, BigIron 8000, and BigIron 15000 switches. These devices are aimed at the LAN/MAN Gigabit Ethernet backbone of large enterprises and service providers.

BigIron switches can be deployed in:

▼ Collapsed backbone

■ Data centers

■ Local area server farms

■ Gigabit Ethernet layer-2 and layer-3 switching

■ IP only or multiprotocol support

▲ PoS on a single platform.

The BigIron layer-3 switches support standards-based routing protocols including RIP, OSPF, and BGP4.

The BigIron family is based on Foundry's IronCore ASIC architecture, which delivers hardware-based, distributed switching and routing, increasing the availability of network bandwidth.

BigIron's nonblocking architecture allows scalable and available network designs to be built. Further, the BigIron family offers a range of interface options, including:

▼ 10/100 Ethernet

■ Gigabit Ethernet

■ Gigabit Ethernet copper

■ PoS

■ ATM

▲ Foundry's Global Ethernet (Layer 2 Ethernet over SONET) technology.

At the top end, BigIron delivers a maximum total switching capacity of 480 Gbps. Further, BigIron can handle 120 nonblocking Gigabit Ethernet ports at a peak performance of 178 Mpps.

BigIron's switching functionality is well suited for enterprises that require line-rate IP or IPX, as well as full multiprotocol support. Further, Foundry's IronWare, the software suite powering BigIron, contains multiprotocol or IP-only support that can process millions of BGP4 routes from hundreds of peers.

BigIron switches reduce their reliance on external routers because Foundry employs an Integrated Switch Routing (ISR) feature that enables VLANs configured on BigIron switches to route layer-3 traffic from one protocol, VLAN, IP subnet, IPX network, or AppleTalk cable to another using virtual interfaces. The use of virtual interfaces allows the network to be reconfigured quickly without needing additional equipment.

BigIron provides fault tolerance with its Management III and Management IV modules. Management III modules include 128MB of SDRAM and a PowerPC 400 MHz processor. Management IV modules include 256MB of SDRAM, a PowerPC 466 MHz processor, dual PCMCIA Type II slots, and an 80MB flash card for configuration and control. In large deployments, the administrator can upgrade the memory to 512MB of SDRAM to support millions of routes with hundreds of peers.

The following highlight some of BigIron's other features:

▼ Eight hardware-prioritized output QoS queues per port adjustable for:
  - Weighted Fair Queuing (WFQ)
  - Strict Priority (SP)
  - 802.1p queue mapping
- Policy-based traffic classification based on:
  - ToS
  - IP precedence mappings
  - Layer-2/3/4 defined traffic flows
- Redundant management modules
- Hot swappable, load-sharing AC and DC power supply options
- Management options:
  - Command line interface
  - IronView network management
  - Telnet
  - Web browser–based GUI

- 10 Gigabit Ethernet readiness

- Modular, chassis-based layer-3 switches for campus, MAN, and LAN/WAN environments

- Up to 120 Gigabit Ethernet ports and 178 Mpps nonblocking performance

- High-density PoS (OC-3c–OC-48c), Global Ethernet (Ethernet over SONET), and ATM

- BGP4 implementation, including two million routes, route reflector, confederation, and route flap dampening

▲ Gigabit Ethernet links up to 150 km

Each member of the BigIron family offers its own level of beefiness. The following sections highlight those differences.

BigIron 4000

Foundry Network's Big Iron 4000 has a four-slot chassis and dual load-sharing power supplies. However, only one power supply is required to power a fully configured chassis; the other is used redundantly. The BigIron 4000 can processes 48 Mpps and switches at rates up to 128 Gbps.

BigIron 8000

Foundry Network's BigIron 8000 has an eight-slot chassis and supports up to four load-balancing and load-sharing power supplies. Only two power supplies are required to power a fully configured eight-slot chassis. The third power supply provides load-sharing capabilities, and the fourth enables N+1 redundancy. The BigIron 8000 processes at 96 Mpps and provides switching at rates of 256 Gbps.

BigIron 15000

Foundry Network's BigIron 15000 has a 15-slot chassis and supports up to four load-balancing and load-sharing power supplies. As with the BigIron 8000, only two power supplies are required to power a fully configured 15-slot chassis. The third power supply provides load-sharing capabilities, and the fourth enables N+1 redundancy. The BigIron 15000 processes 178 Mpps and provides switching at rates of 480 Gbps.

Table 6-7 compares the attributes of each BigIron product.

	BigIron 400	BigIron 800	BigIron 1500
Slots	4	8	15
Maximum gigabit ports per system	32	64	120
Nonblocking backplane throughput	64 Gbps	126 Gbps	240 Gbps
Total switching capacity	128 Gbps	256 Gbps	480 Gbps
Routed/switched throughput	48 Mpps	96 Mpps	178 Mpps

Table 6-7. Comparison of the BigIron Family of Switches

This chapter barely scratches the surface on the optical networking products available. We tried to touch on the offerings of some of the biggest names in optical networking. For each internetworking need, there are a range of products from which to choose. Your decision can be based on a number of factors, including the device's capacity, cost, availability, and compatibility with your existing gear.

Even though we've tried to talk about the big-name products out there, it is important to be aware that new companies with the "next big thing" spring up all the time. What might be top of the line today will be superceded by a new product tomorrow.

CHAPTER 7

Optical Networking
Applications

Optical networking isn't limited to local area networks (LANs), wide area networks (WANs), or long-haul networking. Truth be told, there are a great number of applications that benefit from the capacity and speed of optical networking.

In this chapter, we look at how fiber optics is used in different applications. For instance, fiber is used at the core of most high-speed networks. It's in place not because of its distance capabilities, but because of its inherent speed. Further, using fiber optics helps make long-distance storage possible, enables Internet Protocol (IP)–based telephony, and bridges the gap between LANs and WANs. Finally, we'll look at an emerging technology that wants to take the fiber out of fiber optics. First, however, is a discussion about connecting continents with strands of fiber.

SUBMARINE SYSTEMS

The popular notion is that long-distance communications are accomplished via satellite. That, however, is not the case. Since these birds are positioned in geosynchronous orbit (and about a tenth of the way to the moon), it takes the signal more than half a second to get to the satellite and back to Earth. This introduces a lag that, in voice networks, is simply unacceptable. The solution is submerged fiber optic cable, linking two continents.

As you remember from our discussion about the history of optical networking, the first transoceanic cable was laid in 1858 between Newfoundland and Ireland. This cable allowed telegraphic connectivity until it was decommissioned in the 1920s. This cable was the first of many to connect North America and Europe. In subsequent years, new cables were placed that provided telephone connections. Each successive cable provided more capacity than the one before it.

In the early 1980s, the TAT-7 was the last electronic cable that was placed. Future cables used optical technology to convey telephone communications. By 2000, undersea cables carried 80 percent of the world's transoceanic and coastal traffic. According to industry researchers KMI, undersea capacity equivalent to 800 million voice circuits will be in operation by 2003.

With the growth of the Internet in Europe (it isn't just happening here, you know), multinational intranets and global e-commerce are expected to feed the growth of undersea cable for at least the next three years. Because of this increase, KMI projects that 70 percent more undersea fiber optic cable will be installed in the next three years than has ever been installed since the late 1980s.

As such, submarine cabling is big business and important in the world of telecommunications. In this section, we study submarine cables, how they are designed and how they are deployed.

Connecting Continents

Most of our discussion about submarine cable has involved the section of North Atlantic Ocean between North America and Europe. But don't let that lead you to believe that only North America and England are connected. In actuality, there is a virtual web of fiber covering the globe.

According to KMI, between 1998 and 2003, 70 percent of the undersea fiber optic cable will traverse the Pacific. That equates to about $US23 billion worth of cable deployed across the Pacific and in interregional systems. Investment is expected to grow from $US20 billion in 1997 to more than $US51 billion through 2003.

The newer fiber optic cables have about 3000 times the capacity of older coaxial cable. Cable capacity is increasing. Consider the following: current cables carry 42 wavelengths of 10 Gbps each, and 68 wavelength systems are deployed. In total, there are about 580,000 km (360,000 miles) of undersea cables spanning the ocean floors. In order to connect such vast distances, it is important to conduct exhaustive research about the landing points and the path along the ocean floor.

Determining where a stretch of optical fiber will be laid takes many months of planning. First, planners must decide which cities will be connected. Then, they must establish which route the cable will take along the ocean floor. Ships are sent out with radar gear to ensure that there are no jagged rocks, undersea volcanoes, wide trenches, or any other obstacle that could damage the fiber.

Often, undersea cables are installed in parallel paths. Spaced widely to prevent total outage in the event one of the cables is damaged, the cables use only about half of their capacity and are able to switch over in the event of calamity. In the event a switchover is necessary, this usually occurs within 300 milliseconds and is largely unnoticeable to the network. Typically, cables that run in east-west directions are laid in pairs. Cables that stretch from north to south are generally single cables.

Submarine cabling is popular to connect continents, but it is also useful in providing connectivity for a single continent.

Festooning

Submarine cabling isn't deployed just to connect the United States to England or Japan to Hawaii. As Figure 7-1 illustrates, submarine cable is often used to connect coastal cities in an installation called *festooning*. Festooning is used to install cable because it is simply easier and less expensive to run the cabling along the coast than to acquire right of way and plant the cable on land.

When fiber is festooned, it is armored to prevent damage from ship anchors, dredges, and fishermen. In a festooned system, the fiber is laid in large loops off shore, generally no more than 150 miles long. The loops make ground at the cities where connectivity is needed. Additionally, amplifiers are normally installed at landing points.

In locations where there are concerns about the integrity and safety of the fiber, a modification to the festooned system is implemented.

Spurs

Optical spurs are used in locations where the fiber optic cable could be damaged, such as in high-traffic fishing waters. As Figure 7-2 shows, optical spurs are lines brought in to shore from the festooned fiber optic cable.

Optical spurs do not provide access to the entire fiber ring. Rather, they bring ashore a specific wavelength that is meant for the node at that landfall point. Then, a new lambda

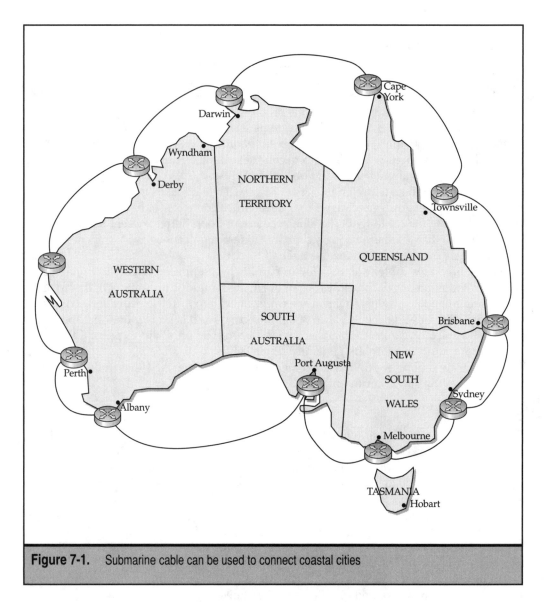

Figure 7-1. Submarine cable can be used to connect coastal cities

is multiplexed onto the fiber and sent back out onto the network. In this type of configuration, the fiber is located about 1000 miles offshore.

Installation

Because submarine systems must endure the crushing pressure of the deep, the fishermens' netting, and hungry sharks, submarine cabling must be extremely well protected. After all, if there is a break in the fiber, it's much more difficult to locate and repair the damaged section in the briny deep than in a dusty ceiling plenum.

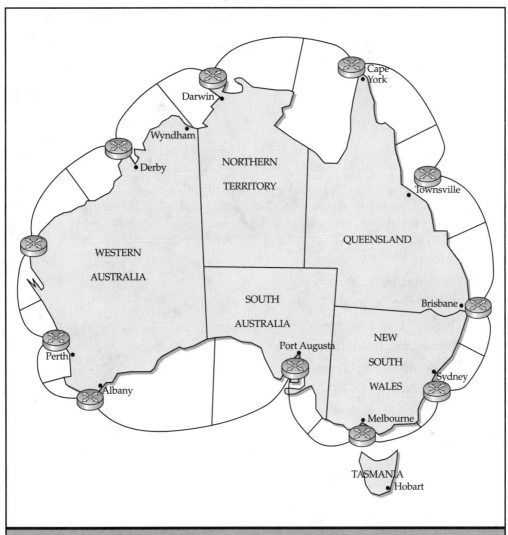

Figure 7-2.   Optical spurs provide reliability in dangerous locations

Physically laying the cable can be done one of two ways:

1. The coastal segment can be anchored to a *beach manhole*. A beach manhole is a concrete vault located at the shoreline. This is where the undersea segment is linked to the land-line cable. Once the segment is anchored at the beach manhole, a small boat carries the rest of the segment to the waiting ship, where it is connected to the rest of the cable.

2. The cable-laying ship approaches the shore as close as possible without grounding. The end of the segment is floated on buoys toward shore. Once the end of the segment reaches shore, three or four strong guys in wetsuits drag it to a landing point.

Near shore, the well-armored cable is normally buried by a device on the ship that tills up the ocean floor, then places and buries the cable. Burying the cable is important, because it prevents the tides from repeatedly smashing rocks against it or swaying out of position.

Fiber Design

The fibers that are laid on the ocean floor are, basically, the same cables used in terrestrial applications, although they are sealed and encased in multiple layers of protective covering. In shallow water, they are subject to the greatest risks. These cables are heavily armored to prevent crushing. The protective layers are complex, as shown in Figure 7-3.

The layers include:

▼ A nylon outer covering*

■ Various polypropylene layers*

■ Layers of steel mesh armor*

■ Hermetically sealed copper tube

■ Elastic cushioning fibers

■ A thick central wire called the *king wire*

▲ The optical fibers themselves

NOTE: The layers marked by asterisks are added to the cable for increased protection when it is placed in shallow water.

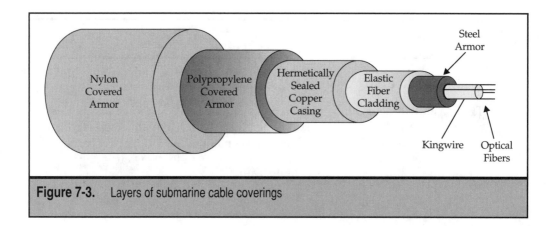

Figure 7-3. Layers of submarine cable coverings

The cable laid on the ocean floor includes only the optical fibers, kingwire, and cushioning fibers, all contained within a copper sheath. This sheath not only protects the fiber, but it can carry an electrical current to any devices that are used along the length of the fiber, such as amplifiers. In deep-sea environments, the cable isn't as heavy as it is near the shore. Otherwise, on its way to the bottom of the sea, it would be so heavy that it would rip itself apart.

Near the shore, the armor-clad cable itself weighs 16 times more than those used on the ocean floor. It is still rather thin, though—near the shore, cables are just three inches in diameter. Undersea, the cables are about an inch and a half thick.

Most fiber manufacturers make special undersea cables. These fibers are designed to have a more constant dispersion across a broad range of operational wavelengths. Dispersion near the edges of the band is reduced, so that those wavelengths operate more like wavelengths in the middle ranges.

Once the cables have been made, they are wound on large, five-meter-diameter spools. A fiber segment is about 80 km (50 miles) in length. As the fiber is loaded onto the ship, it is unwound and amplifiers are added between segments. Couplers are added at each end of the segment. Couplers weigh 300 kg (650 pounds), chiefly because of their dense beryllium-copper housings. It is then sent to the ship's hold where it is stored for the voyage.

Not only is submarine cable speedier than satellite communications, undersea cables are designed with a 25-year lifetime. Satellites, on the other hand, have a life span of 10 to 15 years. In the event a fiber needs to be repaired, it is much easier to pull the fiber up and fix it than it is to go into space and fix a satellite. If the correct ship is near a failed cable, it can be fixed in less than a week. Generally speaking, cables tend to outlive their life expectancies. Coaxial cables laid in 1960 by the United States Navy are still functional today.

Another important issue with undersea fibers is their inherent security. Satellite transmissions can be (and are) intercepted and eventually decoded. Coaxial cables can be tapped without detection. However, undersea fiber optic cables cannot be tapped into because of the enormous pressures at the bottom of the ocean, or near the coasts, because of the thick layer of armor protecting them.

Amplification and Regeneration

When optical fiber is placed on the seabed, the systems must be carefully designed to take into consideration geographical traits, distance, and noise. Long spans must be amplified, but the downside to amplifiers is that they also amplify noise. Therefore, the amplifiers must be included judiciously. To reduce this problem, submarine amplifiers tend to have less gain, allowing more of them to be installed along the route. Further, in a dense wavelength division multiplexing (DWDM) system, the amplification must amplify all the wavelengths in the span.

As Figure 7-4 shows, amplifiers are added between segments of cabling. Lambdas that enter the fiber are amplified by the erbium-doped fiber amplifier (EDFA). The light waves that are traveling in the opposite direction are given the same treatment. The system employs four 980 nanometer (nm) pump lasers, two for each direction. The WDM

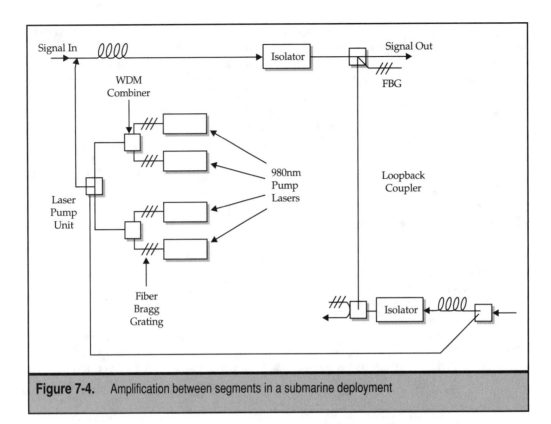

Figure 7-4.   Amplification between segments in a submarine deployment

combiner is employed with the pump lasers to provide a redundant system, ensuring that the system will continue to work in the event that one of the lasers fails. The filter removes the 980 nm signal once it has completed its task. The fiber Bragg gratings (FBGs) stabilize the lasers and select the light to loop back.

Unfortunately, there must also be an optical-electrical-optical (OEO) conversion in long-haul systems. Although the amplifiers try to do a good job, the signal must also be regenerated from time to time. Typically, after every eight amplifiers, a regenerator is installed, which keeps the signal clean.

Submarine cable is an expensive, arduous undertaking. However, this application has already proved that it can bring a world closer together—first, by making long-distance telephony a more efficient technology, and then by transporting data across those same fiber links that connect continents.

METROPOLITAN AREA NETWORKS

Bandwidth has exploded on the LAN, thanks to such technologies as Gigabit Ethernet and ever-beefier applications. WAN traffic has also increased, fueled by the amazing growth of the Internet. To bridge the gap between the two, metropolitan area networks (MANs) have been filling the bill.

Over the past year, MANs have evolved as an important part of the overall network infrastructure. In addition to the bandwidth demands, there are also increasing burdens on architecture, protocols, and technologies.

The maturation of dense wavelength division multiplexing (DWDM), the rise of optical infrastructure, and the push toward voice and data convergence are all pressures on the existing internetwork infrastructure.

MANs aren't a new architecture. They've been around since the early 1990s, when they started as proprietary time division multiplexing (TDM) rings. By the mid-1990s, asynchronous transfer mode (ATM) became the prevalent WAN technology. This conversion was due, largely, to the promise of converging data, voice, and video. Now, however, it seems that ATM isn't really up to the task and TDM solutions like Synchronous Optical Networking/Synchronous Digital Hierarchy (SONET/SDH) are more difficult and expensive than new technologies.

In this section, we study MANs. We talk about how they are built, which optical technology is best, and how the next generation MANs will use a combination of optical technologies for optimal efficiency and service.

The MAN

MANs channel traffic within a metropolitan area (i.e., interbusiness, interoffice, and so forth) as well as to and from large long-haul points of presence (POPs). Because of this design, MANs are driven by two key features:

▼ Customer demands

▲ Technology

Furthermore, MANs are characterized by a broad range of networking protocols and channel speeds, due to the diversity of customer applications and needs.

The most prevalent technology used by MANs is SONET, using point-to-point or add/drop multiplexer (ADM) ring topologies. Connections tend to be permanent or semipermanent, with access speeds between OC-3 and OC-48.

Figure 7-5 illustrates what a basic MAN looks like.

Though SONET has been rather useful in this capacity, newer technologies are challenging its effectiveness.

SONET Versus DWDM Round III

The chief technology in place in many MANs is SONET. Though this technology was quite useful when it was first introduced, its limitations are becoming evident.

SONET uses self-healing rings, which provide excellent redundancy and reliability. That, along with its well-established standards that ensure multivendor compatibility, has made SONET the most popular, prevalent, and established optical technology.

However, as telecom networks are being asked to move data in addition to voice (and more of it), SONET becomes less than the perfect solution.

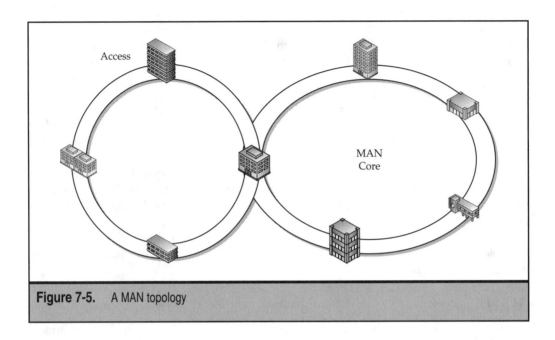

Figure 7-5.   A MAN topology

The increase in long-haul capacity, fueled by DWDM and coupled with the amazing increase of access bandwidth demand, has placed MANs at a crossroads. The existing TDM infrastructure faces challenges in efficiency and scaling. Furthermore, enterprises are demanding the high bit rates of OC-48 connections, which causes the line between access networks and metro networks to blur. The result will be a demand for capacity that existing SONET deployments won't be able to handle.

Scalability and Provisioning

A major problem is one of scaling. With SONET, additional capacity requires additional fiber and nodes to be installed. Because Internet use (as one measure of bandwidth consumption) increases at about 300 percent per year, carriers would constantly be installing additional fiber and other infrastructure.

SONET installation is notoriously slow. Truck rolls—the terminology used to describe the physical installation of new hardware and burying of fiber—can take 18 months, or more.

Further, equipment is not cheap. The cost of additional add/drop multiplexers (ADMs) and SONET cross-connects can be extremely expensive for carriers.

Design

Like so many other technologies that have data shoehorned into them, SONET networks were not designed with data in mind. Rather, they were meant to carry voice traffic.

SONET is a multiplexing technology, which must enforce a strict TDM hierarchy. This works fine with a telephone network that ensures connectivity by assigning a specific time-slice of bandwidth to each connection. However, it is not the flexible, scalable creature that data requires.

As you saw in Chapter 3, to conform with the SONET infrastructure, the slowest channel is a VT1.5, which runs at about 1.7 Mbps. The next highest increment is the STS-1, which carries a payload of 51.84 Mbps. Because there would be unused capacity in these channels, there is an inherent inefficiency. As the ratio of data traffic increases, this inefficiency becomes more pronounced.

DWDM to the Rescue

MAN vendors are looking to DWDM as the answer to SONET's MAN limitations.

Scaling was a problem with SONET (truck rolls required months of planning and installation before the additional capacity was complete), but bringing DWDM on board resolves scaling issues. Rather than add more fiber, a multiplexer is added at one end, and a demultiplexer at the other; the existing fiber can then handle much more capacity.

Instead of pulling new fiber, the idea is to upgrade the whole ring with DWDM. DWDM nodes sit in the basement of the customer premises, just like SONET ADMs. Two fibers are normally pulled into the DWDM chassis from the metropolitan ring. As with SONET, one fiber is used as the primary ring, and the other as the backup ring. The DWDM chassis has multiple slots for cards. Each card allows the unit to drop one or more wavelengths onto the ring. It also contains single-mode and multimode fiber interfaces for delivering services to end users.

Of course, DWDM is less than perfect. One of the barriers to introducing true DWDM networking into the metro is the high cost of OEO conversions. While all-optical networking offers the means to minimize and even eliminate these conversions, situations exist that still make them necessary: wavelength translation (to avoid blocking and stranded capacity) and regeneration (to ensure signal integrity). One approach is to construct the network from all-optical domains where OEO conversion is performed only at the edge. To build such a network, the nodes must satisfy the following requirements:

1. Nodes must be able to support at least four or five access rings or be connected to four or five neighboring nodes. Each fiber connection must be able to handle at least 80 wavelengths.

2. Any wavelength from any input fiber must be able to be switched to any output fiber, without using an OXC.

3. The nodes must be able to receive switching instructions from the operations system.

4. Path integrity must be guaranteed, using fault handling, performance monitoring, reporting, and power equalization.

Furthermore, the nature of DWDM networking (large granularity, circuit-switched) presents a problem. Because access network protocols tend to be smaller-bandwidth and packet-switched, the efficiency problems SONET faced are being revisited on DWDM.

However, this problem can be alleviated by the use of Gigabit and 10 Gigabit Ethernet protocols.

The Next Generation MAN

In order to deal with the necessities that heterogeneous internetworks require, MANs must come into the new millennium. For a MAN to be useful and successful, service providers seem to agree, several attributes must be present:

▼ **Interoperability**   The chief concern is one of interoperability with legacy equipment throughout the MAN's deployment. This means the ability to connect with equipment at the central office (CO), POPs, and customer premises.

■ **Multiprotocol support**   MANs must be capable of handling a plethora of protocols and have the capability to deal with them from a single platform. Alternatively, deploying multiple infrastructures is simply not feasible, especially for service providers that need to provision services quickly. There are a number of benefits for such a system. First, multiprotocol systems will allow providers to leverage existing infrastructure and technology with a new architecture. Further, costs are cut down because legacy equipment can be maintained.

■ **Solid architecture**   An architecture is needed that provides the dual ring protection of SONET. Further, there is a need for the intelligence that comes with layer-3 devices. Redundancy and intelligence ensure that the MAN will continue to function in the event of a failure. The architecture can further be bolstered by configuration into a mesh (which we will talk about later in this section).

■ **Management**   In multiprotocol networks such as MANs, network management is extremely important. In spite of all the protocols being supported, network administrators will still insist on standards-based, bit-rate-independent management solutions that will allow for integrated configuration, fault locating, and performance monitoring.

■ **Cost and billing**   Naturally, cost is a factor in the design and deployment of a MAN. Cost concerns are not limited to the price and maintenance of equipment but extend to total cost involved in a deployment. Providers also want the ability to offer and charge for services at differing levels. (See Chapter 9 for more information on service level agreements, which are contracts between the customer and the ISP.)

■ **Provisioning**   At the access ring level, provisioning is also a concern. Service providers provide not only data but also voice and video services. The goal is to provide between 1 and 10 Mbps in increments that are easy to configure from a central location. Furthermore, customers are increasingly asking for the ability to do this themselves.

■ **Quality of Service (QoS)**   QoS piggybacks on provisioning, in that it ensures that customers receive the amount of bandwidth that they are promised. QoS also assures that crucial bandwidth is not absorbed by any one customer or application.

▲ **ISP flexibility** The ability to connect to two separate ISPs is important, because it ensures a level of redundancy and excellent response times. Additionally, the customer can select specific service packages for critical and less-than-critical traffic.

Provisioning

A crucial component of any MAN is the ability to quickly and smoothly provision bandwidth as more customers come on board. In a traditional SONET topology, provisioning time is measured in months. This involves time to plan the new ring and conduct a truck roll. However, when DWDM is applied to existing SONET rings, provisioning becomes much more feasible.

Providers want to be able to provide such tiered services as traffic classification and segregation on a per-user and per-flow basis. As the demand for bandwidth increases, providers will have to have a way to supply bandwidth quickly.

Intelligence In addition to the ability to provide bandwidth to customers, it is necessary to respond to network conditions on a moment-by-moment basis. To most efficiently deploy a MAN, intelligent wavelength channel provisioning is needed.

Intelligence will come only with a mesh topology, which has the capacity to provide new routes for traffic. A mesh DWDM architecture provides these resources (link wavelengths and nodal processing capabilities).

Because MANs are a much more dynamic environment than long-haul networks, IP traffic engineering protocols such as multiprotocol label switching (MPLS) are good tools to extend into the MAN. Further, QoS tools can be used to ensure that bandwidth isn't being squandered.

Subrate Provisioning Although there is an overall demand for high rates of bandwidth, MANs will also have to cater to those customers who want smaller channel capacities. Obviously, it is not at all cost effective or efficient to devote a single wavelength to a low-rate signal. Further, given the mix of clients and protocols, it doesn't make sense to dedicate a specific wavelength for each protocol. A better plan is to modularly provision subrate channels and multiplex them into a single, high-capacity wavelength. This approach is illustrated in Figure 7-6.

Not only does subrate provisioning allow providers to attract customers who would use lower amounts of bandwidth, but it also helps with the "pay-as-you-grow" philosophy that providers look for. By offering subrate services, providers can save money and attract more customers, which bolsters their business so that they can add more capacity, thus attracting more customers, and so forth.

Blend

A popular solution for MANs is to combine the reliability and guaranteed latency of SONET with the capacity of DWDM and the low cost of Ethernet.

The heart of this type of MAN is the direct provisioning of multiple Gigabit Ethernet channels over DWDM fiber, which is configured in SONET-like rings. This creates a

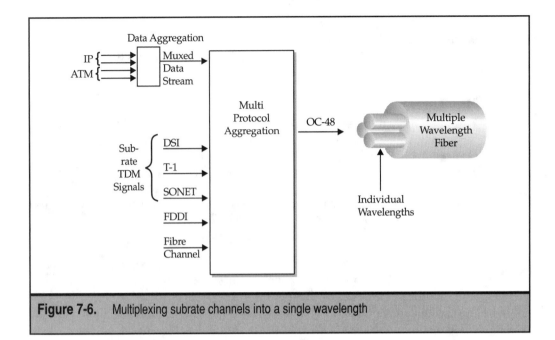

Figure 7-6. Multiplexing subrate channels into a single wavelength

data-optimized optical ring, which is scalable and provisionable. This blend of architectures and technologies eliminates overhead and reduces the equipment costs.

Protocols   Employing Gigabit and 10 Gigabit Ethernet as the predominant protocols on the DWDM rings makes sense for two very important reasons:

▼ Ethernet is so widely dispersed in networks that it has become the *de facto* standard. No other networking protocol has the wide acceptance of Ethernet. Further, because it is so popular, network administrators who grew up on 10/100 Ethernet already understand the basics, so migration to a speedier version isn't as taxing as learning a new system.

▲ Gigabit and 10 Gigabit Ethernet will scale well onto DWDM rings. As opposed to subrate capacities, these protocols are already beefy enough that they can fit on the fiber without wasting space in STS packets.

Of course, as we mentioned before, new generation MANs will require support for a broad range of protocols. However, the best results will be achieved via Gigabit and 10 Gigabit Ethernet.

Topologies   Blending DWDM and SONET brings a number of benefits. The chief benefit is the ability to use existing SONET infrastructure with the new DWDM technology. In this type of configuration, optical ADMs are required to add or remove certain lambdas or let them pass through. This type of configuration also allows the fault protection of SONET's rings to be beneficial.

However, a ring topology is more of an evolutionary step than a final destination. A ring topology is not ideal for scaling, nor is it ideal to cover large geographical areas. There are ring topologies that allow for several rings to overlap each other. Though overlapping rings will allow more nodes to be included in a network, they still require truck rolls, massive planning, and implementation steps.

Using DWDM with existing SONET infrastructure is an ideal way to realize a cost savings and use existing fiber. A better solution is to deploy a mesh topology. Using optical cross-connects (OXC) makes network elements more flexible and capable of using existing point-to-point and ring-based topologies.

A mesh topology provides a better fit for layer-2 protocols, such as IP and ATM. Mesh topologies are more efficient and require less up-front planning of service providers. Furthermore, additional nodes can be added and dropped with no deleterious impact on the rest of the network.

A mesh network also allows migration to future technologies, which are likely to employ a mesh.

Table 7-1 lists the merits of various MAN topologies.

There isn't likely to be any sort of standard MAN deployment in the years to come. Though the MAN is rather important as capacities increase and as the lines between access networks and core networks blur, there will be many different designs and implementations of the MAN. One can chalk this up to existing SONET infrastructure, new mesh deployments, and the choice between SONET and DWDM.

Condition	SONET	DWDM over Optical Ring	Optical Mesh
Cost	Low	Medium	Medium
Efficiency	Low	Medium	High
Protection time	Fast	Fast	Fast
Provisioning time	Slow	Fast	Fast
Topology flexibility	Low	Low	High
Demand scalability	Low	Low	High

Table 7-1. Comparison of MAN Topologies

VOIP

Voice over IP (VoIP) is a means to provide telephony through computers and mostly avoid the public telephone system. Basically, it allows telephone conversations to be converted into IP packets, then sent across the internetwork to their intended destination.

VoIP isn't a perfect way to get rid of your organization's desktop telephones, but it is a viable technology and something that you can use to communicate with a branch office or even with an old high school friend, living on the other side of the continent. Furthermore, in networks using fiber, VoIP becomes more effective and usable than in copper-based environments.

In this section, we delve into the issues and technology surrounding VoIP, and how fiber optics can help deliver on VoIP's promise.

Introduction

One of the early promises of the Internet was the prospect of making free long-distance telephone calls. In theory, calls would be encoded by one computer, transmitted through the Internet, and then decoded by the receiver. Further, there would be the need for only one type of network—the IP network. This would do away with the need for both dedicated voice and data networks. In practice, however, this technology had a long way to go.

The main problem was one of resources. In order for the call to go through, packets had to be received in the correct order, or Internet phone calls would come through as gibberish. Too often, packets were received in a random order, making the calls hard to understand and revealing the technology not to be the panacea all had hoped for. VoIP needed a technology such as Real Time Protocol (RTP) to put a sequence number and time stamp on packets so that the reassembler could not only put packets back into the correct order but provide interpolation of the speech waveform, if possible, should packets either be dropped or arrive later than the buffer depth. In an optical deployment, however, the packets arrive at their destination much more quickly and therefore in the correct order so that VoIP can function properly.

The public telephone network looks more and more like a data network as the lines between telephony and data transmission blur. Today, CO switches are a lot like big computers, like the routers used to form the Internet. What differences exist will start to vanish as VoIP becomes the predominant way to make a telephone call. This might seem like a radical notion, but there doesn't seem to be a cry of "foul" from the masses when they upgrade from an analog cellular telephone to a digital one, or when television stations began stereo broadcasts.

How It Works

Just what happens when you make a VoIP call? Let's take a look at the process, following the steps by the numbers:

1. The session application part of VoIP generates a dial tone and waits for the telephone number to be dialed.

2. The user dials the telephone number; those numbers are stored by the session application.

3. Once enough digits are entered to match a configured destination pattern, the telephone number is mapped to the IP host. This step is accomplished via the dial plan mapper. At this point, the IP host has made a connection to either the destination telephone number or a Private Branch Exchange (PBX) that will complete the call to its destination on the public network.

NOTE: A PBX is a device located within an organization that routes incoming telephone calls to the desired extension. It also supplies additional features such as voice mail or call forwarding. We'll talk more about PBXs later in this chapter.

4. Transmission and reception channels are established when the session application runs the H.323 protocol or the Session Initiation Protocol (SIP). If a PBX is managing the call, it forwards the call to the destination telephone. If the Resource Reservation Protocol (RSVP) has been configured, the RSVP reservations are made.

NOTE: RSVP clears a path across the routers between the two telephones. RSVP is one way to achieve the desired Quality of Service over an IP network.

5. The codecs are enabled for both ends of the connection, and the conversation proceeds using RTP/UDP/IP as the protocol stack.

NOTE: The User Datagram Protocol (UDP) is designed for applications where you don't need to put sequences of packets together. It fits into the system much like TCP. There is a UDP header. The network software puts the UDP header on the front of your data, just as it would put a TCP header on the front of your data. Then UDP sends the data to IP, which adds the IP header, putting UDP's protocol number in the protocol field instead of TCP's protocol number.

6. Any call-progress indicators (or other types of signals that can be carried in-band) are connected through the voice path once the end-to-end audio channel has been established.

NOTE: *Codecs* (coders/decoders) are hardware only or hardware with software devices that translate analog voice signals into digital signals that can be transmitted across the network. After digitization takes place, digital signal processors can perform compression. Compressed or uncompressed, the resulting signal is then packaged with the appropriate IP/RTP/UDP headers to be transmitted.

7. As soon as the phone call has ended (once either end hangs up), the RSVP reservations are torn down (if RSVP is used), the connection is broken, and the session ends. At this point, each end becomes idle, waiting for an "off hook" signal or an incoming IP phone call.

In addition to transporting the packets, the IP network must also ensure that your conversation is transported across the media in a manner that delivers the best voice quality. If packets are received in a different order than how they're sent out, then the conversation will be garbled and, ultimately, useless. The impact on fidelity varies with number of packets lost or delayed too long, and the compression level used. It would be worthwhile to point out that VoIP typically doesn't support dual tone multifrequency (DTMF) tones, fax, and modem traffic due to the effects of compression and packet misordering. Finally, the IP telephony packet stream might have to be converted by a gateway to another format. This is necessary either for the sake of interoperation with a different IP-based multimedia system or if the phone call is terminating on the conventional public telephone system.

Making the Connection

In the public network (also known as the PSTN, or *public switched telephone network*), signaling uses the familiar touch-tones that you hear when you punch in someone's telephone number. To compare the public telephone network to an internetwork, it is helpful to explain the protocol in use. Signaling System #7 (SS7) employs 64 kilobit per second (Kbps) packets that establish your telephone call, then transport your voice every time you make a phone call. SS7 is the protocol that is used between switches to convey call setup and takedown information.

With the public telephone network, the process of making a telephone call is much like the process that takes place when packets are sent across the Internet, as shown in Figure 7-7.

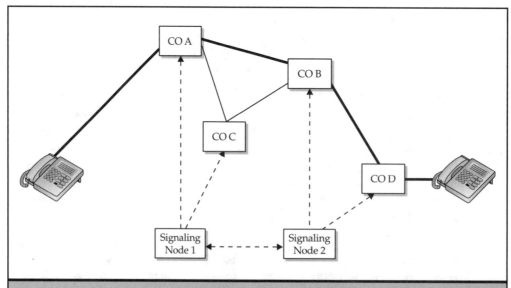

Figure 7-7. The public telephone network makes its connections similarly to routers in the Internet

As you make a telephone call, the route is established between COs until the call is connected to the receiving end. The main difference, you'll notice, is that unlike the Internet, where the routers talk to each other and determine the optimal route for your packets, in the public telephone system, the best route is determined by signaling nodes.

Building VoIP Networks

Before we discuss the specific uses of fiber (which will be covered later in this section), let's cover the construction of a VoIP system. Understanding the basics of VoIP will make the integration of fiber easier to understand.

There are three basic types of VoIP systems. They are designed around the user's specific needs and suit a particular market.

▼ **Simple toll bypass**   The most basic, straightforward use for VoIP is using it to make telephone calls without having to use the public telephone system. This is ideal if you just want to use IP to transport calls between branch offices within the corporate network. This design requires minimal change to existing PBX, cabling, and handset infrastructures; it is relatively easy to develop; and it has no PSTN integration issues to worry about.

■ **Total IP telephony**   This design relegates your existing voice systems to the dumpster. No longer will desktops have conventional telephone handsets—instead, they're traded in on IP telephones that plug into Ethernet ports. You'll use LAN servers to provide the majority of the features your PBX now provides. This is the Holy Grail of VoIP and not a journey to begin on a whim.

▲ **IP-enabled PBXs**   This solution isn't as gutsy as total IP telephony, but you still get a mélange of functionality. You don't have to change the existing cabling or handsets, but you will upgrade the PBXs so that your organization's core systems can speak IP telephony protocols. PBX users will be able to communicate with other IP telephony users, but the limitation is that your PBXs will have to rely on IP telephony gateways to communicate with the conventional, public telephone system.

The easiest solution to implement is simple toll bypass, so let's take a closer look at how that works; then we'll add some of the elements from the other two design concepts.

Simple Toll Bypass

VoIP toll bypass solutions are reasonably easy to implement. Before we start making changes, let's take a closer look at what you're likely to be starting with. Figure 7-8 shows two interconnected PBXs.

A PBX is a device located within an organization that connects phone calls coming in on trunk lines from the PSTN to their designated extensions. PBXs are also able to switch calls to extensions located on other connected PBXs. Most PBX interconnections are digital, and they may even be T1 circuits, which are dedicated for the sole purpose of interconnecting PBXs. Most likely, however, they are channels set up on a TDM backbone. The TDM divides bandwidth between voice and data.

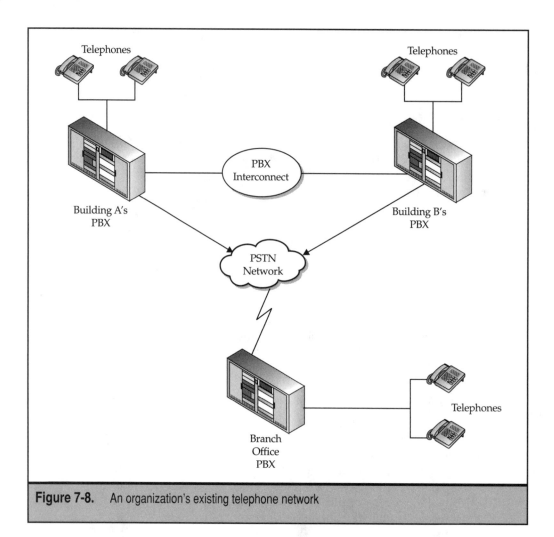

Figure 7-8. An organization's existing telephone network

The problem in having both dedicated voice and multiservice TDM lines is that bandwidth must be permanently allocated for each trunk voice circuit, even though the voice circuits are not always in use. A better way to manage resources is to put all traffic, voice and data, into packets so that all traffic can be commingled and use bandwidth more efficiently. This is where VoIP makes its entrance.

The easiest way to deploy a VoIP solution is to simply unplug the lines to the PBX and plug them into a separate unit that converts the voice signaling and transport into an IP format. Such a unit, referred to as a *VoIP relay* or *gateway*, connects into a router for transport over an IP network, as illustrated in Figure 7-9.

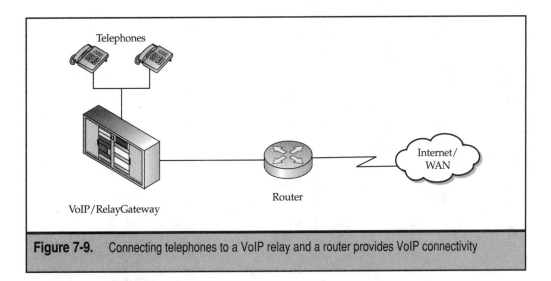

Figure 7-9. Connecting telephones to a VoIP relay and a router provides VoIP connectivity

You do not, however, have to buy a separate VoIP relay and router. But if you want a separate VoIP relay and router, you can certainly configure your VoIP solution that way. No matter which route you choose, there are three basic design concerns you must address:

▼   Make sure that the VoIP gateway will relay sufficient signaling information to support the features in use on the PBXs.

■   Make sure you know which standards your solution is using. Even though some products promise H.323 compliance, there are still a number of proprietary schemes.

▲   Make sure you figure out how you're going to supply the necessary voice quality. This issue comes down to a combination of which encoding scheme you use and the QoS capabilities of your network.

VoIP Solution

The toll bypass system we discussed is a straightforward, cost-saving scenario that you can hook up with little or no headache. But if you want to get adventuresome, consider the design in Figure 7-10.

In a full IP telephony solution, all end-user devices (PCs and phones) are connected to the LAN. The telephone that users will come to know and love can be one of two types:

▼   Hardware IP phones that look and act just like regular telephones, except that they are plugged into the network

▲   Software IP phones that rely on client software running on the PC

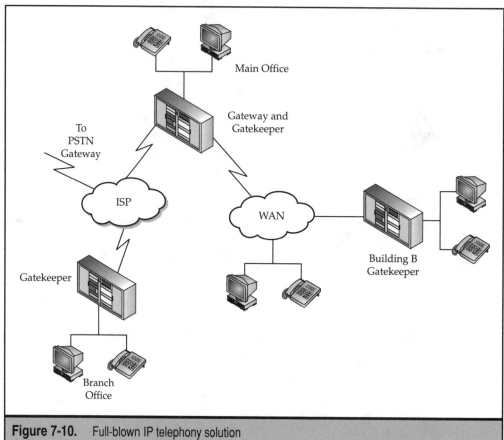

Figure 7-10. Full-blown IP telephony solution

For instance, if Keith in Custodial Services wants to call Pat in Accounting, he picks up the IP phone and they communicate across the LAN using an IP connection. However, if Keith needs to order a drum of floor wax, his call goes through the network using an IP connection, then is linked to a gateway. The *gateway* or *clearing house* is a device that links VoIP calls to the public phone network.

Last, there are servers that support IP telephony. These servers provide both basic call setup functions as well as the advanced features users have come to expect from traditional PBXs, such as voice mail, hold, and call forwarding. Let's take a closer look at IP phones, gateways, and servers.

IP Telephones   At its simplest, you can set up an IP telephone by plugging a speaker and a microphone into the PC. However, people come to expect their telephones to look and feel like telephones. As we mentioned earlier, there are hardware and software IP phones. That "telephone feel" can be accomplished with a telephone that speaks IP and can be plugged directly into a switch (a hardware phone). Alternatively, users can simply plug a specially designed handset into their PC to take advantage of the software solution.

Each of these phones offers the same sorts of features that a telephone connected to a PBX offers. Naturally, there are disadvantages to these solutions. Hardware IP phones will need a jack on the switch (watch out, you can run out of connections fast), and they also need their own power supply.

These pitfalls can be avoided by using a software-based IP telephone. This can be done by either plugging a telephone into a serial or USB port or plugging a plain old desktop analog telephone into a PC card or external adapter.

If you decide to use a software-based IP telephone, you must also get client software that can support IP telephony. The software can either be a stand-alone product, standards-based (make sure you buy the one that matches your phone's standards), or it can be part of a package, like Microsoft's NetMeeting.

There are three issues you should keep in mind when selecting an IP telephone:

▼ When considering hardware IP telephones, make sure that the phone won't limit your ability to integrate with the desktop environment.

■ Make sure that the phones support appropriate codec and signaling standards.

▲ Make sure that the phone and your network will be able to share QoS priorities.

Gateways   Gateways serve as interfaces between PSTN telephone calls and IP telephony. PSTN consists of two separate networks—one for transporting the voice conversations and one for transporting signaling information (using the SS7 protocol).

Let's pause for a moment to consider some of the basics of the public telephone system that will be important to know for the sake of understanding gateway functionality:

▼ **Central office**   The *central office* is where local phone lines first connect into the public network.

■ **Central office switch**   This is the local switch in the central office.

▲ **Tandem switch**   Switches of this kind interconnect between central office switches in a local area network.

A central office switch connects both voice and SS7 signaling trunks, and SS7 connects to signal transfer points (STPs). STPs are the message switches that route SS7 signaling information. These two trunks are kept separate to aid in the setup and teardown of voice calls, as well as to streamline the network during periods of peak usage. SS7 is also necessary for the provisioning of 800 and 888 numbers and makes such perks as call forwarding, caller ID, and last-call return possible.

Using SS7 is not necessary for an IP telephony–to–PSTN gateway connection, as long as there is in-band signaling on voice trunks. But this provides only for a telephone call from an IP telephony device to a telephone on the PSTN network. If additional functionality (call forwarding and the like) is desired, another gateway is needed: the SS7–to–IP telephony gateway.

Servers   A basic IP telephone call occurs when one IP telephone connects to another. However, a number of "behind the scenes" functions must be managed, including such features as call routing and billing. These functions cannot be performed by either of the end users; rather, they must be performed by an IP telephony server (or several servers, depending on the size of the network). Under the H.323 protocol, this set of functions is performed by a gatekeeper. Gatekeepers may also include support for such extras as voice messaging and voice conferencing in the same IP telephony server.

Using Optics

This discussion about VoIP, PSTNs, and SS7 may be all nice and well, but how, exactly, is fiber optics involved? The answer lies in the connections between devices. First, let's take a closer look at the relationships between devices and protocols.

NOTE: Fiber isn't used on a large scale only between devices like COs and PBXs. FDDI can be brought to the desktop to ensure end-to-end fiber connectivity if that is so desired.

In the future, the CO switch is likely to be a traditional circuit switch. However, the switch is likely to be joined by another router whose sole duty is to handle IP packets. Even though we are talking about VoIP here, the IP packets could contain any kind of information, including data or even video. The data packets would be sent to and from the Internet or internetwork, while voice packets will be sent to the PSTN. This process is shown in Figure 7-11.

VoIP is not going to use SS7—there's simply no reason for it. IP packets are not the same as SS7 packets, and it is unnecessary to make IP mimic SS7. SS7 is optimized for the public telephone network, which is 64 Kbps voice. At this point in VoIP's development, there doesn't seem to be any industry standard for IP phone calls. However, there are two protocols that are becoming *de facto* standards: H.323 and SIP.

The most difficult step involves making sure that VoIP users will be able to place and receive calls from the PSTN by translating H.323/SIP packets to and from SS7. This PSTN/IP blend must allow for the cohabitation of CO circuit switches and voice-enabled routers. A gateway exists that allows a standardized conversion of these packets to GR-303.

NOTE: Directory telephone numbers (411) and their IP addresses will be handled by extensions to the domain name system (DNS), then coupled with the Lightweight Directory Access Protocol (LDAP).

As shown in Figure 7-11, packet voice can be sent over an IP connection or the public telephone network. Packet voice can be sent to the CO through the GR-303 gateway or isolated and sent through the voice-enabled router. Once in the voice-enabled router, the data is sent to a "softswitch" that translates between H.323/SIP and SS7. Next, the data is sent on to the Internet and the voice traffic is sent to the PSTN.

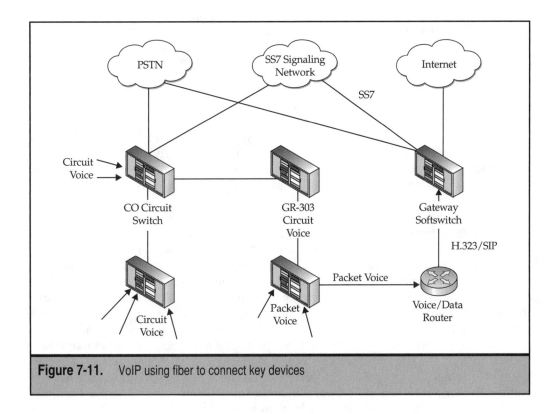

Figure 7-11. VoIP using fiber to connect key devices

You'll notice that voice traffic has two ways to get to the PSTN. Which is selected depends on how far the service provider is along the circuit voice–to–packet voice migration path.

Where optical networking and DWDM become involved is the connectivity between the CO switches and the gateway softswitch, PSTN, and SS7 networks. In Figure 7-11, there are five links to the various networks. In most configurations, these will be separate links. These links are where fiber optics can be used. Those links are:

▼ CO to PSTN voice

■ CO to SS7 signals

■ Softswitch to PSTN voice

■ Softswitch to SS7 signals

▲ Softswitch to Internet voice/data

A DWDM optical network requires that all the connectivity be mapped to a single DWDM ring. As the circuit handles less and less of the voice traffic using legacy techniques, and the VoIP portion of the network handles more and more of the network's resources, the speed of each wavelength can be adjusted for an easy transition. It is unnecessary to be concerned about the relative speed and capacity of the infrastructure between two COs.

STORAGE AREA NETWORKS

In the last section, we talked about how the convergence of voice and data into a single circuit is a goal for many organizations' internetworks. But as more and more data and traffic cross the network, there will be a larger demand for storage. Unfortunately, conventional means of data storage—disk arrays and tape backups connected to the server—aren't enough to keep up with the challenge.

Further, with the moniker "Information Age" comes the burden of storing all that information. And it wouldn't be so bad if the term "information" were limited to pages of the printed word, punctuated with the occasional photograph. But in recent years, "information" has evolved to mean rich multimedia content, mixing both graphics and sound.

As wonderful as multimedia is, the storage requirements of these files are taking their toll. Conventional network storage gear is finding itself incapable of maintaining all this information. And if that wasn't enough, transferring large amounts of data creates its own problems as network bandwidth is continually challenged with other loads.

Having endured almost two decades, the parallel Small Computer System Interface (SCSI) bus that has facilitated server-storage connectivity for LAN servers is imposing limits on network storage. Adding to the limitations of SCSI is the traditional use of LAN connections for server storage backup, which takes away from usable client bandwidth.

One solution to the storage dearth is implementing a *storage area network (SAN)*. SANs are networks that are designed, built, and maintained to store and transmit data. The key to moving all that data to and from a SAN is using fiber. In this section, we'll talk about SANs in general terms, then how you can design a SAN for your own internetworking needs.

Storage Needs

With the popularity of the Internet and the massive increase in e-commerce, organizations are scrambling for a means to store vast amounts of data. A popular way to maintain terabytes of information uses SANs, which interconnect storage devices with Fibre Channel hubs and switches, even though data storage is cheap—you can add a 60GB hard drive for a couple hundred dollars.

However, this is a reactive response to storage shortages. By creating a patchwork of hard drives, you cause your internetwork's overhead to escalate and you slowly lose control. SANs, on the other hand, allow you to manage all your storage needs in a proactive manner while maintaining the high availability that you need. Figure 7-12 shows an example of how a LAN and a SAN work together.

As organizations and their computing needs grow, so will their reliance on data storage. For instance, as more and more companies add server farms to manage their internal

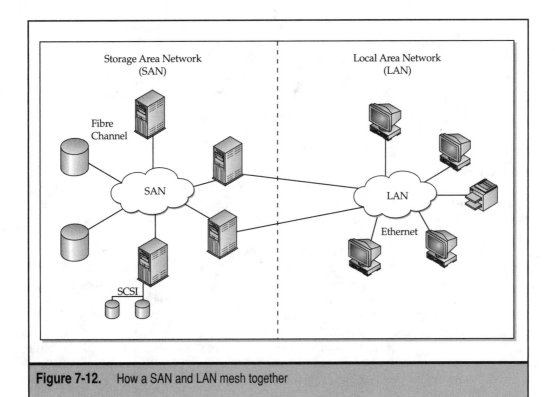

Figure 7-12.   How a SAN and LAN mesh together

and external affairs, the internetwork must become that much more reliable. To ensure high availability, servers sharing storage pools in a SAN can fail over with no hiccup in service. Further, because fiber optics is the backbone of SANs, disaster recovery is pared from several hours to a few minutes.

By combining LAN networking models with the core building blocks of server performance and mass storage capacity, SANs eliminate the bandwidth bottlenecks and scalability limitations imposed by previous SCSI bus–based architectures. In addition to the fundamental connectivity benefits of SAN, the new capabilities, facilitated by its networking approach, enhance its value as a long-term infrastructure. These capabilities, which include clustering, topological flexibility, fault tolerance, high availability, and remote management, further elevate a SAN's ability to address the growing challenges of data-intensive, mission-critical applications.

There are three primary components of a storage area network:

▼   **Interface**   The *interface* is what allows storage to be external from the server and allows server clustering. SCSI and Fibre Channel are common SAN interfaces.

- ■ **Interconnect** The *interconnect* is the mechanism these multiple devices use to exchange data. Devices such as hubs, routers, gateways, and switches are used to link various interfaces to SAN fabrics.

- ▲ **Fabric** This is the platform (the combination of network protocol and network topology) based on switched SCSI, switched fiber, and so forth. The use of gateways allows the SAN to be extended across WANs.

Fibre Channel

Fibre Channel is an industry-standard, high-speed serial interface for connecting PCs and storage systems. Fibre Channel provides attachment of servers and storage systems across distances up to 10 km (which is about 400 times farther than parallel SCSI interfaces). This allows the storage facilities to be located on another floor, in another building, or six miles away.

Fibre Channel carries five times more bandwidth than SCSI (100 Mbps versus 20 Mbps). Further, Fibre Channel supports multiple standard protocols (like TCP/IP and SCSI) concurrently over the same physical cable. This is useful because it simplifies cabling and keeps down infrastructure costs. Because Fibre Channel allows standard SCSI packets to be transported across the fiber optic lines, existing SCSI devices can be maintained and used alongside the Fibre Channel devices.

For the sake of reliability through redundancy, Fibre Channel SANs should be built around hubs and switches. This ensures that no single point of failure exists and performance bottlenecks are ameliorated. This should sound familiar, because it is a key consideration when designing a LAN.

Going the Distance

SCSI storage solutions had to be located next to the server. This proved to be troublesome, especially if space in a server room was at a premium. Because Fibre Channel allows for long-distance location between servers and storage devices, the two pieces of equipment can be up to 10 km apart.

In practice, however, the ability for data to travel long distances can be useful if a storage center was constructed to maintain all the data for several departments. Further, several servers located in one campus could send their data to a central storage facility in a separate building. This trait allows for the creation of modular and scalable storage pools.

Increased Connectivity

Using Fibre Channel also simplifies the connectivity of multiple systems accessing a shared storage device by overcoming the limitations of parallel SCSI, including distance and number of devices per bus. Fibre Channel supports eight times more devices per loop than parallel SCSI. In practice, however, it may not be realistic to put so many devices on a single loop. However, the capability now exists for large numbers of servers to access storage devices like RAID arrays or tape libraries.

NOTE: RAID (Redundant Array of Inexpensive Disks) is a fault-tolerant system that protects data through a series of redundant disk drives.

Designing and Building a SAN

When it comes down to designing and building a SAN, it's necessary to consider several important factors before plugging fiber into routers. You should consider such issues as what kind of applications you'll be using, the best design for the backbone, how you'll configure your topology, and what mechanisms you'll use to manage your SAN. Let's take a closer look at each of these issues.

Application Needs

When developing and designing a SAN, the first step is to figure out which applications will be served. No matter if you're designing a common data pool for a bank of Web servers, a high-performance data-streaming network, or any other system, you must pay special attention to the SAN infrastructure. You have to take into consideration such issues as port densities, distance and bandwidth requirements, and segmentation. These are all variables that are affected by the application.

NOTE: In a mixed environment, it's important to evaluate the platforms that will compose the SAN. Hardware and software support for SANs varies depending on which platforms you use. Once you have addressed these fundamental questions, you can begin constructing the SAN.

A SAN's construction is similar to a typical Ethernet infrastructure. A SAN comprises a few basic components: the Fibre Channel disk storage and tape libraries, fiber hubs and switches, host bus adapters (HBAs), and some form of SAN management.

Backbone

As you design your SAN, a critical architectural hardware decision is whether to use an arbitrated loop or switched fabric.

▼ **Arbitrated loop**   Shares bandwidth and employs round-robin data forwarding. At one time, it was the only choice for SAN backbones.

▲ **Switched fabric**   Dedicates full bandwidth on each port and allows simultaneous data transfers to a single node.

Your choice will be decided largely by your scaling and performance needs. If you have modest storage needs, a simple hub should be enough to get the job done. On the other end of the spectrum, larger storage environments almost demand fiber switches.

In small groups, a good foundation is a Fibre Channel hub in an arbitrated-loop configuration. Hubs are well suited for this environment because they provide a high level of interoperability for a reasonably low price. Hubs support an aggregate bandwidth of 100 megabytes per second. Hubs can support up to 127 devices, but for optimal results, you should limit the number to about 30 devices. Further, because the per-port costs of a switch are higher than those of a hub, a hub is best to fan out the core switch ports to the connecting servers.

One of the main reasons hubs are limited in their scalability is because of the way devices are added into the loop. In order to recognize other devices in the loop, each loop must perform a *loop initialization sequencer (LIP)* when it is first attached to the network. When this action is performed, the loop is suspended while the entire membership on the loop acquires or verifies the port addresses and is assigned an *arbitrated loop physical address.* Although the recognition process is very fast, time-sensitive traffic (like VoIP or data backups) can be negatively affected by these performance speed bumps.

On the other hand, hubs are useful because they are inexpensive, are easy to configure, and interoperate well with other hubs and other vendors' products.

Fiber

If SANs are so fantastic, why aren't they everywhere? The main factor that has brought SANs into play as a viable technology is the use of switched fiber.

Fiber switches support 100 Mbps full duplex on all ports. Unlike hubs, which as we mentioned earlier require an LIP, a fiber switch requires nodes connected to its ports to perform a *fabric logon.* The switch is the only device that sees this logon, and this fact allows devices to enter and exit the fabric without providing an interruption to the remaining devices.

Devices on an arbitrated-loop hub, which is cascaded off a switch, are not fundamentally compatible with other devices on the fabric. Unlike in a switched LAN environment, devices in a switched SAN environment must perform a fabric logon to communicate with other devices. However, those devices that are not built with fabric support usually cannot operate over fabric because they don't perform a fabric logon. Rather, they use a LIP.

Configuration

Just as in a LAN, there are several ways to configure switches, providing different levels of performance and redundancy. In a SAN, the basic configuration design is the tree-type model. In this scheme, switches cascade off one another and fan out throughout the SAN, shown in Figure 7-13.

The main problem with this model is its scalability constraints, due to the latency inherent with the single-port interface. This also limits bandwidth and is not ideal, because it can be pinpointed for a single point of failure. This type of design is best as an alternative to fiber hubs for a SAN that has just a single-tier cascade.

For larger, more intricate SANs, the best choice for both high availability and performance is the mesh model. The mesh makes a large network of switches: each switch is connected to every other switch, thereby eliminating the opportunity for a single point of failure. The mesh also reduces bottlenecks and latency. The mesh model is illustrated in Figure 7-14.

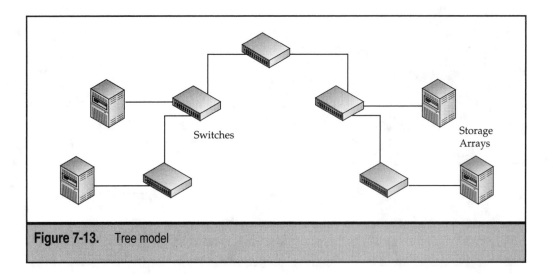

Figure 7-13.   Tree model

But a mesh isn't perfect. The biggest problem is that meshes don't scale very efficiently. As you can tell, as more switches are added, the number of ports required to connect to all the available switches will use up most of the ports on each of the switches. But
given that limitation, the mesh's strength is a good choice for midsize SANs with five or
fewer switches requiring a maximum guaranteed uptime and optimal performance.

Scalability and redundancy are brought together in the next model, as shown in
Figure 7-15. To ensure a redundant data path, each switch is connected to two other
switches. Each switch has two different paths through the SAN, thereby eliminating a
single point of failure. This configuration is an ideal solution for enterprise-class SANs.

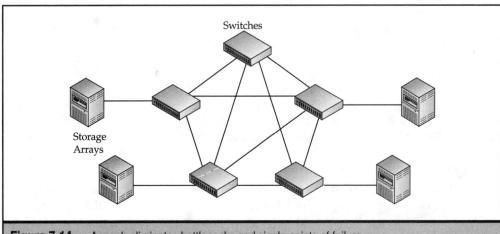

Figure 7-14.   A mesh eliminates bottlenecks and single points of failure

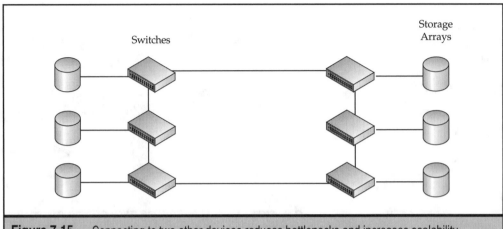

Figure 7-15. Connecting to two other devices reduces bottlenecks and increases scalability

Management

For a SAN to work at its peak, it must use centrally managed devices. SAN management is mainly a security device that ensures servers see only the intended devices and storage arrays, reducing the chance for data corruption. There are two basic ways to manage your SAN's hardware: port-level zoning and logical unit (LUN)–level zoning.

▼ **Port-level zoning**   Port zoning partitions devices by which ports they are using on the hub or switch. Attached nodes won't be able to communicate unless individual ports are shared in a common zone.

▲ **LUN-level zoning**   This is similar to port-level zoning, but it increases the granularity, thereby making it possible to partition nodes by their device ID. LUN-level zoning gives you more flexibility when it comes to communicating with devices on the edge of a SAN.

Data storage can be an ever-changing environment. Storage needs may differ drastically from one day to the next. Happily, however, managing a SAN is helpful because it gives you the ability to dynamically allocate storage to the different pools, without having to reboot the servers in your storage cluster. Additionally, you can add more storage to your SAN and reallocate it as you wish, again with no interruption.

Storage Options

When it comes down to deciding what you'll use as the storage component of your SAN, there isn't an abundance of options. An easy option, especially if you already have SCSI RAID or disk shelves, is to buy an external SCSI-to-fiber bridge. A bridge will allow you to connect almost any SCSI device to your SAN. The downside of this is that you waste all the speed that a natively attached fiber device would deliver. Bridges push between 15 Mbps and 40 Mbps.

This leads to the second option: native fiber-attached storage. Fibre Channel storage is becoming more and more popular, and—as is the case with technology—the price is coming down. Fiber storage can push 100 Mbps (200 Mbps full duplex). But even though prices are coming down, they aren't nearly as inexpensive as a SCSI RAID solution. Costwise, the hard drives are on par with SCSI drives. It's the external Fibre Channel RAID controllers, at anywhere from $US15,000 to $US50,000, that jack up the price.

Backup

Fiber optic backups are just the thing for administrators who manage networks with co-pious amounts of data. Not only can they off-load backups from the network, but they can also share a single library among multiple servers scattered throughout several different departments. Further, resources can be allocated to the departments that have the greatest backup needs. In addition to drives, tape libraries can use SCSI-to-fiber bridges. Though tape libraries don't come close to the speed of drives and may seem a waste of fiber resources, many organizations implement tape libraries into their SANs because backups are easier to perform.

Routers are just starting to come into their own in the world of SANs. Routers in a SAN are intelligent devices that can execute a direct disk-to-tape backup without the middleman of the server processing the information first. As you can imagine, backing up information without the server not only releases the server to perform other tasks, but it reduces backup times by removing any bottlenecks that might occur as the data filters through the server. Further, routers have the technology integrated with them to handle error recovery, as well as the capability to report problems to the backup software.

FIBERLESS OPTICS

Though vital to the bandwidth needs of cities, the discussion about building fiber optic meshes in metropolitan areas may be a moot point in a few years. As fast and as much capacity as fiber optic networks provide, they still suffer the same physical limitations that conventional networks face—there is still a physical medium connecting two devices.

Wireless networking devices are proving to be a solution for conventional networks, but what about optical networking? Can the impressive speeds of fiber be met without the fiber?

Some vendors, like Terabeam of Seattle, Washington, think so. Terabeam squashes the Last Mile problem by using free space optics to deliver IP traffic at up to gigabit per second rates—all without being tethered by a strand of optical fiber.

NOTE: Terabeam isn't the only company developing fiberless optic solutions, though it is the leader in the field. Other companies, including AirFiber of San Diego, California, and TellAire of Dallas, Texas, also have technology that eliminates fiber and carries roughly the same amount of data as Terabeam.

In this section, we discuss fiberless optics: how they work and why they may be the future of MANs and access networks.

Basics

The only difference between fiber and fiberless optics is that instead of using thin glass fibers as the conduit for transmitting data, fiberless uses air. As Figure 7-16 shows, lasers are fired between office buildings or over places where fiber is difficult to lay down, such as rivers.

In the past, transmitting a laser-based digital data signal from point to point was deemed inefficient. However, fiberless optics resolves this by using what Terabeam calls a "point-to-multipoint" implementation. Terabeam's shared hub system allows the service to be carried throughout a city from a single origin point. Point-to-multipoint achieves the economies of scale needed to make the solution practical.

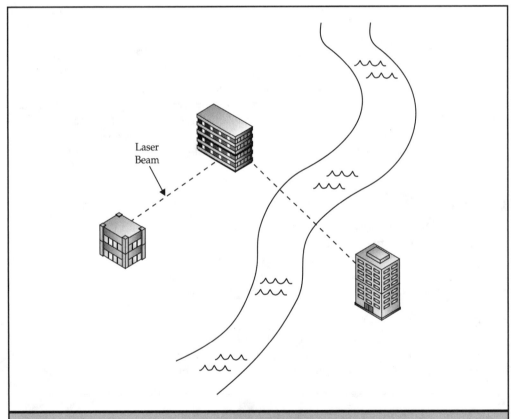

Figure 7-16.   Fiberless optics connect buildings with high-speed links, but without fiber

Other fixed wireless solutions, such as microwave, require licensing a band of the spectrum for a distribution service and erecting a 150-foot antenna on the roof—both of which are extremely expensive. Deploying laser optics takes a fraction of the time and the cost.

Fiberless optics offers speeds of (at the low end) 5 Mbps, which is equivalent to 3 T-1 lines, up to 1 Gbps, enough to transmit 100 high-definition television channels simultaneously.

No Cables, no Red Tape

By using lasers in the 1550 nm frequency spectrum, the technology allows for networking speed, without having to deal with a mess of bureaucratic red tape that has ensnarled traditional wireless, cellular, and fiber networks.

Terabeam transmits data over a spectrum that is free of charge and requires no licensing from the Federal Communications Commission. This avoids the expense of having to bid on a spectrum license. Further, Terabeam works through window glass, so there is no need to install antennae on a roof or dig up First Avenue to bury fiber. The price for such a system is roughly equal to that of a T-1 connection.

Terabeam's first commercial network was started in February 2001 in Seattle. In March of the same year, they added Denver to their list of operational sites and expect more cities to be added in the months to come.

A Network Without Wires

So how, exactly, does a fiberless optic network operate? The system involves unique hardware and employs a mesh of laser beams fired from site to site, forming the network. On the organization's end, this configuration connects with a LAN through a normal Ethernet connection. Let's take a closer look at the components and the design of such a network.

Networking

The fiberless optical network starts inside a window in an office building. This is where the transceiver—Terabeam calls theirs a *holographic photon collector*—sits. The transceiver collector is about five feet tall and has a dish at the top that sends and receives IP traffic. It is plugged into an Ethernet connection, which leads to the organization's LAN.

Next, the laser beam is projected out of the transceiver. The light beam is able to penetrate tinted glass and will even work if a curtain is closed or if a bird flies through the beam. The laser's destination is a hub site that is usually located in a city's POP, where many large carriers converge. The hub site is set up similarly to the client site. At the hub, a transceiver is located in the window of the POP. Those wavelengths are transmitted to the fiber optic connections of the telecommunications carrier over a conventional wired connection.

Weather Worries

Depending on the demand, the weather, and the geography, the number of hub sites will differ from city to city. Wireless optic signals are not affected very much by rain (like wireless and cellular signals) or snow, but fog can be problematic because it diffuses the laser light.

NOTE: Lasers running at 1550 are less affected by weather than either 1310 or 850 nm optics.

For example, Denver needs three hub sites, but Seattle requires five times as many hubs. Shortening the distance between hubs and clients can ameliorate the problem.

With hardwired connections comes a sense of security and reliability. Just seeing the cable provides a reassuring sense that the network is connected and not susceptible to problems. However, fiberless optics vendors claim that their networks are between 99.99 percent and 99.999 percent reliable. In one test, AirFiber fired a laser through a heavy rainstorm and found a signal loss of 45 decibels per kilometer (dB/km). Transmissions would not be totally blocked, however, unless losses reached 200 dB/km. Another test conducted by Washington's Infrared Communication Systems in an undetermined southwestern United States city measured 99.9879 percent reliability over the course of a month. That month included five days of heavy rain and two thunderstorms. The source of the loss, it was determined, had nothing to do with the weather conditions or the distance between transceivers. Rather, the loss was blamed on a dirty lens, because the transceiver was placed too close to an exhaust vent.

NOTE: Vendors are able to compensate for environmental factors inside the building by installing heating and cooling units to manage condensation, along with a solar shield to protect the lens from sunlight. They also use Gortex-patched holes to maintain a consistent level of humidity inside the unit.

Given clear weather conditions, the range for a fiberless optical network is about 10 miles between nodes. This limit is due not to the limitations of the laser, but rather to the curvature of the Earth. Optimally speaking, however, the ideal range for fiberless optics is about 200 meters between transceivers in foggy cities (like Seattle or London) or 450 meters in clear cities (like Rio de Janeiro or Tokyo).

Another concern about fiberless optics is the potential for deleterious effects to humans or birds that happen to get in front of the beam. The laser light used in these technologies is infrared and invisible to the naked eye, however, and is not like microwaves that could cook a human being or a bird.

NOTE: There are both U.S. and international safety standards for power limits for these lasers. Discussions are in progress to converge these standards to just one. While the wavelengths used are indeed invisible to the naked eye, it should never be implied there is no risk of eye damage should you be in the direct line of fire from these lasers.

Cost

Like so many other things in life and in networking, the bottom line is usually price. Whichever technology provides good service but comes in with the lowest price tag is likely to win in a bidding war. Fiberless vendors say that their solutions are much more cost efficient than having to install a conventional optical network.

According to numbers by AirFiber, a fiber optic network would cost between $US50,000 and $US200,000 per building. Conversely, a fiberless optics solution would cost $US20,000 per building. A mesh system in the city of Boston connecting 200 buildings would cost about $US4 million using a fiberless optics system and between $US10 million and $US40 million for a fiber deployment.

One of the main cost savings for fiberless optics comes from spectrum savings. Because these lasers operate in the terahertz range, they are not subject to FCC licensing.

NOTE: Lasers in the terahertz range are not subject to licensing, because they do not create interference with other devices.

Because the cost of fiber is upward of $US150,000 and because it takes a year to connect a building with fiber, vendors are looking to Europe and Asia as a popular place for fiberless technology. Because local authorities are less likely than their American counterparts to allow competitive bidders to tear up congested streets, fiberless optics provides a high-speed solution for these environments.

If fiberless optics is such a fantastic technology, why aren't there a mesh of laser beams in every city in the developed world? The main reason is that it is such an emerging technology. Vendors are small start-ups (though Terabeam is boasting $US526 million in funding, including a $US450 million investment by Lucent) with small sales and marketing departments. But the word is getting out. Such organizations using fiberless optics include:

▼ Seattle's Avenue A

■ New York's Riker's Island Prison

▲ Hawaii's Servco Pacific

As bandwidth demands increase and as organizations push their own networks to meet those demands, there will be more and more call for fiber optics. The applications that will serve those needs are in varying forms of development. Mostly, the process is evolutionary. As the demand changes, so will the specifics of the application.

PART III

Practical Optical Networking

CHAPTER 8

Building Optical Networks

Building an optical network requires understanding its own set of disciplines, techniques, and technologies. It makes little sense to go ahead and start blindly running fiber optic cable through the ceiling plenum unless you understand the big picture on fiber optic network construction.

In this chapter, we talk about building optical networks, construction tips that will help in a deployment, and how you can leverage your existing network technology by fitting fiber optics into it.

First, we will discuss some construction tips that are important to any network—electrical or optical. Then, we will talk about what you should do to understand your existing network. By understanding what you have, you will be better able to know what you need to improve and where that enhancement needs to take place. Next, we'll move on to a discussion of technologies that are important to optical networking. By understanding these technologies, you will be better able to build a network from scratch or—as is most likely—be able to adapt an existing infrastructure with a minimum of headache. Finally, we'll talk about specific designs and ways fiber optics is used in local area networks (LANs), metropolitan area networks (MANs), wide area networks (WANs), service provider networks, and backbone networks.

DESIGN BASICS

Networks are largely geographical by nature, so most design practices have to do with matching topology to needs. The layout of an internetwork largely dictates how it will perform and how well it can scale. In networking, *scale*, or *scalability*, means how much an internetwork can grow without having to change the basic shape of its topology (that is, without having to replace or excessively reconfigure existing infrastructure).

This section examines how a network's topology affects the overall network, methods you can use to develop a stronger network topology, and some of the equipment that you would use in an optical network.

The Three-Layer Hierarchical Design Model

Hierarchical topologies are inherently better than flat ones for a number of reasons, the main one being that hierarchy restricts traffic to its local area. The rule of thumb designers use is that broadcast traffic (that is, traffic sent to every node on a network) should not exceed 20 percent of the packets going over each link—the implication being that segmentation will naturally boost throughput by isolating traffic to its most likely users.

A flat topology—one in which each device does more or less the same job—increases the number of neighbors with which an individual device must communicate. This increases somewhat the amount of payload traffic the device is likely to carry and greatly increases overhead traffic. For example, each time a router receives a broadcast message, its CPU is interrupted. For many small internetworks, a flat topology is sufficient, and the added expense and complexity that hierarchy requires isn't warranted. But it doesn't take many LAN segments to hurt an internetwork's performance and reliability, with devices and hosts bogged down in unnecessary traffic.

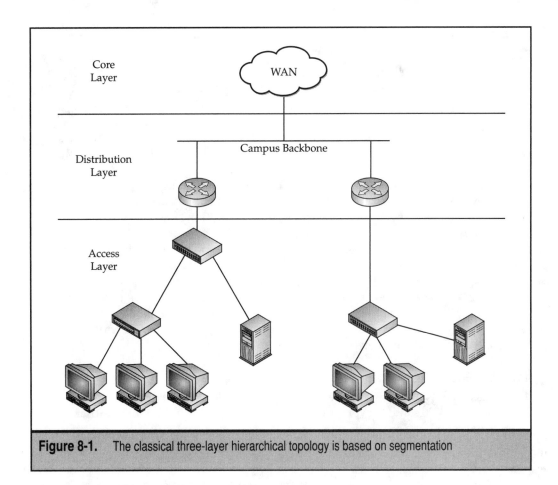

Figure 8-1. The classical three-layer hierarchical topology is based on segmentation

This is why the industry adheres to a classical hierarchical design model. The model has three layers: the access, distribution, and core layers. This separates local traffic from high-volume traffic passing between LAN segments and areas, and lets network devices at each layer concentrate on doing their specific job. The hierarchical model is depicted in Figure 8-1.

Hierarchy is made possible by segmentation—the practice of dividing hosts into smaller LAN segments. Twenty years ago, most LAN segments were actual cable spans running through walls and ceiling plenums; today, most are formed by hubs and access switches. Segmentation and hierarchical topology yield several benefits:

▼ **Performance**   Traffic is isolated to source areas, thereby narrowing Ethernet packet collision domains and speeding throughput. (We'll talk about Ethernet and collisions in more detail later in this chapter.)

■ **Reliability**   Most faults are isolated to the segment from which the problem originated.

- ■ **Simplicity** By separating dissimilar areas, network elements can be replicated as needed throughout the internetwork.

- ■ **Scalability** Modular design elements can be added as the internetwork grows over time, with minimal disruption of existing networks.

- ▲ **Security** Access can be controlled at well-defined junctures between the layers.

Internetworks naturally tend toward a two-level hierarchy. Hubs and switches connect host devices into LAN segments, and the backbone connects the segments into a local network, whether within a floor, a building, an office campus, or even a metropolitan area. This is a relatively flat topology in the sense that, even though collision domains are limited, excessive broadcast traffic still chews into available bandwidth. This makes the distribution layer the key. By isolating traffic, the distribution layer also isolates problems and complexity.

Hierarchy also helps reduce costs. By dividing hosts and traffic, variations are limited to fewer LAN segments, or even a single segment. Variations include such things as desktop protocols (IP, Ethernet), traffic volumes (workgroup versus backbone), and traffic type (big graphical files, e-mail, HTTP). Hierarchy allows the network designer to tune the configuration for the particular job at hand. Adjustments are made in the model of network device purchased and in how it is configured in terms of memory, modules, software, and config file parameter settings.

The Access Layer

The access layer is made up mostly of hubs and switches, which serve to segment host devices such as PCs and servers into many LAN segments made up of either shared or switched bandwidth. This is where media access control (MAC)–layer filtering can take place.

NOTE: The MAC layer is the protocol that controls access to the physical transmission medium on a LAN, be it fiber or copper. The MAC layer is built into the network adapter. Common MAC layer standards are the Carrier Sense Multiple Access with Collision Detection (CSMA/CD) architecture used in Ethernet and the token passing methods used in Token Ring and Fiber Distributed Data Interface (FDDI). The MAC layer is synonymous with the data-link layer in the OSI model.

If an internetwork has remote sites, such as branch offices or home offices, the access layer would also include access servers. WANs must use some type of long-distance transmission medium. There is a wide selection of media now, such as SONET rings, T1 or T3 lines, and Frame Relay public digital networks. Dial-in remote users employ analog modem lines and, in certain areas, higher-bandwidth technologies such as Digital Subscriber Line (DSL) and Integrated Services Digital Network (ISDN). Figure 8-2 shows access-layer functionality.

In large internetworks, the access layer can include routers. These internal routers serve mostly to isolate overhead, control traffic, and enhance internal security. The access

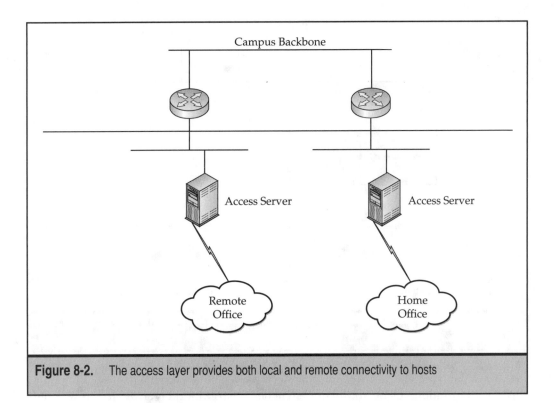

Figure 8-2.   The access layer provides both local and remote connectivity to hosts

layer encompasses a mix of technologies in most internetworks. Dial-on-demand routing (DDR) has become popular for remote connections because it keeps a link inactive except when traffic needs to be sent, thereby reducing telecommunication costs.

The Distribution Layer

The distribution layer is made up mostly of routers. They're used to separate low-speed local traffic from the high-speed backbone. Traffic at the access layer tends to be bandwidth-intensive because that's where most LAN and host addresses reside. Network overhead protocol traffic for discovery protocols, routing protocols, and other network control systems is heavier at the access layer.

Because routers are intelligent enough to read network addresses and examine packets, they also improve performance by sending traffic as directly as possible to its destination. For example, distribution-layer routers define broadcast and multicast domains across LAN segments. Domains are, by default, limited to LAN segments; routers can extend domains across segments as the hierarchy design dictates. Figure 8-3 depicts distribution-layer functionality.

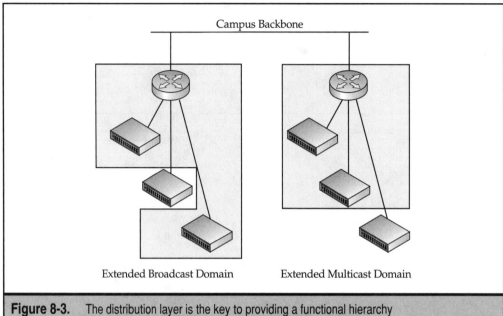

Figure 8-3. The distribution layer is the key to providing a functional hierarchy

In configurations using multilayer switches, distribution-layer devices route messages between VLANs. (VLANs behave like traditional LANs, even though the devices are on different LAN segments.) *Multilayer switching* is a relatively new technology in which packets are filtered and forwarded according to both MAC and network addresses. Cisco's Catalyst 6000 family of switches includes examples of multilayer switches with optical capabilities, incorporating route switch modules (RSMs) in addition to those with typical switch electronics.

Most value-added services are provided by devices at the distribution layer. Address translation takes place at this layer, usually on a gateway router or a firewall (itself a type of router). Address aggregation also takes place here, as well as area aggregation if the internetwork is running OSPF routing domains. Other services are also performed on distribution-layer routers, including: translation between protocols such as IPX and IP; encryption for VPN tunneling (that is, providing a secure tunnel between two nodes); and traffic-based security using access lists and context-based firewall algorithms.

The Core Layer

The core layer is the backbone layer. In large internetworks, the core incorporates multiple backbones, from campus backbone LANs up through regional ones. Sometimes special backbone LANs are configured to handle a specific protocol or particularly sensitive traffic. Most backbones exist to connect LAN segments, usually those within a particular building or office campus. Figure 8-4 depicts how the core layer might look in a typical large enterprise internetwork.

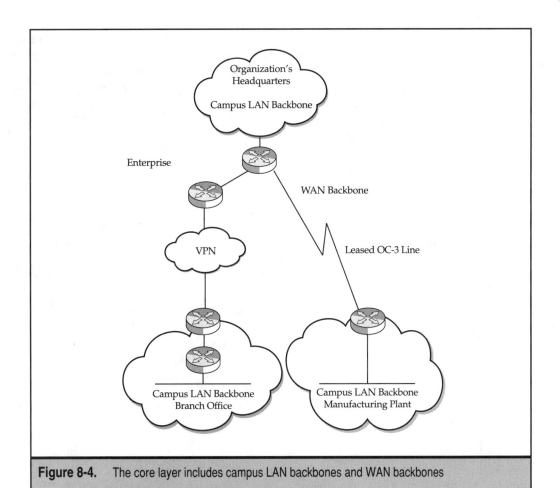

Figure 8-4.   The core layer includes campus LAN backbones and WAN backbones

To run fast, a backbone LAN should be configured to experience a minimum of interruptions. The goal is to have as many backbone device CPU cycles as possible spent transferring packets among segments. The distribution layer makes this possible, by connecting workgroup LAN segments and providing value-added routing services. A minimum of packet manipulation should occur at this level. This is why most newer backbones are switched LANs. The need for address interpretation at the core is minimized by the processing already performed by distribution-layer routers, so why not use switching technology to move data over the backbone much faster?

ATM (Asynchronous Transfer Mode) and Gigabit Ethernet are doing battle to become the switched backbone technology of choice. ATM has an edge for multimedia applications because it uses fixed-sized cells and supports QoS instead of Ethernet's variable-length packets. The obvious advantage of Gigabit Ethernet switched backbones is easier compatibility with the millions of Ethernet LANs already installed throughout the world.

ATM is an international cell relay standard for service types such as video, voice, and data. The fixed-length 53-byte cells speed data transfer by allowing processing to occur in hardware. Although ATM products exist to take data all the way to the desktop, the technology is optimized to work with high-speed transmission media such as OC-48 (2.5 gigabits per second [Gbps]), T3 (45 megabits per second [Mbps]), and T3's European counterpart, E3 (34 Mbps).

Design Methods

Over the years, the networking industry has developed a set of concepts and best practices for use in internetwork design. Most internetworks are works in progress; very few are designed from a clean sheet of paper. As internetwork topologies evolve through time and circumstance, it becomes difficult to maintain a rigorous hierarchical network design—especially in large enterprises with distributed management structures, or in shops that have high personnel turnover in their network teams.

Redundancy and Load Balancing

Redundancy is the practice of configuring backup equipment. This is done to provide fault tolerance, where traffic will shift to the backup device if the primary unit fails, a process called *failover*. For example, most high-speed backbones have dual-configured switches at each end in case the primary switch goes down. Another common safeguard is to have redundant power supplies within a device, so that if one fails, the device keeps running.

Because redundant configurations are expensive, fault-tolerant configurations are usually limited to critical devices. Redundancy is most commonly configured into backbone devices and firewalls, where device failure would have the broadest effect on the overall network.

Load balancing is a configuration technique that shifts traffic to an alternative link if a certain threshold is exceeded on the primary link. Load balancing can be achieved through various means, such as tuning routing metrics in router config files within routing protocol domains.

Load balancing is similar to redundancy in that an event causes traffic to shift directions, and alternative equipment must be present in the configuration. But in load balancing, the alternative equipment isn't necessarily *redundant* equipment that operates only in the event of failure.

Topology Meshing

A good design will incorporate a meshed topology to achieve redundancy and load balancing. A *mesh* is where two network devices—usually routers or switches—are directly connected. In a fully meshed topology, all network nodes have either physical or virtual circuits connecting them to every other node in the internetwork. You can also have a partially meshed topology, in which some parts of the topology are fully meshed, but some nodes are connected to only one or two other nodes. Figure 8-5 depicts the two topologies.

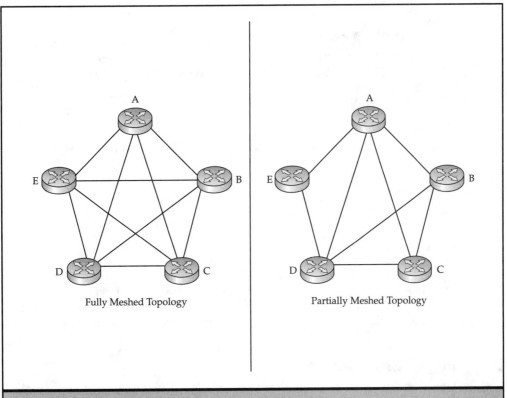

Figure 8-5.   Fully meshed versus partially meshed topologies

At first blush, all meshing seems to be an inherently good thing. Looking at the example in Figure 8-5, you can readily see the benefits in the full-mesh topology:

▼ **Performance**   It's only a single hop to any network attached to one of the other routers, and the fewer the hops, the faster the speed.

■ **Availability**   Having redundant paths means that if any one router goes down, one or more alternate routes are always available.

▲ **Load Balancing**   Alternate paths can also be used for normal operations, where routing parameters can be configured to use alternate paths if a preset traffic load is exceeded on the primary router.

The partially meshed internetwork to the right of Figure 8-5 doesn't have these advantages. For example, to go from router E to router B takes two router hops, not one. If routers on both sides of router E go down, it will be unable to communicate with the rest of the internetwork. Also, fewer mesh connections reduce opportunities for load balancing. However, although meshing can bring benefits, it must be used carefully; it comes at a cost:

▼ **Expense**   Every router (or switch) interface dedicated to meshing is one that can't be used to connect a LAN segment. Meshing consumes hardware capacity.

■ **Overhead traffic**   Devices constantly advertise their services to one another. The more mesh links a device has, the more advertisement packets it broadcasts, thereby eating into payload bandwidth.

■ **Vulnerability**   Meshing makes it more difficult to contain problems within the routers' local area. If a misconfigured device begins propagating indiscriminate broadcast messages, for example, each element in a mesh will cause the broadcast storm to radiate farther from the source.

▲ **Complexity**   Additional connections make it more difficult to isolate problems. For example, it would be harder to track down the device causing the broadcast storm in a fully or heavily meshed internetwork, because there would be so many trails to follow.

For these reasons, few internetworks are fully meshed. The general practice is to fully mesh the backbone portion of topologies to provide fault tolerance and load balancing along these critical links, but only partially mesh the access- and distribution-layer topologies.

Backdoor and Chain Configurations

Circumstance sometimes dictates deviating from the strict hierarchical model. The two most common topology deviations are so-called backdoors and chains. A *backdoor* is any direct connection between devices at the same layer, usually the access layer. A *chain* is the addition of one or more layers below the access layer. Figure 8-6 depicts the two.

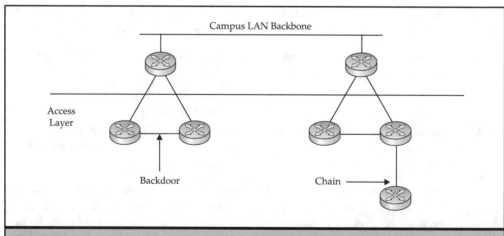

Figure 8-6.   Backdoors and chains violate the ideal three-layer hierarchical topology

Sometimes it makes sense to configure a backdoor. For example, you might want to directly link two remote sites if the links to the distribution-layer routers are costly or slow. Backdoors also provide a degree of redundancy: if the backdoor link goes down, the two remote sites can fail over to the distribution-layer router and keep communicating. More often than not, however, backdoors and chains emerge because of poor network planning or a renegade manager who installs networking equipment without involving the network team.

Designing and building networks is largely a matter of making choices. Most of the choices have to do with selecting the right technologies and products for the job. Even design elements over which you have no control may still leave choices to make. For example, if the company's art department uses AppleTalk and has no intention of changing, you must decide whether to run it over multiprotocol links or break it off into one or more AppleTalk-only LAN segments.

Once the present and future needs of the enterprise have been researched and documented, the next step is to choose technologies for various functional areas:

▼ **Backbone technology selection**   A variety of backbone LAN technologies exist, chosen mostly on the basis of the size of the internetwork and its traffic characteristics.

■ **Protocol selection**   It's assumed here that IP is the network protocol, but choices remain as to which routing and other network control protocols to use.

▲ **Access technology selection**   A mix of hubs and switches is usually configured to best fit the needs of a workgroup or even a particular host.

After the underlying technologies are chosen, specific products must be configured to run them. After that step, more design work must be done to implement the configuration. For example, an IP addressing model must be configured, a name services subsystem must be set up, routing metrics must be tuned, security parameters must be set, and so on.

Optical Networking Gear

We've already given some ink to some of the tools used, specifically, for optical networks. Though we've already talked about such devices as optical cross-connects and optical add/drop multiplexers, in this section we'll talk about some of the pieces that compose an optical network. Many of these devices are the types of things that you would expect to see in a conventional copper-based network. However, when dealing with optical networks, specific tools and devices must be used.

NOTE: This section is meant as just a brief overview. We talk about specific vendors and their products in Chapter 6.

Switches

Quite often, optical switches are designed and built with both optical and electrical ports. Switches may also offer modules that you can plug into the switch to provide optical capabilities. This blend of electrical and optical is beneficial because the switch might have to be deployed in a mixed environment. Also, the switch might be used to aggregate traffic from electrical sources into an optical uplink.

Optical switches are also designed to handle a variety of protocols. For instance, there are optical switches designed to handle ATM traffic, and there are switches that are designed to be compatible with the different flavors of Ethernet. These options are available so that you can match the device with the technology of your choice.

Routers

Optical routers are intelligent devices. These are the devices that must be able to determine across which path IP packets will be sent. They must also be able to groom packets for introduction into the internetwork. For instance, if Quality of Service (QoS) mechanisms are in place, it is the router's job to make sure that packets are being sent out as fast or as slow as necessary. Because routers are required to process millions of packets every second, the more robust the network is, the more robust the router must be.

Since routers are key for MAN and WAN deployments, it is important that they operate at extremely high rates. In fact, when we talk about OC-192 and OC-768 rates, these are the devices that must transmit and receive traffic at such speeds.

But not only do these routers need to be able to handle high-speed optical data streams, but they must also be backward compatible enough to join into the LAN and provide internetwork connectivity. For example, the Cisco 7600 series router not only provides OC-48 connectivity, but it can also interface down to 10 Mbps Ethernet, if necessary.

Cabling

The type of fiber optical cabling used is also rather important in networking construction. Mixing and matching fiber optical cabling cannot be done without ill effects. For instance, if your optical switch uses 62.5-micron multimode fiber to connect with other devices, you cannot splice in 50-micron multimode fiber or 9-micron single-mode fiber. Furthermore, the type of connector you must use is also important (it will be dictated by the device to which you are connecting).

For example, the type of cabling used in Fibre Channel is FC cable. FC cables are a pair of fibers with specialized connectors on each end. The fibers in an FC cable cross so that the input at one end of the FC cable becomes the output at the other end, and the connectors are designed to ensure proper orientation for connections. FC cables that connect to infrastructure cabling must match the fiber type of the infrastructure cabling. For example, if a 50-micron FC cable connects a server to a wall outlet, the infrastructure cabling that runs to that wall outlet must also be 50-micron. A mismatch (connecting a 50-micron FC cable to 62.5-micron infrastructure cabling) can cause severe degradation of the optical signal and could result in marginal operation or an unreliable connection. Cable assembly suppliers can provide custom cables with unique combinations of length, connector type, and fiber type to mate with infrastructure cabling.

Color	Fiber Size	Mode
Yellow	9 micron	Single-mode
Orange	50 micron	Multimode
Slate Gray or orange	62.5 micron	Multimode

Table 8-1.   Color-Coding Schemes for Different Types of Fiber Optic Cabling

NOTE: We explain cabling types, designs, and choices in more detail in Chapter 11.

To aid in the process of matching cabling types, the industry has developed color-coding standards that help, at a single glance, to tell what type of fiber has been placed. Table 8-1 explains what those fiber colors are.

DESIGNING TO FIT NEEDS

You'd be surprised how many internetworks—even big sophisticated ones—have grown haphazardly. Unmanaged network growth occurs for any number of reasons. The most common one is that things simply happened too fast. Keep in mind that those realities we now take for granted—client/server computing, intranets, the Web, extranets—were mere concepts until the 1990s. This left many IT managers unprepared to formulate well-researched, reasoned strategic network plans for their enterprises.

Methodologies have been developed to help bring network planning under control. Not surprisingly, these bear a strong resemblance to data processing methodologies. First and foremost, of course, is to fit the solution to the business needs through some form of needs assessment—both present and future.

Understanding Existing Internetworks

As mentioned earlier, few network designs start from scratch. Although it would be nice to work from a blank sheet of paper, most designs must accommodate a preexisting network. Most are incremental redesigns to serve more users or to upgrade bandwidth capacity, or both. A common upgrade, for example, is to insert a layer of routers between the LAN backbone and the layer at which hosts access the network. This is being done in many enterprises to improve performance and accommodate projected growth. Whatever the change, the preexisting infrastructure must be thoroughly analyzed before even considering a purchase.

The next section describes methods for network planning and design. They focus on establishing a baseline of how the network will look upon implementation. To refresh on the subject, a baseline is a network's starting point, as expressed in traffic volumes, flows, and characteristics. Allowances are made for margins of error and projected growth over and above the baseline.

If designing an entirely new network area, you must arrive at a design baseline based on well-researched assumptions, often derived from paperwork or other nonnetworked data traffic already in place. If an existing network topology is being upgraded, the baseline is taken by measuring its characteristics. If the design scenario encompasses nonnetworked and networked elements, then the two must be compiled together. Whatever the case, the principles and methods of good network design remain the same.

Characterizing Networks

There are several methods for understanding an internetwork well enough to formulate a proper design. These methods apply whether it's an existing internetwork or a topology to be built from scratch. As you might expect, the methods focus on geography and traffic—in other words, where network nodes are and what travels among them. A network node is any device in the topology, including network devices such as routers and payload hosts such as servers. For our purposes, when designing a network from scratch, a node could be a noncomputer entity such as a desk or a file cabinet. The point is to identify where the users are and what they're using.

Understanding Traffic Flow

Understanding and documenting traffic flow is the first step in network design. Drawing an analogy to highway design might seem too obvious, but the two are remarkably similar. A road designer must know where the roads should be, how wide, covered with what type of surface, and what traffic control rules are to be applied. All these things are largely a function of traffic flow.

Traffic characteristics are largely a matter of directionality, symmetry, packet sizes, and volumes. A unidirectional flow does most communicating in one direction; a bidirectional flow communicates with roughly the same frequency in both directions of a connection. An asymmetrical flow sends more data in one direction than the other; a symmetrical flow sends roughly equal amounts of data back and forth. For example, an HTTP session's flow is bidirectional and asymmetric because a lot of messages are sent both ways, but data is mostly downloaded from the Web server to the browser client.

Identifying Traffic Sources   To understand traffic flow, you must know its sources. This is done by identifying groups of users, not individual persons. In the parlance of computer methodology, a group of users is often called a *community*.

An inventory of high-level characteristics, such as location and applications used, should be gathered. This isn't to say that one would go around with a clipboard gathering the information. Most network designers would pull this information off a database from such tools as Netuitive, EcoSCOPE, or NetSys Baseliner. Table 8-2 shows what type of data you might gather.

Community	No. of Persons	Locations	Applications	Host Type
Accounting	31	St. Paul	AR, AP, GL	Unix
Customer Service	200	Washington, DC	Call Center	Windows XP

Table 8-2. Traffic Sources

You can gather whatever information you want. For example, you might not want to document the type of host the group uses if everybody has a Pentium PC. On the other hand, if there's a mix of dumb terminals, PCs, and souped-up Unix workstations, you might want to know who has what. This information can help you more accurately calculate traffic loads.

Identifying Data Sources and Data Sinks   Every enterprise has major users of information. The experts identify these heavy data users as *data sinks* because it's useful to trace back to the data sources they use to help identify traffic patterns. The most common sources are database servers, disk farms, tape or CD libraries, inventory systems, online catalogs, and so on. Data sinks are usually end users, but sometimes servers can be data sinks. Table 8-3 shows information to gather on data sinks.

Documenting which communities use each data sink enables you to correlate traffic. You can now begin connecting user desktop hosts to data sink servers. Combining the information in the preceding two illustrations lets you begin drawing lines between client and server. Correlate every user community to every data sink, and an accurate profile of the network's ideal topology begins to emerge.

Identifying Application Loads and Traffic Types   Most network applications generate traffic with specific characteristics. For example, FTP generates unidirectional and asymmetric traffic involving large files. Table 8-4 is a sampling of typical message types and their approximate sizes. Obviously, sizes can vary widely, but these are good rules of thumb for estimating traffic loads.

Data Sink	Locations	Applications	User Communities
Server farm 3	St. Paul	AR, AP, GL	Accounting
CCSRV	Washington, DC	Call Center	Customer Service

Table 8-3. Data Sources and Data Sinks

Message Type	Approximate Size
Web page	50KB
Graphical computer screen (such as a Microsoft Windows screen)	500KB
E-mail	10KB
Word processing document	100KB
Spreadsheet	200KB
Terminal screen	5KB
Multimedia object (such as videoconferencing)	100KB
Database backup	1MB and up

Table 8-4.   Typical Message Types and Sizes

Beyond traffic loads, it's also useful to know the traffic type. Traffic types characterize the kinds of devices connected and how traffic flows between them:

▼ **Client/server**   Usually a PC talking to a Unix or Windows 2000 server, this is the standard configuration today. In client/server types, traffic is usually bidirectional and asymmetrical.

■ **Server-to-server**   Examples include data mirroring to a redundant server backing up another server, name directory services, and so on. This type of traffic is bidirectional, but the symmetry depends on the application.

■ **Terminal-host**   Many terminal-based applications run over IP, even IBM terminal connections to mainframes. Another example is Telnet. Terminal traffic is bidirectional, but symmetry depends on the application.

▲ **Peer-to-peer**   Examples include videoconferencing and PCs set up to access resources on other PCs, such as printers and data. This type of traffic is bidirectional and symmetric.

Understanding what types of traffic pass through various links gives a picture of how to configure it. Table 8-5 shows information used to identify and characterize traffic types.

Frequently, a link is dominated by one or two traffic types. The Bandwidth Required column in the preceding table is usually expressed as a bit-per-second estimate and could be Mbps or even Gbps. Once all the applications in an internetwork are identified and characterized, the designer has a baseline from which to make volume-dependent configuration decisions.

Application	Traffic Type	User Community	Data Sinks	Bandwidth Required	QoS Policy
Web browser	Client/server	Sales	Sales server	350 Kbps	CAR
TN3270	Terminal	Purchasing	AS/400	200 Kbps	WRED

Table 8-5.   Identifying Application Loads and Traffic Types

Understanding Traffic Load

After the user communities, data sinks and sources, and traffic flows have been documented and characterized, individual links can be more accurately sized. Listing the traffic flow information ties down the paths taken between sources and destinations.

Designing internetworks to fit needs is more art than science, though. For example, even after having totaled the estimated bandwidth for a link, you must go back and pad it for soft factors: QoS priorities, anticipated near-term growth, and so on.

OPTIMAL OPTICAL TECHNOLOGIES

In constructing an optical network, it will be necessary to decide which technologies you will use to transport your data. There are a number that you can choose between, each providing different qualities and attributes than another. By understanding the technologies that are key to optical networking, you can save a lot of headache by adapting your current network to work well with your optical upgrade.

For instance, if your organization's LAN is already based on Ethernet (which most LANs are), it would make the most sense to implement Gigabit Ethernet as part of your optical upgrade. Likewise, if you have been charged with developing an off-site storage solution, you might find that connecting via Fibre Channel will make the process easier to build and manage.

In this section, we take a closer look at the leading technologies that you can use to build your optical network. We examine existing fiber optic solutions like FDDI and Fibre Channel, and also the latest flavors of Ethernet, which are proving that they can break their LAN mold and move on to bigger, faster things.

FDDI

The Fiber Distributed Data Interface (FDDI) technology is a 100 Mbps, token-passing, dual-ring topology that uses fiber optic cabling in LANs. Often, FDDI is used in high-speed backbones because it can support a high amount of bandwidth for greater distances than copper.

Like SONET, FDDI employs a dual-ring architecture. Traffic flows in opposite directions (in networking parlance this is known as *counter-rotating*) along the primary and secondary rings. FDDI is not nearly as complex as SONET, however. During normal operation, traffic flows around the primary ring and the secondary ring remains idle. In the event of an outage, the rings wrap around and the secondary ring is used. This is depicted in Figure 8-7.

FDDI isn't as popular as it once was; however, you may discover that it suits your needs, or you may be dealing with an existing FDDI deployment that needs to be added on to or modified.

Overview

FDDI was developed by the American National Standards Institute (ANSI) in the mid-1980s because high-speed engineering workstations were taxing LAN bandwidths that relied on Ethernet and Token Ring. Additionally, FDDI was developed to address issues of reliability.

FDDI uses optical fiber as its primary transmission medium. Fiber was chosen because of its immunity to electrical interference, its security, and its speed. Furthermore, fiber allows for a stretch of 2 km between stations using multimode fiber and even further distances using single-mode fiber.

NOTE: Copper Distributed Data Interface (CDDI) uses the same technologies as FDDI but uses copper cabling instead of optical fiber.

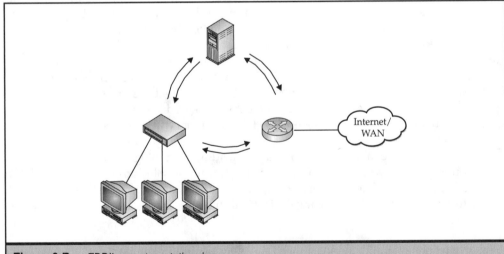

Figure 8-7.   FDDI's counter-rotating rings

Basically, FDDI is a stretched version of Token Ring. However, the elongated rings make FDDI well suited for MANs, because they can reach 100 km. There are differences between Token Ring and FDDI, but the basic technology was the same—there is a token passed around a ring. The token is nothing more than a frame that is passed around the ring. The station holding the token is allowed to send a transmission.

By the nature of the token, throughput is somewhat limited on an FDDI ring. If a station wants to send something, it must wait until it gets possession of the token. Then, the frame will be filled up and sent around the ring. To expedite this process, FDDI adds a method called *fast token release*. This allows the sender to generate a token frame while waiting for the information frame to traverse the ring. Token passing technologies avoid the collision-based nature of Ethernet, which is not desirable with heavy loads. However, smaller loads suffer on token-passing rings.

FDDI typically uses multimode fiber with a wavelength of 1300 nanometers (nm). Light emitting diodes are normally used as transmitters, and PIN photodiodes are used as receivers.

Attachments

FDDI is unique in that there are a number of different ways to connect FDDI devices. FDDI defines three different types of devices:

▼ **Single attachment station (SAS)**   The SAS attaches to just the primary ring via a concentrator. The primary advantage of connecting SAS devices is that the devices will have no effect on the ring if they are disconnected or powered off.

■ **Dual attachment station (DAS)**   FDDI DAS devices have two ports (A and B). These ports are used to connect the device to both primary and secondary rings. If a DAS device is disconnected or powered off, there will be an effect on the ring.

▲ **Concentrator**   An FDDI concentrator is the main component in an FDDI network. It is connected to both the primary and secondary rings, and in the event of an outage, the concentrator will not bring down the ring. For instance, a concentrator allows a PC to be turned off without the entire network going offline.

Figure 8-8 shows all three elements—SAS, DAS, and concentrator—connected to an FDDI ring.

Reliability

As we've mentioned in earlier chapters, the key to FDDI's reliability is in its rings. Like SONET, if there is a failure on a particular device, the backup ring snaps into play, wrapping around and providing connectivity for the rest of the network. But there are other means, which help to keep FDDI operational should a problem arise.

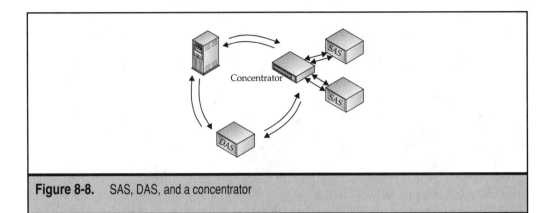

Figure 8-8.   SAS, DAS, and a concentrator

Optical Bypass Switch   Another technology used in FDDIs is the *optical bypass switch*. These switches provide continuous dual-ring operation if a device on the ring fails. The switch accomplishes this task through the use of mirrors that pass the wavelength from the ring to the DAS device during normal operation. If there is a problem with the DAS device, like a power down or some other failure, the optical bypass switch passes the light through itself using internal mirrors, maintaining the ring's integrity. The benefit of this is that in the event of a failure, the ring does not enter a wrapped-around state. Figure 8-9 shows an optical bypass switch.

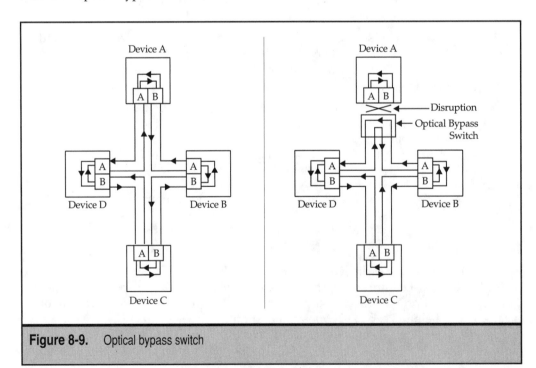

Figure 8-9.   Optical bypass switch

Dual Homing   Another means of reliability in FDDI is called *dual homing*. Constructing your optical network with dual homing is especially useful on critical devices, like routers or servers. In a dual homing scenario, the mission-critical device is connected to two concentrators, as shown in Figure 8-10.

In this figure, the router is connected to two different concentrators: one connection is known as the *active link;* the other is the *passive link.* The passive link remains in back-up mode until the primary link fails. If the active link fails, then the passive link automatically kicks in.

When FDDI was developed, engineers knew that 100 Mbps Ethernet would be coming, but they didn't know when it would arrive. As such, FDDI was used widely in backbone LANs but has lately been replaced by other technologies. However, FDDI is still out there, and you might find yourself in a situation where expanding the FDDI deployment is your best option.

Gigabit Ethernet

It's more than likely the computer network you use everyday is Ethernet-based. This is because Ethernet is an extremely popular technology, which has become the *de facto* standard for computer networks. In the past, Ethernet was suitable only for LAN applications. This was due to inherent speed and distance limitations. However, with the advent

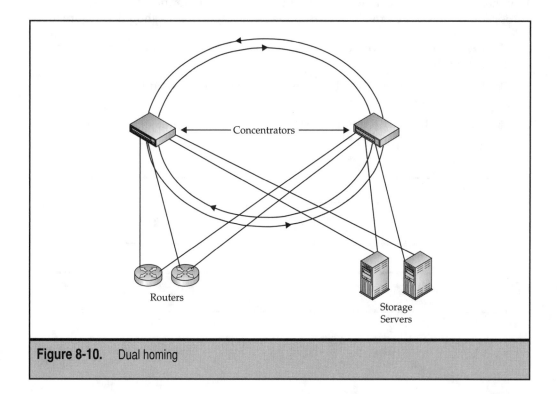

Figure 8-10.   Dual homing

of Gigabit Ethernet and the coming 10 Gigabit Ethernet, Ethernet makes itself perfectly useful in WAN and MAN applications—it is also especially useful in optical networks.

Ethernet's roots are at the University of Hawaii as its ALOHA network a quarter century ago. The first Ethernet, developed by Xerox, was based on this network and carried 2.94 Mbps and connected more than 100 workstations on a 1 km cable. This network was so popular that in 1980, Xerox, DEC, and Intel developed a 10 Mbps standard, which became the foundation of the IEEE 802.3 standard.

Ethernet's functionality is based on a protocol that requires nodes to *listen* to the medium. If there is a signal on the medium, then a node must wait until the medium is clear. If two senders transmit at the same time, then a *collision* has occurred. When a collision occurs, then transmitting stations will wait for a bit, and then try again.

When the Ethernet standard was developed in 1980, 10 Mbps was a lot of bandwidth. Since then, as you know, bandwidth demands have increased, and in 1995, the IEEE adopted the 802.3u standard governing *Fast* Ethernet, which operates at 100 Mbps. Fast Ethernet brought full duplex capacity (full duplex means that nodes can send and receive at the same time).

In 1996, *Gigabit* Ethernet (802.3z) was added, and slated for a 2002 release is the 10 Gigabit Ethernet standard (802.3ae).

The Ethernet Packet

Ethernet has a very specific way to carry data. The frame format (which is consistent across all versions of Ethernet) consists of the following fields, as shown in Figure 8-11:

▼ **Preamble**   This seven-octet preamble pattern of alternating 0s and 1s is used for synchronization.

■ **Start frame delimiter (SFD)**   This field containing the sequence 10101011 is used to indicate the start of a frame.

■ **Address fields**   Each frame contains the destination and source addresses. These addresses are 48 bits long.

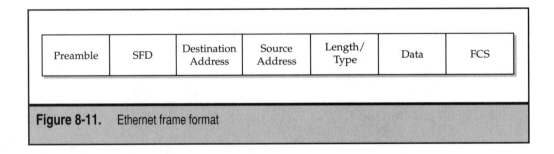

Figure 8-11.   Ethernet frame format

- **Length/type**   If the number is less than the maximum valid frame size, it indicates the length of the MAC client data. If the number is greater than or equal to 1536 decimal, it represents the type of the MAC client protocol.

- **Data and padding**   Padding is necessary only when the data packet is smaller than 38 bytes to ensure the minimum frame size of 64 bytes as specified in the existing standards. In Gigabit Ethernet, the minimum frame size is 512 bytes.

- ▲ **Frame checking sequence (FCS)**   The FCS field contains a 32-bit cyclic redundancy check.

Not only are the Ethernet frames alike, but so is MAC layer functionality. Where Gigabit Ethernet differs from its brothers is at the physical layer—the layer that governs what media are being used in the network.

Physical Layer

The physical layer defines the electrical and optical signaling, line states, clocking guidelines, data encoding, and circuitry needed for data transmission and reception. Contained within the physical layer are several sublayers that perform these functions, including the physical coding sublayer and optical transceiver or physical media–dependent (PMD) sublayer for fiber media. We'll explain these sublayers in more depth later.

The 1000Base-X standard is used in optical deployments. In fact, 1000Base-X is based on the Fibre Channel physical layer. The physical layer of Gigabit Ethernet employs an amalgamation of technologies from the original Ethernet and the Fibre Channel specification—particularly the lowest layers of Fibre Channel. Those layers are:

- ▼ **FC-0**   This layer governs interfaces and media.

- ▲ **FC-1**   This layer governs encoding and decoding.

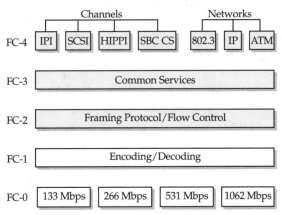

By borrowing those layers from Fibre Channel, Gigabit Ethernet is able to interface cleanly and efficiently with fiber optical cables and devices. Specifically, the 1000Base-X standard employs three types of media:

▼ **1000Base-SX** Uses an 850 nm laser on multimode fiber. The "S" in SX stands for *short* wavelength.

■ **1000Base-LX** Uses a 1300 nm laser on single-mode and multimode fiber. The "L" in LX stands for *long* wavelength.

▲ **1000Base-CX** Uses short-haul copper "twinax" STP cable.

The cabling and their supported distances are listed in Table 8-6.

Obviously, we're most interested in the importance of optical fiber in this discussion; however, for the sake of completeness, it is important to point out that the other standard for Gigabit Ethernet is 1000Base-T. This concerns data transmission over copper wire, specifically unshielded twisted pair (UTP). Data can traverse the copper medium between 25 and 100 m over four pairs of Category 5 UTP, 250 Mbps per copper pair.

MAC Layer

At the MAC Layer of Gigabit Ethernet is the same protocol as Ethernet: CSMA/CD. The length of the cable segment used to connect stations is governed by the CSMA/CD protocol. This length is determined because of the collision-based nature of Ethernet. For example, Ethernet has a minimum frame size of 64 bytes. This size is used because it prevents a station from completing the transmission of a frame before the first bit has reached the far end of the cable. Therefore, the minimum time to detect a collision is the same time it takes for a signal to reach the receiving end of the cable. This amount of time is known as the *slot time. Slot size*, on the other hand, is the number of bytes that can be transmitted in one slot time. In Ethernet, slot size is 64 bytes, which is the minimum frame length.

Cable Type	Distance
Single-mode fiber (9-micron)	5 km using 1300 nm laser (LX)
Multimode fiber (62.5-micron)	300 meters using 850 nm laser (SX)
	550 m using 1300 nm laser (LX)
Multimode fiber (50-micron)	550 m using 850 nm laser (SX)
	550 m using 1300 nm laser (LX)
Short-haul copper	25 m

Table 8-6.   Gigabit Ethernet Cabling and Its Supported Distances

The maximum length of cable allowed in Ethernet is 2.5 km. As the bit rate increases, the sender transmits a faster frame rate. In light of this, if cable lengths and frame sizes remain constant, a station may send a frame too quickly and not detect the collision at the other end of the cable. To prevent this from happening in faster incarnations of Ethernet, there are two options:

▼   Maintain the maximum cable length and increase the slot time (and, as a result, the minimum frame size).

▲   Maintain the slot time and decrease the cable length.

Alternatively, both solutions can be employed in tandem.

In Fast Ethernet, the maximum cable length is reduced to 100 m, yet still maintaining the frame size and slot time.

Gigabit Ethernet maintains the minimum and maximum Ethernet frame sizes but uses a larger slot size of 512 bytes. If the frame is shorter than 512 bytes, it is padded with extension symbols so that it will maintain compatibility with Ethernet. These symbols (which are specialized and cannot appear in the payload) are part of a process called *carrier extension.*

Carrier Extension   One of the main attractions of Gigabit Ethernet is its capability to interoperate with existing Ethernet networks. By using a carrier extension, the 802.3 standard can be maintained while still allowing usable distances to be employed.

In extended frames, the non–data extension symbols are included within the *collision window.* In other words, the entire extended frame is considered for collision and dropped. However, the FCS is computed only on the original frame. The extension symbols are removed before the FCS is checked by the receiver. Therefore, the logical link control (LLC) layer is not even aware of the carrier extension.

Figure 8-12 shows the Ethernet frame when carrier extension is used.

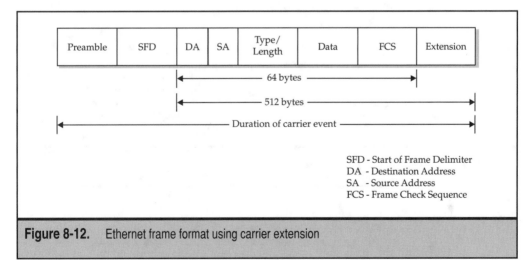

Figure 8-12.   Ethernet frame format using carrier extension

Packet Bursting   Carrier extension works well, but it should be obvious that it is not very efficient and wastes a lot of bandwidth. In fact, up to 448 bytes could be wasted on padding, resulting in low throughput. A way to combat this wastefulness is through *packet bursting.*

Packet bursting is used in conjunction with carrier extension. When a station has several packets to send, the first packet is padded to the time slot using carrier extension. The packets that follow are sent back-to-back, with the minimum interpacket gap, until a burst time expires. As a result, packet bursting increases the throughput. Figure 8-13 shows how packet bursting works.

GMII   The MAC and physical layers need something to act as a go-between so that they can communicate. As you can see in Figure 8-14, which depicts the Gigabit Ethernet protocol architecture, the Gigabit Media Independent Interface (GMII) provides that interface.

The GMII is an extension of Fast Ethernet's Media Independent Interface (MII) and Ethernet's Attachment Unit Interface (AUI). This interface employs eight-bit-wide transmit and receive paths, so it can support full duplex operation.

The GMII gives two media status signals that indicate:

▼   The presence of a carrier

▲   The absence of a collision

The reconciliation sublayer (RS) maps these signals to physical signaling (PLS), which is understood by the MAC sublayer.

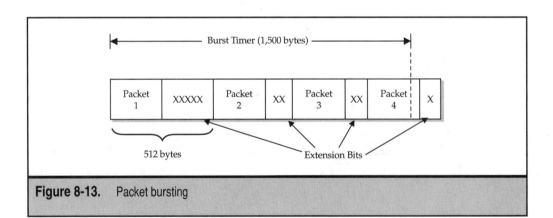

Figure 8-13.   Packet bursting

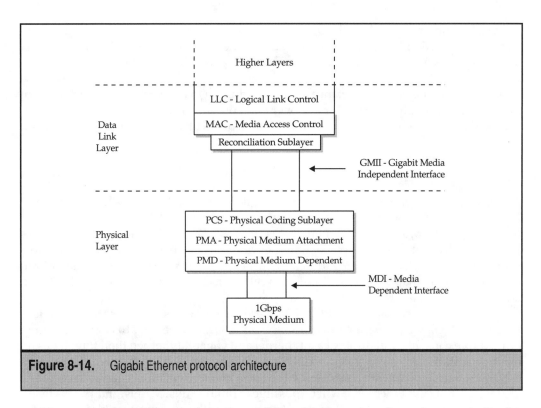

Figure 8-14.   Gigabit Ethernet protocol architecture

Because of the GMII, one can connect different types of media and transmit Gigabit Ethernet, including STP, UTP, single-mode fiber, and multimode fiber, all the while using the same MAC controller.

The GMII consists of three sublayers:

▼   **Physical coding sublayer (PCS)**   This sublayer provides a uniform interface to the reconciliation layer for all physical media. It uses the same coding as Fibre Channel. Carrier sensing and collision detection indications are also generated at this layer. It also governs the network speed with which the network interface card (NIC) communicates with the network and the mode (half- or full duplex).

■   **Physical medium attachment (PMA)**   This sublayer provides a medium-independent means for the PCS to support serial bit-oriented physical media.

▲   **Physical medium dependent (PMD)**   This sublayer maps the physical medium to the PCS. At this layer, signaling is defined and the actual physical attachment (cabling, connector type, etc.) is defined.

In GMII, no connector is defined, so the optical transceiver cannot be an external device. This restriction was put in place because of the parallel nature of Gigabit Ethernet transfers. By using external devices, cables would be hard to control with high frequencies and bit rates.

Gigabit Ethernet is an important and useful addition to the world of networking. Not only does it support high rates of speed over fiber, but it is also based on an existing technology that is well entrenched in organizations worldwide. But as powerful as Gigabit Ethernet is, its big brother is even more impressive.

10 Gigabit Ethernet

Just as Gigabit Ethernet is making its presence felt in networks everywhere, 10 Gigabit Ethernet will soon come along and speed things up another notch.

At 10 and 100 Mbps speeds, Ethernet was used as an access technology. However, as 10 Gigabit Ethernet enters the scene, Ethernet can move from an access technology to a simple, fast, cost-effective aggregation and backbone network technology. And, as you remember from Chapter 7, it will be an excellent technology to use on SONET and DWDM deployments.

10 Gigabit Ethernet uses the IEEE 802.3 Ethernet media access control (MAC) protocol, the IEEE 802.3 Ethernet frame format, and the IEEE 802.3 frame size. 10 Gigabit Ethernet is full duplex, just like full duplex Fast Ethernet and Gigabit Ethernet; therefore, it has no inherent distance limitations. Because 10 Gigabit Ethernet is still Ethernet, it minimizes the user's learning curve by maintaining the same management tools and architecture.

Using 10 Gigabit Ethernet, it will be possible to build LANs, MANs, and WANs using Ethernet as the end-to-end layer-2 transport—something that was not possible in the past.

The technology will support distances of 100 m to 300 m on multimode fiber and more than 40 km on single-mode fiber. Because of this reach, simple, low-cost MANs using layer-3 and layer-4 switches will be possible.

For comparison's sake, Table 8-7 lists the spans necessary for different applications.

10 Gigabit Ethernet uses the same MAC protocol, frame format, and frame size as its Ethernet brothers. Because it is full duplex, there are no distance limitations. Thanks to the distances made possible by 10 Gigabit Ethernet, it is being targeted at three different environments: LANs, WANs, and MANs. To tackle these applications, the 10 Gigabit Ethernet Task Force is defining appropriate physical layers.

LANs

Within a LAN application, 10 Gigabit Ethernet will be used to interconnect server clusters; aggregate several Gigabit Ethernet segments into 10 Gigabit Ethernet links; and switch links for high-speed connections between backbone or data center switches.

In this application, the distance requirement is not as hefty as it is in MANs and WANs; however, cost is an issue. These users want inexpensive technology for high-speed networking. Because 10 Gigabit Ethernet is backward compatible, it doesn't plunge existing LAN equipment into obsolescence.

Application	Distance
Local storage network	100 m
Remote storage network	40 km
Disaster recovery facilities	40 km
Enterprise networks	100 m
Enterprise aggregation facilities	550 m
Campus backbone	10 m
Enterprise backbone	40 km
Internet service provider	100 m
Internet aggregation facility	40 km
Internet backbone facility	2 km

Table 8-7.   Applications and Span Needs

At the LAN level, the PMD sublayer changes the incoming data stream into light pulses, destined for fiber optics. Several PMDs have been suggested for campus and backbone applications, including one based on DWDM that supports installed multimode fiber backbones by transmitting, muxing, and demuxing four optical wavelengths coming across a 62.5-micron multimode fiber up to 300 m long.

MANs

10 Gigabit Ethernet is a beautiful technology for MANs. At this level, the task force is trying to get the protocol to reach over 40 km.

The medium-haul markets include campus backbones, enterprise backbones, and storage area networks (SANs). In this case, the distance requirement ranges from 2 km to 40 km. In these deployments, the media most likely already exist, so once again 10 Gigabit Ethernet's backward compatibility saves money and a bit of a learning curve.

Using this technology, service providers could build Ethernet networks using layer-3 or layer-4 switches over dark fiber, but without having to use SONET or ATM, and while provisioning Ethernet, Fast Ethernet, and Gigabit Ethernet at low costs.

WANs

The task force has also defined a physical layer that can connect with an existing WAN SONET infrastructure. The intention is to establish a SONET-compatible physical layer that will operate at a rate compatible to OC-192.

In this market, those served include ISPs and backbone facilities. The access points for long-distance transport networks will require OC-192 speeds, so a key requirement will be compatibility with 9.95 Gbps speeds. In this case, 10 Gigabit Ethernet will fit in nicely. Though OC-192 is not exactly 10 Gbps, the standard is likely to include a mechanism to allow for its compatibility. This interface will allow 10 Gigabit Ethernet switches and routers to connect SONET access gear and use the existing SONET infrastructure for layer-1 transport.

NOTE: The very nature of Ethernet and its collision-based technology prevent it from achieving its full capacity in a practical setting. Because of all the collisions going on, networks are lucky to achieve 50 percent of the bandwidth that Ethernet promises. However, because 10 Gigabit Ethernet will most likely be used in point-to-point deployments, it will be able to use more of its bandwidth than the Ethernet in complex deployments.

Expect to see prestandard 10 Gigabit Ethernet equipment by the fall of 2001; however, it will not, technically, be standardized. The final standard should be completed by March 2002.

Fibre Channel

Fibre Channel was developed as a practical, inexpensive, and expandable way to quickly transfer data between workstations, mainframes, storage devices, and other devices.

Fibre Channel is not a traditional networking protocol, like Ethernet. Rather, it is more akin to the Small Computer System Interface (SCSI), used to connect hard drives and scanners to a computer. But don't let that lead you to believe that Fibre Channel is any kind of a slouch. Fibre Channel runs at 100 Mbps, 200 Mbps, 400 Mbps, 1 Gbps, or 2 Gbps.

Unfortunately, Fibre Channel speeds are not particularly well aligned with other LAN or WAN speeds. To make understanding Fibre Channel speeds even more confusing, Fibre Channel speeds are expressed differently than other technologies. Table 8-8 lists the conversion between mega*bits* to mega*bytes*, giga*bits* to giga*bytes*, and what they are called in Fibre Channel parlance.

What should stick out as being odd from Table 8-8 is that the conversion of bits to bytes in Fibre Channel is not straightforward. The conversion includes what is known as 8B/10B encoding, and it also adds overhead from frame headers and other miscellaneous bits. This is how, in the world of Fibre Channel, 133 Mbps translates into 12.5 MBps.

Ports

When connecting a Fibre Channel device, there will be two ports—input and output. All Fibre Channel devices must be configured with a line coming in and a line going out. In fact, as we mentioned earlier, the type of fiber used in Fibre Channel is actually two fibers bundled together.

Fibre Channel Terminology	Speed	Fibre Channel Speed
Eighth Speed	133 Mbps	12.5 megabytes per second (MBps)
Quarter Speed	266 Mbps	25 MBps
Half Speed	531 Mbps	50 MBps
Full Speed	1.063 Gbps	100 MBps
Double Speed	2.126 Gbps	200 MBps
Quadruple Speed	4.252 Gbps	400 MBps

Table 8-8.   Fibre Channel Speeds

Fibre Channel devices use different types of ports. The type of port depends on the topology and the device's role within that topology. On a basic level, two devices, each with *N_Ports* connect together via a pair of fiber cables. In an arbitrated loop topology, the devices would use *L_Ports*.

The most prevalent type of port is used in fabric configurations. A Fibre Channel fabric uses a central switching device that employs *F_Ports*. The switch's F_Ports connect to the *N_Ports* on other devices. F_Ports require N_Ports to enable a login/logoff capability as devices are powered on and off.

As Figure 8-15 shows, a number of Fibre Channel devices connect via the switch's F_Ports. The Fibre Channel switch can allow traffic flow in two different ways:

▼   **Blocking**   Once Fibre Channel frames start flowing through the switch from one N_Port to another, no other N_Ports can communicate.

▲   **Nonblocking**   Once frames start flowing through this fabric, the switch is fast enough to allow other N_Ports to communicate.

Topologies

Fibre Channel architecture offers three topologies for network design: point-to-point, arbitrated loop, and switched fabric. Each of these topologies is based on gigabit speeds, with 100 MBps throughput.

Though we're interested in the fiber optic medium, it is useful to point out that each topology allows for both copper and fiber optics. The maximum allowable distances are:

▼   30 m for copper

■   500 m for multimode fiber (770–860 nm, also known as *short wavelength lasers*)

▲   10 km for single-mode fiber (1270–1355 nm, also known as *long wavelength lasers*)

Let's take a closer look at each of these topologies.

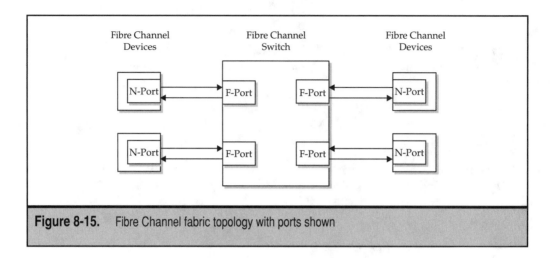

Figure 8-15. Fibre Channel fabric topology with ports shown

Point-to-Point *Point-to-point* is a simple, straightforward connection between two devices. This type of configuration is used for minimal server/storage configurations. Generally speaking, point-to-point cabling runs between devices without a hub separating the two. If additional devices are needed, the topology can be extended. However, since the medium is no longer under the control of just two nodes, an arbitrated loop protocol must be used to negotiate access to the medium. Figure 8-16 shows what a point-to-point topology looks like.

Arbitrated Loop As you've seen in FDDI and SONET deployments, loop designs allow the two communicating nodes to possess the shared medium for just the duration of the transaction. With an arbitrated loop, however, an additional subset of Fibre Channel commands are used to govern the negotiation of access to the loop and specific sequences for assigning loop addresses to the nodes. An arbitrated loop is shown in Figure 8-17.

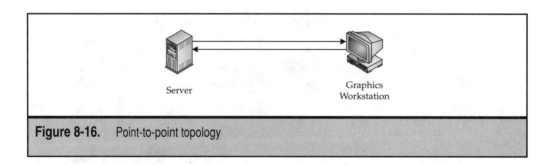

Figure 8-16. Point-to-point topology

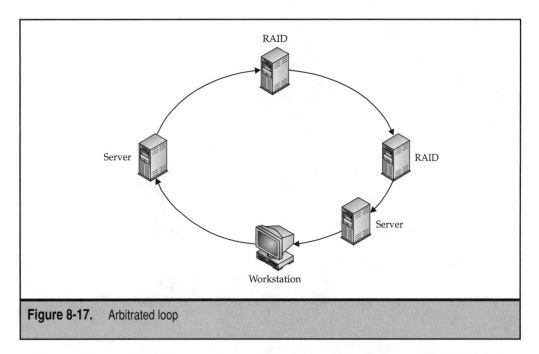

Figure 8-17. Arbitrated loop

Arbitrated loops connected transmit and receive ports between several nodes, thus creating a ring topology. However, since the connections formed a single ring, the entire ring was vulnerable if there was a break or failure along the chain. A failure could cause the entire ring to come down.

This vulnerability can be ameliorated if a hub is added to the center of the ring, forming a hybrid star/ring topology. Arbitrated loop hubs provide improved control and reliability over loops with no hub. The hubs employ bypass mechanisms at each port, which prevents faulty nodes from bringing down the entire network.

Fabric   A *fabric* topology is akin to a star topology. It is a particularly reliable deployment, especially in the event a number of devices are to be used. Like the other Fibre Channel topologies, fabrics connect with devices via two runs of fiber—one on which to send data, the other on which to receive data.

Unlike a loop, in the event the fiber is damaged between the switch and a node, the remaining devices can still function properly. A fabric configuration is shown in Figure 8-18.

Fibre Channel Layers

Fibre Channel employs a five-level stack for its functionality. These layers, illustrated in Figure 8-19, provide for the use of different types of transmission media, different protocols, and different encoding and decoding rules. A more detailed explanation of the layers follows Figure 8-19.

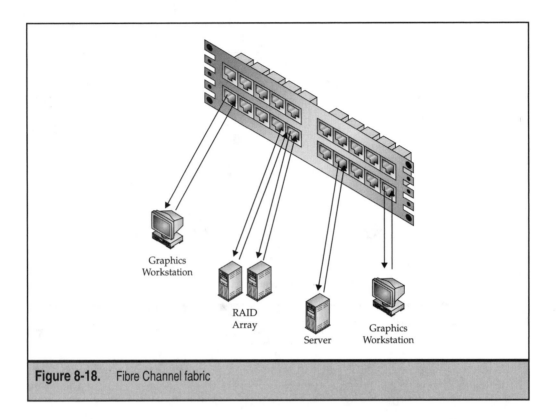

Figure 8-18. Fibre Channel fabric

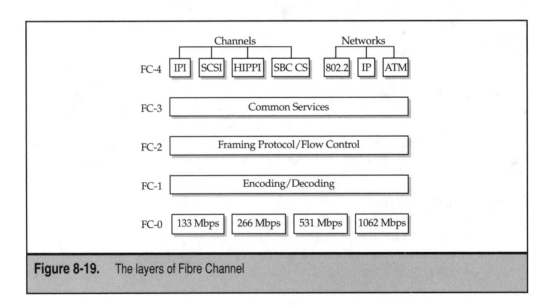

Figure 8-19. The layers of Fibre Channel

FC-0   The FC-0 layer is the lowest layer of the stack. At this level, the physical system (including the fiber, connectors, and optical parameters for a variety of data rates) is established. The physical level is designed to meet the broadest range of technologies.

FC-1   At the FC-1 layer, the transmission protocol is defined, including encoding and decoding procedures, special characters, and error management. Information to be transmitted across a fiber is encoded eight bits at a time into a ten-bit *transmission character.* A transmission code is used to improve the transmission of information across a fiber.

FC-2   The FC-2 layer is also known as the *signaling protocol level,* which serves as the transport mechanism for Fibre Channel. At this level, the following characteristics are defined:

▼   The framing rules of the data to be transferred between ports

■   The various mechanisms for controlling the service classes

▲   The means of managing the sequence of a data transfer

To aid in the transport of data across the link, the following building blocks are defined by the standard:

▼   Ordered Set

■   Frame

■   Sequence

■   Exchange

▲   Protocol

FC-3   The FC-3 level of the standard provides the common services required for such features as:

▼   **Striping**   This is used to multiply bandwidth using multiple parallel ports for transmission of a single flow of information across multiple links.

■   **Hunt groups**   This provides the ability for more than one port to respond to the same alias address. This allows for speed and efficiency by making more than one port available.

▲   **Multicast**   A multicast delivers a single transmission to several destination ports. Multicasting includes broadcasting or just a select subset of the ports on the fabric.

FC-4   The highest level of the FC standard defines the application interfaces that can be used over Fibre Channel. It established mapping rules for the upper layers to the FC layers below. The following list outlines the network and channel protocols that are specified for use in Fibre Channel:

▼   Small Computer System Interface (SCSI)

■   Intelligent Peripheral Interface (IPI)

- ■ High Performance Parallel Interface (HIPPI) Framing Protocol
- ■ Internet Protocol (IP)
- ■ ATM Adaptation Layer for computer data (AAL5)
- ■ Link Encapsulation (FC-LE)
- ■ Single Byte Command Code Set Mapping (SBCCS)
- ▲ IEEE 802.2

Use of Fibre Channel

As we mentioned in Chapter 7, Fibre Channel is widely used in SAN applications. By connecting a single-mode fiber and using a 1310 nm laser, the distance between Fibre Channel devices can be as long at 10 km. Often, this distance is about the range between one organization and its ISP. Furthermore, SANs can be constructed with the RAID devices located well off-site, thus ensuring an additional layer of reliability.

DWDM is an excellent tool to use for extending SANs over great distances. Because DWDM traffic is independent of bit rates and coding methods, it is the only technology capable of extending SANs outside of the simple loops provided by Fibre Channel. Unfortunately, Fibre Channel rates do not align well with Ethernet or SONET. They do, however, fit with DWDM, as Figure 8-20 illustrates.

The DWDM switch in Figure 8-20 could be located on a customer's site, or at the ISP. Any two of the links could be up to 10 km apart. Furthermore, because DWDM employs multiple wavelengths, both switches could actually be the same switch, just so long as

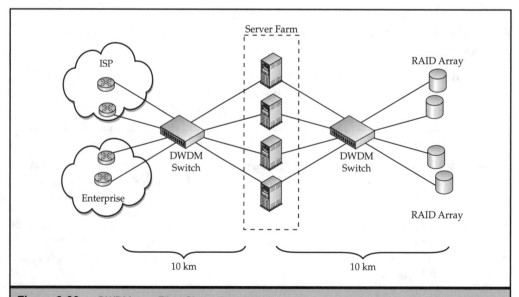

Figure 8-20. DWDM over Fibre Channel

there are enough wavelengths at your disposal. Using this model, it is possible for the ISP to offer both access and storage services.

MODELS

Optical networks can be employed in many different scenarios. Once the province of carriers and tier-one service providers, optical networks are now available for LANs, MANs, and WANs. At each different level of networking, fiber can be employed to produce a range of results. Obviously, the first, most important feature is to deliver the levels of speed that were unheard of a decade ago.

In this section, we examine some different types of networks and suggest how fiber optics can be used within those environments. Whether your organization needs a speedier WAN, you're thinking about hooking up to a MAN, or you need blazing speeds to the desktop, there is an optical fiber solution out there for you.

Service Provider

Service provider networks have the unenviable task of trying to keep up with customer demand, attracting new customers, and squeezing every bit possible out of their system. As customer demand grows and as the capacity of the network reaches its limit, service providers must be able to scale their networks to accommodate new customers and more robust access demands. Service providers not only serve as points of presence for customers, but they also link into Internet backbones and must be able to accommodate the speeds the Internet demands.

Next Gen Ethernet

At the risk of banging 10 Gigabit Ethernet's drum too loudly, the technology is perfect for service provider deployments.

Ethernet has been an extremely functional technology in LAN applications. At 10 and 100 Mbps and—to an extent—1 Gbps, Ethernet has been a fixture in organizations. This is due to Ethernet's ease of use and the fact that the employees' knowledge base is so entrenched in Ethernet technology. However, as Ethernet looks to meet 10 Gbps when the standard is released, the latest flavor of Ethernet might be too beefy for most LAN deployments. In this case, Ethernet will move quite well to WAN and core network applications.

10 Gigabit Ethernet operates over optical fiber. This will work just fine for service providers who will be able to leverage their existing optical fiber installations in an upgrade to 10 Gigabit Ethernet. Not only that, but because Ethernet is so prevalent, the learning curve for such a system will not be too sharp.

This capacity growth (carriers have evolved from 1 Mbps to 1 Gbps and now to 10 Gbps) is rather important because of the ever-increasing demand of customers who want to be able to send large files, view movies, and have VoIP conversations. Since the demand seems only to be increasing, 10 Gigabit Ethernet is a good way to scale networks easily and economically.

NOTE: Because of existing fiber, dark fiber, and DWDM implementations, some estimates say that by 2002 an additional 1.6 million lines will be created in North America.

Furthermore, because there are so many SONET implementations, it will be possible to use existing SONET installations to frame data and move it across optical backbones. SONET is still very attractive to service providers because of its reliability and performance.

Construction

A new version of the POP based on 10 Gigabit Ethernet is shown in Figure 8-21. There are three areas of interest in this design:

▼ The switches in this model can aggregate high numbers of lower-speed Ethernet links, which then feed into wide area 10 Gigabit Ethernet systems.

■ Routers in this solution must also have high-speed 10 Gigabit Ethernet ports. These routers make network routing and outbound networking choices at extremely high rates.

▲ The optical core of this solution is transparent to the MAC layer of Ethernet. However, it must be equipped with the appropriate terminations. Switching, routing, and optical transport act as one system that help carriers deal with scalability, reliability, and cost.

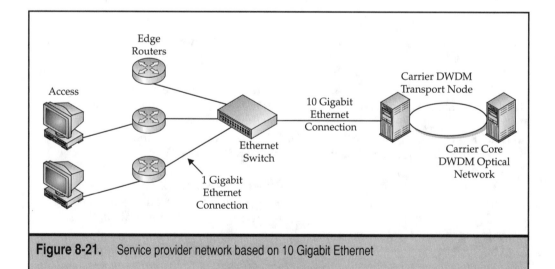

Figure 8-21. Service provider network based on 10 Gigabit Ethernet

Backbones

Backbones are used to connect major peer network nodes. A backbone link connects two particular nodes, but the term *backbone* often is used to refer to a series of backbone links. For example, a campus backbone might extend over several links.

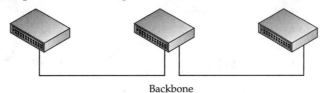

Backbone

Backbone links move data between backbone devices only. They don't handle traffic between LAN segments within a site. That's done at the distribution layer of the three-layer hierarchical model by LAN switches and routers. Backbones concentrate on moving traffic at very high speeds over land.

Campus backbones obviously cover a short distance, usually via underground fiber optic cabling. WAN backbones—used by big enterprises and ISPs—move traffic between cities. So-called Internet backbone providers operate most WAN backbone links, although many large enterprises operate their own high-speed long-distance links. WAN links run over high-speed fiber optic cable links strung underground, on electrical pylons, and even under oceans. Regardless of transport medium, and whether it's a campus or WAN backbone, they share these characteristics:

▼ **Minimal packet manipulation**   Such processing as access control list enforcement and firewall filtering are kept out of the backbone to speed throughput. For this reason, most backbone links are switched, not routed.

■ **High-speed devices**   A relatively slow device would not be configured onto a high-speed backbone. The two ends of a backbone link generally operate over fast routers.

▲ **Fast transport**   Most high-speed backbones are built atop transport technology of 1 Gbps or higher.

The two main backbone technologies now are ATM and Gigabit Ethernet. FDDI is more widely installed than either, but with a total capacity of only 100 Mbps, few new FDDI installations are going into high-speed backbones.

ATM Backbones   Asynchronous Transfer Mode (ATM) uses a fixed-length format instead of the variable-length packets Ethernet uses. The fixed-length format lends itself to high-speed throughput because the hardware always knows exactly where each cell begins. For this reason, ATM has a very positive ratio between payload and network control overhead traffic. This architecture also lends itself to QoS—a big plus for operating critical backbone links.

Gigabit Ethernet Backbone Although Gigabit Ethernet is a much newer technology than ATM, many network managers are turning to it instead of ATM for their backbone needs. A Gigabit Ethernet backbone can be configured using the same platforms as for ATM. This is done by configuring Gigabit Ethernet modules instead of ATM modules. Note, also, that the same fiber optic cabling can be used for Gigabit Ethernet, but the adapters must be changed to those designed to support Gigabit Ethernet instead of ATM.

As you might imagine, the technology-specific modules and adapters represent the different electronics needed to process either variable-length Ethernet packets or fixed-length ATM cells. It can only be assumed that 10 Gigabit Ethernet will fit into this model as well.

LANs

Mostly, fiber optics has been used in long-haul and backbone environments. It is only recently that LANs have been the site for optical deployments. The cost of fiber, itself, was not prohibitive; it was the cost of terminating the cable to a connector and the equipment for the necessary optical-electrical-optical (OEO) conversion.

Furthermore, one of fiber's biggest plusses is its ability to function across great distances. Obviously, in a LAN, this is not much of an issue. Even though technologies like Ethernet can carry LAN traffic for a couple kilometers, there are very few that actually need this type of distance.

But workstations demanded greater bandwidth, and fiber was increasingly viewed as an option. Another attraction for fiber was the increasing use of backbone LANs. Backbone LANs are used only to connect smaller, departmental LANs, hubs, switches, and routers. No clients or servers are connected to a backbone LAN. If your organization has these small LANs and devices spread across a large campus or between several buildings, you can see the need for fiber.

Optical LANs are constructed in much the same way as a conventional LAN. The chief differences consist in the purchase of optical equipment (or optical modules), rather than conventional equipment. Upgrading to an optical solution will depend largely on you organization's need. Are you adding more workstations, thereby calling for a beefier connection to your backbone LAN or Internet connection? Or does your organization have high-speed needs at the desktop? The following scenarios address the different needs in a LAN.

Server-Switch Connections

In a "typical" LAN configuration, workstations are connected to a hub or switch. The switch aggregates those conversations and is, itself, connected to the server. Because of increasing bandwidth demand, more workstation connections, or a combination of these things, the connection between the server and the switch can be taxed.

This connection is an excellent location for an optical Gigabit Ethernet upgrade. As Figure 8-22 shows, the hubs connecting workstations can be connected (using twisted

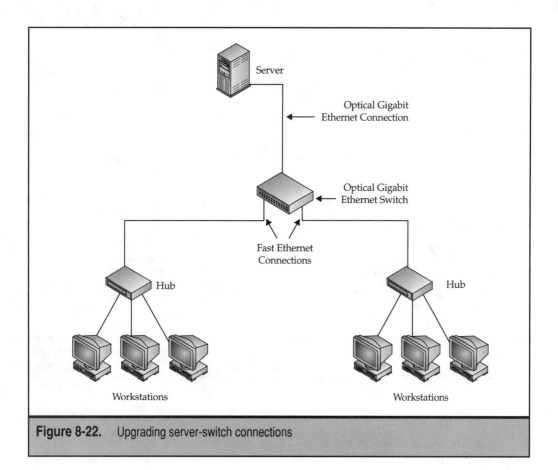

Figure 8-22.   Upgrading server-switch connections

pair copper wire) to ports on a Gigabit Ethernet switch. Then, an optical connection can be made to the server, using the switch's optical port. This way, the Fast Ethernet connections can be easily combined into a Gigabit Ethernet connection.

Backbone

A Fast Ethernet backbone switch aggregates several 10/100 Mbps Ethernet switches. It can easily be upgraded to a Gigabit Ethernet switch, thereby supporting multiple 100/1000 Mbps switches, as well as routers and hubs with optical Gigabit Ethernet interfaces. As soon as the backbone has been upgraded, servers with Gigabit Ethernet connections can be added directly to the backbone, as shown in Figure 8-23.

This modification will go a long way toward giving applications the high bandwidth they need.

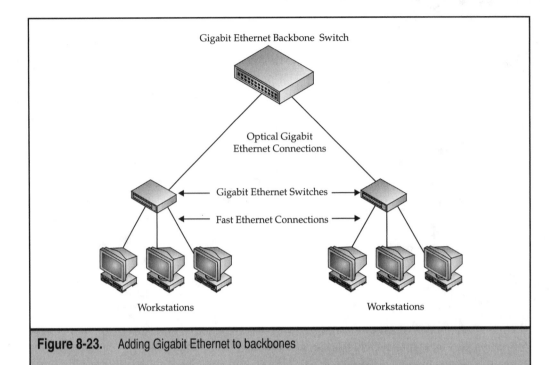

Figure 8-23. Adding Gigabit Ethernet to backbones

The Desktop

If your organization is such that you need high-speed connections right to the desktop, again, Gigabit Ethernet can help. High-performance workstations need only connect to Gigabit Ethernet switches. This upgrade can be performed either with fiber or by using the existing cable, which is already in place.

You may choose to upgrade to optical cable for a number of reasons, including avoiding electromagnetic interference or getting ready for future upgrades.

MANs

As you remember from the last chapter, MANs occupy a position where they functionally overlap both LANs and WANs. MANs are defined as being less than 100 km from end to end; however, most MANs are much smaller than that, usually about a fifth to a third of that size.

If you wanted to construct a MAN, there are a number optical networking technologies you could use to do so. It is possible to employ an FDDI architecture, which would make use of the most likely available fiber arrangement—existing SONET rings. On the other hand, Gigabit Ethernet and Fibre Channel are also means that could be employed to develop a MAN, which would provide high speeds and a good match with your existing network.

Developing a MAN doesn't necessarily mean that you have to deploy your own fiber infrastructure. It may very well be that there is already fiber in place and all you must do is connect to it.

Dark Fiber and the MAN

When connecting buildings, an attractive choice is *dark fiber*. Dark fiber is fiber that has been run but is not actively in use. There are a number of reasons dark fiber exists. Anyone who owns some right of way (cities, utility companies, and so forth) has been busy planting fiber, whether he or she has immediate plans to use it or not. It makes sense, to a degree, that there is so much dark fiber. After all, if a city is ripping up Main Street to install a new sewer system, it makes perfect sense to be a little proactive and place a run of fiber. In the event an organization wants to create a MAN (or connect to an existing MAN), the fiber is already in place and the city can charge for the fiber's use. But as useful as correctly placed dark fiber can be, there seems to be more than enough of it in place. Some estimate that at least 90 percent of the deployed fiber is dark fiber.

Construction

The physical layout and construction of a MAN depends largely on the fiber. If it is already in place, most likely it is configured in rings. This harks back to the early days to SONET, in which rings were a critical part of a MAN's functionality. This works well for FDDI, and can also be adapted for Fibre Channel and Ethernet.

FDDI   FDDI is known largely as a technology for backbone LANs. However, FDDI has migrated into the world of the MAN. By using single-mode fiber, the reach of FDDI can be extended up to 60 km, as shown in Figure 8-24.

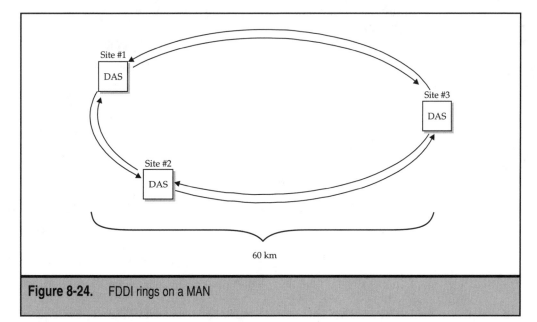

Figure 8-24.   FDDI rings on a MAN

It is FDDI's reach that makes it an especially attractive technology for MANs. However, in this scenario, there are more than 200 km of fiber and it is more than likely that the organization will have to purchase space on the fiber from a service provider. Since most service providers are going to be operating SONET on that ring, this can cause a problem in terms of cost and efficiency. At its lowest level, OC-1 operates at about 51.84 Mbps. Since FDDI operates at 100 Mbps, this is obviously not a good match. The next level is OC-3, which is 155.52 Mbps. If the organization tries to run FDDI over this link, approximately one-third of the available bandwidth will go to waste.

A better way to develop this scenario is to use DWDM. Rather than have a big chunk of unused bandwidth, FDDI can run across DWDM. A DWDM wavelength can carry the FDDI signal and not waste any bandwidth.

Fibre Channel and Gigabit Ethernet   Though Fibre Channel is most commonly associated with SANs, and Gigabit Ethernet is used in LANs, MANs, and WANs, many network administrators would rather connect all their facilities using the same protocols. Not only would this simplify their network topologies, but it would also make the network more scalable and manageable.

But developing Fibre Channel to work as part of a MAN requires a number of enhancements:

▼ Distance can be problematic because even if the two buildings to be connected are only 10 km apart, the cable run may be 40 or 50 km apart. This is because fiber links are run through COs and must follow rights of way, resulting in some roundabout paths.

■ Quality is another issue, because along the way, the fiber cabling might be spliced in a number of places and through who knows how many patch panels and connectors.

■ The organization must also have enough switching capacity to handle the fiber deployment. There must be enough ports and bandwidth to support the MAN. It is important that the SAN's Fibre Channel hub, fabric, or loop have enough ports.

■ To achieve the distances required for MAN fiber links, the correct laser is important. The preferred laser in this capacity is a distributed-feedback (DFB) laser, rather than a Fabry-Perot or vertical-cavity surface-emitting laser (VCSEL), which is normally used in SAN fiber installations. The choice of a DFB comes down to power and attenuation. Because of the distances in MANs, it is best to emit a laser at 1550 nm, where attenuation in fiber optic cabling is the lowest. VCSELs emit their laser at 850 nm, which is best for short distances. Fabry-Perot lasers emit at 1310 nm, with an attenuation of about 0.3 dB/km. DFB lasers, on the other hand, have an attenuation of about 0.2 dB/km.

▲ DFB lasers were developed for the telecommunications industry. But it wasn't until recently that DFB lasers were available in a form that could be adapted into a MAN environment. DFB lasers have been integrated into gigabit-interface converter (GBIC) modules. Because GBICs are hot-swappable, the network can be expanded without any downtime or disruption in service.

The abundance of dark fiber, along with the conjunction of laser and interface technologies for extending Gigabit Ethernet and Fibre Channel across long stretches of fiber will be a boon to MANs. The ability to connect remote LANs and SANs within the same company can save customers a considerable amount of money.

10 Gigabit Ethernet over DWDM   As 10 Gigabit Ethernet starts to become more and more available in the coming months, it can be used as an important part of a MAN. Because the number of Fast Ethernet links at the network edge is increasing, so does the need to aggregate Gigabit Ethernet links to the backbone. Not only will 10 Gigabit Ethernet be a somewhat convenient way to aggregate these signals, but it will also be necessary.

In a MAN, 10 Gigabit Ethernet can be deployed over fiber to support such requirements as serverless buildings, remote hosting, off-site storage, and disaster recovery. By using 10 Gigabit Ethernet, service providers can build backbones with less complex and expensive POPs.

Figure 8-25 shows the various components of a MAN. By using 10 Gigabit Ethernet:

▼   Slower links can be aggregated.

■   Providers can use the technology in their backbones.

▲   Provide WAN access.

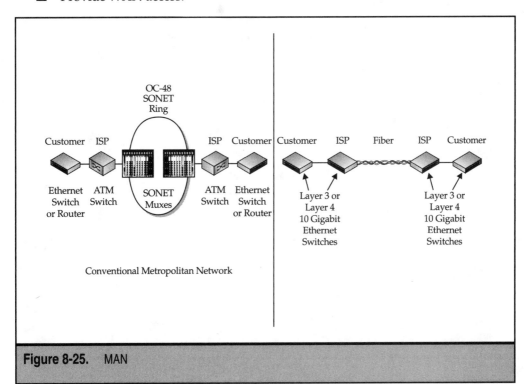

Figure 8-25.   MAN

10 Gigabit Ethernet over DWDM provides a way for a proven, popular technology (Ethernet) to be deployed over the sorts of distances that MANs demand. Further, by employing DWDM, multiple wavelengths can be used, adding capacity to an exploding network.

Constructing an optical network is no small feat. There are a number of variables that must be balanced in order to either develop a new optical network or beef up your existing network with optical capabilities. Once you've constructed your optical network, the work is not over. You will have the responsibility of managing it.

CHAPTER 9

Optical Network
Management

Once a network has been planned, designed, and built, still more tasks must be attended to. Network management—whether of a conventional or optical network—is an ongoing process to which attention must be paid.

Management is critical because without someone overseeing the network, first it will lose its optimization and after a while the network will be unusable. This is because networks are a lot like automobiles. Unless the oil gets changed and air checked in the tires, the car will not perform to its optimal capacity. Given time, the unmanaged automobile will burst into flames, destroying the vehicle, and probably voiding the warranty. That isn't *likely* to happen to your network, but never underestimate the positive effects of some tweaking and tuning.

By implementing a management system, administrators can provision their networks for applications and users with special demands. Further, management ensures that all the networking devices are performing at their best. Because networks are in a state of evolution, management is an ongoing process.

In this chapter, we examine the issues behind network management and talk about tools and techniques you can use to manage your network. We start off with an overview of network management. This describes, in more detail, the reasons why management is so important and how network management started. Next, we talk about service level agreements (SLAs). If you are a provider, you've likely run into these agreements in the past. If you are part of an organization that is using or considering using a service provider, this section will help explain why a contract between yourself and your service provider is a good thing. From there, we'll move into a discussion about Simple Network Management Protocol, which is the predominant standard for network management. From there, we talk about Telecommunications Management Networks (TMNs). These are useful because Synchronous Optical Networks (SONET) cannot be managed by SNMP. TMNs were designed specially for managing all kinds of telecommunications networks. Finally, we'll round out the chapter with a quick overview of some network management tools that you might find useful for your own network.

OVERVIEW OF NETWORK MANAGEMENT

Network management can be confusing to newcomers. By its nature, the field involves a daunting list of tasks. Figure 9-1 outlines the range of tasks performed by the typical network management team. As this figure shows, the process of network management is a never-ending circle. The question those new to the world of network ask is, "Where do I jump in?" The answer is: "Anywhere."

Internetworks must be planned, modeled, budgeted, designed, configured, purchased, installed, tested, mapped, documented, operated, monitored, analyzed, optimized, adjusted, expanded, updated, and fixed. That's a lot. No single tool can do all these things, at least not yet. Suffice it to say that network management products and services constitute an industry unto itself, composed of a complex array of technologies, products, and vendors providing everything from simple protocol analyzers that measure a single link to worldwide network command centers.

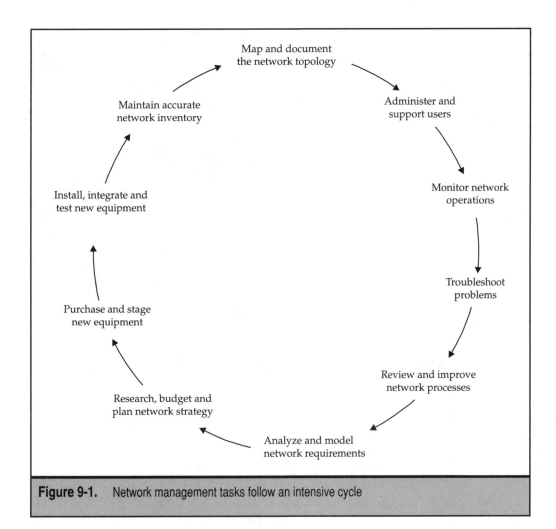

Figure 9-1. Network management tasks follow an intensive cycle

NOTE: You may have noticed that the term "network management" is used in connection with internetworks (almost nobody manages just one LAN any more). The term has held on since the rise of internetworking and is still universal. There is no real difference between network management and internetwork management.

The Roots of Network Management

Historically, the problem with computer management tools has been delivering true multivendor support. In other words, it's hard to find a single tool that can handle equipment from different manufacturers equally well. Multivendor configurations—the norm in virtually all enterprise IT (information technology) infrastructures today—are tough to manage using a single tool because of subtle differences in each manufacturer's equipment.

Computer management tools have evolved from opposite poles of the computing industry: systems and networks. The goal is to bring all computing assets under the management control of a single tool, and the prevalence of placing host systems on networks is driving existing system and network management tools into one another's arms.

Traditional System Management Consoles

Sophisticated computing management systems called *system consoles* have been around for decades. These consoles were generally hooked up to mainframes sitting in a data center and used to schedule jobs, perform backups, and fix problems. Over time, they developed more and more capabilities, such as managing remote computers.

The best-known product from the data center mold is Unicenter from Computer Associates (CA). Unicenter is actually an amalgamation of products that CA has woven into a single management solution. Unicenter evolved from a sophisticated console for managing IBM mainframes and disk farms to an integrated management system with support for all the important hardware and software platforms. Most Unicenter product growth has been achieved by acquisition, understandable given the product scope.

The key to Unicenter and other system consoles is the ability to handle the various computer architectures that enterprises are likely to put into a configuration.

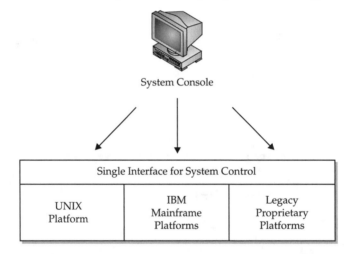

System Console

Single Interface for System Control

| UNIX Platform | IBM Mainframe Platforms | Legacy Proprietary Platforms |

Network Management Systems

Over the past decade, a second breed of management tool emerged in the form of network management systems. These tools focus on network infrastructure instead of the data center. They use the networks they manage as the platform for monitoring events and are controlled from a console referred to as the network management station (NMS).

The leading NMS is OpenView from Hewlett-Packard (HP). There's a bit of history as to how HP ended up in this enviable position. HP had committed to Unix as its strategic operating system in the mid-1980s—years earlier than other enterprise platform vendors. (Don't give HP too much credit; they did so out of desperation because their proprietary 16-bit operating system had run out of gas.) By that time, Unix and IP had become closely linked in the market, mostly because IBM and other big system vendors were still pushing their proprietary networking schemes. Around 1990, HP seized the moment and OpenView rode the Unix bandwagon to become the predominant network management tool. There are now over 100,000 OpenView installations that range from small local area network (LAN) systems to large, optical service provider networks.

As with Unicenter, the key to OpenView's success is its ability to work with devices from various manufacturers. But HP had a built-in design advantage in the form of a then-new IP network management standard called Simple Network Management Protocol (SNMP). Instead of having to design to dozens of proprietary interfaces, HP was able to let the network equipment vendors design products to the SNMP standard. OpenView was the first major management product to implement SNMP.

Network Management Station (e.g., HP Open View, IBM Net View)					
Device Inventory	Configuration	Topology Mapping	Device Monitoring	Troubleshooting	Analysis
SNMP/RMON					
Routers	Switches	Hubs		Access Servers	Servers
Cisco Works 2000		Bay Networks' Optivity		Others (e.g., Castle Rock, Corvis, Lucent)	
Resource Manager Essentials	CWSI				

The defining difference between system and network consoles is the level at which they operate. System management tools focus on operating systems, transactions, data files, and databases as they exist across servers, storage controllers, and disks. Network management tools focus on packets and connections as they exist over network devices, network interfaces, and transmission links.

System and network consoles are now converging into a single technology class some call enterprise system management (ESM) tools. Convergence into ESM is inevitable as the line between network and computer blurs and enterprises complete the shift to client/server architectures that move resources from the data center out into their internetwork topologies.

Network Management Tools Today

It has proved to be very difficult to manage an internetwork using a single tool. The problem has been the inability to collect consistent data from the variety of devices that exist in most enterprise IT infrastructures. The problem isn't so much old versus new equipment, although that's part of it. The major hang-up is that most network management systems are shallow in their implementations; in other words, they can manage only a few aspects of device operation, and they leave some devices unmanaged altogether.

This is so despite the fact that all major network equipment makers bundle SNMP into their device operating systems. The base SNMP infrastructure is there, but device manufacturers seldom implement it fully in their products. There are a variety of reasons for this:

▼ **Consumption of resources by network management**   Every CPU cycle spent gathering a measurement or sending an SNMP message is a cycle not used for payload traffic. Network management extracts a cost in either slower performance or extra hardware.

■ **Spotty standards support by manufacturers**   It would be expensive for device makers to build complete compliance into their products. Device hardware would need to be beefed up to handle the additional SNMP work, pushing up prices in the process. In addition, some manufacturers prefer a dash of SNMP incompatibility to steer customers toward standardizing on their product line because implementing SNMP from one manufacturer is easier than bringing devices of different manufacturers under the same management regime.

■ **Labor**   A lot of time and attention is required for enterprises to implement and operate a network management system. Management teams are hard pressed just to keep up with network growth. Few have the manpower to make greater use of SNMP-based systems.

▲ **Price-conscious customers**   Customers are fixated on low price points. The network half of IT shops is regarded as infrastructure, and managers demand commodity pricing. The relentless focus on driving down the cost per port looks good on paper but incurs hidden costs in the form of poorly utilized assets.

For these reasons, most SNMP implementations gather only high-level information. Fewer processes—called *objects*—are monitored, samples are smaller, polling cycles are less frequent, and so on.

Often, even when an enterprise *does* want more network management controls, blind spots are still created by noncompliant devices. Blind spots occur when a policy cannot be enforced in part of a network because a device doesn't support it. Blind spots often occur at backbone entryways, especially to switched backbones. Take the scenario depicted in Figure 9-2. The part of the topology on the bottom has implemented a policy to manage traffic usage between a pair of communicating hosts. But the router in the middle is not configured to monitor that, leaving that SNMP policy unenforced beyond the router.

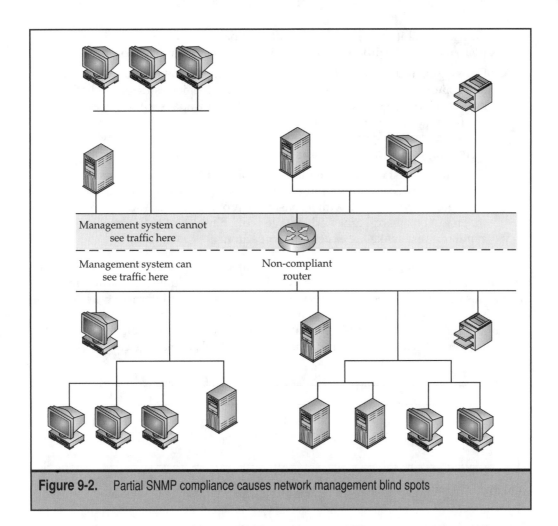

Figure 9-2.   Partial SNMP compliance causes network management blind spots

The Internet Engineering Task Force (IETF) is responsible for the SNMP standard, and it has a tough job. The implementation of any standard requires coordinated acceptance from both manufacturers and users. This is difficult to pull off because manufacturers are wary of market acceptance and the potential loss of competitive advantage. Understandably, then, standards setting is always a tricky process. Yet the goal of an integrated NMS console has proved to be particularly elusive for these reasons:

▼ **Hardware dependencies**   Any computer standard must contend with various architectures used for CPUs, buses, device interfaces, drivers, and the like. This both complicates the standards-setting process and makes it more expensive for manufacturers to comply. The problem is exacerbated by the internetworking industry's habit of using so many different parts in their product lines. Remember all the different CPU architectures that go into Cisco's router line?

■ **Converging technology**   Until recently, telecommunications, data networking, and computing were viewed as separate and distinct industries. Each had its own industry bodies, standards, and so on. But nowadays, all of this equipment has fallen under the purview of network managers. This has increased the scope of the standards and brought together different engineering fields, which creates increasingly more complex work environments for network managers.

▲ **Technology onslaught**   Relentless technology advances in all quarters of computing (telecommunications, operating systems, CPUs, cabling, and so on) have presented the IETF with a constantly moving target. And a manufacturer that has won a hard-earned advantage is often reluctant to fall into line with standards and make life easier for competitors.

Progress has been slow. Yet the lack of integrated management hasn't impeded the explosive growth in the size and use of networks. To accommodate this conflict, management teams use several products to track different parts of their internetworks. Most big enterprises have an ESM, but they augment it with dedicated tools to manage critical parts of internetworks. Figure 9-3 illustrates a typical scenario, with OpenView used to watch the overall network and manufacturer-specific tools to manage critical assets.

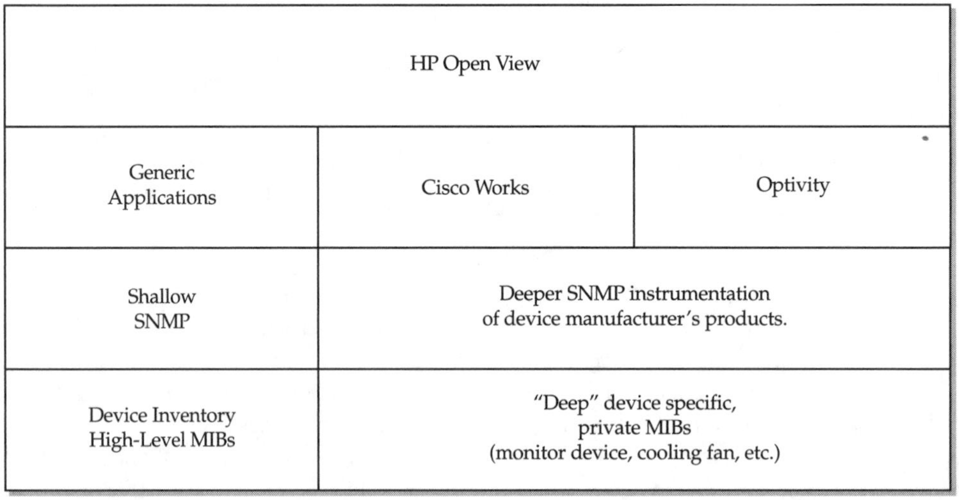

Figure 9-3.   Most network teams use several tools to manage their internetworks

Trends in Enterprise System Management

ESM tools have been criticized as difficult to implement, labor intensive, expensive, slow, and ineffective. They're priced up to $250,000 and cost at least that much again to implement. As far as specialized management hardware, Remote Monitoring (RMON) probes can cost over $10,000 each. The expense has left most small to medium-sized internetworks relying on multiple tools of more or less equal importance, each usually specific to the major equipment manufacturers used in the configuration. A second result is that fewer things are monitored, diminishing proactive network management.

But the market for tools is robust anyway, because the potential for savings from NMS tools is enormous. Some estimate that during a typical IT infrastructure's lifecycle, 75 percent or more of all costs are spent on operations. There is a double benefit of enabling network administration personnel to be more productive and getting better results in available bandwidth. NMS tools help enterprises reduce costs and boost service at the same time.

Competition is heating up in the NMS arena. There are now over a dozen major NMS tools. In addition to OpenView and Unicenter, other notables are IBM's Tivoli NetView (IBM acquired Tivoli Systems a few years ago), Platinum Technology's ProVision, Cabletron System's Spectrum, Nortel Networks Optivity, Loran Technologies' Kinnetics, Bull Worldwide's OpenMaster, and Sun's SunNet Manager.

Microsoft has tentatively entered the fray with the introduction of Microsoft Management Console (MMC), introduced in Windows 2000. MMC is a key to the company's server strategy in that corporate computing must have management capability. It's just a bare-bones framework for a few Microsoft applications for now, but rest assured that Microsoft will be pushing hard to get vendors to snap their management applications into the Microsoft Management Console. Figure 9-4 charts how different management tools interrelate.

The cast of contenders comes from three sources: computer platform makers such as HP and IBM; network device manufacturers Cisco and Nortel Networks; and software companies in the form of Microsoft, Castle Rock, and others. Who prevails will tell which is most important: the wire, the desktop, or the mainframe. Regardless of vendor, NMS technology is headed toward these goals:

▼ **More coverage**   Where greater management control is placed on devices and network processes, doing this will require faster device hardware.

■ **Simplicity**   As internetworking has exploded in popularity among small and medium-sized enterprises, more networks are being operated by nonexperts.

■ **Automation**   As underlying network management technologies improve, more management tasks are being automated to improve Quality of Service (QoS).

▲ **Proactive management**   A new breed of tools helps isolate emerging problems and avert major network problems by taking early corrective action.

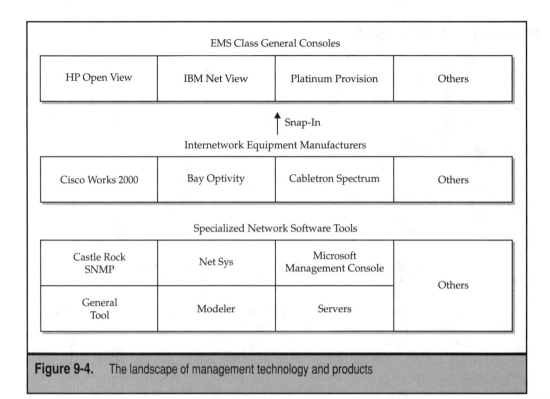

Figure 9-4. The landscape of management technology and products

Nearly all progress in computing results directly or indirectly from industry standards. Internetworking ushered in the era of open computing with the help of several standards: the seven-layer OSI reference model, IP, Ethernet, Unix, Wintel (the Windows + Intel desktop standard), HTTP, SQL, and others. Now it's time to bring it all under control with integrated management technology driven by SNMP.

SERVICE LEVEL AGREEMENTS

Network management is all well and good, but what happens to resources out of your control? What if you've got your network optimized within an inch of its life, yet data runs into a mean bottleneck once it leaves your organization and enters your service provider? Not only is that a fair and reasonable question, but it is also a big enough issue that many organizations have unleashed their lawyers on their providers to come up with a solution.

Organizations can ensure that they have significant resources to accomplish mission-critical tasks through an agreement with their service provider. Service level agreements (SLAs) are contracts that an organization and service provider enter into, which guarantee specified levels of service.

According to research from IDC, almost 97 percent of companies with 2500 or more employees required a SLA for network availability in the next year. SLAs are critical to ensuring consistent QoS, performance, and uptime in important computer-centric environments. Furthermore, IDC predicts that the market for managed- and hosted-service SLAs will grow from $278 million in 1999 to $849 million by 2004.

NOTE: This section is not meant to imply that you should enter into some combative relationship with your service provider. Quite the contrary. By understanding your system needs, your budget, your provider, and your provider's capabilities, a SLA can help ensure that you and your provider will develop a positive relationship based on mutual respect.

Benefits

A SLA is, in essence, a contract that lists what networking resources your service provider guarantees to be available.

Simply deciding which service provider will house your online resources isn't enough. You may expect a certain level of network availability and resources, but your service provider may not. For example, let's say that you expect to connect two branch offices across a wide area network (WAN). You expect constant uptime and a high rate of speed in your connection. "Constant" and "high rate of speed" are very fuzzy concepts; both these terms are relative. Over at your service provider's office, they might have two dozen other customers who expect the same level of service that you do. Because of constraints on the provider's network, bandwidth might have to be provisioned such that everyone can at least have some measure of access. Though the provider has seriously scaled back the amount of bandwidth available, in the provider's opinion, they are providing "constant" service at a "high rate of speed." However, because you did not spell out specific levels of service, there is nothing you can do, because you did not have a SLA.

Guaranteed Levels of Service

The SLA is a contract between the service provider and its customers. The SLA defines the acceptable levels of network performance, including response time, availability, downtime, and repair response.

With a SLA, customers can establish defined requirements for IT and network services and weigh them against costs. In the event the SLA is breached by the provider, the most common punishment is a credit for service—but we'll talk about penalties later.

SLAs benefit different members of an organization in different ways:

▼ Network managers can get an accurate picture of their network and understand exactly how they are meeting objectives. They can also spend less time justifying network costs to the end users and have tangible evidence why money needs to be invested in the network to senior management. Further, SLAs can also be used in evaluating vendors' services and wares. Because managers can look at specific goals and requirements, they have solid numbers that can be used when evaluating or buying vendors' products. Finally, managers can also evaluate different applications, including priorities, bandwidth reservation, or special packet handling.

▲ End users benefit because they will see their network being more responsive, costs are minimized, and critical applications will have the resources that they need. By employing a SLA, users will be able to determine, conclusively, when the network is dipping beneath a desired threshold, rather than the ubiquitous "the network is slow today."

The Penalty Phase

When a service provider is unable to meet the terms of a SLA, the financial implications can be steep. In a severe example, the penalty can be three times the monthly charges for each hour the line is down (beyond what is stipulated in the SLA). That means that if a service is down for 13 hours (the SLA allows one hour of downtime per year), the service provider will have to give three years worth of credit. Naturally, the expense can be rather high, so the service provider wants to ensure that the service is up to snuff before entering into any such agreement.

Even with a solid SLA, organizations can still suffer. Case in point, a major airline felt comfortable with their service provider because a harsh, punitive SLA had been crafted. In the event the service provider violated the SLA, it would award the airline a large sum of money. Everyone at the airline felt confident that the SLA would protect the organization if there was ever a network problem. However, the worst-case scenario struck and the airline's computer network was down for six hours, keeping aircraft grounded worldwide during that time. It took 12 hours to get critical systems back online and the airline's schedule was thrown into disarray for five days. Sure, the SLA paid off, but the sum was inconsequential compared to the lost revenues and image damage that the airline suffered.

Though credit is a common penalty against providers, the organization should decide if credit is enough to make up for bad performance or failed connectivity. Remember the example of the airline we used earlier: the airline lost far more in revenues and image damage than the provider had to recoup.

There are instances where a service provider has actually issued a check to an organization for a SLA violation—however, those are rare cases. It is better for an enterprise to come up with a penalty that would cause their service providers a measure of pain for the violation, rather than trying to apply a specific dollar amount. Pain can be a good way to keep a service provider from violating a SLA.

Network SLAs

Your SLA should cover the important connection and security characteristics of the network. The SLA will identify the IP performance levels that your provider will guarantee. Some organizations will buy "best effort" delivery methods via the public Internet. This means that they will get the best service that the provider can give, given the availability of Internet resources. They may get abundant bandwidth sometimes; most often they won't. Other organizations will insist that their provider offer service over a private IP network that allows specific guarantees for application availability and is tweaked for specific customer needs.

The SLA should define what type of network infrastructure the service provider will deliver. By understanding the physical design of the network, providers can help establish customer expectations about the level of service they will receive. The SLA will also measure, in terms of bits per second, such issues as:

▼ Uptime

■ Network availability

▲ Throughput

It would be fantastic if an organization could achieve 100 percent uptime, but it is more realistic to strive for 99.5 and 99.9 percent uptime. Spread over a year, that equates to roughly 43 and 8 hours of downtime, respectively. It is important to note when that downtime will be counted. An important element in specifying penalties for downtime is establishing a differentiation between downtime during business hours and overall downtime. For instance, if your system goes out at 2 P.M., it can cause major upheavals. However, if it goes down at 2 A.M., it might only interrupt the night watchman's online Quake tourney. On the other hand, if your network is an e-business system that doesn't have a "closed" sign that gets flipped over at 6 P.M., an outage at any time will be unacceptable.

Another important part of your SLA will be spelling out acceptable data losses and latency along with bandwidth provisioning.

▼ Data loss, which occurs in highly saturated IP networks, is often outlined in SLAs as being no less than 99 percent. Again, this seems like a pretty high bar, but real-time applications like Voice over IP still suffer at this level. In environments where users will primarily Web-browse, 5 percent is more average.

■ Data latency is also critical in VoIP environments, where data delays can have a deleterious effect of the application. A standard benchmark is that real-time applications require response times of 100 milliseconds (ms) or less. Those environments where Web browsing is more the speed see latency levels at 250 ms.

▲ Security SLAs define such attributes as applications, data, and services, which are protected while being transported over the provider's network. In this case, the security portion of the SLA doesn't contain etched-in-stone metrics. Rather, whether or not the service provider is meeting his or her goal is subjective.

SLAs can contain a large amount of metrics to be guaranteed and monitored. In the next section, we'll take you through the process of researching and drafting a SLA.

Preparing a SLA

When you set out to prepare a SLA, it is unnecessary (and somewhat over the top) to presume that your entire organization will be covered by the terms of the SLA. It is simply unattainable to establish an all-encompassing SLA. At the very least, your IT department will spend more time on policing and establishing performance metrics than they will on their actual jobs. Therefore, it is best just to set up SLAs for the most mission-critical functions of your organization.

When setting up a SLA, there are four major processes:

▼ Recognizing business and user needs

■ Establishing a baseline

■ Establishing metrics and negotiating trade-offs

▲ Drafting the SLA

The following sections detail these processes.

Recognizing Business and User Needs

In order to establish business objectives, it is necessary to work with senior management as well as the business managers. This will help establish the organization's goals and how the IT department fits into those goals. By getting the line managers' input, it is possible to define goals for specific applications and performance levels necessary for each department. Ultimately, the goal is to establish the network and application priorities while also understanding the organization's willingness to pay for reliability and performance levels.

At this stage, the IT department has the unenviable role of acting as arbiter between management and the service provider. It is in everyone's best interest if the IT department plays the game straight and recognizes the realistic capabilities of the service provider, then helps management to understand what, exactly, the system's capabilities are. This prevents management from expecting more than the provider can deliver.

Establishing a Baseline

Next, the organization's existing capabilities are measured and recorded as a baseline. This is the basis upon which future performance will be measured. Without a baseline, it will be impossible to quantify what improved and what did not.

First, individual applications that are deemed to be mission critical are measured. This measurement should be conducted over a period of time so that trends can be identified and analyzed. This sample should include such high-traffic times as:

▼ End of the month

■ End of the quarter

▲ End of the year

This is necessary because if you measure performance in the middle of the month for just a couple days, then you won't get an accurate picture of your network's needs. For example, if you are measuring the performance of a network used in retail sales, it is useless to measure system performance during a lone week in June.

However, if it is simply not reasonable to measure a year's worth of performance (or a half year, or a quarter), then reasonable estimates should be made and performance still measured to make adjustments as needed.

Establishing Metrics and Negotiating Trade-Offs

Next, it is necessary to determine which metrics will be used in the SLA. There are three main criteria for metrics. The metrics must:

▼   Be measurable

■   Define performance goals

▲   Be meaningful

For example, bit error rates are measurable; however, they aren't meaningful to users in the accounting department. On the other hand, the number of application time-outs would be meaningful to the users in the accounting department. Because the SLA is an agreement between the organization and the provider, it must not simply contain jargon useful only to the IT department. For the organization to buy into the idea of a SLA, there need to be meaningful measurements. This can be established by talking to the end users and finding out what is important to them.

The SLA should include as much network information as possible. However, it is not necessary (nor even possible) to track and monitor the 30,000-odd events that are typical in today's large network. Detailed data events should be available, but they are not useful unless condensed into simple summaries that identify whether the network is okay, or if there are problems that require attention. This necessitates that the information be organized hierarchically—that is, with simple summaries at the top and the information getting more and more precise as one drills down.

The SLA should be able to identify dangerous situations, such as a router suddenly tripling its load, or a user doing something unseemly, such as trying to reconfigure the firewall. These are a couple of the events that are so critical that when they occur, the IT department should be notified immediately.

It is also at this stage that the question of cost arises. The terms and cost of the SLA can be directly connected to management and user requirements. But if the price tag is too large for the organization to stomach, it might be necessary to reduce performance goals if the SLA does not work within budgeted amounts. In this case, it is important that the IT department work with management to prioritize the list of metrics.

Drafting the SLA

Once the details have been established, it is necessary to commemorate those measurements in the written word. This is the stage at which the SLA contract is drafted. This document establishes such details as:

▼ Minimum levels of performance

■ Reliability

■ Scalability

▲ Cost

The metrics used to gauge success or failure must be quite precise. Table 9-1 shows an example of some SLA metrics and their associated performance guarantee.

Metric	Performance Guarantee
Reliability	No more than 2 hours of unplanned downtime during the year, excluding servers and hosts. Servers will experience no more than 1 hour unplanned downtime per year. Hosts will experience no more than 1 hour of unplanned downtime per year.
Utilization	The system will support 48 simultaneous users at peak times. Ethernet segments will not be more than 30 percent utilized during the peak hour, averaged over a 1-minute period. E-mail will constitute no more than 3 percent of network traffic during the peak hour.
Performance	95 percent of users will have a network response time of 2 seconds or less during the peak hour. Application timeouts will be limited to one every 50,000 sessions. Internet users will be able to load a 100-kilobyte database file in less than 10 seconds during the peak hour. Other parameters include maximum frame size, burst size, rate, traffic policing, traffic within committed rate, and traffic outside committed rate.

Table 9-1.   Metrics and Performance Goals

Most SLAs today deal only with resource availability and not performance. However, this is the direction that things are going and it is a good idea to make sure you're working proactively.

Maintenance

Establishing a SLA is just the start of a process of continual fine-tuning and adjustment. Occasionally, the procedures used for measuring SLA metrics must be reviewed. Reviewing the individual metrics and how well those metrics are being met serves as a means to evaluate not only your service provider, but also how you gauge your organization's performance. For instance, in Table 9-1, we use as an example that a 100-kilobyte database file must be loaded in under 10 seconds. That is fine, but if your organization no longer uses database files of that size, this metric is meaningless and the SLA is not serving your organization.

As Figure 9-5 shows, the process of evaluating the SLA and your metrics is an ongoing process. You can review your metrics as often as you like; however, a monthly review is normally sufficient.

NOTE: If your organization undergoes quick periods of business needs change, you might wish to review your metrics more frequently.

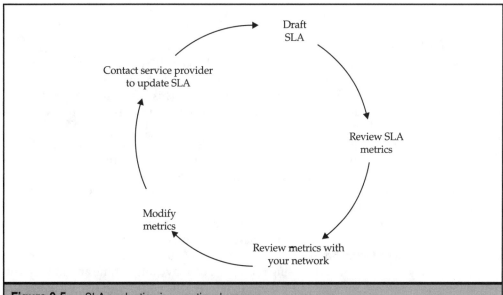

Figure 9-5.   SLA evaluation is a continual process

Once you've conducted your review, make a note of any exceptions and trouble spots. Then, determine if these exceptions are really problems or just aberrations that can be chalked up to a seasonal variation. Investigate what caused the exception. Is there a new application on the network? Does the network slow down every day at 4 P.M. when the users play Half Life on the LAN?

Like a network, your SLA should be constantly evolving. What is important today may not be important tomorrow.

Measurement

To conduct your performance monitoring, there are tools out there that can track a plethora of details. The tools must be able to provide continuing and state performance measurements. Further, the information must be useful and able to relate to the SLA metrics.

Performance measurement tools must be able to show end-to-end performance so that it is possible to monitor specific devices and the metrics identified in the SLA. It might not be possible to find a single application that can track all the metrics in your SLA. In this case, it might be necessary to purchase multiple tools that can keep track of all the data you need to monitor.

Ideally, the best SLA tools let IT managers view network performance in the same way that the provider does. Such SLA management tools as ViewGate Networks' Inteligo are widely used by service providers but can also be used by organizations via a Web browser. This allows an organization's IT personnel to monitor network performance. Tools should also monitor and manage SLA metrics in real time, rather than just as historical views showing past performance. That way, you can stay up to date on your network's performance and not act in a strictly reactionary way.

What Really Matters

If you remember the example of the airline, you will recognize a fundamental mistake a number of organizations make when establishing a SLA. Not only do they set specific metrics, but there are also penalties that are put in place. This is all fine and good; however, if the network goes down, then the penalty may not be enough recompense for the downtime.

It isn't enough just to penalize the service provider if there is an outage. Better, you should spend the time early in the process and recognize which metrics are the most important for your organization. This will fine-tune your attention to the mission-critical processes, plus you won't have to monitor a thousand issues when there are only a dozen that really require your attention.

For example, performance monitoring and availability management tools are not always able to find the precise cause of a problem. They can narrow it down to the source, which is a good place to start and helps alleviate lots of running around and searching down blind alleys. Furthermore, by using them, you can save lots of time and money you would have spent doing something like adding more bandwidth or paying for another wavelength when all you had to do was reconfigure the router.

What to Look for in a SLA

When you decide which service provider to select, you should be aware of a number of issues and have the answers before you sign on the dotted line. Be sure to check out your service provider, first. Here are a few of the most important things to look for:

▼   Cost should be secondary to services and quality. Too often companies lazily look at service providers that are in their price range, then try to piece together an offering from there. The service provider's ability to deliver is the most important thing. If you go with something because it's less expensive, you'll be paying for it in the long run.

■   The service provider should be strategically and financially sound. Don't be afraid to dig around and ask questions. If you're dealing with small firms, a good way to gauge their quality is by how regularly the bills arrive. If they're three months late, they have a problem. On the other hand, with large companies, strategy shifts are a common problem that can inconvenience your organization.

■   Ask about packet loss and latency figures and even perform "ping" tests, where a packet Internet groper puts intentional stress on the network to test its stability. Be sure to check out network infrastructure, too.

■   Make sure your service provider will be there for you. Round-the-clock service is just as important as performance. If your system goes down, your service provider should be able to get it back up quickly.

■   The provider should offer all the essentials of a solid provider: physical security, redundant power grids, dual tier-one ISP connections, and internal change control processes. Ask the provider where single points of failure could result in loss of service, and what could be done to minimize/eliminate them.

■   The service provider should offer the right options. This should be true not only for where your organization is today, but for where it wants to be next year and the year after that. An ISP should offer access options such as plenty of points of presence, dedicated access for different speeds, and Frame Relay or ATM networks. It must offer security services that meet your needs, no matter if that means off-the-shelf products or managed firewall servers. It should already have—or at least be developing—service options such as news feeds, network management, intranets, or virtual private networks (VPNs).

▲   Talk to your colleagues. Use personal experience, especially from people you know. Most often service providers are chosen by someone calling a friend in an IT position.

Finding a service provider isn't as easy as opening the Yellow Pages and looking up "ISPs." Certainly, the expanding nature of the Internet makes it tricky to find the latest and most complete list of ISPs out there. However, you can search a list of ISPs by area code by visiting www.ispworld.com. You can find local service providers, national service providers with a local presence, and service providers with an 800 number you can dial into.

SNMP

Almost all modern internetwork management suites are built atop the Simple Network Management Protocol (SNMP). SNMP is widely used to gather information about a network. It can be used to find out how many packets are being sent out, if any links are down, or any of hundreds of other details about the network.

In this section, we look at SNMP in greater depth and explain what it does, why it does it, and how your network can benefit from it.

What Is SNMP?

SNMP is a TCP/IP protocol purposely built to serve as a communications channel for internetwork management operating at the application layer of the IP stack. Although SNMP can be directly operated through the command line, it's almost always used through a management application that uses the SNMP communications channel to monitor and control networks. As Figure 9-6 shows, SNMP has two basic components: a network management station and agents.

Agents are small software modules that reside on managed devices. They can be configured to collect specific pieces of information on device operations. Most of the infor-

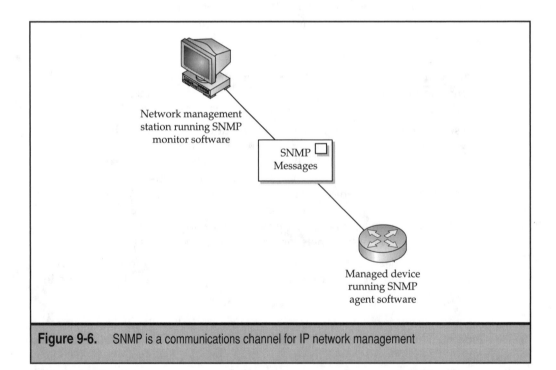

Network management
station running SNMP
monitor software

SNMP
Messages

Managed device
running SNMP
agent software

Figure 9-6.   SNMP is a communications channel for IP network management

mation consists of totals: total bytes, total packets, total errors, and the like. Agents can be deployed on a panoply of devices:

▼   Routers

■   Switches

■   Access servers

■   Hubs

■   Servers (Windows, Unix, Linux, MVS, VMS, and so on)

■   Workstations (PCs, Macs, and Unix desktops)

■   Printers

▲   UPS power backup systems

The idea is to place agents on all network devices and manage things according to the status information sent back. A piece of equipment with an SNMP agent loaded onto it is referred to as a *managed device* (also called a *network element*).

The Network Management System (NMS) is the internetwork's control center. Usually, there's just one NMS for an autonomous system, although many large internetworks use more than one NMS—usually arranged in a hierarchy. Most NMSs today run on dedicated Unix or Microsoft Windows servers.

SNMP Polling and Managed Objects

SNMP is a fairly simple request/response protocol. It works by having the NMS periodically poll managed devices for fresh information. The polling frequency is a matter of configuration choice, but it usually takes place once every few minutes or so. There are three types of polling:

▼   **Monitor polling**   To check that devices are available and to trigger an alarm when one is not responding.

■   **Threshold polling**   To detect when conditions deviate from a baseline number by a percentage greater than allowed (usually plus or minus 10 percent to 20 percent) and to notify the NMS for review. This is also called threshold crossing alerts (TCAs).

▲   **Performance polling**   To measure ongoing network performance over longer periods and to analyze the data for long-term trends and patterns. This is also called performance monitoring (PM).

The agent responds to the poll by returning a message to the NMS. It's able to do this by capturing and storing information on subjects that it has been configured to monitor. These subjects are usually processes associated with the flow of packets. A process about which the agent collects data is called a managed object. A *managed object* is a variable characteristic of the device being managed. The total number of UDP connections open on a managed device, for example, could be a managed object. One open UDP session on a specific interface is an *object instance,* but the total number of simultaneously open UDP sessions on the device (say, a router) is a managed object. Figure 9-7 shows our example UDP connections as managed object and instances.

Managed objects are usually operating characteristics of managed devices. The managed devices can be anywhere in the topology—backbone devices, servers, or end systems. Most objects are physical pieces, such as a network interface. But a managed object isn't necessarily a physical entity. An object could also be a software application, a database, or some other logical entity.

The MIB

The agent stores the information about objects in specialized data records called *MIBs (management information bases).* A MIB is the storage part of the SNMP agent software. Information stored in MIBs is referred to as *variables* (also called *attributes*). MIBs usually collect information in the form of totals for a variable during a time interval, such as total packets over five minutes. Figure 9-8's example shows variables being extracted from

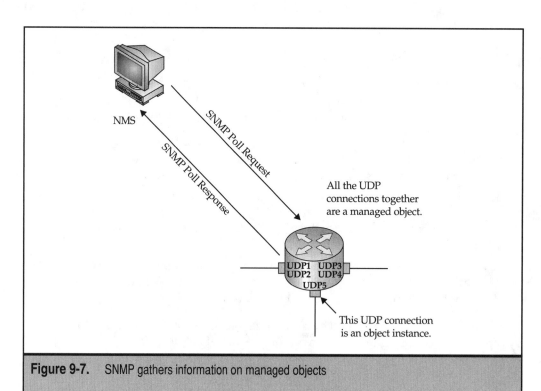

Figure 9-7. SNMP gathers information on managed objects

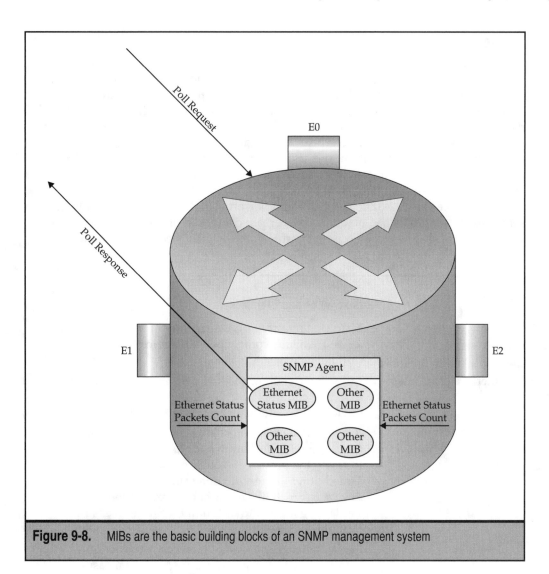

Figure 9-8. MIBs are the basic building blocks of an SNMP management system

instances and processed through managed MIBs and the managed object—in this example, a count of total Ethernet packets going through a router's interface. Again, the packet count from each interface is a managed object instance; the count for all three interfaces is the managed object.

By collating data from multiple objects, the MIB lets the agent send the NMS information concerning everything on the device that is being monitored.

Types of MIBs

MIBs are prefabricated to perform specific jobs. They're often called MIB objects. Basic MIBs usually come packaged inside the network device operating system.

Generally, MIBs are named using a convention that indicates the MIB category. For example, a Cisco MIB object that deals with a specific network interface will have *if* in its name (from the letters *i* and *f* in interface). The ifInErrors MIB object monitors incoming packet errors on an interface; ifOutErrors monitors the outgoing errors. sysLocation reports a device's network location, and so on. In and Out specify whether the MIB object is to measure incoming or outgoing traffic. Table 9-2 shows five basic MIB categories used in most SNMP systems.

It is possible to set a MIB to gather information on a single object instance only, called a *scalar* object. Most managed objects, however, are composed of several related instances. This practice, called *tabular* objects, is the rule in most MIBs because it's more efficient to

Category	Description and Examples
Configuration	MIBs that report basic management information such as device name, contact person, device location, and uptime.
Interface error rates	MIBs that monitor specific interfaces. Packet errors are a normal condition, but watching their trends indicates device health and helps isolate faults.
Bandwidth	ICMP is a layer-3 protocol that reports on IP packet processing. It's best known for its **echo** command used to verify the presence of other devices by pinging them. Timed pings are used to determine how far away a device is (much like in the submarine movies). SNMP sends ping input and output messages to measure available bandwidth.
Traffic flow	Performance management is largely a matter of measuring traffic flow. There are MIBs to measure traffic rates both as bits per second and packets per second.
Unreachable address	The object to measure how often a router is asked to send messages to an unreachable address.
SNMP data	There are even objects to measure how much time the router spends handling SNMP messages.

Table 9-2.   Basic MIB Objects Commonly Used in SNMP Implementations

manage as much as possible from a single data collection point. As the name implies, a tabular MIB keeps the information straight by storing it in rows and tables.

Optical MIBs

MIBs are not just used in electrical networks. Optical networking gear has its own set of MIBs for network management. Like electrical networks, vendors define their own MIBs for optical devices, but generic MIBs exist for optical devices. For example, Table 9-3 lists some of the MIBs defined by the IETF for SONET/SDH interfaces (specifically, IETF Request for Comment [RFC] 2558).

This is a just a brief taste of the dozens of MIBs identified by this particular RFC. There are thousands of MIBs that handle any number of functions that occur on your network.

What Makes SNMP Machine-Independent

We don't want to get too technical in this book, but you should understand how the SNMP standard makes itself machine-independent. In other words, how is it able to run on different brands of equipment, each with its own proprietary operating system?

The SNMP standard requires that every MIB object have an object ID and a syntax. An object ID identifies the object to the system, and tells what kind of MIB to use and what

MIB	Description
ifPhysAddress	Circuit identifier or octet string of zero length.
ifAdminStatus	Supports read-only access. The desired administrative status of the interface.
ifOperStatus	This object assumes the value is down, if the object sonetPathCurrentStatus has any other value than sonetPathNoDefect.
ifLastChange	sysUpTime at the last change in ifOperStatus.
ifName	Textual name of the interface or an octet string of zero length.
ifLinkUpDownTrapEnable	Default value is disabled. Just read-only access may be supported.
ifHighSpeed	Set to rate of SONET/SDH path in megabits per second.
ifAlias	The (nonvolatile) alias name for this interface as assigned by the network manager.

Table 9-3.   Some MIBs for SONET/SDH Interfaces as Defined by IETF RFC 2558

kind of data the object collects. Syntax means a precise specification a machine can understand in binary form.

To understand a field's contents, the operating system must know whether the field contains a number, text, a counter, or some other type of data. These are called data types. *Data types* specify the syntax to be used for a data field. A *field* is any logical piece of data, such as a model number or temperature reading. In the same way that a field has its own box on an input screen, it has its own position in a computer file. A file represents data in binary (zeros and ones), and a set of binary positions are reserved for each field within the file. All fields must be declared as some data type or another, or else the machine cannot process the data held there.

Computer hardware architectures, operating systems, programming languages, and other environmentals specify the data types they're willing to use. A data type represents the layer where software meets hardware. It tells the machine what syntax to use to interpret a field's contents. Different syntaxes are used for floating-point numbers, integer numbers, dates, text strings, and other data types.

SNMP makes itself independent by declaring its own data types. It does so in the form of the Structure of Management Information (SMI) standard. SMI is a standard dedicated to specifying a machine-independent syntax for every data type. These data types are independent of the data structures and representation techniques unique to particular computer architectures. SMI specifies the syntax for data types such as object IDs, counters, rows, tables, octet strings, network addresses, and other SNMP elements.

MIBs are programmed by vendors using an arcane programming language called ASN.1, created just for programming SMI data types. ASN.1 (for Abstract Systems Notation One) is an OSI standard, from the same people that brought us the seven-layer reference model. Figure 9-9 shows how SMI data types universalize MIB information.

SMI tries to let vendors code "write-once, run anywhere" MIB objects. In other words, someone should be able to write a single piece of MIB software—a packet counter, for example—and the counter MIB should be able to run on any device that supports the SMI syntax definition for a counter.

SMI data types are SNMP's building blocks at the lowest level. They are used to construct MIB object formats in a syntax any machine can understand. From there, object instances are measured and rolled up into managed objects, which in turn are reported by the SNMP agent to the NMS. This is how NMSs can operate across disparate device architectures.

Standard MIBs and Private MIBs

The current MIB standard is MIB-II (RFC 1213), which has nearly 200 standard MIB objects. The standard is implemented as a hierarchy that starts from a root and continues to branch down from the source MIB to the root Internet MIB. Looking at Figure 9-10, you see that each branch is marked both by a name and a number (the numbers are used to build object IDs).

Figure 9-10 also shows the players in the history of the Internet. ISO is the International Standards Organization, and DoD is the U.S. Department of Defense (which started it all with ARPANET). CCITT is the Consultative Committee for International

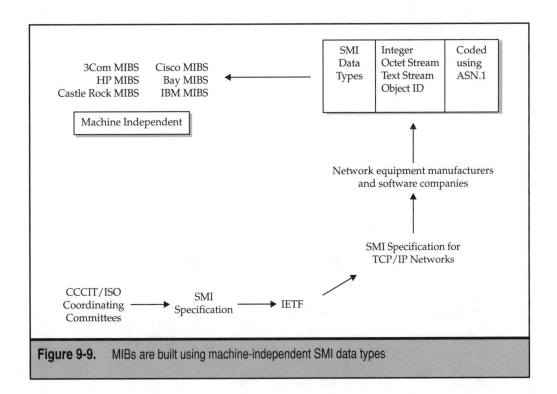

Figure 9-9. MIBs are built using machine-independent SMI data types

Telegraph and Telephone. The CCITT is only a distant cousin of the Internet, handling telephony and other communications standards. The CCITT is now known as the ITU-T (for Telecommunication Standardization Sector of the International Telecommunications Union), but you'll still see the CCITT acronym attached to dozens of standards.

Because they're more user-friendly, text strings are usually used to describe MIB objects in directories. Object IDs are mainly used by software to create compact, encoded representations of the names. Let's use Cisco as an example.

Working from the tree structure in Figure 9-10, the Internet root's object ID is 1.3.6.1, named iso.org.dod.internet. The two main branches beyond the Internet root are the management and private MIBs. Industry-standard MIBs go through the management branch to become iso.org.dod.internet.mgmt.mib with the object ID 1.3.6.1.2.1. Private MIBs become iso.org.dod.internet.private and 1.3.6.1.4. Cisco's private MIB is represented as iso.org.dod.internet.private.enterprise.cisco, or object ID 1.3.6.1.4.1.9. Vendors can build private MIBs by extending standard MIB branches. In this way, they can customize MIBs to better fit their particular needs.

Many of the object groups within the Cisco Management, Temporary Variables, and Local Variables subgroups measure Cisco proprietary technology. For example, the Cisco Environmental Monitor group in the Cisco Management subgroup—object ID 1.3.6.1.4.1.9.9—looks after such things as operating temperature inside the device. This

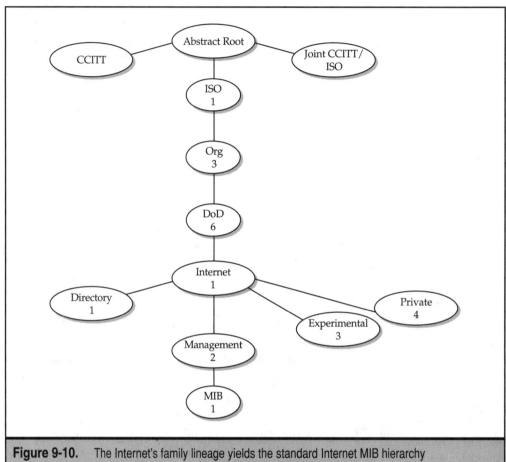

Figure 9-10.   The Internet's family lineage yields the standard Internet MIB hierarchy

type of information is the "deep" stuff we were talking about that management applications from other manufacturers have trouble getting at.

Another important aspect is support for legacy desktop protocols. Novell NetWare IPX, VINES, AppleTalk, DECnet, and even Xerox XNS networks can be managed using MIBs. These are legacy in that the IP LAN specification seems to be steamrolling the market, but the others are still in use and therefore important to their customers.

Polling Groups and Data Aggregation

MIBs are frequently placed into polling groups to facilitate SNMP data collection. A *polling group* is a set of logically related managed objects that are reported and analyzed as a cohesive entity. For example, Figure 9-11 shows polling groups for three different classes

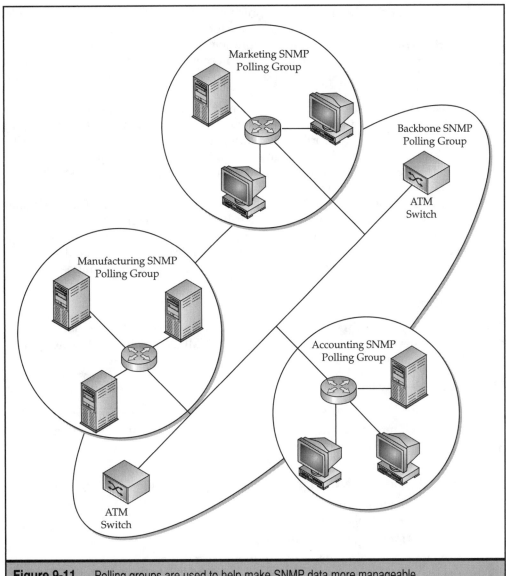

Figure 9-11.   Polling groups are used to help make SNMP data more manageable

of equipment in an internetwork: the backbone switches, routers, and application servers. Different MIB variables are likely to be collected for each type, so each gets its own polling group. In this way, logically related management information is compiled and stored into the SNMP database under group names.

Grouping simplifies the network administrator's job. In the Figure 9-11 example, thresholds can be set to fit tolerances appropriate for each group. For example, a network team is likely to set alarm variables to be more sensitive for the backbone switches, because trouble with them could bring the entire internetwork down. Polling similar MIBs en masse simplifies SNMP operations and helps assure data that's consistent, trustworthy, and easier to assimilate.

Groups also make it easier to limit the amount of information stored in the NMS database. SNMP could build mountains of data on every device in a network, but doing so would be neither practical nor worthwhile. Storing information on related MIB groups facilitates the movement of raw data through a cycle of aggregation and purging. Figure 9-12 shows a typical scenario, in which MIB variables in a group are polled and stored in the NMS database every five minutes. Each midnight, the data is aggregated into minimums, maximums, and averages for each hour, and stored in another database. The data points are purged from the database weekly, leaving behind only the aggregated data.

The collect-aggregate-purge cycle has several benefits. It keeps disk space open on the NMS server for storing new MIBs and maintains statistical integrity of the data record, but at the same time it keeps a consistently fresh picture of network operations.

SNMP Commands

The *simple* in Simple Network Management Protocol comes from the fact that the protocol has just six root commands. They're used to set SNMP parameters within the device's config file. Here are the root SNMP commands:

▼ **Get**   Used by the NMS to retrieve object instances from an agent.

■ **GetNext**   Used to retrieve subsequent object instances after the first instance.

■ **GetBulk**   Introduced in SNMP version 2, only one **GetBulk** operation is necessary to retrieve both the first and all subsequent instances in a managed object (replaces the need for iterative **GetNext** operations).

■ **Set**   Used to set values for object instances within an agent (such as a threshold).

■ **Trap**   Used to instruct an agent to unilaterally notify the NMS of an event (without being polled).

▲ **Inform**   Introduced in SNMP version 2, this command instructs one NMS to forward-trap information to one or more other NMSs.

NOTE: Most of the time, SNMP commands are used by computer programs rather than by people directly. For example, if an administrator enters the location of a router in an inventory screen in the Essentials console, a process is launched from Essentials that invokes the **set snmp location** command in IOS inside that router.

SNMP needs to be simple in order to make itself supportable by disparate architectures. Doing so is a practical requirement for SNMP interoperability.

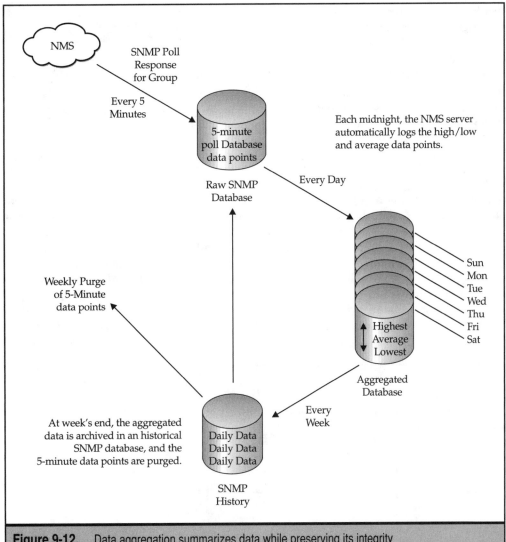

Figure 9-12.   Data aggregation summarizes data while preserving its integrity

Thresholds

A *threshold* defines an acceptable value or value range for a particular SNMP variable. When a variable exceeds a policy, an *event* is said to have taken place. An event isn't necessarily an either/or situation, such as a switch going down. Events are usually operational irregularities that the network team would want to know about before service is affected. For example, a network administrator may set a policy for the number of packet errors occurring on router interfaces in order to steer traffic around emerging traffic bottlenecks. Thresholds can be set either as a ceiling or as a range with upper and lower bounds. The two types of thresholds are depicted in Figure 9-13.

The shaded portions of the graph in Figure 9-13 are called *threshold events*. In other words, an event is when something has taken place in violation of the set policy. A *sampling interval* is the period of time during which a statistic is compiled. For example, a MIB object can store the total number of packet errors taking place during each five-minute period. Intervals must be long enough to gather a representative sample, yet short enough to capture events before they can substantially affect network performance.

Events and Traps

When an event occurs, the network administrator can specify how the SNMP agent should respond. Either the event can be logged, or an alarm message can be sent to the NMS. An SNMP alarm message is called a *trap*, so named because it catches (or traps) the event at the device. A trap contains information about the event.

Alarms can take many forms. They're often configured to show themselves as a blinking icon on the NMS console, but you could have a noise generated. Networks that don't have administrators present at the NMS all the time have the trap dial a pager or send a priority e-mail to alert the person on response duty at the time.

Traps aren't used just to send alarms. As an internetwork grows in size, SNMP overhead traffic will increase along with it. Network managers can reduce SNMP overhead

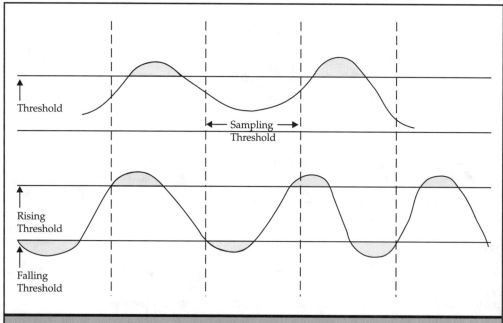

Figure 9-13. Thresholds set a normal operating range for a managed object

by stretching the polling frequency, but doing that makes the NMS less responsive to emerging network problems. A better way to limit SNMP overhead is to use traps. Given that they're unsolicited messages instead of SNMP poll responses, traps consume a negligible amount of bandwidth.

A number of SNMP traps are enabled in the config file. This tells the SNMP agent on the device to send trap messages if anything changes. The last line gives the IP address of the NMS, so the agent knows where to send the trap messages.

SNMP is the most prevalent and popular way to manage network resources. Because it is so popular, it is possible to manage network devices from different vendors. This cuts back on an organization's expenses and does not require them to buy different management tools for each device—assuming, of course, that they can be managed via SNMP.

SNMP Versions

As we mentioned before, SNMP is based on three ideas: agents, managers, and MIBs. No matter what the configuration, at least one management node runs the SNMP management software. Agents are installed on the devices to be managed, including routers, switches, transceivers, and so forth. The agents are responsible for providing access to a local MIB of objects that represents the resources and activity at a MIB's particular node.

These capabilities are good for basic network management systems. To make this functionality even more useful, SNMP was updated in 1993 and 1996. SNMP version 2 added bulk transfer capacity and other useful extensions. But the biggest problem with SNMPv1 and SNMPv2 was that neither offered security functions. To be more specific, SNMPv1 and SNMPv2 could not authenticate the source of a management message, nor could they provide encryption. In the absence of authentication, users could apply unauthorized SNMP commands. Further, it was possible for users to snoop on management information as it was passed between managed systems and management nodes.

To ameliorate the security problems of SNMPv1 and SNMPv2, SNMPv3 was introduced in January 1998. SNMPv3 builds off of SNMPv2 and adds administration and security features.

SNPv3 adds three important services:

▼ Authentication

■ Privacy

▲ Access control

To deliver these services in an efficient fashion, SNMPv3 introduces the concept of a *principal*. A principal is an entity on whose behalf services are provided or processing takes place. A principal can be:

▼ An individual acting in a particular role

■ A set of individuals, each acting in a particular role

■ An application or set of applications

▲ Combinations of these

Basically, a principal operates from a management station and issues SNMP commands to its agents. The principal and the target agent work together to determine the security measures, including authentication, privacy, and access control. By using principals, security policies can be customized to the specific principal, agent, and information exchange.

TMN

Although SNMP is well suited for applications that are much higher in the IP stack (like Ethernet), a better means of managing SONET is the Telecommunications Management Network (TMN).

Think of a telecommunications network as one of those Air Force bombers that never lands. For a while, it does just fine. It flies around on its own, just waiting for the command to drop its load. But, world peace being what it is, the command to drop the bombs never comes. Since the bomber has to stay in the air, it will fall out of the sky unless it is refueled. To accommodate this, a fueling plane is sent up which assists the bomber in its mission. Without having to land, the bomber is refueled.

In the world of telecommunications management, think of a telecommunications network (like the public phone network) as the bomber and the TMN as the refueling plane. Though the two are separate entities, the TMN assists the telecommunications network in its mission.

According to the TMN Standard M.3100, Principals for a Telecommunications Management Network, the TMN standards exist *"to provide an organized architecture to achieve the interconnection between various Operations Support Systems (OSSs) and/or telecommunications equipment for the exchange of management information."*

Originally designed by the ITU-T, TMN is built around the OSI reference model and its associated standards, including the Common Management Information Protocol (CMIP) and the Guidelines for the Development of Managed Objects (GDMO). A TMN is a separate network that links with a telecommunications network (like SONET or ATM) at numerous points.

In this section, we'll give a brief overview of a TMN's architecture. To be sure, the subject of the TMN could fill (and has filled) entire books. That is out of our purview here, but for the sake of a basic understanding of TMNs, we hit the highlights.

Overview

The purpose of a TMN is to support operators in managing telecommunications networks and services. Such support includes:

- ▼ Planning
- ■ Provisioning
- ■ Installation
- ■ Maintenance
- ▲ Administration

TMN is important because as telecommunications services carry multimedia, multi-party, and mobile services, it is necessary to manage these resources. This is especially necessary as providers enter into Service Level Agreements with customers.

A TMN is a data network that carries only management traffic. Though portions of it may share physical space (like a server room or an equipment closet) with components of the telecommunications network, a TMN is logically separate from the network that is managed. Though logically separate, it connects in a number of places for monitoring and control operations.

The idea behind a TMN is to provide a framework for interoperation between management applications (known in TMN circles as operations systems [OSs]) and the telecommunications hardware that is being managed. This is accomplished through an architecture with a set of interfaces that support object-oriented message exchanges over established protocol stacks. Because this is all standardized, it is possible for administrators to build TMN systems from different vendors.

The relationship between the TMN and the telecommunications network being managed is depicted in Figure 9-14. On a telecommunications network, the user plane simply supports transmission, e.g., making phone calls. In order to manage that network, that capacity must be added for data to be added. This capability is provided through Signaling System No. 7 (SS7).

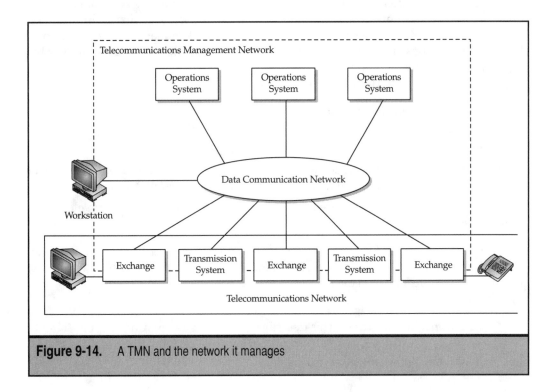

Figure 9-14.   A TMN and the network it manages

In this example, there are three planes on which the action is happening:

▼ **User plane**   This plane is where user information is transferred (be it voice, multimedia, or data).

■ **Control plane**   This plane is where calls and connections are established, operated, and released.

▲ **Management plane**   This plane plans, installs, configures, and provisions the network infrastructure so that the user and control planes can function as efficiently as possible.

TMN management applications generally run on computer systems, which are attached to the telecommunications network or reside in local networks, which are attached through internetworking units. Though Figure 9-14 depicts the TMN boundary as one restricted to managing equipment on the telecommunications network, it might also extend to manage equipment in the customer premises.

As Figure 9-14 shows, the interfaces between the TMN and the telecommunications network are formed by exchanges and transmission systems. These exchanges and transmission systems are connected via a data communication network (DCN) to one or more OSs.

The OSs perform most of the network's management functions. These functions can be managed automatically, or manually by an operator. Further, a single management function can be carried out by multiple OSs. The DCN is used to exchange information between OSs. The DCN can also be used to connect network management workstations. Because workstations are meant to interface with users, they define the end of the TMN, logically, functionally, and physically.

Key requirements for TMN systems include:

▼ Minimizing management reaction times to network events

■ Minimizing management traffic load, especially when it is carried by the telecommunications

■ Allowing for geographic scattering of management functions over a wide area, like a large SONET ring with nodes in major cities throughout a region

▲ Improving service assistance and interaction with customers through electronic interfaces

A TMN is built around different architectural layers. They start with functional designs, which is a way of understanding how blocks interrelate and work their way to the point where they are managed by users at computer consoles. A TMN manages networks at several levels:

▼ **Functional architecture**   This describes the management functions of a TMN.

■ **Physical architecture**   This defines how these management functions can be implemented into physical equipment.

- ■ **Information architecture**   This describes concepts that have been adopted from OSI management.
- ▲ **Logical layered architecture (LLA)**   This includes a model showing how management can be allocated according to different responsibilities.

Functional Architecture

TMNs are not just defined by their physical construction. At their lowest, basic level, TMNs have a functional architecture, which defines what behavior the TMN will exhibit once it's built out. The basic element at this level is the *function block.*

There are five types of function blocks (see Figure 9-15), which are defined by TMN's functional architecture. All five blocks need not be present in each TMN configuration, but it is common for multiple types of function blocks to be present.

The function blocks, which are depicted in Figure 9-15, are:

- ▼ **Network element functions (NEF)**   A telecommunications network is made up of exchanges and transmission systems. In TMNs, these are known as *network elements (NEs).* The functions of an NE are called *network element functions (NEFs).* These functions include:

  - ■ **Primary functions**   These functions are the subject of management and support the exchange of data between users of the telecommunications network.

  - ■ **Management functions**   These functions allow the NEF block to operate specifically in an agent's role.

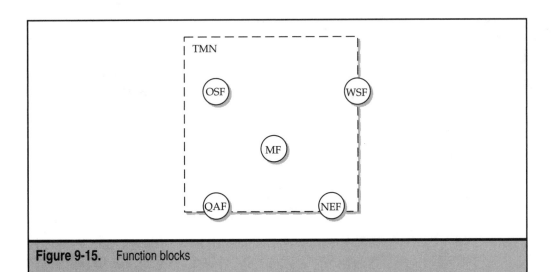

Figure 9-15.   Function blocks

- ■ **The operations system functions (OSF)**   This block initiates management operations and receive notifications. In a manager-agent model, the OSF can be considered as the manager. A single TMN can have multiple OSFs. Further, OSFs in different TMNs can communicate with each other.

- ■ **The Mediation Function (MF)**   This block is located within the TMN and acts on information that is passed between NEFs or QAFs, and OSFs. A MF block can be used to connect single and multiple NEFs and QAFs to an OSF. The MFs that can be recognized include those that:

  - ■ **Augment OSFs**   Including storage and filtering of management information.

  - ■ **Augment NEFs**   Including those that transform local representation of management data into a standardized form.

- ■ **The work station function (WSF)**   This block allows TMN information to be decoded for the manager.

- ▲ **The Q adaptor function (QAF)**   This block connects the TMN with entities that do not support standard TMN reference points.

Connecting the function blocks are a number of reference points. When used together, the function blocks and reference points define a *reference model* for the TMN. The logical functionality of the TMN can be described in a reference configuration composed of function blocks and reference points. Figure 9-16 shows how these two components work together.

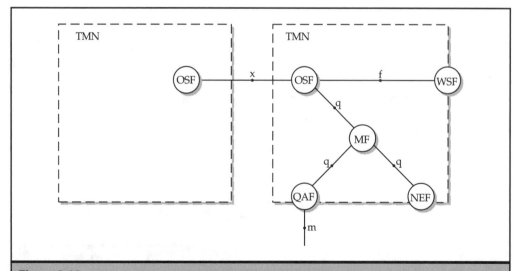

Figure 9-16.   Function blocks communicate via reference points

The TMN defines the types of reference points, which are listed in Table 9-4. Those reference points inside the borders of the TMN (q_3, q_x, f, and x) are standardized so that systems and devices can be easily interconnected.

Physical Architecture

In addition to its functional architecture, TMN also employs a physical architecture. The physical architecture is where the rubber hits the road in a TMN. This architecture shows how TMN's functions are implemented by equipment. The physical architecture details how function blocks should be mapped to physical equipment and how reference points are implemented.

Interfaces are the physical implementations of the TMN reference points. Reference points can generally be compared with the underlying service; interfaces can be compared with the protocol stacks that implement those services.

Most often, reference points and interfaces have a direct mapping. However, no interfaces exist for reference points that:

▼   Connect function blocks that are deployed inside a single building block

▲   Exist outside the TMN

Two facets characterize interfaces:

▼   **Conceptual facet**   This facet is designated by the reference point and is characterized by the M-Part (Message Part).

▲   **Physical facet**   This facet is characterized by the P-Part (Protocol Part).

Reference Point	Description
q_3	Joins OSFs to NEFs; QAFs, MFs, and OSFs to OSFs.
q_x	Joins MFs to "weak" QAFs, NEFs. Also joins MFs to each other in a hierarchical manner.
x	Joins OSFs to OSFs between TMNs.
f	Joins WSFs to OSFs and MFs.
g	Presents information to the user in a graphical form.
m	Joins QAFs to *foreign* managed elements, for instance those supporting SNMP.

Table 9-4.   TMN Reference Points

The M-Part defines the structure of the message, which is transmitted or received from a managed object (for instance, a Common Management Information Service [CMIS] message). The P-Part defines the protocol stack, which is used for message transfer.

NOTE: Reference points are denoted by lowercase letters (e.g., q_3), while interfaces are written with uppercase letters (e.g., Q_3).

Within TMN's physical architecture are the following building blocks:

▼ Network element (NE)

■ Mediation device (MD)

■ Work station (WS)

■ Data communication network (DCN)

■ Q adaptor (QA)

▲ Operations system (OS)

Though there seems to be a lot going on with TMN's architectures, it is somewhat easy to keep track of the building blocks of the physical architecture, because they maintain the same names as the function blocks. For example, the physical Q Adaptor actually performs Q Adaptor functions.

Furthermore, it is possible to merge several function blocks into a single building block. For example, the operations system can be used to implement multiple OSFs. Building blocks can also merge several dissimilar function blocks into one building block; an operations system can implement an OSF, an MF, and a QA. In the case of a multiple deployment, the most predominant function determines the building block's name.

Figure 9-17 shows which function blocks can be implemented together.

A unique building block is the DCN block. This block is not used to implement any TMN functions; rather, it is used by other building blocks for the exchange of management information. The DCN acts as a transport network.

Information Architecture

A TMN's information architecture uses an object-oriented approach and is based on the OSI Management Information Model. Using this model, the management information of a managed object is visible at the managed object boundary. The management view at this boundary is described in terms of:

▼ **Attributes**   These are the object's characteristics.

■ **Behavior**   These are shown in response to operations.

■ **Operations**   These are performed on the object.

▲ **Notifications**   These are sent out by the object.

	NEF	MF	QAF	OSF	WSF
NE	M	O	O	O	O^x
MD		M	O	O	O
QA			M		
OS		O	O	M	O
WS					M
DCN					

M = Mandatory
O = Optional
O^x = Only if OSF or MF is present

Figure 9-17.   Which function blocks can be mixed together

Managed objects reside within managed systems and include agent functions to communicate with the manager. TMN employs the same agent-manager features as OSI.

Logical Layered Architecture

The TMN management framework moves from a flat management paradigm to a multi-layered, hierarchical, distributed paradigm. Because of this stratification, abstraction is increased and encapsulation occurs at the higher levels. The functionality of a layer is built upon the functionality of the layer beneath it.

Each layer can contain sublayers. The functionality of the layer and sublayers is supported by one or more OSFs. These OSFs could have peer-to-peer relationships when in the same layer or a hierarchical relationship when in different layers. Each OSF presents an information model to superior OSFs, which then build on it to present different information models of higher abstraction to their superiors. To that end, a layer in this architecture builds on the information model presented by the layer beneath.

For example, between layers 1 and 2 the management view of layer 2 is presented to layer 1. This view contains management information that is contained within the agent at layer 2. For simplicity's sake and ease of functionality, not all information is passed through the layers. In this case, only layer 2 shows the information relevant to layer 1.

As Figure 9-18 shows, the information models at each level represent manageable resources at different levels of abstraction. At the lowest level of the hierarchy, managed network elements contain resources of the finest granularity, like access points, interfaces, and call endpoints. At the higher levels, objects represent resources of a higher abstraction, like subnetworks, networks, and services.

The important feature that characterizes the TMN is that each layer builds off the functionality of of the layer beneath. This hierarchy allows the levels to be blissfully ignorant of issues that are irrelevant to it. Thus, the lower levels are unaware of the goings-on at the higher level. They just respond to management requests made by higher-level layers.

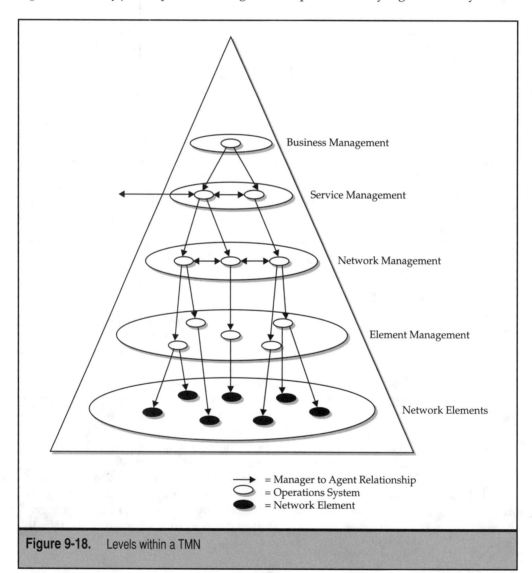

Figure 9-18.   Levels within a TMN

Within the TMN, a hierarchy of management responsibilities exists. This hierarchy is talked about in terms of layers, and—in TMN—those layers are known as the Logical Layered Architecture (LLA). Management in a telecommunications network (such as SONET) can be so complex that it is best conducted in a series of logical layers.

The following sections explain the layers of the LLC in greater detail.

Network Elements

This layer defines each manageable element in the network on a device-by-device basis. Network elements include routers, switches, firewalls, and so forth.

Element Management

This layer manages the characteristics of the elements that are defined by the network element layer. Information at this level includes activity log data for each element. This layer also stores the actual element management systems responsible for the management of each device or set of devices in the network.

Examples of the functions performed at this level include:

▼ Measuring power consumption

■ Measuring equipment temperature

■ Measuring resource usage (CPU time, buffer space, queue depth, etc.)

■ Detecting equipment errors

▲ Logging data

It is worthwhile to note that an OSF in the element management layer and a NEF can be implemented in the same piece of equipment or within different pieces of equipment.

Network Management

The network management layer has the ability to monitor the entire network via information provided by the element management layer. At the element management layer, NEFs are deployed in single pieces of hardware. At the network management layer, the relationships between those pieces of hardware are managed. Because, at this layer, the internal structure of a network element is not visible, such details as router capacity and switch temperature cannot be managed.

Some of the functions performed at this layer include:

▼ Routing table modifications

■ Fault detection

■ Link utilization monitoring

▲ Dedicated path creation

At this layer, OSFs use vendor-independent management information that is provided by the OSFs in the element management layer. Thus, the OSFs in the network management layer act as managers, while the OSFs in this layer act as agents.

Services Management

The services management layer responds to information provided by the network management layer to deliver services including accounting, provisioning, fault management, configuration, and security services.

This layer is concerned with management of the network aspects that can be seen by the users of the telecommunications network. These users are both the telecommunications network customers and the service providers.

Some of the functions performed at this layer include:

▼ Accounting

■ QoS management

■ Adding and removing users

▲ Address management

Business Management

The last layer is the business management layer. It manages the entire organization, including applications and the processes that provide strategic business planning and tracking of such customer details as SLAs.

This layer is very broad in its responsibilities, and communications management is just a part of it. Business management is often likened to goal setting, in that it is more akin to strategic planning than to operational planning.

OPTICAL NETWORK MANAGEMENT APPLICATIONS

When you decide the time is right to buy an application with optical network management in mind, there is no lack of tools on the market. Network management tools come in all shapes and sizes—some offer proprietary tools for specific vendors; others use such technologies as SNMP to be as universal as possible.

Such software tools are especially useful when monitoring your network's usage. They can show you where resources are being used, how they are being used, and what you can do to improve network performance. Further, when the time comes to expand your network, these are good tools to help build your network in a logical, well-planned fashion.

Network management applications add value to your network not only because they help you build a better network, but because you will also be able to save money by squeezing all the bits out of the network that you possibly can. The use of a network management application can help you do that. For example, by managing your network with one of these applications, you can find out which devices on the network are performing optimally. By doing this, you can be proactive and ferret out problems, rather than being reactive and responding to crashes and failures.

The following four applications are meant as a quick overview of different tools that can help manage an optical network. In this section we take a closer look at some of the offerings from Lucent, Cisco, Corvis, and Sun. The first three tools have basic optical network management in mind; the Sun Solstice, on the other hand, is a tool meant for use in TMN deployments when it is necessary to build your own agents.

Lucent WaveWrapper

In addition to its popular WaveStar management tool, Lucent also offers the WaveWrapper, which is being highly touted as the basis for an optical management standard. WaveWrapper is unique in that it can manage individual wavelengths.

Using WaveWrapper, service providers can offer faster, more efficient data services. WaveWrapper offers network management functions on a per-wavelength basis. Some of its features include:

▼ Optical layer performance monitoring

■ Error correction

▲ Ring protection

These capabilities help WaveWrapper carry packet-based traffic like IP, ATM, and Gigabit Ethernet directly over the network's optical layer. WaveWrapper works in conjunction with its WaveStar OLS 400G DWDM optical transmission system that transmits at 10 Gbps.

WaveWrapper "wraps" the optical data stream within a digital "wrapper." The wrapper carries information to be used for monitoring individual wavelengths within a DWDM-encoded optical stream and performs forward error correction (FEC) and channel performance monitoring as needed, without the need for retransmission.

The wrappers carry such information as:

▼ Restoration signals

■ The type of traffic contained in the wavelength

▲ The wavelength's destination

Based on this information, the WaveStar system can determine the health of the signal, whether it needs to be rerouted, and if the necessary equipment exists to receive the signal at its destination.

The WaveWrapper technology is based on the ITU standard for underwater FEC. The use of FEC allows a greater number of channels to be used in each fiber, a higher bit rate on each wavelength, and greater distances between regenerators. WaveWrapper has been so popular and useful in its approach, that it is under consideration as a prototype to define digital wrapper techniques.

Cisco Transport Manager

Cisco's entry into the optical networking management world is the Cisco Transport Manager (CTM). It is designed to work with Cisco's 15000 series of products. The CTM is a carrier-class element management system (EMS) that aims to lower the cost of optical network operation, administration, maintenance, and provisioning.

The CTM provides the following types of management functionality:

▼ Fault management

■ Configuration management

■ Performance management

▲ Security management

Scalability and Ability

Built on a client/server platform, the CTM scales to 1000 network elements and up to 100 simultaneous users. This minimizes the number of server platforms that need to be purchased and administered for a given network size, thus saving capital and operations costs.

CTM provides support for SONET, SDH, DWDM, IP, and Ethernet, which is ideal in multiservice networks. Because CTM uses open interfaces to Operations Support Systems (OSS) using Transaction Language-1 (TL-1), SNMP, and CORBA, CTM allows service providers to leverage their existing legacy equipment and well as set the stage for next-generation OSS networks. Once deployed, CTM acquires and maintains network information, making it available to the back office by means of open communications protocols.

By utilizing CTM and its sister Cisco ONS 15000 series products, the need to deploy multiple EMSs (one for each transport technology) is eliminated. Not only does this make the network easier to manage, but it is also less expensive than having to deploy a number of EMSs.

CTM is based on a philosophy popular with service providers; it's "Pay as You Grow." This pricing model allows providers to buy a basic starter kit with sufficient client and NE licenses, at which point out-of-the-box domain management is possible. Then, as the network grows, additional licenses can be purchased.

Scalability is also enhanced through CTM's ability to cross not only borders, but oceans. Because of its model-awareness, CTM can manage ANSI and ETSI network elements with a single CTM server instance. This allows CTM to be used on a global scale.

A sample screen of the CTM application is shown in Figure 9-19.

Availability

CTM is built for popular platforms, including Sun Solaris, Oracle8, and Microsoft Windows. This broad functionality allows network operators to leverage the cost of their existing network operating systems, while still coupling them with optical networking technology.

These are the operating requirements of the Cisco Transport Manager client:

▼ Cisco Transport Manager client runs in the Java runtime environment version 1.2.2.

■ The Intel version needs a Pentium III–class PC or better with Windows 95, 98, NT 4.0 (450 MHz CPU, 128 MB RAM, 50 MB free disk space).

▲ The Sun version needs a Sun Ultra5 workstation or better with Solaris 2.7 and CDE (333 MHz CPU, 256 MB RAM, 50 MB free disk space).

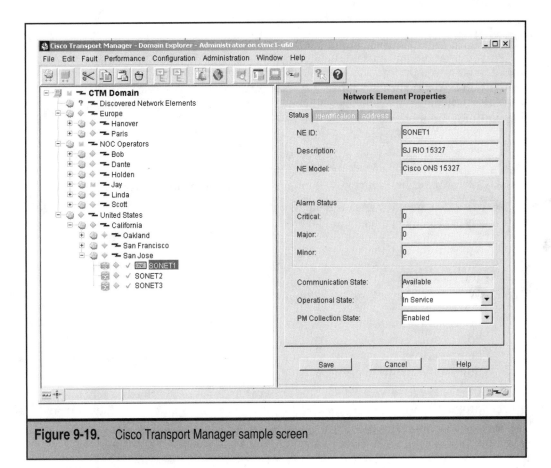

Figure 9-19. Cisco Transport Manager sample screen

These are the operating requirements of the Cisco Transport Manager server:

▼ The Cisco Transport Manager server runs on Sun Solaris 2.7.

■ It requires a Sun Ultra60/80 with up to 2 × 450 MHz CPUs, 2 GB RAM for up to 200 NEs.

▲ Alternatively, it runs on a Sun Enterprise 450 with up to 4× 400 MHz CPUs, 4 GB RAM for up to 1000 NEs.

These are the operating requirements of the Cisco Transport Manager database:

▼ Industry-standard Oracle 8.1.6

▲ Optional database distribution to local server

Corvis CorManager

Corvis's tool for optical network management is its Corvis Network Management Suite. This amalgam of applications combines Corvis network elements into an end-to-end, all-optical network. The CorManager tools are meant to help service providers beef up the speed of their service delivery and generate more revenue, at the same time reducing expenditures for equipment and capital resources.

The following highlights some of the features of CorManager:

▼ Integrated element management

■ Performance monitoring, fault management, and configuration management

■ Automated end-to-end wavelength planning and provisioning for both active and protective paths

▲ Fast initial setup

The CorWave Suite

The CorWave Suite consists of the following applications:

▼ **Corvis Wave Planner**   This application is used for network planning and optimizing carrier services by distributing planned and provisioned traffic demands over the network. According to Corvis, this reduces provisioning time from months to minutes.

■ **Corvis Provisioning Tool**   This application is for network engineers to provision and validate services over entire networks quickly, without errors.

■ **Corvis Network Manager**   This application performs integrated fault, configuration, performance, and security management. Carrier-grade system surveillance includes alarm and event monitoring, aggregation, and correlation.

▲ **Corvis Element Interface**   This application is the graphical user interface (GUI) that provides common access to Corvis Network Elements for configuration, monitoring, and troubleshooting.

Working Together

The network planning process starts with the Corvis Wave Planner, which helps plan and engineer large-scale networks. This application helps deploy planned services and equipment as efficiently as possible.

Though the Wave Planner is a good tool for arranging a network, planners are able to provide their own input and say-so in matters of network deployment. They can veto the Wave Planner's choices if they have other thoughts for more capacity and specific routes.

The Wave Planner can glean its information directly from the Corvis Network Planner, which would contain accurate network configurations. Using this information, the Wave Planner can analyze the data and prepare several hypothetical scenarios.

Corvis's Provisioning Tool is used by network managers to provision wavelengths across an entire network in just minutes. The Provisioning Tool aims to remove the complexity of provisioning from the process by providing its functionality from a central location. Thus, network engineers and managers need not provision the network from a number of locations. This not only speeds up the process, but it also reduces human error. Finally, the Provisioning Tool is also able to identify equipment and generate reports. This is useful is determining what additional equipment would be necessary for new capacity or increased network efficiency.

Sun Solstice Enterprise Manager

Sun Microsystems' entry into the world of network management includes the Solstice Enterprise Manager. This application is based on the TMN standard and designed for telecommunications industry needs.

Some of the features of Solstice Enterprise Manager include:

▼ **Granular graphical presentations**   Network elements are displayed and manipulated as graphical icons. Elements can be displayed superimposed on a map projection, allowing elements to be shown at actual physical locations (even down to specific streets).

■ **Fully distributed data and management**   The Management Information Database can be distributed across any number of servers, which can be located anywhere on the network. Multiple management applications can access this database from multiple locations. The distributed database allows multiple servers to share the workload, provides redundancy, and can be used to reduce network traffic. Management applications residing anywhere on the network have full access to all data.

■ **Multilevel, highly granular security**   Solstice Enterprise Manager allows security to be controlled down to the feature level within applications. Individuals or groups can be granted specific rights to specific objects. This means that the Operations Center personnel can be granted rights to modify settings across the entire network, while a local technician can be granted rights to monitor (but not modify) settings and statuses of a certain set of switches.

■ **Intelligent event management**   Alarms can be filtered according to specified parameters, and automatic responses or actions (such as e-mail, pager, script execution, and so forth) can be generated for specific alarm conditions.

■ **APIs for extensibility**   The Portable Management Interface (PMI) API enables developers to take advantage of the distributed services provided by Solstice Enterprise Manager when developing new applications. The developers' edition includes these APIs for writing custom applications (to add management support to legacy elements).

▲ **Management Protocol Adapters (MPAs) for CMIP, Remote Procedure Call protocol (RPC), SNMP, and legacy agents**   MPAs provided with Solstice Enterprise Manager enable communication with agents using CMIP, RPC, and SNMP management protocols. Additional MPAs can be added to support new and legacy protocols.

Figure 9-20 shows a sample screen from Solstice Enterprise Manager.

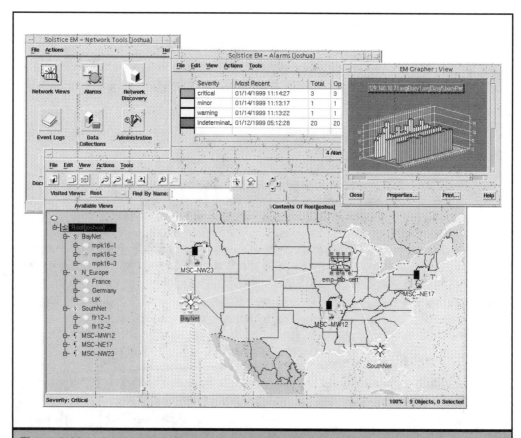

Figure 9-20.   Sun Solstice Enterprise Manager application

The following points outline the system requirements for the Solstice Enterprise Management application:

▼ **Operating system**   Solaris 7 and 8 Operating Environment on the SPARC platform.

■ **Minimum configuration**   A minimum configuration of an Ultra 2 system with 192 MB of memory and 1 GB of disk space is recommended.

▲ **Suggested configuration**   A two-CPU UltraSPARC-II (300MHz) system with 256 MB of memory, 512 MB of swap space, and 4 GB of disk space.

Employing a tool like Sun's Solstice allows you to manage your TMN and ensure that your resources are being used in the most efficient way possible.

Optical network management is something that cannot be overlooked, no matter if the network is a small LAN or a large service provider deployment. Because networks are always in a state of flux, and because their needs are constantly being taxed, it is in the administrator's best interests to get as much out of his or her network as possible. By understanding and utilizing network management techniques, you assure that a network can reach its fullest potential.

CHAPTER 10

Optical Maintenance and Tuning

In the last chapter, we talked about the importance of network management and why constant vigilance is important to keep packets flowing smoothly. Tending to your network doesn't stop there, however. There are a number of maintenance and tuning issues that will both creep up over time and hit you out of the blue.

For instance, as your network develops and grows, it is more than likely you will add nodes wherever you can manage. Unfortunately, these additions will come at the expense of a perfect network design. Switches will be cascaded off other switches, and routers will be configured to get the job done. This piece-by-piece process of addition is a lot like junk building up in your attic. At first, a couple boxes stashed here and there aren't much of a problem. After time, however, a look at the entire attic uncovers piles of forgotten stuff. The same is true in networking. All the little details will add up, and one day you'll look over the network and wonder where all the misconfigurations came from.

But not every problem will have built up over time. Some problems will be entirely out of your control. For instance, bums cooking their beenie weenies under a bridge and burning through your fiber optic cable isn't something you can plan for, but it is a problem you will have to remedy.

In this chapter, we talk about network maintenance and tuning. Specifically, we cover correcting the errors that can slow down your network, dealing with fiber cuts, adding connectors to fiber, and dealing with the "little things" that have built up over time.

LOGICAL MAINTENANCE AND TUNING

Within your network, there are bound to be changes and upgrades that you can make without leaving the office. In the formative stages of your network, for instance, you can decide on which technology you will base your network—Synchronous Optical Networks (SONET) or Dense Wavelength Division Multiplexing (DWDM). You can also decide how you will optimize your data flow.

In this section, we talk about strategies that you can use to make your network as durable as possible. We'll talk about network designs that will make a more reliable network and talk about what you can do to solve problems that creep up after your network has had a chance to grow.

Network Design

One of the critical components in ensuring network stability starts in its design. When a network is designed with reliability in mind, a disaster like a fiber cut or a router failure won't bring all network traffic to a grinding halt.

But it isn't just an unplanned event or a failure that can cause packets to stop flowing. As more nodes are added to a network, or maintenance is being performed, then it is possible for an outage to occur without any sort of network disaster. One way to ensure inherent maintenance and reliability is by basing your infrastructure on a technology that will compensate for outages.

Just by virtue of its nature, SONET avoids the pitfalls that can bring a lesser network to its knees. Point-to-point networks without route diversity, for instance, would be crippled if there were a major outage caused by a cable cut.

SONET Versus DWDM IV: SONET Strikes Back

In previous chapters, we've explained some of the ups and downs in SONET and DWDM deployments. Though both have their merits (SONET is widely deployed, DWDM provides more capacity), SONET is inherently better in its construction for purposes of maintenance and reliability.

For example, consider the five nodes in Figure 10-1. All five need to communicate with one another, and using a point-to-point connection over DWDM is just fine, unless the fiber (without route diversity) is cut, for instance between routers two and three.

Not only has the cut prevented routers two and three from communicating, but every router before two and every router before three is cut off from communicating across the cut. Traffic between one and two is still possible, as is traffic between three, four, and five.

However, if SONET rings are deployed, as shown in Figure 10-2, then the network is more reliable because a fiber cut between routers two and three isn't the end of the world. Rather, traffic switches over to the secondary ring until the primary ring can be repaired.

NOTE: The same holds true for Cisco's proprietary Dynamic Packet Transport (DPT) system. As you remember from Chapter 3, DPT uses a structure similar to SONET's dual rings. However, DPT uses both rings for network traffic, rather than sending traffic along just one primary ring.

SONET's ring-based architecture ensures uptime in the event of a fiber cut or a router failure. Because of its built-in backup mechanism, maintenance teams need not rush out, worrying about downtime in the event of a failure.

Benefits of a Mesh

DWDM isn't left totally out in the cold. To the contrary. DWDM can enjoy SONET-like reliability when built on top of SONET rings. That way, if one ring fails, the backup ring can kick in. Better yet, DWDM enjoys a higher level of reliability when configured in a mesh topology. Though we've talked about mesh topologies in Chapter 7, a reminder of some of their usefulness is in order.

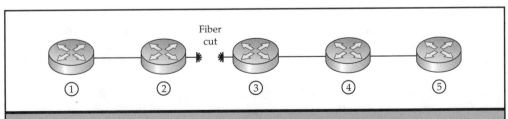

Figure 10-1.   Point-to-point connections provide little security in the event of a fiber cut or a failure

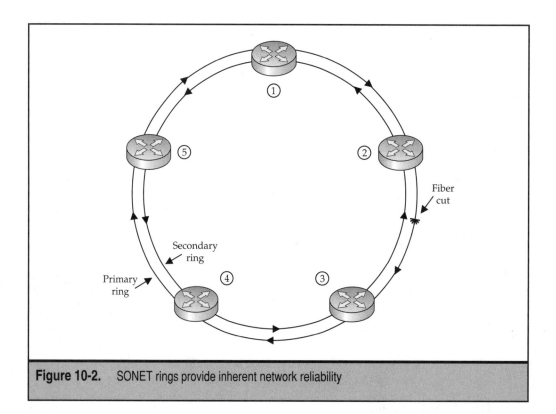

Figure 10-2.   SONET rings provide inherent network reliability

A mesh is the same sort of topology that the World Wide Web is built on. As Figure 10-3 shows, a mesh connects one router with several others. Each of those routers is connected to several others, and so forth.

This sort of connection provides a high level of reliability. In the event one router fails or goes down, traffic can be routed around the failed device. In this way, a mesh is even more dependable than SONET rings, because traffic has many more routes across which it can travel. If there is a failure, traffic isn't just relegated to a single path. Rather, it can use the path of least resistance.

Routing

For traffic to be redirected, it is necessary to know that a router has failed or is no longer in contact. Once the failed router has been detected, the neighboring routers must be able to compute an alternate path across which packets will travel. This is accomplished through the use of *routing protocols*.

A routing protocol formalizes the ongoing exchange of route information between routers. Messages called *routing updates* pass information used by routing algorithms to calculate paths to destinations. A *routing algorithm* is a system of rules that controls a

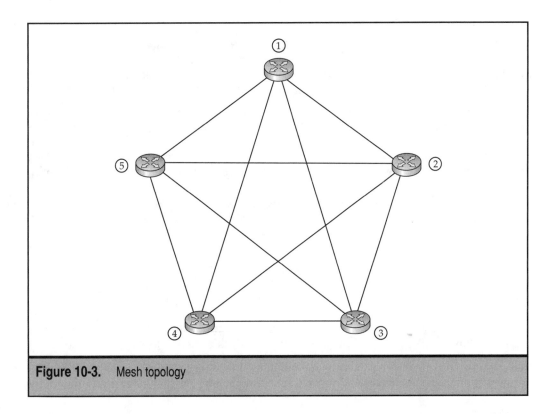

Figure 10-3.   Mesh topology

network's behavior in such a way that it adapts to changing circumstances within the network's topology. Ongoing changes include such things as which links are up and running, which are fastest, whether any new equipment has appeared, and so on. Each router uses its own copy of the algorithm to recalculate a map of the internetwork to account for all the latest changes from its particular perspective.

Routing protocols use a peer arrangement in which each router plays an equal role. There is no routing protocol server to centrally manage routing processes. Ongoing routing table maintenance is handled in real time through an arrangement in which each router makes its own route selection decisions. To configure a routing protocol for an internetwork, the routing protocol process must be configured in each router that will be involved in the arrangement. Properly configured, the routing protocol is able to collectively influence all these machine-made decisions so that they work in harmony. The area within which routing information is exchanged is called a *routing domain*.

Of the many routing protocols, some are standards-based and others are proprietary. Several are old and fading from use, a few are used only within narrowly defined market niches, and others are in such wide use that they are de facto standards. Routing protocols also differ in the types of internetworks they're designed to manage, and in the sizes of internetworks they can handle. Naturally, these differences are manifested in each routing protocol's algorithm. Yet all their algorithms share these two basic processes:

▼ Routers send one another update messages advising of changes in internetwork topology and conditions.

▲ Each router recalculates its own routing table based on the updated information.

Updating one another helps each individual router know what's going on. More important, it helps orchestrate a network's routers by maintaining a common set of information with which to operate.

Table 10-1 compares the following routing protocols:

▼ Routing Information Protocol (RIP)

▲ Enhanced Interior Gateway Routing Protocol (EIGRP)

Statistical Multiplexing

In Chapter 3, we talked about the process of multiplexing. For instance, SONET uses time division multiplexing (TDM) to divvy up its wavelength so that different customers can share it. Wavelength division multiplexing (WDM) is a means to get several colors of

Routing Protocol	Best Topology	Metric	Routing Update
RIP	Well suited for topologies with 15 hops or less between source and destination.	Best measurement is hop count, and the maximum hop count is 15. The best route is the one with the fewest number of hops.	The routing path is updated, by default, every 30 seconds. This value can be reconfigured as needed.
EIGRP	Well suited for large topologies having 16 hops or more between source and destination.	Best measurement is distance information, which is based on a neighboring router's distance.	"Hello" packets sent every 5 seconds. Additionally, updates are transmitted when the state of a destination router changes.

Table 10-1.　Routing Protocols Compared

light on a single length of fiber, which increases the sheer number of wavelengths that can be sent across the fiber. Another type of multiplexing, and the focus of this section, is called *statistical multiplexing*.

Statistical multiplexing is a method of sharing a transmission channel by using statistical techniques to allocate resources. A statistical multiplexer can analyze traffic density and dynamically switch to a different channel pattern to speed up the transmission. At the receiving end, the different signals are sorted out and merged back into individual streams.

Statistical multiplexing allocates bandwidth dynamically, only when a user has data to send or receive. If no one else is using it, a single customer can take advantage of all the bandwidth offered by the high-speed pipe. This is perfect for data traffic.

Statistical multiplexing works because the bursty traffic of user applications leads to peaks and valleys in the data rates required by a network. Because these peaks and valleys are not going to occur simultaneously in several networks, statistical multiplexing exploits this fact and allows additional resources to be allocated from one data flow and applied to another. Statistical multiplexing addresses this issue by never letting the transmission line go idle as long as any user has data to send.

For instance, as Figure 10-4 shows, there are four organizations served by SuperService Provider, Inc. Each organization has been allocated a pipe of 2.5 Gbps, and the service provider has guaranteed that level. However, Organization A has cut a deal with the service provider so that if there is additional bandwidth available at any given time, it will be sold to that organization. Since Organizations B through D don't come close to using 2.5 Gbps consistently, the excess is sold to Organization A. Thus, Organization A is able to use the scraps from the other organizations to get a much larger piece of bandwidth. That doesn't mean that the other organizations are getting shorted on their bandwidth, however. If Organizations B through D decide that they need to use up to 2.5 Gbps, the bandwidth is available to them. However, at that moment, Organization A will not have any extra bandwidth to buy.

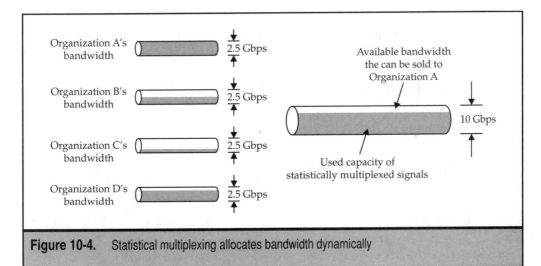

Figure 10-4.   Statistical multiplexing allocates bandwidth dynamically

As you can tell from the preceding example, statistical multiplexing pays off twice for the service provider. Not only is it getting paid for the guaranteed levels of service to all its organizations, but it is able to milk all the bandwidth it can out of the system and get paid twice for the same bandwidth.

The downside to statistical multiplexing is that every transmission needs to carry an address, since ownership can no longer be deduced by the time at which a transmission arrives.

Statistical multiplexing is found most commonly in video applications, but it can also be used in optical networks. For example, ATM uses statistical multiplexing to compress signals from a variety of sources. This optimizes the use of bandwidth generated by SONET. You will find specific devices for this purpose (called statistical multiplexers), and some routers even have statistical multiplexing capabilities.

Errors

A sure-fire sign that there is trouble in your network rears its head in the form of errors. You may see errors that affect your LAN or some that have a broader impact, causing problems on metropolitan area networks (MANs) or wide area networks (WANs).

Understanding the errors that impact your network is important. By understanding what is wrong, you can take the necessary action to fix what may be broken. The most likely places for errors to occur are at layer 2 of the Open Systems Interconnect (OSI) stack and, specifically, with Ethernet.

NOTE: Although Ethernet is predominantly a LAN technology, as Gigabit and 10 Gigabit Ethernet become popular in WANs, these same errors are likely to occur in large deployments, as well.

This section describes the errors that you might encounter while running Ethernet. Also, we talk about some data link–level (layer-2) errors and how those can be ameliorated.

Ethernet

The most prevalent network technology in wide deployment is Ethernet. Whether at 10, 100, 1000, or 10,000 Mbps, Ethernet is Ethernet. With that common platform comes a common understanding of the technology. As you are likely to deploy such a system, there will come a time when it is necessary to tune and maintain your system.

As your network grows and expands, so is the likelihood that errors will start to creep into the system. The following outlines some of the major Ethernet errors you are likely to encounter and where you might investigate their sources.

Out-of-Window Collisions   Out-of-window collisions occur when a station receives a collision signal while still transmitting, but more than 51.2 ms after transmission began. There are two conditions that cause this type of error:

▼   The network's physical length exceeds the specifications in IEEE 802.3x.

▲   A network node is transmitting without listening for carrier sense.

Giants *Giants* are packets that are larger than the maximum Ethernet packet size (1518 bytes). Giants generally occur when there is a jabbering node on a network—that is, a node that is continuously transmitting or transmitting intermittently long data bursts. This is due, most likely, to a bad network interface card (NIC).

Furthermore, packets that have been improperly inflated by the addition of garbage signals, or by the corruption of the bits used to indicate frame size, can also cause giants.

Alignment If a packet is *misaligned*, then it contains any number of bits less than one byte. A misaligned packet can stem from a problem at the media access control (MAC) layer, or from a cabling problem, causing a corruption or loss of data. Also, misalignment can occur when packets pass through more than two cascaded, multiport transceivers.

Alignment problems usually show up in packets that have cyclic redundancy check (CRC) errors.

Cyclic Redundancy Check *CRC errors* occur when packets are damaged in transit. As packets are transmitted, the MAC layer of the transmitting device computes a frame check sequence (FCS) value, which is derived from the contents of the packet. The receiving station performs the same check, and if the two FCS values differ, the packet is thought to be corrupted; thus a CRC error has occurred.

CRC errors can be caused by a MAC-layer hardware problem, which causes the FCS value to be incorrectly computed, or some other transmission problem that has scrambled the contents of the packet.

Runts A *runt* packet is similar to a giant packet in that the error deals with size. Whereas the giant packet dealt with oversized packets, the runt packet deals with those packets that are undersized. In this case, they are smaller than the minimum Ethernet frame of 64 bytes.

The size of the packet is tied to the maximum propagation time of an Ethernet network segment.

Runts can result from collisions and can be quite natural in a very busy Ethernet environment. On the other hand, they can also indicate the following problems:

▼ Hardware, resulting in bad packet formation

■ Transmission, resulting in corrupted data

▲ Network design, including more than four cascaded repeaters

Cause and Effect If (and when) Ethernet errors poke their heads up, nipping the problem in the bud is a good way to keep your network operating at peak efficiency.

Table 10-2 lists common Ethernet errors and some possible causes.

Data Link

The data-link layer is the second level in the OSI model. It specifies network and protocol characteristics including physical addressing, network topology, error notification, sequencing of frames, and flow control. The data-link layer establishes the rules for sending and receiving information from one node to another between systems.

Problem	Possible Causes
FCS or CRC or alignment errors	Bad cable crimpsElectromagnetic interference (if using copper wire)Incorrect spacing between taps
	Make sure the correct type of cable is used. Ensure that hub/switch port settings are not set to "auto negotiate."
Remote collisions	Overloaded segmentCable segment too long
Excessive local collisions	Overloaded segmentCable segment too long Full duplex set in a shared environmentLooped network at layer 1
Late collisions	Cable segment too longToo many repeating hubs or repeaters in the network (three maximum)
	Make sure that hub/switch port settings are not set to "auto negotiate."
Excessive collisions	Watch for bad cabling or connectors
Jabbering errors	Caused by a constant transmission from a network interface card. Most likely a faulty NIC or transceiver.
Runt errors	Caused by collisions
Giant errors	Faulty driversBad NIC

Table 10-2.   Ethernet Errors and Likely Sources

Structure   The basic function of the data-link layer is to transform a raw transmission facility into a line free of transmission errors. Reliable error control between adjacent nodes should be one of its many goals. The physical layer (layer 1) accepts and transmits bit streams without regard to meaning or structure.

The IEEE splits the data-link layer into an upper sublayer, Logical Link Control (LLC), and a lower sublayer, media access control (MAC). The LLC sublayer manages communications between devices over a single link of a network. The MAC sublayer manages protocol access to the physical network medium. MAC addresses allow multiple devices to uniquely identify one another at the data-link layer.

Data-link layer implementations can be categorized as either LAN or WAN specifications. The most common LAN data-link layer implementations are:

▼ Ethernet

■ Fast Ethernet

■ Fiber Distributed Digital Interface (FDDI)

▲ Token Ring

On a WAN level, the most common data-link layer implementations are:

▼ Frame Relay

■ Link Access Procedure, Balanced (LAPB)

■ Synchronous Data Link Control (SDLC)

■ Point-to-Point Protocol (PPP)

▲ SMDS Interface Protocol (SIP)

NOTE: In this discussion, SIP (SMDS Interface Protocol) should not be confused with the multimedia protocol Session Initiation Protocol (SIP).

At the data-link layer, transmitted data is broken into data frames. These frames are composed of predefined amounts of bytes. In addition to the transmitted data, senders analyze acknowledgment frames sent back from the receiver, and incorrectly received frames will be retransmitted.

Problems Several problems can arise at the data-link layer. Problems occur with acknowledgment frames for traffic from node A to node B that are competing against data frames from node B to node A when a line is transmitting data both ways.

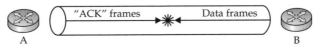

Another problem occurs when a fast transmitter floods a slow receiver in data. Some sort of traffic regulation mechanism must be employed to tell the transmitter how much buffer space the receiver has.

A noise burst on the line can destroy an entire frame. When this occurs, the data-link layer must retransmit the frame. However, if multiple frames are transmitted, the risk of duplicate frames exists. Duplicates can occur, for instance, if the acknowledgment frame from the receiver is destroyed. It is up to the data-link layer to solve problems cause by damaged and duplicate frames.

When data leaves the network device, there is a much greater chance that corruptions will occur. Because of this, in most applications it is necessary to incorporate a way to detect when a transmission error occurs, but also a way to obtain a copy of the damaged frame. This process is called *error control*.

The majority of errors at the data-link layer are caused by:

▼ **Noise**   This is the addition of extraneous signals to the transmitted frame, which, if strong enough, can lead to altered bit values. Noise comes from the following sources:

   ■ *Crosstalk* from signals on adjoining lines, further characterized as near-end crosstalk (NEXT) and far-end crosstalk (FEXT)

   ■ *Thermal* noise from nearby heat sources

   ■ *Impulse* noise from lightning, switches, and components acting intermittently

   ■ *Electromagnetic* noise from adjacent sources of electrical energy

   Naturally, noise generated by these sources will not occur within a fiber system. The very nature of fiber prevents crosstalk, impulse noise, and electromagnetic noise from disrupting transmissions. However, heat sources can have an adverse effect on fiber, because temperature changes can cause the fiber to stretch and the cladding to distort, thereby changing the wavelength, attenuation, and dispersion enough to cause a disturbance. Subterranean fiber cables provide more consistent performance than aerial cables.

■ **Distortion**   This occurs to signals due to the different physical characteristics of individual lines. Varying levels of resistance in each line can result in skewing in parallel data transmission.

▲ **Others**   Some errors may be the result of faulty components that function intermittently, breaks in the transmission path, and so forth.

The duration of the interference will cause the error to affect just a single bit or many groups of bits. Quite often, the receiver won't know that the data has been corrupted. That's why it is important that the data link contain a means of error detection. The two main types of error detection are:

▼ Parity bits

▲ CRCs

These methods are good for identifying that an error has occurred, but they are not necessarily good ways to correct the error. Error detection and correction requires the use of complex algorithms called *forward error correction (FEC)*. Different implementations of FEC provide varying degrees of both detection and correction. The larger the span of bit disturbance that can be detected and corrected, the more complex the FEC. This also results in a larger overhead, reducing the traffic payload as a consequence, and adding computational complexity to the receiving device.

PHYSICAL MAINTENANCE AND TUNING

In the last section, we talked about the sort of maintenance that is delivered or in the design, construction, or configuration of your network. However, there are other factors that influence the stability of your network than what can be controlled from a computer console.

As with any network that relies on cabling (electrical or optical), situations arise where the cable is inadvertently cut or—more routinely—cabling has to be terminated to a connector.

In this section, we talk about the methods that can be used to avoid (or at least shorten) outages that are caused because of physical problems. We discuss not only fixing damaged cable, but also what steps you need to follow when terminating a length of fiber that will go into a networking device.

Solving Fiber Cuts

Two of the primary enemies of optical networking are hungry gophers and misdirected backhoes. In the event your network suffers an outage due to cut fiber, you can minimize the problem by doing two things:

▼   Having a redundant network topology

▲   Reconnecting the fiber

Let's take a closer look at each of these steps.

Routing

First, the problems of a cut fiber optic cable can be lessened if there are sufficient routes available around a node.

Earlier in this chapter we talked about the merits of SONET rings and mesh topologies. These are the first line of defense when an errant backhoe driver digs up the fiber optic link in your MAN. But even if your line is cut, that doesn't mean your network will cease functioning—at least not if you have a solid infrastructure that can redirect traffic around problems.

There is no need to rehash what we discussed earlier in this chapter as to the merits of SONET rings, mesh topologies, and routing protocols. But it cannot be stressed enough that the difference between a weakly designed network topology and a strong topology can be measured in the number of days it takes to get your network back up and running. By ensuring a redundant, reliable network, a cut in optical cabling will not bring your network to its knees. SONET standards require that cuts be detected within 10 ms, and switching occur within 50 ms. Some devices using UPSR rings can detect and switch in the submillisecond range.

Splicing

When it comes time to physically repair the fiber, this is most commonly accomplished by splicing the two ends of fiber back together. In an electrical network, splicing the cable is a reasonably straightforward operation. Since electrons don't care how the wire is connected (just that it *is* connected), splices don't have to worry about alignment or positioning.

In an optical network, however, the process is much more involved. First, the fiber is extremely tiny and impossible to reconnect with the naked eye. A microscope is usually employed to ensure that the fiber is going together properly. Second, optical fiber must be reconnected as precisely as possible to mitigate line loss. If the cores are out of alignment by even a couple of microns, the signal can be lost. Contamination is another concern during splicing. A single speck of dirt or dust can be enough to impede the signal coming down the fiber. Normally, splicing in the field takes place in the back of a van that is set up for this particular function.

Two types of splices are used to conjoin fiber:

▼   **Fusion splicing**   This method is done by welding two fibers together, normally with an electrical arc. Its benefits are low loss, high strength, low optical return loss, and lengthy reliability.

▲   **Mechanical splicing**   This method uses an *alignment fixture* to mate the fibers. Then, an index gel is used to minimize optical return loss. Some mechanical splices use bare fibers in an alignment bushing, while others look a lot like connector ferrules (but without the mounting hardware).

NOTE: We talk about epoxies in greater detail later in this chapter.

The aforementioned splices are illustrated in Figure 10-5.

The quality of the splice relies heavily on the quality of the *cleave* on the fibers being spliced together. Cleaving is done with a very sharp blade by scoring a surface blemish on the glass fiber, then pulling on the fiber until a crack spreads across the fiber. Good fusion splices are accomplished when both fiber ends are made perpendicular to the fiber axis. With a good, perpendicular cleave, fused ends can be welded together properly and with a minimum of loss.

With a mechanical splice, the fibers are pressed together and an index-matching epoxy glues them together. However, index matching is not perfect, so some reflection is likely to occur. By cleaving fibers at an angle, the reflected light will be absorbed in the cladding, thus reducing back reflections. To get the desired angle, special cleavers have been designed.

Loss   Loss in a splice is minimized when the two fiber cores are perfectly aligned. The size of the fibers being spliced is very important. The two important measurements are:

▼   **Numerical aperture (NA)**   This is a measure of the maximum angle at which a light source can be from the center axis of a fiber in order to collect light.

▲   **Core diameter**   This is the physical measurement of the optical fiber core.

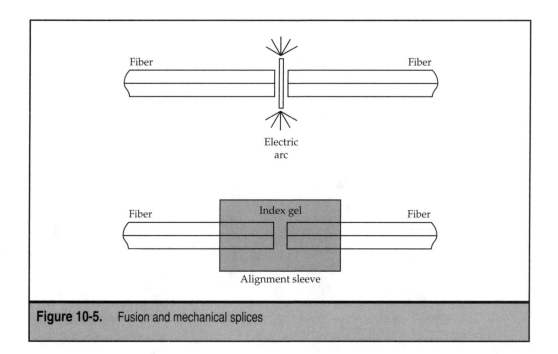

Figure 10-5.   Fusion and mechanical splices

Differences between these two create loss in systems depending on which way the light is flowing. Light from a fiber with a larger NA will be more sensitive to angularity and gap. Therefore, transmission from a fiber with a larger NA to one with a smaller NA will suffer more loss than light moving from fiber with a smaller to a larger NA.

Similarly, light from a fiber with a larger core diameter will suffer loss when spliced into a fiber with a smaller core diameter. In this case, loss is dependent of the direction of propagation. However, a fiber with a smaller core diameter can be spliced to a fiber with a larger core diameter with only minimal loss, because it is much less sensitive to end gap or lateral offset. This is shown in Figure 10-6.

Naturally, it would be ideal to match fiber sizes exactly. If the fibers are the same size, loss is usually independent of direction of propagation. However, there are situations where fiber mismatch simply cannot be avoided. For instance, you might be splicing into a system with older multimode fiber that simply cannot be matched. Also, there are production variances that are properly dimensioned, but suffer internal variances. A good rule to remember is that if the direction of propagation is from a smaller fiber to a larger one, the splicing loss will be minimal (maybe about 0.3dB). However, if the direction of propagation is from a larger fiber to a smaller one, expect to suffer substantial losses. This is due not only to the smaller core sizes, but also the smaller NA of the smaller fiber.

Table 10-3 lists the losses that can be expected (assuming a perfect splice) when mismatching fibers. It is also important to note that if the transmitting fiber is closer to the source, the loss will be higher. If the fiber is near steady state conditions, the loss will be less.

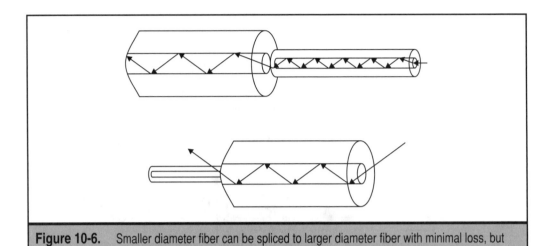

Figure 10-6.   Smaller diameter fiber can be spliced to larger diameter fiber with minimal loss, but the converse is not true

NOTE: When using a different fiber with a system, you should also make note of the differences in fiber bandwidths. Even though the system should work, if there is insufficient bandwidth, expect trouble.

Cleanliness   It is very important to make sure the work area is kept clean and free of cable fill compound, coating, and stray fiber ends. Also, the equipment you use must also be kept clean and free of dust. Any particles of dirt or dust (no matter how large or small) will have an adverse effect on your splices and result in bad fiber alignment.

The stripper is important to keep clean because any debris on the stripper can damage the fiber. Also, try to take as few passes as possible with the stripper, which could damage the fiber. After the fiber has been stripped, debris should be wiped away using an alcohol wipe. Discard the wipe after each use.

Receiving Fiber	Transmitting Fiber		
	62.5/125	85/125	100/140
50/125	1.6–1.9	3–4.6	4.7–9
62.5/125	–	0.9	2.1–4.1
85/125	–	–	0.9–1.4

Table 10-3.   Expected Loss When Connecting Dissimilar-Sized Multimode Fibers

The cleaver should have a sharp blade that is perpendicular to the fiber axis. If, during your splicing, more than a couple of bad cleaves occur, you should clean the blade. If the problems persist, the blade should be replaced.

Conversely, after cleaving, the fiber end should not be cleaned with the alcohol wipe. This could leave debris on the face of the fiber, which will lead to problems during splicing.

Solving Bad Fiber Connections

Another source of loss can be where a fiber is terminated. Connectors are used to terminate fiber; that is, connectors are attached to fiber so that the fiber can be plugged into a device or to another run of fiber. There are a number of different types of connectors (which are explained in greater depth in Chapter 11).

Let's take a closer look at connectors and how they are attached.

The Right Connector

One of the prime culprits in data loss is the connection point between a fiber and a component or between two fibers. To ensure that a good connection is made, connectors employ a *ferrule*. Within each ferrule is a spring that presses the cables together.

Most connectors employ a cylindrical ferrule to capture the fiber. The ferrules are aligned together so that the fibers touch, as shown in Figure 10-7.

However, because the spring applies a small force between the ferrules (about 0.9 kilograms), the ends of the ferrules can become deformed. In some cases, this deformation is a good thing, because the deformation can allow the fibers to mate better. Further, imperfections on the face of the fiber can be compensated for.

Connectors are used to join two ferrules that are used to mate two lengths of fiber. If these components aren't precise, the mating will be off and loss will occur. But no matter how well these components are made, there are still some eccentricities that prevent the fibers from mating exactly. The leading cause of insertion loss is a lack of concentricity in the construction of the ferrule, as Figure 10-8 illustrates.

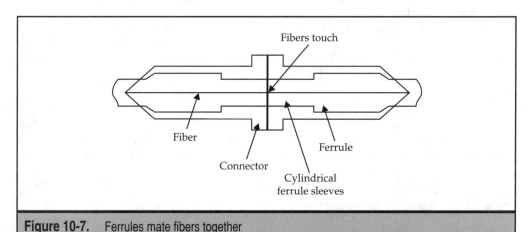

Figure 10-7.   Ferrules mate fibers together

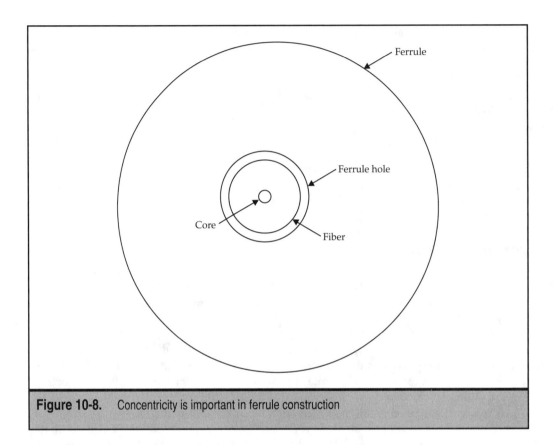

Figure 10-8.   Concentricity is important in ferrule construction

If the ferrule is not concentric, then the fibers will not align well. When you consider the size of the fiber in a single-mode fiber, a ferrule that is off by just 1 or 2 microns can have a huge impact.

The problem can also be worsened if the size of the hole in the ferrule is too large. This can cause the fiber to sit off-center and, again, cause a misalignment. Ferrules should be built with a diameter of 125 μm, but to make the manufacturing process easier, many are built with a 126 μm diameter. The best way to beat this problem is to make sure you buy connectors from reputable vendors who specify ferrules with 125 μm holes.

Another important consideration is the epoxy used. Epoxy is used to secure the fiber within the ferrule (we talk about different types of epoxies and adhesives later in this chapter). Even though secured within the ferrule with epoxy, the fibers can still shift. This is called *fiber pushback* or *pistoning* of the fiber and is caused by the force from two sources:

▼ Normal (longitudinal) force on the ferrule and fiber by the connector springs

▲ Thermal expansion (shear) force between ferrules and fiber

The most important parameter of epoxy is its glass transition temperature, which correlates to its shear strength over temperature. Studies have shown that epoxies with a lower glass transition temperature (noted as T_g) may experience fiber pistoning soon after termination when placed back in the curing oven. Other studies have shown that fiber pushback occurs within the first few hours of deployment.

Another detrimental factor that epoxy can have on a termination is the presence of air bubbles. This can cause inconsistent pressures on the fiber, possibly even fracturing the fiber. It is also helpful to understand that the geometry of the ferrule is rather important in the reliability of a connector. The optimal shape for a ferrule is a convex surface.

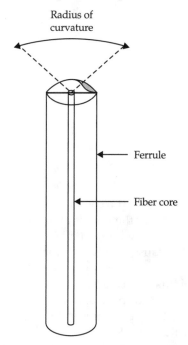

A convex surface is used to ensure that the fibers touch when they are mated. This avoids any air gap that could cause a signal degradation. The size of the surface is talked about as the *radius of curvature*. This specifies just how much curvature (from one side to the other) there is on the end of the ferrule. Smaller radii of curvature mean there will be a smaller contact area, which results in more deformation of the fiber and the ferrule. This causes more stress on the epoxy, which can increase the likelihood of fiber pushback. On the other hand, more pressure and deformation can compensate for fibers that have been undercut.

Larger radii of curvature result in a flatter end and in less deformation. The ideal size for a ferrule's radius of curvature is 7–25 mm.

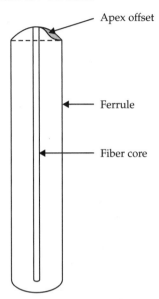

Apex offset describes how far from the center the highest point of the convex end is. This offset should be minimal so that the fiber is at the highest point of the end of the ferrule. If you are using two connectors whose ferrules have a pronounced apex offsets, the problem is only exacerbated because they won't mate properly. An apex offset of less than 50 μm is ideal.

Positive and negative heights describe how the fiber is situated within the fiber. As Figure 10-9 shows, positive height (or protrusion) occurs when the fiber peeks just over the top of the ferrule, and negative height (or undercut) occurs when the fiber does not quite reach the tip of the ferrule.

Generally speaking, both types of positioning can aid in the mating of two fibers. A bit of protrusion can help two ends mate, while some undercut can improve durability. Also, when the springs in the ferrules press together, the ferrules can deform slightly, allowing undercut fibers to touch, which is highly desirable. However, when there is too much protrusion, the durability is decreased and can even lead to fiber fracture. Undercut, though less of a problem than protrusion, can cause a poor connection and cause higher insertion loss. Optimally, there will not be more than 50 nm of undercut or protrusion.

Replacement

In the event that you need to replace a connector or are working on a new installation and must put a connector on a length of fiber, the process is not as straightforward as connecting an RJ-45 jack on some Category 5 cabling. When dealing with fiber, there are some important steps that you must adhere to.

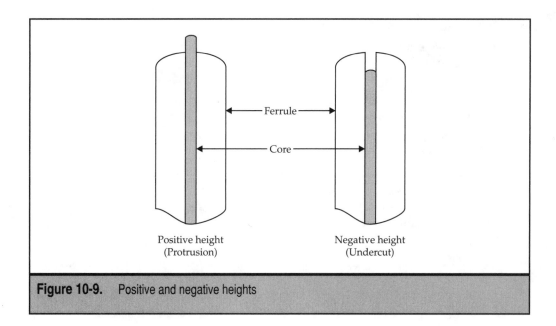

Positive height
(Protrusion)

Negative height
(Undercut)

Figure 10-9.   Positive and negative heights

Steps to Making a Connector   Since the connector can be a primary source of loss, it is a good idea to understand what goes into attaching a connector to the end of a fiber cable. Twenty years ago, affixing a connector to a length of cable involved: applying epoxy to the end of the fiber with a cotton swab; inserting it into a connector; curing; cleaving; and finally polishing. This process took about 20 minutes per connector.

Today, the process is largely similar, but the epoxies have been improved, the epoxy application process has been enhanced, and polishing films and tools have been tweaked for better performance. Not only that, but connectors have been designed that enable one to affix a connector to a cable in less than two minutes. In this section, we talk about different cable termination methods and the pros and cons of each.

First, let's go over the basic steps that are used when using epoxy to attach a connector to bare fiber:

NOTE: This series of steps assumes that you have already stripped cable to its bare fiber.

1. Combine resin and hardener. Premeasured packets are available that facilitate the combination process by allowing you to mix the resin and the hardener right in the package. Also, premixed epoxy is available in syringes, but it most be kept frozen until ready to use. The advantage of premixed epoxy is that no air bubbles will be present.

2. Load the mixed epoxy into a syringe (unless it's premixed).

3. Inject the epoxy to the end of a ferrule.

4. Insert the prepared cable into the connector so that the bare fiber is inserted into the ferrule hole. Push the cable in until the cable seats inside the connector. The bare fiber will protrude from the front of the ferrule about a half-inch.

5. If the fiber is jacketed, it is necessary to crimp on the connector. Crimping requires a crimp sleeve, and for best results, two crimps are needed.

6. Place the cable with the crimped connector into a curing holder. The holder protects the protruding fiber from any damage.

7. Place the connectorized cable and curing holder into an oven. Ovens for this purpose are basically a hot plate with a dozen holes for the curing holder. Any kind of oven will work as long as it can reach the desired temperature for the correct amount of time.

NOTE: If you wind up using a conventional oven, make sure that the curing holder is positioned so that the mating end of the connector is facing the floor. This configuration avoids *wicking*, which occurs when the epoxy flows from the back end of the connector and into the strength members of the cable. This is undesirable because the absorbed epoxy can cause brittleness and degrade the cable.

8. Cleave the protruding fiber as close to the ferrule tip as possible. Remove the excess fiber with a straight pull (it is important not to twist the fiber).

NOTE: Put the trimmed fiber piece on a piece of masking tape before tossing it out. Though small and seemingly insignificant, a piece of glass jammed in your finger or in your eye can be especially unpleasant.

9. Polishing the fiber is critical because it is important to get as smooth a surface as possible. If the tip of the fiber is not smooth, light will be lost. Polishing is done in a series of grades of polishing film. The first step uses a coarse grit film and removes excess epoxy. Subsequent steps use gradually finer grades of film so that the fiber can be smoothed out. Polishing should be done with the longitudinal axis of the fiber 90 degrees to the polishing film. Deviations as slight as one-half degree can result in significant loss.

10. Clean the ferrule tip. This can be done with a lint-free wipe dipped in 99 percent reagent-grade alcohol, followed by a swipe with a lint-free wipe.

11. Check your work. It is a good idea to look at what you've done so far to make sure that the polishing and cleaning were completed as well as possible. This is not only important to ensure that the connector is affixed in an optimal way, but it also prevents damage from occurring to a good connector when a bad one is mated with it. Inspection can be done with a number of microscopes designed for this purpose. They are designed to hold the fiber in place while you examine your work.

12. Finally, you should test your work. Different types of fiber demand different kinds of testing:

- Multimode fiber requires only an *insertion test.* This test measures how much light is passing through the connection.

- Single-mode fiber requires that *return loss* is also tested. This test measures how much light is being reflected as a result of the connection.

Epoxies and Adhesives   The epoxy you use will depend on many factors—cost, the time you have to make the connection, and the amount of epoxy you will use. The choice of epoxy to use is a personal choice, to an extent, but it will also depend on the application and the environment. For instance, will it be acceptable for a fiber link to be down for several days? Will time be an issue? What if the fiber is being connected in northern Canada? What about a connection in Panama? Will temperature be a factor?

The following points explain the different attributes of different types of epoxy:

▼ **Heat-cured epoxy**   These are good epoxies to use because they achieve an optimal resistance to extreme environments (hot, cold, and humid). However, they take a long time to terminate (about 10 minutes) and a long time to cure (about half an hour). To make the process even more difficult, an oven is needed for these types of installations.

■ **Room temperature–cured epoxy**   This type of epoxy is similar to heat-cured epoxy, except that it cures at room temperature. This means that connections made in the field can be easier and without the need for power or an oven. However, this type of epoxy has a short *pot life.* That means that once the epoxy is mixed, the clock is ticking before it becomes unusable. The rule of thumb is that only about 10 connectors can be terminated before the epoxy starts to harden. Not only does the installer have to work in small batches, but he or she also has to work quickly to make the best use of the epoxy. Room temperature–cured epoxy also has a long cure time, three hours.

■ **Preinjected epoxy**   This method used heat-cured epoxy, but the manufacturer has already injected the epoxy into the connectors, thus eliminating a lot of headache and mess. An installer must apply heat to the connector to soften the epoxy, then the fiber is inserted. Because the connector has to be heated, an oven is needed and the installer must handle hot connectors. Finally, polishing tends to take longer because there is a large bubble of epoxy that forms on the tip of the ferrule after the epoxy has cooled.

■ **Ultraviolet (UV) adhesive**   This type of epoxy requires a UV light source for curing. Polishing tends to be easier with this type of adhesive because no adhesive pools on the ferrule as do epoxies. This method tends to be fast (about 45 seconds of cure time), and an oven is not necessary. The downside is that the UV light source can cure the adhesive only if the light can get to it. Therefore, opaque ferrules cannot be used. Instead, special ferrules with a glass capillary are needed. Also, this type of adhesive is not as resilient to environmental extremes as epoxies.

- **Cyanoacylate adhesive** This method speeds up the curing process by spraying an *accelerator* on the ferrule tip after inserting the cable. By using the accelerator, the curing process takes about a minute. Further, the polishing process is rather quick. However, the downside is that it might be too quick. The adhesive can harden before the fiber can be fully inserted into the ferrule. Also, it is not as resistant to environmental extremes as epoxy.

- **Anaerobic adhesive** This is similar to cyanoacylate adhesive, except rather than spraying on an accelerator, the tip of the bare fiber is dipped in an activator. As the bare fiber enters the ferrule hole, the lack of oxygen (hence, anaerobic) causes the curing to begin. This method is convenient because no oven or UV light source is needed. As with cyanoacylate adhesive, the downside is that this type of adhesive can be too fast—the adhesive can harden before the tip is inserted all the way through the ferrule. Also, it is not as resistant to environmental extremes as epoxies. Finally, the adhesive has just a three-month shelf life (as opposed to other methods' year shelf life).

- **Acrylic adhesive** This type of adhesive is as fast as the anaerobic method, but it does not start to harden immediately, so getting the fiber into the connector shouldn't be as much of a race. It is also more resilient to environmental extremes than other adhesives. It does not require an oven or UV light source, and its shelf life is on par with epoxies (12 months).

- ▲ **No Epoxy** This type of connector includes a length of fiber that has been preepoxied to the connector and prepolished at the factory. A length of fiber extends from the back of the connector and is then spliced onto the existing cable. The splicing requires a special cleaver to ensure that the cut is acceptable. It also employs several different crimping mechanisms so that the cable is as strong as possible. The primary advantage to this method is that there are no epoxies needed and there is no polishing needed.

Table 10-4 compares each of these adhesion methods.

Checking Your Work

One of the last steps when terminating or splicing fiber optic cable is to inspect your work. Since fiber optic cabling is so small, this cannot be done with the naked eye. Instead, microscopes are generally employed to see the tiny connections.

Don't underestimate this step. Examining the surface of a connector is a great way to determine the quality of the termination and to locate any potential problems. A well-made connector will have a smooth, polished, scratch-free surface, and the fiber will not show any signs of cracking or pistoning.

The best magnification for examining fiber is generally between 30 and 100 power. Lower magnification will not be enough to judge the finish on the connector. On the other

Method	Source of Cure	Termination Time (in minutes)	Connector Cost	Environmental Resistance	Special Tools
Heat-cured epoxy	Oven	10 30 minutes cure	Low	Excellent	Oven
Room temperature-cured epoxy	Air	10 120 minutes cure	Low	Good	None
Preinjected epoxy	Oven	8 30 minutes cool down	Medium	Good	Oven, cooling rack
UV adhesive	UV light	5	Medium	Fair	UV light
Cyanoacrylate adhesive	Air	3	Low	Fair	None
Anaerobic adhesive	Activator	3	Low	Fair	None
Acrylic adhesive	Activator	2.5	Low	Fair	None
No epoxy	NA	1.5	High	Good	Special cleaver and crimp tool

Table 10-4.   Epoxies and Adhesives Compared

hand, if the magnification is too high, small, inconsequential faults will look worse than they are.

There are three ways to inspect the connector:

▼   Viewing the end of the polished surface with side lighting

■   Viewing directly with side lighting and light transmitted through the core

▲   Viewing at an angle with lighting from the opposite angle.

Viewing directly with side lighting allows you to determine if the ferrule hole is the correct size, if the fiber is centered in the hole, and if a proper amount of adhesive has been used. Viewing this way tends to make only the largest scratches visible. If you add light to the end of the fiber, cracks made by pressure or heat during the polishing process will be visible.

Viewing the fiber at an angle with lighting coming from the opposite side at the same angle provides the best environment to inspect the quality of the polish and possible scratches. Because of the shadowing effect of angular viewing, the light contrast makes the scratches much more apparent.

NOTE: Be cautious not to be overly critical when inspecting connectors. Especially at high magnification, problems can look larger than they really are. The only place to be concerned about damage is on the fiber core. Chipping at the glass around the outside of the cladding is common and won't have any adverse effect on the core. Similarly, scratches on the cladding won't cause loss.

Durability

An important factor when affixing connectors is the durability of the connection. This is proved by its ability to endure multiple matings with minimal loss or deformation. Testing your connectors' durability is a simple enough process—repeatedly mate and demate your connector pair while measuring loss. Generally speaking, loss is a function of both the connectors and the alignment sleeve, so loss could be attributed to any of these sources.

For example, plastic alignment sleeves—when used with ceramic connectors—will wear out quickly, because the plastic will be shaved off, causing increased loss. During durability tests, occasional checks of the connector end faces and ferrules with a microscope will help uncover any wear.

Loss Testing

Once you've spliced fiber together or added a connector to the fiber optic cable, it is necessary to test the line for loss. Not only is loss testing important for new splices and connections, but it is also important when trying to track down problems in your network.

This section talks about the process of testing for loss within a fiber optic system. We talk about the basics of power meters, establishing a baseline (the measurement against which readings will be compared), and performing the actual loss tests.

Measuring with a Power Meter

When testing power in a fiber optic network, it is easy to think of that power as like the voltage in an electrical circuit. The photons inside the optical network are what make everything happen, just like the electrons in a circuit. But it is important to strike a balance. If there are too many photons, then the network won't function. Likewise, if there aren't enough photons, the system won't function.

To measure power in an optical network, you need an optical power meter and an adapter for the connector. It is important to remember when measuring power that the meter must be set to the proper range (normally dBm) and the correct wavelength.

To measure the power, attach the meter to the cable at the transmitter by checking a length of test cable (this is explained in the next section) and then connecting to the source as shown in Figure 10-10.

Next, turn on the source and make a note of the power that your meter measures. Then, compare that reading with the specified power for the system and ensure that you are working within the guidelines for power established by your device's vendor.

Establishing a Baseline

The first step in testing optical power loss is to calibrate your power meter by mating the cable to a good, known reference cable. This step is important because it establishes a baseline for your network's performance.

You must establish the test conditions by calibrating the reference cable. Clean your power meter connectors and set up the equipment in this manner:

1. Turn on the source and select the wavelength you wish to test.

2. Turn on the meter and select the "dBm range," then select the wavelength you will be testing.

3. Measure the power at the power meter. This reading will be your reference power level for all loss measurements. Your reference power must be high enough so that future measurements won't exceed the range of your meter.

4. If your source power is adjustable, set the power to around –30 dBm for light emitting diodes (LEDs) and –10 dBm for lasers in single-mode fiber.

NOTE: In the past, setting the reference power was done by using both the launch and receive cables mated with a splice bushing. It is best not to do that, because if either the launch or receive cable is bad, setting the reference with both cables hides this and you'll get skewed readings. Further, you could underestimate connector loss by one connector, compared to how the measurement should be made.

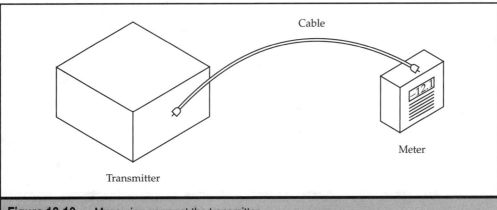

Figure 10-10.   Measuring power at the transmitter

Testing Loss

Two methods are used for measuring loss:

▼ **Single-ended loss**   This uses only the launch cable for its measurement.

▲ **Double-ended loss**   This uses the launch and receive cables for measurement.

The methods are explained in more detail under the headings that follow.

Single-Ended Loss   Single-ended loss is measured by mating the cable to be tested with the reference cable (plugged into the launch port) and measuring the power at the far end with the power meter. Doing this measures:

▼ The loss of the connector mated to the reference cable.

▲ The loss of the fiber, any splices, and connectors present in the fiber optic cabling.

This process is shown in Figure 10-11.

NOTE: It helps to keep your reference power the same for all measurements. This eliminates confusion during your testing.

After this measurement has been completed, reverse the cable to test the connector on the other end.

NOTE: Reversing the cable is not necessary for single-mode fiber.

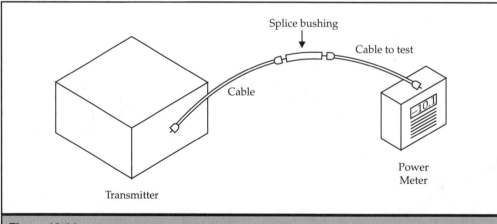

Figure 10-11.   Single-ended loss testing

Double-Ended Loss A double-ended loss test attaches the test cable between two reference cables—one is attached to the source, the other, to the meter (as shown in Figure 10-12).

A double-ended loss test measures two connectors' losses, one on each end, plus the loss of all the fiber in between.

> **NOTE:** Before testing any cables, make sure you use the single-ended test to measure the loss in all your reference cables before you start testing. If the cable loss is too high (0.5dB or greater), don't use them.

How Much Loss Is Acceptable? Different components of an optical network will generate different levels of loss. For instance, a connector will account for more loss than a splice. Fiber itself accounts for varying levels of loss. Table 10-5 lists different sources and amounts of loss.

When approximating the loss of a cable plant, here's a quick formula for making your calculations:

(0.5dB × the number of connectors) + (0.2dB × the number of splices) + total fiber loss on the entire length of cable = approximate power loss.

Troubleshooting If you measure a length of cable and discover a high level of loss, make sure you reverse it and test the fiber in the opposite direction. Because a single-ended test just tests the connector on one end, this can help you isolate a bad connector. In this scenario, the bad connector will be the one on the launch end of the cable.

If you encounter high loss in a double-ended test, it can be isolated by reversing the direction to check if there is a bad connector. If the loss is the same, you should test each segment separately to isolate a bad segment. If the fiber is long enough, you might have to use an optical time-domain reflectometer (OTDR).

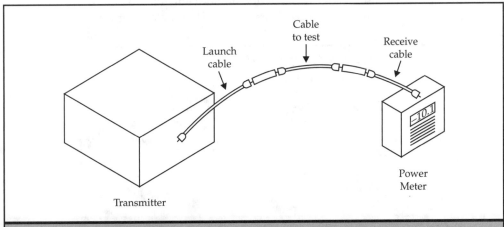

Figure 10-12. Double-ended loss testing

Source of Loss	Amount of Loss
Connector	0.5–0.75 dB
Splice	0.2 dB
Multimode fiber	*850 nm*—3 dB per km (or 0.1 dB per 100 feet)
	1300 nm—1 dB per km (or 0.1 dB per 300 feet)
Single-mode fiber	*1300nm*—0.5 dB per km (or 0.1 dB per 600 feet)
	1550 nm—0.4 dB per km (or 0.1 dB per 750 feet)

Table 10-5.   Sources and Amounts of Loss in an Optical Network

NOTE: An OTDR is an instrument that analyzes the light loss in optical fiber. An OTDR injects a short, intense pulse of laser light into the fiber and measures the backscatter and reflection of light as a function of time. Since the propagation speed of light is known, it is very easy to convert time to a distance. The reflected light characteristics are analyzed to determine the location of any fiber optic breaks or splice losses.

Tunable Lasers

One way to boost capacity while decreasing costs is by employing tunable lasers. These lasers are still a young technology, but as the number of wavelengths in networks increases so will their importance.

Fixed-wavelength lasers, which dominate the market today, require equipment makers to purchase many laser components to transmit data over a broad range of colors. An easy way to think about what a tunable laser does is to look at the picture in Figure 10-13.

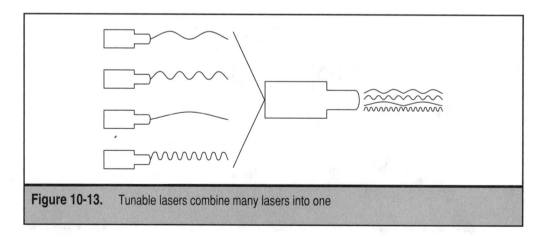

Figure 10-13.   Tunable lasers combine many lasers into one

A tunable laser is able to emit many wavelengths from a single device. Currently, to introduce the multiple wavelengths that are possible in a DWDM system, multiple lasers were necessary. However, a tunable laser allows for the selection of a single wavelength to be generated from a palette of many. This benefits both the manufacturer and the user, who don't have to stock or purchase lasers that can generate only a single wavelength to cover the number of lambdas needed for a particular DWDM network. Each specific wavelength in the network is separated from the next by approximately 0.8 nm (this is often referred to a 100 GHz spacing, the frequency separation). A single tunable laser can serve as a spare for up to 100 nontunable lasers.

Most tunable lasers are designed to operate on the same principles as nontunable lasers and incorporate a grating like those used in a distributed feedback laser, but they are much more complex. These gratings can be manipulated so that the wavelengths are changed. Technologies based on vertical cavity surface emitting lasers (VCSELs) allow the cavity ends to be adjusted so that the emitted wavelength is also altered.

Tunable lasers are very well suited for DWDM deployments. Tunable lasing will make it possible to isolate, route, and manage individual wavelengths to serve specific traffic and services in line with demand. This will be useful when truly all-optical routers and switches become a reality. Further, tunable lasers can alleviate the expensive inventory management that comes with fixed wavelength lasers. Ultimately, this will result in improved service, better performance, and reduced costs.

For manufacturers, tunable lasers can also be beneficial. They need only produce one type of laser instead of eight (look for even more lambda capabilities in the future). Ultimately, that cost savings should be passed on to the organization, because if the manufacturer is saving money in the laser's construction and the provider is saving money on the cost of the laser, then the organization should save money on the service.

But tunable lasers aren't a perfect solution, just yet. The primary problem is one of power. The more tunable a laser, the less able it is to transmit a powerful pulse, and so the shorter the distance the signal can travel without amplification. As a result, tunable lasers might be more useful for metropolitan areas, rather than in long-haul deployments.

TOOLS

Finally, in this chapter, we'll take a quick look at the tools you can use to perform system maintenance and checks. There are a score of vendors out there with products on the market, but the following companies (LightWave, Acterna, and Fluke) are three of the most prominent.

Your organization will realize a cost benefit much as it does with the purchase of any other worthwhile piece of test equipment. Without a device to test connections, inspect packets, or search for other problems, not only will your network suffer through outages, but it will lack the sort of tuning that is necessary to keep it working at peak performance.

The following sections talk about their specific products and how they are useful for your organization's network.

Digital Lightwave Network Information Computers

Digital Lightwave's line of test equipment is called its Network Information Computers. These computers provide analysis of global DWDM, SONET, T-Carrier, PDH, ATM, and Packet over SONET (POS) networks. This equipment is used for verification and qualification of service during network installation and troubleshooting deployed networks.

The NIC Plus is Lightwave's top-level test computer. The NIC Plus is joined by the NIC ASA 312, the NIC 10G, and the NIC 2.5G.

The models, starting at $US175,000, offer the following functionality:

▼ Simultaneous testing of SONET/SDH, T-Carrier, PDH, ATM, and POS. Separate protocol processors for OC-1/STM-0 through OC-192/STM-64, ATM, DS0/DS1/DS3, and 64K/E1/E3/E4

■ Alarm/error generation and analysis

■ Auto configuration to pattern level

■ Trouble scan

■ A 12.1-inch active matrix color display with touch screen

■ Dual-slot PCMCIA interface for modem or memory storage

■ Built-in optical power and frequency measurement

■ Test set configuration with graphical switch matrix

■ DS1/DS3 and E1/E3 drop/insert from SONET/SDH, built-in M13/E13

■ OC-192/STM-64 through mode with overhead manipulation

■ OC-192/STM-64 1310/1550 nm wavelength laser

■ OC-48/STM-16 1310/1550 nm dual-wavelength laser option

■ POS for 10G and 2.5G rates

■ Remote control GUI

■ Firmware upgradable via Web connection

▲ Three slots for future expansion

With the Digital Lightwave portable devices, it is possible to meet current maintenance needs as well as plan for future additions. The NICs boast an easy-to-use interface that allows technicians to maintain all sorts of optical networks.

Acterna CycloneCore IP Optimizer

The Acterna CycloneCore IP Optimizer is used for IP-traffic engineering and troubleshooting for testing Packet over SONET (POS) networks. The CycloneCore is also able to monitor QoS functions and help maintain POS networks.

CycloneCore, priced starting at $US70,000, combines remote features with a real-time, customizable flow classification engine to test and monitor at wire speeds within carrier-scale IP networks. The CycloneCore is able to monitor core IP– and Multi Protocol Label Switching (MPLS)–enabled networks.

The CycloneCore offers the following features:

▼ Event analysis through all seven OSI layers

■ IP analysis of up to 32,000 conversations

■ Frame-based data link analysis

■ Direct or remote control via 10/100 Mb Ethernet and internal/external modem

■ Verification of network and device interoperability at both the data and control flow level

■ Ability to make network modifications quickly and easily

■ Ability to pinpoint the exact source of network congestion

■ Ability to view physical-layer alarms as soon as they occur

■ Monitoring of core IP- and MPLS-enabled networks with real-time monitoring of 128,000 data flows

■ Identification of traffic patterns, network bandwidth, and congestion

■ Packet filter/capture/decode functionality

■ Reduction in mean time to repair (MTTR) as a result of reduced mean time to understand (MTTU) the root cause of problems

▲ Remote, single-point management of multiple devices

Additionally, CycloneCore can be used to identify control plane protocol activities within autonomous systems and peering networks. Further, its event logging function allows a view of handshaking parameters that are helpful in locating trouble spots.

Fluke FiberInspector

Fluke Networks offers a number of devices for checking network systems. For fiber networks, one of Fluke's tools is the FT300 FiberInspector. Its claim to fame is that it can be used in tight, formerly inaccessible, quarters and won't contaminate any fibers.

This tool, priced at about $US3500, is a portable video microscope that works by inserting a probe and inspecting installed fiber connectors through bulkhead adapters, without the need to access the backside of the patch panel. This is beneficial because it allows fiber inspection without running the risk of contamination with dirt or dust. Further, it allows inspection of installed connectors and critical fibers on hardware devices with the FT300 FiberInspector.

The FiberInspector employs a handheld LCD display unit and a small, lightweight probe containing an LED light source and a closed-circuit display camera. The probe adapter tip mates with the connector and projects images of microscopic debris and end-face damage on the LCD display. The video display allows you to look at a fiber end face without looking into the fiber, eliminating the chance of harmful laser light penetrating your eye.

NOTE: We talk about fiber safety in general, and the adverse effects of laser light in particular, in Chapter 11.

In addition to improving the ease of inspecting hard-to-reach fibers and connectors, the FiberInspector reduces the chances of contaminating fibers. Because the FiberInspector does not touch the termination point, the risk of contamination is reduced.

The FiberInspector includes the following components:

▼ Fiber probe

■ Fiber display

▲ Probe adapter tips (ST, SC, FC, and a universal 2.5 mm patch cord tip)

To return to the analogy used in the beginning of this chapter, stacking a few boxes in one's attic may not be problematic at first—indeed, it might be a perfectly acceptable solution for a few stray boxes that have no home. But after time, so many boxes will be added that it becomes necessary to clean out the attic. Likewise, it is important to keep an eye on your network and continually maintain and upgrade the system, because after time, so much "junk" will have been added to the network that the system can no longer run optimally.

Also, there are important considerations and skills that network engineers must develop when physically adding to the network. When new components are added, it will be necessary to terminate new runs of fiber so that they can be connected to the new devices. These skills are also important when fiber is cut and the two end of damaged fiber must be spliced together.

Maintaining and tuning an optical network is a balance both of logical considerations (how things like errors affect the network) and physical considerations (how, for instance, fiber is spliced and terminated). Networks need constant attention on both fronts to ensure not only optimal network deployments but also uptime.

CHAPTER 11

Optical Fiber

Throughout this book, we've talked about the basics of optical fiber, but we held on to a lot of specifics for this chapter. Fiber is a very complex product. Because of fiber's intricate design, it is very difficult to manufacture. Further, it is difficult to handle and install properly. Many problems occur during the installation of fiber, though recent cable designs have lessened this problem.

In this chapter, we look at the different types of fiber that are used in modern networks, how fiber is made, how it is terminated, and how it is installed in a range of environments, from mild to wild.

CABLES, CONSTRUCTION, AND CONNECTORS

The first section covers the different types of fiber. In earlier chapters, we have talked about different types of fiber, specifically multimode and single-mode fibers and the type of traffic they can handle. Here, we take a little more time to drill down into the specifics of each fiber and explain the different types of multimode and single-mode fibers. Further, we talk about plastic fibers, which cannot handle the capacity of glass fibers but come with a much lower overall price tag.

After discussing the types of fiber, we'll talk about how those fibers are constructed. Because there are so many important layers in optical fiber, it goes without saying that fiber is not an easy thing to build. Finally, we'll cover the different types of connectors that can be applied to the end of a piece of optical fiber.

Types

In earlier chapters, we talked about the differences between single-mode and multimode fiber, but we really covered only some of the basics. In this section, we talk more specifically about the types of optical fiber and how one might use them in an optical network.

First, we talk about the different types of multimode fiber. From there, we'll cover some of the issues facing single-mode fiber, and we'll wrap it up with an overview of plastic fiber.

Multimode Step-Index

Step-index refers to the fact that there is a uniform index of refraction throughout the fiber core. As such, there is a step in the refractive index where the core and cladding meet. As Figure 11-1 shows, when two modes travel through the fiber, they wind up traveling different distances to arrive at their destinations. As such, one mode arrives at its destination first, the other arrives later. This disparity between the arrival times is called *modal dispersion*.

Modal dispersion results in poor signal quality at the receiving end and ultimately limits the transmission distance. Distance is limited because the mode's route is only magnified as the fiber spans great distances; this is why multimode fiber is not used in long-haul communications.

As a result of modal dispersion, step-index fiber is found most commonly in LANs and other short-distance applications. Even though modal dispersion can be problematic

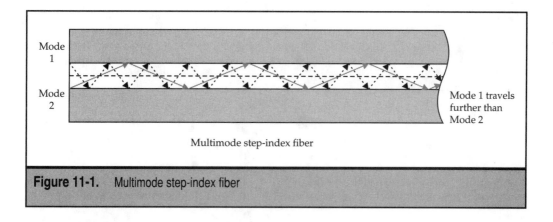

Multimode step-index fiber

Figure 11-1. Multimode step-index fiber

in long-haul environments, it is not much of an issue in LANs, because it is a faster option than competing, electrical technologies.

The length of a fiber span is a very important characteristic. Essentially, the shorter the step-index fiber, the more bandwidth is available. The longer the span, the less bandwidth is available. The relationship between bandwidth and distance is sometimes expressed as the "bandwidth.distance" product of the fiber. Because waves of light are analog signals, bandwidth is expressed in terms of megahertz (MHz). The rule of thumb is that so long as the distance of the fiber span does not exceed the bandwidth.distance product measurement, the fiber should work just fine.

For instance, bandwidth in 62.5/125 multimode fibers is 1000 MHz.kilometer (km). Therefore, on a 10 km stretch of fiber, 10 MHz can be used for information transfer. Another way to look at it is that, if 500 MHz of bandwidth is needed, the fiber can be only 2 km in length.

NOTE: Bandwidth.distance applies only to multimode fiber. It is not a factor in single-mode fibers that do not have to deal with modal dispersion.

Multimode Graded-Index

Because of the distance limitations of step-index fiber, *graded-index* fiber was invented. Graded-index refers to the fact that the refractive index of the core is graded—gradually it decreases from the center of the core outward, in a way also referred to as radially graded, in a parabolic profile. Rays that stay near the core center and follow nearly straight paths, travel relatively slowly because they are in a region of high index. On the other hand, rays that make wide excursions toward the cladding traverse longer paths, but they travel faster because they spend time in a lower-index material. By careful control of the index profile, the travel times for all rays can be made nearly equal. This typically results in at least two orders of magnitude improvement over multimode step-index fiber in the bit rate carried before attenuation begins.

Figure 11-2 illustrates graded-index fiber.

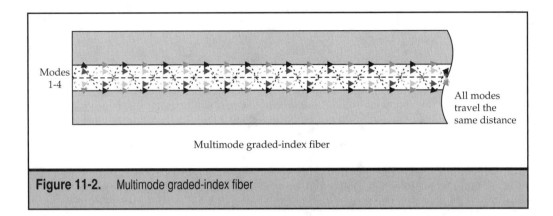

Figure 11-2. Multimode graded-index fiber

For example, if a pulse of light enters a span of step-index fiber, its modal dispersion will cause the modes to arrive at the opposite end at different times. However, in graded-index fiber, the lambdas will arrive at the same time, due to the grading.

Because grading requires a precise and exact construction, it is more expensive than other types of multimode fiber.

Single-Mode

The first, most obvious thing that should strike someone looking at pieces of multimode and single-mode fiber is the differing sizes of the core widths. Where multimode fiber cores are normally about 50 or 62.5 microns (µm) in diameter, single-mode is much smaller, only 9 µm. This size is important because it allows just one wavelength into the fiber core.

NOTE: Multimode and single-mode are relative terms, however. It all depends on the wavelength being used with the fiber. For instance, given a long enough wavelength, multimode fiber will be able to handle only a lone wavelength. In a single-mode system, a wavelength of 600 nm will allow multiple modes to be transmitted. As such, single-mode fibers have what is called a *cutoff wavelength*. Below this wavelength, the fiber becomes multimode. The cutoff wavelength for most 9 µm fibers is 1100 nm.

When the proper wavelength is used with single-mode fiber, reflection no longer occurs at the juncture of the core and the cladding; light travels directly down the center of the fiber. In practice, this is much harder than it sounds. Because the numerical aperture (NA) is so small, much of the light is lost to *insertion loss*. Also, about 20 percent of the light actually travels in the cladding. This effect is called *waveguide dispersion*. Because of this trait, single-mode fiber is often talked about in terms of its *mode field* or *mode field diameter* instead of the actual core diameter. The mode field diameter depends on the difference in the refractive index (RI) between the core and the cladding, which is much less in single-mode fiber than in multimode fiber (remember, light doesn't need to bounce off the walls of single-mode fiber, and the purer the glass, the further the signal will travel).

Because single-mode fiber cores are so small, they experience high loss when bent around corners. If the bend exceeds the recommended bend radius, light will be lost into the cladding.

NOTE: We talk about the specific dangers of bending fiber later in this chapter.

We've listed many of single-mode fiber's downsides, but certainly there must be some reason it is so popular. The main explanation is that attenuation in single-mode fiber is very small—about half that of multimode fiber. The chief cause of attenuation comes from the dopants used to make RIs different between core and cladding. Again, because RI is not much of an issue in single-mode fiber, dopants need not be used (the glass is purer), thereby giving single-mode fiber better levels of attenuation. As such, single-mode fibers are best used in WANs, where they can make the long hauls that are demanded of such deployments.

The best wavelength for single-mode fiber is at 1310 nanometers (nm), which is the so-called *zero dispersion point* of single-mode fiber. This is also the prime reason why Synchronous Optical Networks (SONET) operated at this wavelength initially, but with the need for greater distances and improved manufacturing capabilities of both the fiber and lasers, 1550 nm became the predominant wavelength. Almost all OC-48 and OC-192 today operate at 1550 nm.

Dispersion-Shifted Fiber   However, most Dense Wavelength Division Multiplexing (DWDM) equipment operates around 1550 nm, because this range has less overall attenuation than 1310 nm. DWDM equipment can run at 1550 nm across single-mode fiber; however, it has a very high dispersion rate, about 17 picoseconds per nanometer-kilometer (ps/nm/km).

It is easy enough to shift the dispersion level in single-mode fiber. Such fiber is called *dispersion-shifted* fiber, for which the zero point is shifted to 1550 nm during the manufacturing process. This is accomplished by controlling the RI of the core and the cladding. In effect, a larger waveguide dispersion effect is added. Because waveguide dispersion happens when light travels in the cladding, the RI core profile is made more complex to compensate for this effect.

Because it has been tweaked to accommodate DWDM equipment, one would think that dispersion-shifted fiber is well suited for DWDM work. Actually, this is not the case. Signals tend to break up more often in dispersion-shifted fiber than in standard fiber. Also, with multiple wavelengths traveling at the same speed, four-wave mixing (FWM) is more prevalent. FWM causes interference between channels and is a real problem.

Non–Zero Dispersion–Shifted   Since FWM causes a problem in DWDM dispersion-shifted fiber, it is a better idea to have a *little* bit of dispersion near 1550 nm. These types of fibers are called *non–zero dispersion–shifted fiber (NZ-DSF)*. These fibers have a very complex RI profile and an accompanying high price tag. However, they are tweaked for DWDM systems. Dispersion in NZ-DSF systems runs at about 4 ps/nm/km between 1530 and 1570 nm.

Plastic

For the last few hundred pages, when talking about fiber, we've referred to fibers made out of silica glass. But that isn't the only material used in the construction of optical fiber. Plastic Optical Fiber (POF) is useful for illumination and low-speed, short data links. Lately, there has been an increased interest in POF because there have been leaps forward in performance, as well as because of its ease of installation and low costs.

POF typically uses polymethylmethacrylate (PMMA), a general-purpose resin, as the core material, and fluorinated polymers for the cladding material. Although glass fiber is widely used for infrastructures, POF has been called the "consumer" optical fiber. This is due to the fact that optical links, connectors, installation costs, and POF itself are much less expensive than their glass counterparts.

Some of the benefits of plastic fiber are:

▼ **POF has a much larger diameter than glass fiber** Most POF has a diameter of 1000 μm (1 millimeter) with a core diameter of 980 μm. (Figure 11-3 compares POF, single-mode, and multimode fibers.) Because POF has such a large core, transmission is not impeded even if the ends are slightly soiled or damaged, or if the light axis is slightly out of alignment. Therefore, parts such as optical connectors need not be built to the same rigid standard as their glass-fiber counterparts. The result is a less expensive product (between 10 and 20 percent the cost of glass connectors) and a simplified installation process.

■ **POF is strong and is hard to overbend** Even when POF is bent to a radius of 25 mm, there is only a small loss. This makes it good to place in walls or other tight locations.

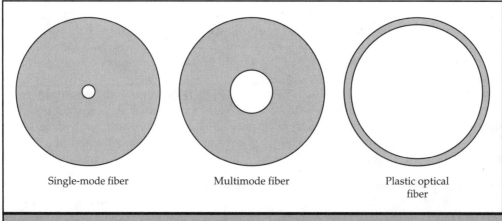

Single-mode fiber   Multimode fiber   Plastic optical fiber

Figure 11-3. Core size comparison of single-mode, multimode, and plastic fiber

■ **Installation is simple**   A common means of terminating POF is called the "hot plate" method. Using this method, the fiber ends are heated until softened, then pushed against a mirrored surface. This method is quick and simple to repeat. Also, it is very easy to simply trim the end of POF with a razor blade.

■ **A 650 nm LED is the light source for POF transceivers**   Because this wavelength is within the visible spectrum of light (red, to be exact), safety is enhanced because one can see if light is coming through the end of the fiber.

▲ **POF transmits a low level of infrared light**   Low levels of infrared light mean that POF can be used in environments where heat would pose a problem, for example in semiconductor manufacturing.

If plastic fiber is so great, why isn't it in wide use? The main reason is that POF is just not suited for long-haul transmissions. As compared with glass fiber, POF has a very high transmission loss. POF has a loss of 0.15–0.2 dB per *meter* at 650 nm, and its bandwidth is limited by its large NA and step-index profile. But POF is good for running short links, such as inside devices or for desktop connections up to 50 meters. Its main bread and butter applications have been within automobiles, where it has become very popular.

Recently, POF has developed to the point where it offers a low NA and higher bandwidth. Further, graded-index POF has been developed that couples the high bandwidth of graded-index fiber with the low cost of POF. The current limit on POF is about 2 Ghz bandwidth at 100 meters.

As you can tell, POF is an excellent choice for desktop LANs. Installed in minutes with a minimum number of tools, it offers a bandwidth that easily exceeds copper connections. Because home and office deployments do not require distance deployments (but require low costs and ease of use), POF is good for these environments.

Fiber Construction

Optical fiber, as you no doubt understand, is extremely thin. Most fibers are a total of 125 μm in diameter. This is only slightly thicker than the human hair, which is about 100 μm in diameter. But remember, 125 μm represents the total thickness of the fiber, including core and cladding! When the buffer is added, it can double the size of the fiber, but that is still extremely thin. How is something this tiny made?

The process starts with something called a *preform*. A preform is a much larger version of the fiber (several inches in diameter and several feet long) containing all the components that will be needed in the final fiber.

Next, the preform is stood on end in a *drawing tower* and heated. Happily, all the layers in the preform soften at the same rate, so the glass can be drawn into fiber thicknesses and lengths. The fiber is then cooled, buffered, cooled again, then wound on reels. This process is shown in Figure 11-4.

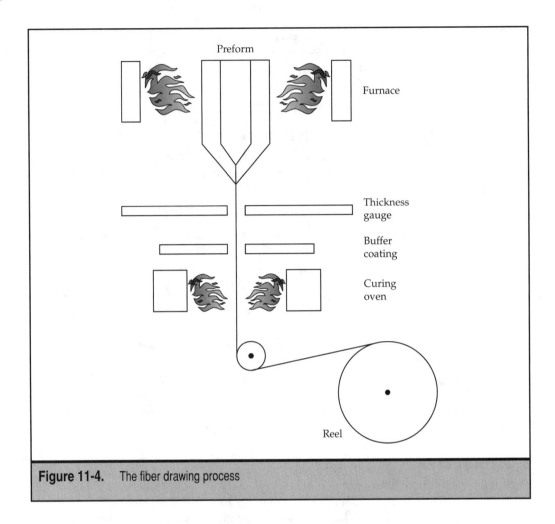

Figure 11-4.   The fiber drawing process

This process is the same for all types of fiber, the difference coming from how the preform is made. There are four main ways that preforms are made:

▼   Outside vapor deposition (OVD)

■   Vapor axial deposition (VAD)

■   Modified chemical vapor deposition (MCVD)

▲   Plasma-activated chemical vapor deposition (PCVD)

The first two methods basically build the fiber from the inside out, and the last two build it from the outside in. The following section explains the preform manufacture process in greater detail.

Outside Vapor Deposition

Outside vapor deposition (OVD) is used primarily in the United States and Europe and is a Corning patent. Construction occurs in three steps: laydown, consolidation, and draw.

1. In the laydown phase, a soot preform is formed by flame hydrolysis reactions, typically using a methane-oxygen flame, to deposit submicron (approx 0.25 micron) soot particles. This continues until the soot is built up layer by layer into a cylindrical porous soot boule. Chemically pure vapors of silicon tetrachloride and germanium tetrachloride are then delivered. These reagents are deposited on the surface of a rotating rod by direct chemical vaporization or with metering pumps. The core material is deposited first, followed by the cladding. Since both core and cladding raw materials are vapor-deposited, the entire preform is extremely pure. This step is shown in Figure 11-5.

2. In the consolidation phase, the target rod is removed from the center of the preform and placed into a consolidation furnace. During the consolidation process, hydroxyl molecules (OH) are removed from the preform. This high-temperature consolidation step *sinters* the preform into a solid, dense, transparent glass blank. The hole left by the target rod is collapsed by the extremely high temperature of the draw furnace.

3. The draw phase is like the draw process we described earlier in this section.

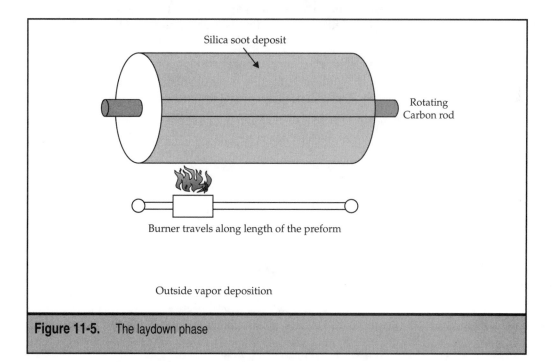

Figure 11-5. The laydown phase

One of OVD's problems comes from water generated by this process. Because water is created, so-called *OH Groups* develop which absorb light at 1385 nm. This absorption makes it crucial that light avoid this particular wavelength.

Vapor Axial Deposition

Vapor axial deposition (VAD) is used primarily in Japan. VAD is an updated version of OVD. Essentially, VAD equipment puts the OVD equipment on one end, and it can make larger performs. As such, up to 250 km of fiber can be drawn from a VAD preform.

Instead of moving the dopant-infused flame to control soot vapor deposition or RI, the preform is slowly pulled upward and rotated. The sintering process takes place further up the preform. This process allows water contamination to be better controlled, and the preform rod can be fed directly into the drawing phase.

Figure 11-6 illustrates the VAD process.

Modified Chemical Vapor Deposition

Chemical vapor deposition is very different than OVD or VAD methods. Whereas the first two methods of preform construction make the fiber starting with the core, chemical vapor deposition works from the outside in. *Modified chemical vapor deposition (MCVD)* is also used in the United States and Europe.

MCVD forms the silica in a premade, rotating silica tube. Gases to be introduced are injected on one end of the tube, and burners move across the length of the tube. As such, the soot is deposited internally, and exhaust gases are released from the other end of the tube. When the process is completed, there is a hole running through the center of the

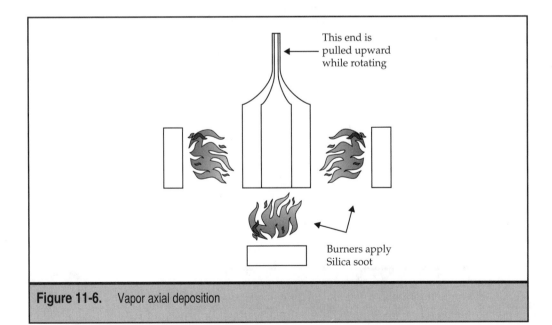

Figure 11-6. Vapor axial deposition

preform. As in the previous methods, this hole is sealed off as the heat is turned up and the cavity collapses.

MCVD has advantages over OVD and VAD:

▼ The RI profile can be monitored very closely.

■ No water is produced, so the OH absorption problem is eliminated.

■ Manufacture is fast and can be integrated into a draw system.

▲ Handling of germanium is simplified, because this element tended to evaporate when the final hole in the fiber core was closed. As a result, there is a risk that the RI profile will change along the axis of the core in OVD and VAD fibers.

Figure 11-7 shows the MCVD process.

Plasma-Activated Chemical Vapor Deposition

Plasma-activated chemical vapor deposition (PCVD) is a faster, improved form of MCVD. Rather than use burners to heat the outside of the premade silica tube, microwaves are used to heat the inside of the tube. Think of it as a kicked-up microwave oven.

The microwaves can be moved quickly along the outside of the silica tube, which itself does not heat up. As such, the microwaves can make thousands of passes, rather than just hundreds. This allows thinner layers to be made, which can have finely controlled RIs.

NOTE: During the preform manufacture, the silica tube *does* undergo some heating. In fact, it can reach 1000 degrees Celsius, as opposed to 1600 degrees Celsius using burners.

Another benefit of PCVD is that the silica tube need not be rotated. The process is more efficient and faster than MCVD, and preforms can produce hundreds of miles of fiber. Figure 11-8 illustrates how PCVD preforms are made.

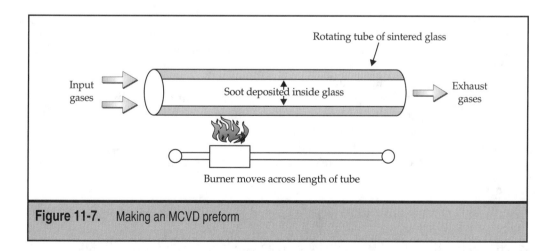

Figure 11-7. Making an MCVD preform

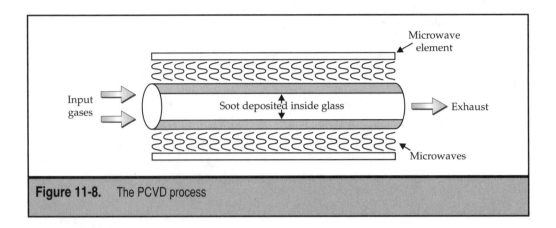

Figure 11-8.   The PCVD process

Fiber Connectors

In Chapter 10, we explained the different methods for terminating optical fiber with a connector. However, we saved a description of the different kinds of fiber connectors for this chapter.

Fiber connectors come in a plethora of different shapes. The trend, lately, has been to use connectors that are smaller, rather than the bigger, bulkier types. Though there are different types of connectors out there, the connections do not necessarily dictate anything special about the network. What are important are the types of fiber that are being connected. Be cautious not to simply look at the connector when joining two lengths of fiber or when connecting an optical networking device. Rather, it's important to know what types of fiber are being brought together.

The following sections describe some of the connectors that are used in optical networking. They are presented here in alphabetical order.

Biconic

A *biconic* connector has two conical mating surfaces that provide accurate mating between two connectors. They are available for both multimode and single-mode fibers. The biconic connector is a medium-performance fiber optic connector that incorporates precision molding techniques to deliver a very small amount of insertion loss. These connectors' loss per mating averages about 0.5 dB with a maximum of 1.0 dB. Return loss of 30 dB is more than adequate to meet the requirements for high bit rate single-mode transmissions. Biconic connectors allow easy plugging and replugging.

These connectors are used for LANs, data processing systems, medical instrumentation, remote sensing, telemetry, and cable television. A biconic connector is shown in Figure 11-9.

E2000

E2000 connectors are also known as FLSH connectors. An important, and useful, attribute of an E2000 connector is the ability to install it at 60-degree angles, making access much simpler. The typical amount of loss in an E2000 connector is about 0.1 dB.

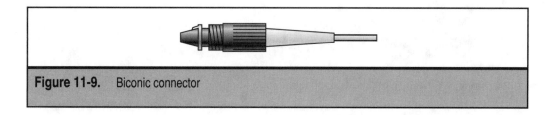

Figure 11-9.   Biconic connector

E2000 connectors are be used for cable TV, LANs, WANs, MANs, test equipment, medical equipment, sensors, and industrial applications. An example of an E2000 connector is shown in Figure 11-10.

FC

Fibre Channel (FC) connectors have a design that is quite like ST connectors (which are explained later in this section). Typical loss for an FC connector is 0.15 dB. FC connectors are also similar to SC connectors. But where SC connectors are square, FC connectors are round. Termination is a little easier because FC connectors can be terminated using the same equipment used for ST and SC connectors.

These connectors are used for Fibre Channel LANs and WANs. An FC connector is shown in Figure 11-11.

FCPC

FCPC connectors are the standard for single-mode fiber. Many equipment vendors, however, are beginning to use SC connectors in place of FCPC connectors because the risk of accidentally switching multimode and single-mode connections exists when the same connector is used for both. FCPC connectors are best when used with single-mode fiber.

FCPC connectors are used for telecommunications, cable TV, LANs, MANs, WANs, test equipment, medical equipment, sensors, and industrial applications.

FDDI

As the name suggests, *FDDI* connectors are used in Fiber Distributed Data Interface (FDDI) networks. The *Media Interface Connector (MIC)* is a two-channel snap-fit connector that combines a loss of about 0.6 dB with positive side-latch mating, polarization, keying,

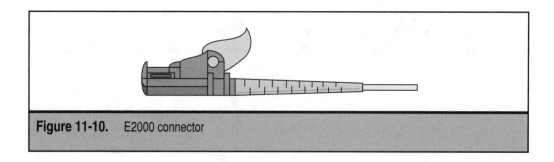

Figure 11-10.   E2000 connector

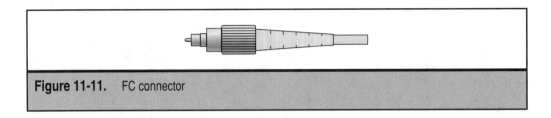

Figure 11-11.   FC connector

and fiber strain relief. FDDI connectors are used in duplex fiber optic systems, building wiring, FDDI backbone networks, or IEEE802.4 token bus.

An example of an FDDI connector is shown in Figure 11-12.

LC

The *Lucent* connector (LC) is a about a half-inch wide—about half the size of industry standards. Borrowing features from the RJ-45 connector, LC connectors provide duplex connections with 50 percent less space than other connectors. The latch makes the connector pull-proof and provides excellent load performance. Because LC connectors fit into an RJ-45 footprint, updating equipment from copper to fiber is possible. These connectors have a typical loss of about 0.1 dB and can be used in cable TV, LANs, MANs, and WANs.

Figure 11-13 shows an LC connector.

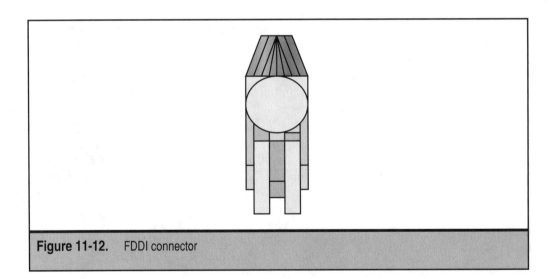

Figure 11-12.   FDDI connector

Figure 11-13.   LC connector

MP

The *multi purpose* (MP) connector is an adaptation of the popular SC connector (which we talk about later). However, connectors of this type differ in that they are designed and built for multiple fibers. MP connectors can terminate between 2 and 12 fibers per connection. MP connectors are most often used in LANs but can be used for especially short distances, such as jumpers. Loss is generally about 0.4 dB.

Figure 11-14 illustrates an MP connector.

MT-RJ

Media termination–recommended jack (MT-RJ) connectors are about half the size of comparable duplex SC connectors (explained later in this section) but still use the same space in patch panels and networking equipment as RJ-45 copper connectors. The connectors, with insertion losses of about 0.2 dB, are designed to be used with dual-fiber, single-jacket cables with diameters from 2.4 mm to 3.1 mm.

MT-RJ connectors are used for LANs and WANs. Figure 11-15 illustrates an MT-RJ connector.

Figure 11-14.   MP connector

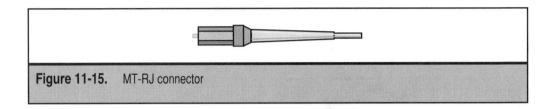

Figure 11-15.   MT-RJ connector

SC

The *subscriber connector* or *square connector (SC)* uses one or two popular standard connectors in a simplex or common duplex housing. The duplex housing not only ensures the polarity of the cable but also provides a smooth insertion and removal. SC connectors are becoming the standard for both host network interface cards and backbone connections. They are normally used for multimode fibers, but one of their disadvantages is that they make it easy to confuse multimode and single-mode fibers. This is bad because the transceiver can be damaged if single-mode fiber is accidentally plugged into a multimode transceiver.

SC connectors are used for Gigabit Ethernet, telecommunications networks, LANs, WANs, MANs, ATM, data communications networks, Fibre Channel and component testing. An SC connector is shown in Figure 11-16.

ST

Straight tip (ST) connectors used to be the standard for multimode connections, but they are quickly being supplanted by SC connectors. Though still in use, ST-connectorized host cards are hard to find. One of the reasons ST connectors lost favor was because they were large and had to be twisted onto a jack, much like a coaxial cable. Normally, this wouldn't be so much of a problem, but if the cable was pulled, the fiber would come out of the connector before the connector would disengage from the equipment. This meant that the fiber had to be reterminated.

ST connectors are used for cable TV, LANs, MANs, WANs, test equipment, medical equipment, sensors, and industrial applications. Figure 11-17 shows an ST connector.

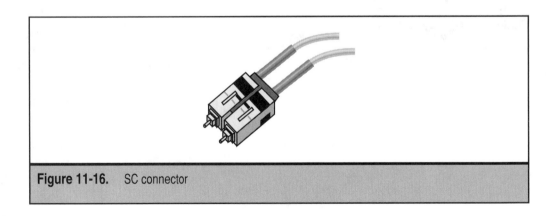

Figure 11-16.   SC connector

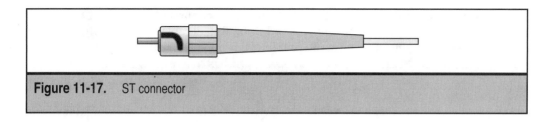

Figure 11-17. ST connector

CABLING AND COMPOSITION

Once optical fiber has been built, it needs to be encased in some sort of cabling for deployment indoors, outside, or underwater. Where the cable will be deployed plays a huge part in the design and composition of this cabling. Furthermore, cable cannot simply be placed somewhere and left without any thought to its safety and security. It is also important to ensure that the cable has been handled properly to avoid damage and deterioration.

In this section, we take a closer look at the environments in which cable will be placed. Additionally, we will examine specific types of cable for specific environments. Next, we'll look at the overall design of optical cable. Finally, we'll wrap up with a discussion about how fiber must be handled to ensure its safety and usability.

Cabling Environments

Fiber optical cabling must survive in a broad range of environments. From the snuggly, warm comfortable environs of a ceiling plenum to a frosty cold trench in Northern Minnesota, fiber must be able to endure it all. As if extreme heat and cold weren't bad enough, fiber is routinely placed at the bottom of the sea, where it faces a whole new set of hazards.

In this section, we take a closer look at the different environments in which fiber might be deployed, and then talk about how cable is built specifically for those applications. In particular, we talk about outdoor cable, indoor cable, undersea cable, and air-blown cable.

Outdoor Cable

Outdoor cable installations have to deal with harsh environments. Whether it is wet, dry, cold, or hot, environmental extremes can take their toll on fiber if it is not adequately protected.

On the least harsh end of the spectrum is the outdoor cable used to connect buildings in a campus deployment. These cables provide LAN connectivity, video conferencing, and the like. Usually, they are transported via ductwork that is owned by the organization and are well protected against the elements inside that ductwork.

However, things get rougher when the fiber leaves the campus environment. For long-distance installations, fiber cable is buried in orange plastic conduit along rights of way. The conduit is buried in a trench or by burrowing a tunnel made by a high-pressure water jet and pushing the conduit through the tunnel. The jet avoids the need to dig a tunnel and can cut through anything short of solid granite.

Outdoor cable, as shown in Figure 11-18, normally contains six gel-filled tubes. It is supported by a central steel cable and often additional steel cables are added for strength on top of the steel jacket surrounding the cable. If the customer requests (and is willing to pay), the jacket can be made from stainless steel, which is rust resistant. Quite often, especially for short distances, the entire cable is made from plastic, rather than steel. In some environments an outer jacket of nylon is added to deter termites.

Gel is often used to fill all the void spaces within the fiber. As we explain later in this chapter, gel is good at cushioning the fibers, while still allowing them to move around, unhindered.

Within each of the six tubes in the example in Figure 11-18 are 8 fibers. This makes the total amount of fibers 42. Thus, 21 can be dedicated to outbound signals, and 21 can be dedicated to inbound signals. It is very likely, however, that the cable is solely dedicated to outbound traffic, with another cable, located elsewhere, handling the inbound traffic.

Though our figure shows just six tubes, there can be as many as 12 tubes carrying up to 288 fibers. Also, if power along the route is necessary, the cable can carry a copper wire that will provide needed electricity for regenerators or other devices.

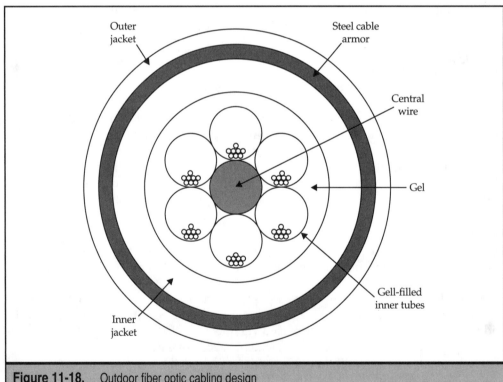

Figure 11-18. Outdoor fiber optic cabling design

Segmented Core Cable   Another type of outdoor cable is called the *segmented-core* cable. This type of cable has a central strength wire to provide durability, and from that core radiate six pieces of plastic, which segment the cable into six pieces. This is shown in Figure 11-19.

Fibers are located between the lengths of plastic (called *channels*), and then the void is filled with gel. In our figure, there are six channels; however, there can be as many as 24 channels. The advantage of segmented core cable is that it provides an additional layer of protection in case there is a breach. Further, segmented core cable is less expensive than other types of outdoor cable. However, it is more cumbersome when it comes time to fill the cable with gel, because rather than a single void in which to inject gel, there can be as many as 24 channels.

Figure 8 Cable   Sometimes, the cable can be attached to a steel messenger cable (as shown in Figure 11-20). Called a figure-8 configuration, this yields a self-supporting cable designed for aerial use in extreme conditions. The top portion of the cable is an asphalt-filled steel cable; the lower half is the optical fiber cable.

One might think that it would be easier just to install a more durable wire down the center of the outdoor cable. However, this results in the wire actually being heavier, increasing stress where the cable must be suspended.

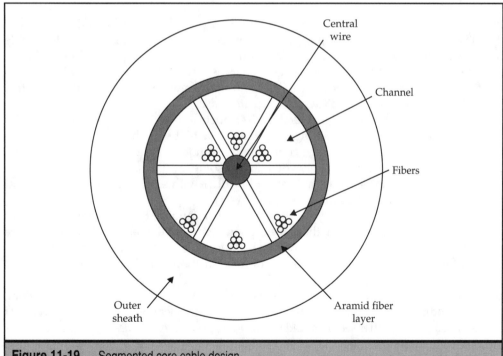

Figure 11-19.   Segmented core cable design

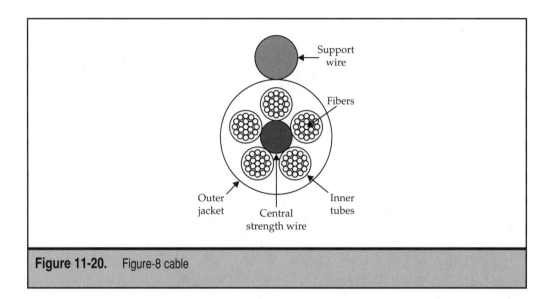

Figure 11-20.   Figure-8 cable

Indoor Cable

Indoor cabling is deployed as the name suggests—inside. It is found in office buildings, in data centers, or in sealed plenum vaults between buildings in a campus. Indoor cable can be used to connect devices (computers, routers, switches, and so forth) situated right next to each other. It can also act as a backbone transport connecting devices along an entire floor, such as a factory. Indoor cabling is normally rated as fire resistant just for this purpose, and it is also referred to as *plenum rated cable.*

Indoor fiber is often found installed in riser ducts to provide backbone connectivity and transport in multitenant buildings. For example, a high-rise that has a number of tenants requires voice, data, and video connectivity. Although various tenants will require differing levels of connectivity, they will all need some level of service.

Indoor cabling consist of a single strand of fiber with additional strength material added and a PVC jacket (as shown in Figure 11-21).

The strength members are typically *Aramid* fibers and lie between the optical fiber cladding and the jacket. In total, the cable is about 2 mm in diameter and these fibers are normally constructed in pairs. This saves on installation time (hardly anyone ever installs just one fiber), as applications generally require both an inbound and outbound fiber.

In the event more than two fibers are joined this way, they are usually situated around a central strength member. Each fiber has its own secondary coating, strengthening material, and color coding. Finally, the whole bundle is encased in a clear outer layer. These types of cables are packed together securely and are known as *tight-buffer cables.* Tight-buffer cables are designed so that the stress of an individual fiber's weight is taken off the fiber and placed on the protective material. We talk about tight-buffer cables in more depth later in this chapter.

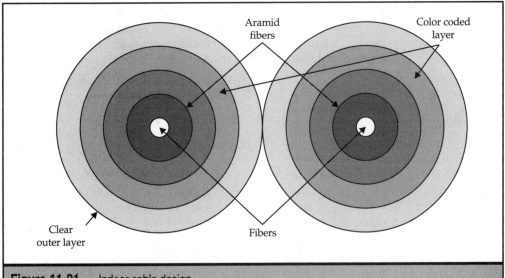

Figure 11-21. Indoor cable design

Air-Blown Fiber

Optical fiber is fragile stuff. At just a few microns in diameter, the fiber cannot withstand a lot of manhandling. In fact, it is the mishandling of fiber during installation that leads to a great many of its problems.

Air-blown fiber (ABF) ameliorates this problem by allowing the crew to simply handle the conduit through which fiber is blown. This type of cabling is especially critical for very light fibers. The main propellant used to blow fibers through conduit is compressed nitrogen. Nitrogen is used because compressed air can be corrosive to the plastic jackets used on fiber. ABF is normally used indoors and can blow between 2 and 18 fibers in a single conduit tube. Though mainly an indoor application, ABF has been used outdoors for distances up to 2 km.

Not only are the fibers used in ABF systems lightweight, but they are also aerodynamic. Fiber floats within the tube and has very little contact with the conduit walls. The heart of the ABF system is a highway of conduit installed in place of conventional inner duct work. Once the infrastructure is in place, lightweight bundles of single-mode or multimode fiber are blown, at speeds up to 50 meters per minute, through a predefined route, using special blowing equipment.

Installation is fast and easy, typically requiring only two technicians. Cable runs may exceed 2000 meters and the fiber path may traverse outdoor, riser, and plenum tubes in a single run. Since the fibers are not pulled, installation damage is no longer an issue. Moreover, point-to-point connectivity eliminates splices—the most common site of network failure.

In most ABF installations, conduit is installed with more cells than are currently required, thus providing a measure of "futureproofing." Unused sections are capped until needed. Network expansion or reconfiguration is accomplished by extending conduit from the nearest distribution unit. Fiber bundles can be upgraded or replaced by blowing fiber through unused sections, or by blowing out old fiber (which can be reused) and blowing in new—all without disrupting the existing network.

Undersea Cable

We talked about undersea cable in great detail in Chapter 7, but this is a good place for a refresher.

The fibers that are laid on the ocean floor are, basically, the same cables used in terrestrial applications; however, they are sealed and encased in multiple layers of protective covering. In shallow water, they are subject to the greatest risks. These cables are heavily armored to prevent crushing.

The layers include:

▼ A nylon outer covering

■ Various polypropylene layers

■ Layers of steel mesh armor

■ Hermetically sealed copper tube

■ Elastic cushioning fibers

■ A thick central wire called the *king wire*

▲ The optical fibers themselves.

NOTE: In the first three entries, these layers are added to the cable for added protection when it is placed in shallow water.

The cable laid on the ocean floor includes only the optical fibers, kingwire, and cushioning fibers, all of which are contained within a copper sheath. This sheath not only protects the fiber, but it can carry an electrical current to any devices that are used along the length of the fiber, such as amplifiers. In deep-sea environments, the cable isn't as heavy as it is near the shore. Otherwise, on its way to the bottom of the sea, it would be so heavy that it would rip itself apart.

Near the shore, the armor-clad cable weighs 16 times more than those used on the ocean floor. These cables are nonetheless still rather thin—near the shore, cables are just three inches in diameter. Undersea, the cables are about an inch and a half thick.

Most fiber manufacturers make special undersea cables. These fibers are designed to have a more constant dispersion across a broad range of operational wavelengths. Dispersion near the edges of the band is reduced, so that those wavelengths operate more like wavelengths in the middle ranges. Undersea fiber optic cable is usually sold as "deep sea" or "coastal" cable. Deep sea cable is meant for environments where the bottom is more than 1000 meters from the surface.

NOTE: Undersea cable avoids obstacles like mountains and lava flows because its route is painstakingly planned ashore weeks before the first bit of cable is placed.

Cable Composition

Glass optical fibers used for fiber optics communications are very stable and reliable. However, they are also very small and, in some sense, delicate. Thus for any practical fiber optic installation, the fibers used to carry the light signal are protected by a cable structure that prevents the fibers from being damaged. There are three ways fiber cables can be constructed:

▼ **Tight-buffer**   Fibers are secured within the cable and not allowed to move around.

■ **Loose-tube**   Individual fibers are housed within a conduit but are not packed tightly. This allows the fibers to "float" within the conduit. This is beneficial because the fibers can realign themselves to prevent kinking and bending.

▲ **Gel-filled**   This type of cable is similar to loose-tube construction, except the conduit is filled with a water-absorbing gel. This acts to cushion the fibers and protect them in case water enters the cable.

The following sections explain the types of cable composition in greater detail.

Tight-Buffer

Tight-buffer cables are designed to hold the fiber securely in place, by virtue of the jacket design. The cables are about 1 mm in diameter, are found mostly in indoor applications, and do not exceed campus application lengths.

The first step in the manufacture of any type of tight-buffer fiber optic cable is to apply an extra layer of plastic to protect the fiber. In most tight-buffer cables, this jacket is 900 μm in diameter (about the thickness of a dime). The plastic jacket adds some rigidity to the fiber and makes it a little more durable when the fibers are routed inside a splice enclosure or patch panel.

After the plastic jacket, the tight-buffer cables are divided into two subcategories:

▼ Break-out cable

▲ Riser cable

Break-Out Cables   In the break-out cable, a layer of Kevlar is applied around the plastic jacket. The Kevlar provides tensile strength to prevent the fiber from being stretched if there is tension on the cable. Within the break-out cable, a plastic sheath of about three millimeters in diameter is applied over the Kevlar coating. At this point, each fiber is individually protected and strengthened. This type of construction with a single fiber is commonly used for jumper cables and patch cords. Since each fiber is individually strengthened with Kevlar, a connector can be attached to the fiber so that the Kevlar will take any strain between the connector and the fiber cable, adding to the cable's durability.

Aside from the obvious application as patch cords, the break-out- or fan-out-style cable is also commonly constructed as a dual-fiber zip cord design or a multifiber cable with an overall sheath. The advantage of easy connectorization makes these cables very useful for short runs. Since the multifiber break-out cables have extra strength members and an overall jacket, they are very rugged and can be tie-wrapped to supports and run in commercial or industrial settings. The disadvantage of the break-out or fan-out cable is that it is relatively bulky, heavy, and expensive for fiber counts above six.

Riser Cables   Riser cables are normally constructed by wrapping 900 µm plastic buffer fibers around a central strength member. Next, a layer of Kevlar is then applied over all the fibers, and an outer sheath finishes the cable.

Riser cables are advantageous because they are small, lightweight, and inexpensive. Of all the cable designs, however, fibers in riser cables have the least protection. Further, the fibers are closer to the surface of the cable, making them less durable than in other cable designs. Because of all this, riser cable installation requires more care than others.

Riser cables are most often used in vertical risers, which is how their name is derived. This deployment is ideal for them because they are lightweight and unlikely to experience any environments where bending or crushing would occur.

Loose-Tube

In spite of the simple-sounding name, loose-tube cables are really rather complex. As Figure 11-22 shows, a number of components make up a loose-tube cable.

At the center of a loose-tube cable is a steel member to provide strength. It is surrounded by a dozen color-coded buffer tubes, each of which contains optical fibers. Within each buffer tube there can be up to 12 fibers, or if installed as a ribbon, there may be 18 fibers per tube. Loose-tube cables need not be extremely large—some contain only two fibers.

NOTE: Ribbons make up special fibers that have been fused into a ribbon assembly. This makes splicing multiple fibers much easier than splicing individual fibers. Ribbon fibers also allow more fibers to be used per tube. However, ribbon fibers must be handled carefully, as they kink easily.

The buffer tubes are next encased in an inner polyethylene jacket and a protective armor coating, which is meant to prevent the cable from being crushed or nibbled on by hungry squirrels. Finally, the cable is coated in an outer polyethylene jacket.

Loose-tube cables are used for long-haul, wide area applications. Because the fibers do not adhere to the outside of the cable, they are not as susceptible to heat fluctuations. Temperature changes can cause changes in the RI of the fibers, so temperature control is important.

Loose-tube cabling also includes ripcords, which are used to tear through the outer layers to access the fiber inside for splicing. It could also contain twisted pair and power leads to be used for amplifiers and other devices.

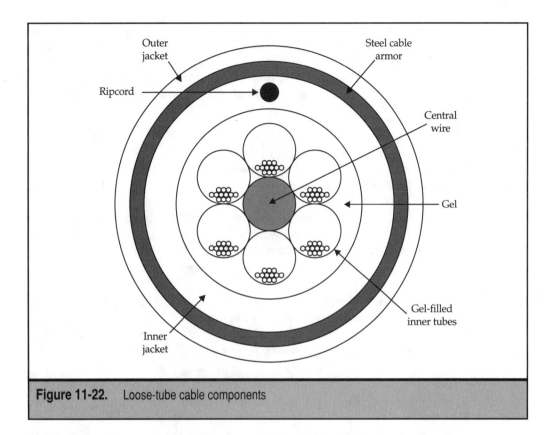

Figure 11-22.   Loose-tube cable components

Since the fibers are loose within the cable, the fibers inside tend to twist around each other. Because of this twist, there is about 5 to 10 percent more fiber than there is tube. For example, if there are 100 meters of cable, there are 110 meters of fiber inside. This is also beneficial because, if the cable is bent or twisted, the fibers have enough give that they are not bent or twisted.

Gel-Filled

Gel-filled fiber is basically the same as loose-tube fiber, except gel is used to fill the cavity. Gel is used for two reasons: First, it acts as a cushion to the fibers, preventing the fibers from chaffing against each other and preventing microbends. Second, it can help protect the fiber in the event the cabling is breached and water starts to enter.

The type of gel used in fiber optic cabling used to be simple petroleum jelly. It was inexpensive and was used for a number of years. However, petroleum jelly experienced a range of viscosity over temperature variations. Gel viscosity is important, because the gel must be thin enough that it will flow easily during cable construction, but it must also be thick enough that the fibers do not settle on the bottom of the cable and it itself does not settle if the cable is installed vertically. Also, it must be viscous enough so that, if the cable is damaged on a hot day, the gel does not leak out.

Synthetic gels have been designed that fulfill these needs and provide the proper level of viscosity. Finally, gel-filled cables are found most often in outdoor cabling.

Fiber Protection

No matter how durably a cable is constructed, damage can still occur if it is mishandled. One of the primary sources of damage to cable comes from inadvertent abuse while installing it. Not only can fiber be rendered useless by poor handling, but it can develop flaws that will take time to develop.

It isn't just installation gaffes that cause trouble to occur. Gophers and work crews can do their fair share of damage. In this section, we talk about some prime sources of damage and also ways one can ameliorate problems with a little understanding.

Pulling

In spite of the care issues we've mentioned over and over, optical fiber is actually stronger than steel. This doesn't mean, however, that fiber optic cable should be mistreated. Optical fiber is especially susceptible to tensile damage. Even if pulling on the fiber does not break it, it can still increase the attenuation level within the fiber.

Bending

The rule of thumb on bending fiber is that the typical bend radius for optical fiber is about ten times the overall cable diameter. If the fiber is bent beyond that radius, the result will be signal loss. Microbends are crimps in the cable that could occur if a desk or other large piece of furniture (for example) is accidentally set on the fiber. This problem is lessened in outdoor or undersea deployments, where the runs tend to be straight and (mostly) obstacle free.

Nature

Mother Nature must have it in for optical cable (that and trailer parks, but that's another story). Animals that like to gnaw (gophers, squirrels, and so forth) seem to have a taste for optical cable. Of course, if the animal stops chewing before it gets to the fiber, then no loss will occur, but there can still be damage if they gnaw too much or if they compromise the protective layers of the cabling.

Water can be another problem for optical fiber. When submerged in water, fiber will absorb hydroxyl ions, which absorb light. If the fiber absorbs enough hydroxyl ions, then it will become opaque and cease working. Further, water can cause *microcracking* in the glass, which scatters photons and weakens the fiber.

NOTE: Water problems occur only in fibers that are not properly waterproofed. Submarine cables are perfectly safe, so long as their waterproofing measures are solid.

Installation

One of the chief threats to fiber safety is a backhoe, cutting fiber in half. This doesn't just happen at construction sites. Interestingly, many cases of fiber damage occur when fiber is being buried next to existing fiber.

When installing fiber, the way that technicians handle the fiber is very important. In the past, how the construction crew handled the fiber was also very important. Some would be very rough with it, while others would be extremely gentle. The result was runs of fiber that didn't work while others did. This isn't so much of a problem now, but it is worth being aware of. For example, even if the crew is being especially gentle, damage can still occur if the fiber is pulled through a long conduit.

CARE, CAUTION, AND COMPANIES

In the last section of this chapter, we'll wrap up our discussion of optical fiber with an overview of the care and caution that needs to be exhibited while working on optical fiber. First, we'll talk about dangers to optical fiber cables as they are deployed. Next, we'll discuss some safety concerns that go hand-in-hand with optical networking. Finally, in this section we will take a quick look at some of the companies making optical fiber and give a taste of their lines of fiber.

Problems

For all the benefits of optical fiber, it is important to remember that there are certain drawbacks to using this medium. Unlike copper wire, which can be manhandled within an inch of its life, optical fiber is a very delicate thing that is susceptible to damage one might not even think of.

If fiber is installed improperly, serious damage to the equipment can occur, and at the very least you will achieve less-than-optimal results. The following will explain some of the dangers optical fiber faces.

Bending

Probably the most serious problem facing fiber results from its bending. This is not due to the fragility of fiber (in a cross section, it has a stronger tensile strength than steel wire), but rather the way light travels within the core. Since light is reflected from the border between the core and cladding, the amount of signal (and therefore signal loss) depends on how much light bounces off this boundary. When the angle is low, light will continue to reflect as need be. However, when the fiber is bent too much, then the light escapes into the cladding and the signal is lost.

This is a big reason why contemporary optical cable is encased in strength members like Kevlar, which is the same material from which the United States makes helmets and flak jackets for the military. By adding additional strengthening materials to the fiber, it is not only beefed up, but it resists the urge to bend too far. This jacketing also makes the fiber easier to see and handle. This jacket does not make the fiber indestructible, however. Serious damage can still occur if the fiber is stepped on.

The degree to which a piece of optical fiber can be bent depends on the fiber and the RI between the core and the cladding. The higher the difference, the tighter the allowable bend. But there are deleterious effects from making the core and cladding too dissimilar, so they tend to be as close in composition as possible, thereby keeping the RI low. As such, fiber cannot be bent too much.

Connection Problems

In the last chapter, we talked about adding connectors and splices. As you might remember, these are prime sources for signal loss in an optical network. The best way to connect fibers is with a fusion splice. This splice actually melts the fiber ends together, making a nearly seamless connection. However, this is very difficult to do, especially in cold climates and outdoors.

Fusion splices are great for permanent connections, but at places where fiber needs to be disconnected and reconnected repeatedly, a better solution is the use of connectors, such as patch panels or devices like switches or routers. Contemporary devices come with short lengths of connectorized fiber with a ready-made plug that is well suited for mating to a connectorized length of fiber. This length of existing fiber, called a *pigtail*, can be the source of a lot of loss.

Multimode fibers are easier to connectorize because of their large cores. Further, in shorter deployments, like a LAN for instance, there can be connectors everywhere. In long-haul deployments, however, connectors can represent too much loss and will be ineffective.

Glass Dangers

Since optical fibers (save POF) are made of silica glass, significant trouble can occur if the glass is damaged. Damage does not simply include shattering or splintering but can come from a number of sources.

Water   If you leave anything in water long enough, water will get into it. For empirical evidence of this, take a look at the Grand Canyon. Optical fiber is just as prone to danger, especially if it is not waterproofed properly.

If there are any air bubbles in a length of fiber and water is able to penetrate the glass, it will fill the air bubbles and the fiber will stop working. This is one reason that undersea cable is encased in layer after layer of protective material.

Radiation   There are two types of radiation that can hurt fiber. Ultraviolet (UV) radiation (which is how we get sunburned) and gamma radiation (which is responsible for creating Spiderman) are two foes of optical fiber.

Aerial fibers are especially susceptible to UV damage, and unless they are properly protected, the radiation can cause a breakdown at the barrier between the core and the cladding. As you remember, this barrier is what makes optical fiber work.

Gamma radiation darkens glass and can cause it to glow. Both of these side effects are bad news for fiber—either cables will stop working because of the opacity, or there will be noise as a result of the excess light.

Strong Electrical Fields   A benefit of fiber is that it is not susceptible to interference from electromagnetic sources. This is why it is better deployed in some environments than twisted pair copper wire. If the voltage gets too high (exceeding 30,000 volts), however, optical fiber tends to discolor and emit light. Thus, when placed next to high-voltage lines, the optical fiber has to be shielded from danger.

Safety

The concept of safety hasn't really come up yet. And why should it? After all, optical fiber doesn't carry an electrical current, just pulses of light. That's harmless enough, isn't it? In all actuality, fiber optic networks can be deceptively dangerous. The hazard doesn't come when you're situated at a computer terminal; rather, if you have occasion to splice, terminate, or test fiber, you could find yourself at risk.

The following sections illustrate the danger areas within an optical network that you should be aware of.

Light

The first, most obvious, source of danger in an optical network comes from the laser itself. Even though the laser presents a danger, with caution it is easy to avoid. As with the old axiom that says you should treat every electrical cable as a live cable, it is best to assume that every piece of fiber has laser light coursing through it, and that it is not dark or carrying an LED signal.

Most every optical system uses infrared light. And as you remember from our earlier discussion, infrared light is invisible to the human eye. Furthermore, you should *not* try to look for the light. One of the big dangers is that, because the light is invisible, the human eye cannot react to it and the pupil will not open or close in response to the light. That means that the intense beam of light will penetrate your eye without any resistance.

To look for infrared light, you can use an infrared detection card that will convert the light into visible light. Caution is still needed, however, because in bright light conditions it might still be hard to view the light. The better solution is to use a light indicator tester that can detect the presence of infrared light.

The danger is quite pronounced when trying to splice fiber. While doing so, be sure to keep the fiber pointed away from you. Typically, splicing does not require you to look directly into the end of the fiber. Also, the fiber is normally covered by a hood in a fusion splicing machine, or held in a sleeve during a mechanical splice. If you're trying to splice fiber and the end is broken or shattered, the risk is not so severe. The shattered end will actually disperse the light. However, a cleanly cleaved end will bring the photons through at full strength.

The prime spot for danger is when inspecting a connector with a microscope. Due to the nature of the job, the fiber's end is close and pointed directly at the eye. Good, high-powered microscopes (those with 300x power) will have a built-in infrared filter. However, cheaper, low-powered microscopes (100x power) might not.

Infrared is on one end of our visible spectrum of light; another source of danger is at the other end, the source of UV light. UV light, though not used as a light source, is used to cure epoxies. Even though UV light isn't, technically, used in optical networks, you might find yourself exposed to it. There are safety glasses that diffuse infrared and UV light. For safety's sake, if you buy a pair, make sure they deflect the wavelengths you'll be working around.

Bare Fiber

Scraps of bare fiber can be quite dangerous if improperly handled. A *bare fiber* is the core and cladding, after the coating has been removed. In an environment where termination or splicing is taking place, hundreds of bare fiber scraps are likely to be around, courtesy of the cleaving process.

Bare fibers are dangerous because they easily penetrate the skin, causing a glass sliver that is difficult to deal with. Even if a magnifying glass is used, it can be extremely difficult to remove fiber slivers. To make matters worse, while the glass fiber is being extracted, it will tend to break off, making removal that much more difficult, frustrating, and painful. More serious problems can be infections, eye injury, or internal injury, if the scrap is ingested.

When splicing or terminating fiber, make sure you can account for every scrap of bare fiber. The best practice is not to leave a fiber around with a bare end protruding. Always trim the fiber back so that it is flush with the coated part. When trimming the end of a fiber, always cut on the coated portion, never on the exposed glass. This prevents the end from flying off like a toenail gone astray.

In the event you notice a piece of bare fiber, keep your eyes on it. Find a piece of tape (held adhesive side down) to pick it up and dispose of it properly. One's first reaction might be to pick it up. However, this will likely cause the fiber to get stuck in your fingers. Then, as human nature dictates, the resulting wound will go to your mouth for comfort. Unfortunately, this is an excellent way to ingest the fiber.

There are two common ways to dispose of bare fibers:

▼ **Fiber scrap containers**   This is a separate trash can specifically for bare fiber scraps. Forward-thinking, safety-minded companies have already produced fiber scrap containers that are prelabeled and set up with spill-proof tops. If you want to save a buck, you can make your own; just make sure you label it properly so everyone knows what's in it.

▲ **Tape**   Two-inch-wide electrical tape is a popular way to dispose of bare fiber scraps. Two-inch wide tape (versus the 3/4-inch tape found in some disposal kits) gives enough surface area that the fiber ends are not protruding.

Other Dangers

As you remember from the last chapter, termination techniques use a fair amount of adhesives and epoxies. If you are sensitive to chemicals, it is a good idea to make sure that you are wearing protective gloves. Also, it's a good idea (no matter your sensitivity to chemicals) to make sure your workspace is properly ventilated.

When working on outside cabling, remember that the cables are encased in a durable metallic sheath, usually steel. Good, tough gloves will keep you from getting cut.

Normally, cabling has a rip cord used to open the jacket. It's a good idea to use pliers to get a good grip on this cord and prevent injury.

Earlier, we said that fiber optic cable is not conductive to electricity, so it does not pose a shock hazard. However, if the cable contains any metallic parts (sheath, and so forth) the cable can conduct electricity and care must be taken. When cable does contain metal, it is normally grounded at the splice points. However, these grounding points may be miles apart, and the closest, most attractive source for grounding may be the technician. Make sure you test the cable for voltage and use a grounding harness (applied to the cable) while working on it.

Manufacturers

The world of fiber manufacture is a small one. There aren't many companies that make fiber optic cabling. As such, competition is fierce. Each company is constantly trying to improve its product by battling the two biggest obstacles native to optical fiber: attenuation and dispersion.

The following sections give a brief look at the major players in the world of optical network fiber construction.

Lucent

One of the big names in fiber optic networking is Lucent, a company that manufactures not only networking devices but also the fiber over which those devices can communicate.

Lucent's product offerings include the popular TrueWave line, which provides fiber for a number of different applications and environments. For instance, TrueWave RS is an NZ-DSF fiber that works best in the third (the C-Band) and fourth (the L-Band) transmission windows. The TrueWave line also offers several fibers that are designed for submarine applications. TrueWave XL submarine fiber is a negative-dispersion, large effective area fiber meant for long-haul submarine environments. TrueWave Submarine Reduced Slope (SRS) is another negative-dispersion fiber used with erbium-doped fiber amplification systems.

Lucent's AllWave operates in the 1400 nm band, which was largely unheard of, but it is able to do so because it contains low levels of hydroxyl. This fiber is well suited for transport of coarse wavelength division multiplexing (CWDM) systems, metro deployments, and hybrid fiber-coax applications.

Corning

The other big name in fiber manufacture is Corning (you might remember that Fiberglas insulation is made by Owens-Corning and is, itself, spun glass). Corning offers a variety of optical fiber from single-mode to multimode.

Corning's single-mode offerings include the Large Effective Area (LEAF) fiber, which is best suited for high-speed transmission in a long-haul environments. For multimode needs, Corning's InfiniCor CL is meant for lengthy, laser-based LAN deployments. InfiniCor is specially suited for Gigabit Ethernet applications. Corning also offers 62.5/125 and 50/125 graded-index multimode fiber, which is meant for both local and wide area applications.

In addition, Corning also offers a line of products for submarine deployments.

Alcatel

Alcatel has the distinction of being the first company to offer Raman amplification in its fiber products. They also boast a very close wavelength spacing on their fiber, even as it travels across great distances. For instance, in one Alcatel trial, they claim to have sent 80 closely spaced channels across a 3000 km piece of fiber. Not only did they transmit so many lambdas, but each lambda ran at 10 Gbps.

Another trial brought 40 Gbps across a 250 km, repeater-free length of fiber. In 1999, the company was able to achieve a 12,000 km nonregenerated transmission between the United States and China.

Boston Optical Fiber

Boston Optical Fiber is the world leader in plastic fiber. As we mentioned earlier in this chapter, plastic optical fiber isn't taken seriously in the high-speed data transmission world, yet it is not without its uses. Again, it is much less expensive than glass fiber and can be much more durable.

According to Boston Optical Fiber, their fiber can carry data at speeds up to 300 Mbps over 100 meters. This doesn't approach the speeds and distances of its glass brothers, but it is certainly useful in LAN applications that don't require the blistering speeds that glass delivers. In the future, Boston Optical Fiber expects to come out with fiber that is capable of carrying several gigabits over 100 meters of plastic optical fiber.

Fibercore

The United Kingdom's preeminent fiber company is Fibercore, which is one of the oldest fiber manufacturers in the world. Their range of products include a polarization-maintaining fiber and a variety of doped fibers.

HiBi polarization-maintaining fiber, introduced in 1982, and the DF1500 series of erbium-doped fibers, introduced in 1988, were among the very first commercially available examples of their technologies and remain key milestones in the history of both Fibercore and fiber optics. In September 2001, Fibercore received the Queen's Award for Enterprise in the International Trade category. This is due to Fibercore's growth by nearly 100 percent every year since 1996.

To provide the blistering speeds that optical networks provide, fibers must be specially made, specially handled, specially installed, and specially used. This can create a certain level of inconvenience; however, when the speeds of optical fibers are weighed against their shortcomings, it is easy to understand why the hassle is endured.

CHAPTER 12

Optical Network Security

It's no secret that network security is a big topic. It would be impossible to cover all of the issues germane to this topic in just one chapter. However, as a way to round out this book, we'll take this opportunity to deal with some of the main issues of network security in general, and how you can secure your optical network, in particular.

First, we will give an overall view of network security. In the second section, we'll examine security protocols and intrusion detection systems. Finally we'll talk about security issues specific to optical networking. The first two sections are relevant to both electrical and optical networks, because they function the same way, regardless of the medium used to share data. However, the last section turns the magnifying glass on optical networks to show where the weak links are and how you can minimize the effects of an attack.

OVERVIEW OF NETWORK SECURITY

Let's take a look at two kinds of network security. One kind is enforced as a background process not visible to users; the other is right up in your face:

▼ **Traffic-based security**   Controls connections requested by a network application, such as a Web browser or an anonymous FTP download.

▲ **User-based security**   Controls admission of individuals to systems in order to start applications once inside, usually by user and password.

Within the realm of traffic-based security systems are two subsets. One kind of security is the use of firewalls to protect autonomous systems by screening traffic from untrusted hosts. The other kind of traffic-based security is router access lists, used to restrict traffic and resources within an autonomous system. User-based security, on the other hand, is concerned with people. This is the kind of security with which we're all familiar—login-based security that asks you for a username and password.

The two types complement one another yet operate at different levels. Traffic-based security goes into action when you click a button in a Web browser, enter a command into an FTP screen, or use some other application command. User-based security asserts itself when an individual tries to log into a network, device, or service offered on a device.

Traffic-Based Security

Traffic-based security is implemented in an internetwork by using firewalls or router access lists. This style of security focuses mainly on source and destination IP addresses, application port numbers, and other packet-level information that can be used to restrict and control network connections.

Until recently, firewalls have focused strictly on guarding against intruders from outside an autonomous system. However, they're now being used in more sophisticated shops to restrict access to sensitive assets from the inside. Access lists have been the traditional tool of choice when enforcing intramural security.

Access List Traffic-Based Security

Routers can be configured to enforce security in much the same way firewalls do. Almost every standard router incorporates the ability to implement access lists. They can be used to control what traffic may come and go through the router's network interfaces, and what applications may be used if admitted. What exactly an access list does is left to how it's configured by the network administrator.

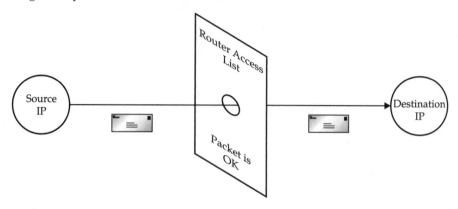

Mostly, access lists are used to improve network performance by isolating traffic in its home area. But a well-configured access list can pretty much behave like an internal firewall, restricting traffic among departments.

Firewall Traffic-Based Security

Firewalls can be looked at as beefed-up routers that screen processes according to strict traffic management rules. However, they use all sorts of additional tactics to enhance security: address translation to hide internal network topology from outsiders; application layer inspection to make sure only permitted services are being run; even high/low counters that watch for any precipitous spikes in certain types of packets to ward off Denial of Service (DoS) attacks such as SYNflood and FINwait.

Firewalls intentionally create a secure passage at the autonomous system's perimeter. As traffic passes through, the firewall inspects packets as they come and go through the networks attached to its interfaces.

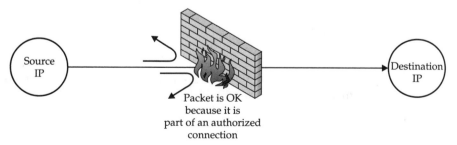

Firewalls read source and destination host addresses, and port numbers (for example, port 80 for HTTP), and establish a context for each permitted connection. The context comes in the form of a session, where packets with a certain address pair and port number must belong to a valid session. For example, if a user tries to connect to a Web server to download a file, the firewall will check the user's source IP address and the application service requested before permitting the packets to pass.

Think of traffic-based security as being like those "easy pass" automated tollbooths used on major toll roads. Vehicles are funneled through a gateway where a laser reads each electronic ID, barely slowing the flow of traffic.

User-Based Security

User-based security evokes a different picture—this one of a gate with a humorless security guard standing at the post. The guard demands to know who you are and challenges you to prove your identity. If you qualify, you get to go in. More sophisticated user-based security systems also have the guard ask what you intend to do once inside and issue you a coded visitor's badge giving you access to some areas, but not others.

Thus, user-based security is employed where a person must log into a host, and the security comes in the form of a challenge for your username and password. In internetworking, this kind of security is used as much to keep bad guys from entering network devices such as routers or switches, as it is to restrict access to content-rich devices, such as servers.

Unlike firewalls, however, user-based security is nearly as concerned with insiders as outsiders. That security guard at the gate has colleagues on the inside, there to make sure nobody goes into the wrong area. You know the routine—there are employee badges and there are visitor badges, but the employee badges let you go more places.

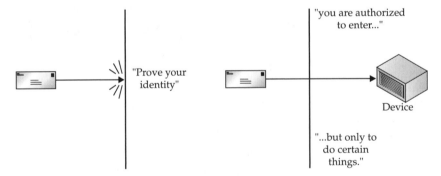

Login/password points are generally placed on every network device and all servers. Because user-based security mechanisms are software, not hardware, they can be deployed at will within an internetwork with little impact on performance or budget.

The trade-off is how much inconvenience you're willing to put network users through, having to log in to gain access to various services. User-based security has four major applications:

▼ To grant remote employees access to the enterprise internetwork

■ To grant on-site employees access to protected hosts and services within the internetwork

■ To let network administrators log into network devices

▲ To let ISPs grant subscribers access to their portals

Because more and more access is from locations that are geographically distant from the server, security often involves remote dial-up connections. The two important pieces in securing dial-up connections are access servers and dial-up protocols.

Access Servers

Entering an internetwork via a dial-up connection is almost always done through an access server. The access server is a dedicated device that fields phone calls from remote individuals trying to establish a connection to a network. Access servers are also called *network access servers* or *communication servers*. Their key attribute is to behave like a

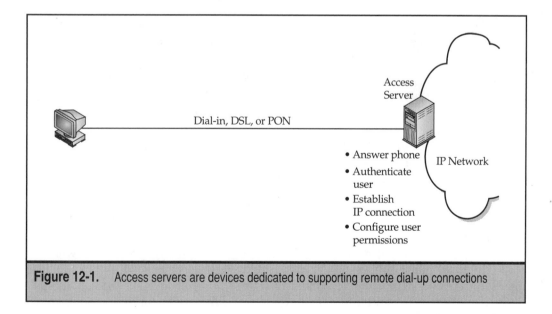

Figure 12-1.   Access servers are devices dedicated to supporting remote dial-up connections

full-fledged IP host on one side, but like a modem on the other side. Figure 12-1 depicts the role access servers play in dial-up connections.

When you connect to an internetwork's host from the enterprise campus, you usually do so over a dedicated twisted-pair cable that is connected to a hub or a switch. Of course, this might also be possible if the user is employing a passive optical network (PON). To make that same connection from afar, you usually do so over a normal telephone line through an access server—a device that answers the phone call and establishes a network connection. Besides making connections for remote dial-up users, access servers can also be used to connect remote routers.

Small office and home office users tap into their enterprise internetworks via an access server, making it perhaps the most basic device in any dial-up network. Low-end access servers are inconspicuous desktop devices resembling a PC without a monitor. When you dial into your ISP to get into the Internet from home, the call is also answered by an access server. As you might imagine, an ISP's computer room is jammed with rack-mounted high-density access servers to handle connections made from thousands of subscribers.

Dial-in Protocols

Making dial-up network connections work properly presents special problems because most telephone company infrastructure was designed to handle voice, not high-speed data. Dial-up protocols exist to handle the point-to-point dial-in connections over normal telephone lines.

▼ **PPP** The Point-to-Point Protocol is the de facto standard for remote dial-up connections to the IP networks; virtually all dial-up connections to the Internet use PPP. Most PPP connections are over asynchronous lines, but a growing number are made over DSL and PONs in areas where they are available.

▲ **SLIP** The Serial Line Internet Protocol is also used to make point-to-point dial-up connections to IP networks from remote sites. SLIP is the predecessor to PPP, but it is still in use in some quarters. You may also encounter a SLIP variant called CSLIP, the Compressed Serial Line Internet Protocol.

In the old days, to make a remote connection, you dialed into a PBX to connect to a mainframe or minicomputer as a dumb terminal. With the rise of internetworking, network-attached terminal servers took over the job of taking dial-up calls. As demand for remote computing grew still more, simple terminal connections were replaced by those made using the SLIP protocol. By that point, many desktops had PCs instead of terminals, but they emulated terminals in order to make dial-up connections. The boom in demand for Internet connectivity drove the market to replace SLIP with PPP, a protocol even more capable of computer-to-computer communications over phone lines.

Types of Attack

The way security is administered is just one consideration of the overall network security puzzle. Another issue to be aware of are the types of attacks than can be perpetrated against a network.

There are a number of ways a network can be attacked. The type of attack can range from an unauthorized person gaining access to restricted files to attacks meant to bring the network down. The following sections describe some of the most common types of attacks that a network can be prone to.

Data Delay

In this type of attack, an assailant would divert or delay data from arriving at its intended destination. This type of attack does not occur in all-optical networks, so we won't go into to the specifics of this type of attack.

Denial of Service and Quality of Service

These types of attacks occur when an attacker floods a network with packets, preventing the network from operating properly. Because of the sheer magnitude of packets being sent, network operations can be dramatically slowed down, or even brought to a grinding halt.

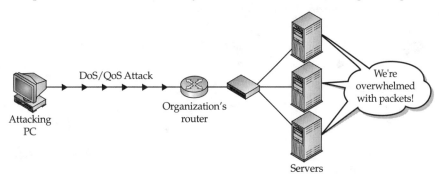

DoS   *Denial of Service (DoS)* attacks are meant to bring the network to a halt. These are very common attacks that you have probably heard about. In fact, they've brought down some big name companies and dot com Web sites in the past couple years.

The thing to remember about DoS attacks is that they assault the network with so many packets that the network spends all its time and resources dealing with the attack, thus stopping normal network operations.

As if DoS attacks weren't bad enough, they have been kicked up even more in the form of *Distributed Denial of Service (DDoS)* attacks. DDoS attacks are very similar to DoS attacks in that they flood a network with packets; however, DDoS ratchets the complexity level up a notch by launching them simultaneously from hundreds of remote-controlled attack servers, to engulf a site in excess traffic.

QoS   *Quality of Service (QoS)* attacks threaten the integrity of the network, slowing down priority packets. Whereas a DoS attack prevents any packets from moving, QoS attacks slow down all a network's traffic.

Both DoS and QoS attacks are known as *service disruption* attacks, and optical networks are just as prone to them as an electrical network. These attacks don't rely on splicing in to the optical fiber or even being near the fiber. Service disruption attacks can be done from anywhere in the world.

A good way to fight service disruption attacks is to tighten up the network's topology and use the latest versions of network components and application software within the network. Hopefully others will do the same to prevent their networks and servers from being the starting point for an attack on your network.

Traffic Analysis and Eavesdropping

Both traffic analysis and eavesdropping are methods of monitoring the traffic and traffic patterns on a network. Attackers can not only glean sensitive information from messages but also study the message transmission process and learn details about the organization through its traffic patterns.

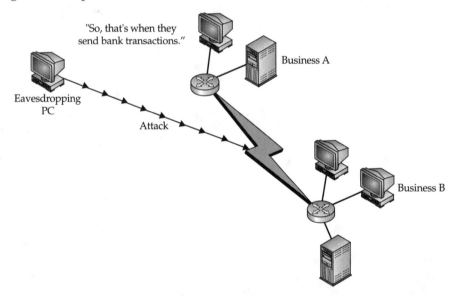

Traffic Analysis   In a *traffic analysis* attack, the interloper will gather information about specific network communications patterns, but not the actual content of the communications. For example, traffic analysis can tell when an organization has the highest amount of activity, or when they access a business-to-business partner's network.

Eavesdropping   An *eavesdropping* attack differs from traffic analysis in that the content of the traffic patterns is collected and analyzed. For example, an attacker can find out credit card numbers or read sensitive documents in transit.

Spoofing

An *IP spoof* occurs when an outside source poses as an internal IP address. The network then becomes confused and sends packets to the wrong IP address. Not only are the packets misdirected, but if they are not encrypted, the packets can be easily read by the attacker.

Spoofing attacks are difficult to do in an all-optical network, assuming encryption methods are used. Pretending to be a trusted entity would be almost impossible without an in-depth knowledge of the network.

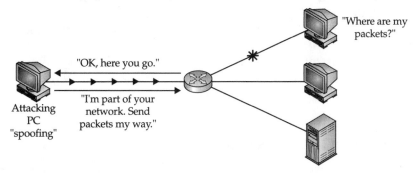

Packet Sniffing

Another way an attacker can get access to sensitive information is by intercepting and reading network packets. When we talk about attackers, the assumption is that someone outside the organization is working with malice in mind. However, the attacker can also be someone inside the organization. In fact, most security breaches come from someone inside the organization. An "inside job" is especially true in the case of packet sniffers.

In this type of attack, there must be a direct link to the network as the data passes back and forth. The most common items stolen thanks to packet sniffing are user accounts and passwords. Because most networks send their packets in a common manner, it is easy to read the packets once they have been intercepted.

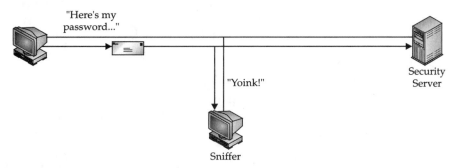

Once packet sniffing has been established, it is very difficult to detect or stop. Because users tend to use the same password and username for so many applications, packet sniffers allow the attacker to get a "skeleton key" that will fit many virtual locks.

As a matter of fact, it's now possible for sniffing to be done on wireless networks. Software programs like AirSnort and WEPCrack have been released into the public domain recently. They sniff 802.11b wireless networks that use Wired Equivalent Protocol (WEP) to secure their traffic from prying eyes. It was thought that WEP was not going to be easily cracked, but programmers were able to exploit weaknesses in the protocol used to encrypt the traffic between the wireless adapter and its Wireless Access Point (WAP). Using a wireless network adapter, the software sniffs enough packets to guess the encryption password. At that point, the wireless network traffic becomes visible to the intruder. It's as if the intruder had an Ethernet port to plug directly into the network—except they might be in a car in the parking lot! Even wired packet sniffers are hard to detect because network administrators use the same sorts of devices to track down and eliminate problems within the network.

Attacks can come in many different ways. We've tried to outline some of the most prevalent, but you can be sure that, as networks evolve, attackers will find more and more ways to assault networks.

PROTECTING YOUR NETWORK

The ultimate goal of network security is making sure that no one can get into your network and cause damage. This is accomplished through a number of tasks, most notably through security protocols (which provide the logical foundation for your network's security) and intrusion detection systems (IDSs), which deal with attackers if they are able to get through your outer layers of protection.

In this section, we examine both security protocols and IDSs and explain their basic functions and how they can be used in your own network.

Security Protocols

As we've mentioned before, protocols are nothing more than a standardized way for communications to occur within and between networks. For instance, the Internet Protocol (IP) allows conversations between different machines, both speaking a common language.

But whereas some protocols are aimed at ensuring the lines of communication are open, security protocols are used to keep out interlopers. This section gives an overview of the most popular security protocols, Secure Sockets Layer (SSL), IPSec, Point-to-Point Tunneling Protocol (PPTP), and Layer 2 Tunneling Protocol (L2TP). The latter three protocols are often found in virtual private network (VPN) deployments and are used as a means to keep data secure between an organization and a remote user, for instance.

IPSec

IPSec is the set of protocols that supports secure exchange of packets at the IP layer. Because IPSec operates at the network layer (layer 3), it can provide secure transport capable of supporting any application that uses IP.

IPSec provides three main areas of security when transmitting information across a network:

▼   Authentication of packets between the sending and receiving devices

■   Integrity of data when being transmitted

▲   Privacy of data when being transmitted

IPSec operates in two modes—transport and tunnel:

▼   In *transport* mode, Encapsulation Security Protocol (ESP) and Authentication Headers (AH) reside in the original IP packet between the IP header and upper-layer extension header information. In some cases, the packet headers are not encrypted, while the payload is encrypted. This allows authentication between sender and receiver, thus ensuring that packets are shared between the proper users. Next, the users' encryption process can translate the payload.

▲   In *tunnel* mode, IPSec places an original IP packet into a new IP packet and inserts the AH or ESP between the IP header of the new packet and the original IP packet. The new IP packet leads to the tunnel endpoint, and the original IP header specifies the packet's destination. You can use tunnel mode between two security gateways, such as tunnel servers, routers, or firewalls.

IPSec tunnel is the most common mode; it works like this:

1.   A standard IP packet is sent to the IPSec device with the expectation that the packet will be encrypted and routed to the destination system over the network.

2.   The first of the two IPSec devices, which in this case would probably be either a firewall or a router, authenticates with the receiving device.

3.   The two IPSec devices negotiate the encryption and authentication algorithms to be used.

4.   The IPSec sender encrypts the IP packet containing the data and then places it into another IP packet with an authentication header.

5.   The packet is sent across the TCP/IP network.

6.   The IPSec receiver reads the IP packet, verifies it, and then unwraps the encrypted payload and decrypts it.

7.   The receiver forwards the original packet to its destination.

Point-to-Point Tunneling Protocol (PPTP)

The *Point-to-Point Tunneling Protocol (PPTP)* enables the secure transfer of data from a remote client to a private enterprise server. PPTP supports multiple network protocols, including IP, IPX, and NetBEUI. You can use PPTP to provide a secure virtual network using dial-up lines, over LANs, over WANs, or across the Internet and other TCP/IP-based networks. In order to establish a PPTP VPN, you must have a PPTP server and a PPTP client.

Layer Two Tunneling Protocol (L2TP)

PPTP is a Microsoft technology, which establishes a virtual connection across a public network. PPTP, together with encryption and authentication, provides a private and secure network. Cisco developed a protocol similar to PPTP, Layer Two Forwarding (L2F), but it required Cisco hardware at both ends to support it. Cisco and Microsoft then merged the best features of PPTP and L2F and developed the *Layer Two Tunneling Protocol (L2TP)*. Similar to PPTP, L2TP provides a way for remote users to extend a PPP link across the Internet from the ISP to a corporate site.

SSL

Web surfers face a real problem every day. It's a problem of privacy. The issue arises when credit card numbers or other sensitive data traverse the Internet. Unless they are somehow protected, this information can fall into the clutches of evildoers.

Happily, RSA Data Security, Inc., has provided a solution that has become an Internet standard for security. In fact, if you've ever purchased anything online, you've no doubt used the *Secure Sockets Layer (SSL)* protocol.

The root of SSL is *public key encryption*, which is widely used for authentication and encryption. Public key encryption is a technique that uses a pair of asymmetric keys for both encryption and decryption. Each pair of keys consists of two parts:

▼ The *public key* is made public by distributing it freely.

▲ The *private key* is never distributed but always kept secret.

Data that is encrypted with the public key can be decrypted only with the private key. Conversely, data that is encrypted with the private key can be decrypted only with the public key. SSL's asymmetrical nature is what makes it so useful.

Authentication   On the Internet, you can tell someone that you're the President of the United States and no one would be able to prove that you're not (unless you're talking to the *actual* President, then he'll know for sure you're lying). During the course of normal Web browsing, this isn't such a big deal, but when it comes time for money to change hands, it's clear that you need to know who you're dealing with. This is where *authentication* helps.

Authentication is the process of verifying identity so that one party can be sure that another party is who it claims to be. Figure 12-2 shows how SSL-based authentication works.

Suppose Larry from accounting needs to buy a gross of number two pencils. He goes to Pencilworld.com, places an order, and is ready to enter a secure site, which maintains his company's procurement information. But before he types in the number, Larry's computer must prove to Pencilworld.com that he's allowed to order supplies from them.

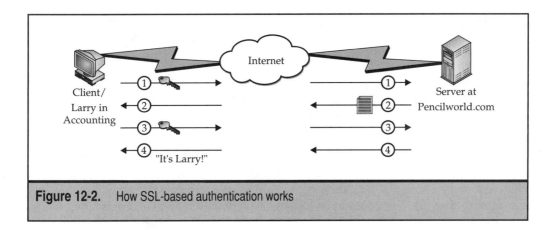

Figure 12-2.   How SSL-based authentication works

Here's how it works:

1. Pencilworld.com wants to authenticate Larry, who has a pair of keys, one public and one private. Larry sends his public key to Pencilworld.com.

2. Pencilworld.com generates a random message and sends it back to Larry.

3. Larry uses his private key to encrypt the message and returns it to Pencilworld.com.

4. Pencilworld.com receives this message and decrypts it using Larry's previously transmitted public key. Pencilworld.com compares the decrypted message with the one they originally sent to Larry. If they match, Pencilworld.com knows they are talking to Larry.

Using this method, an imposter wouldn't know what Larry's private key is and would be unable to properly encrypt the random message for Pencilworld.com to check.

Certificates   However, the method just described is not foolproof. Someone else can go to Pencilworld.com and say he is Larry in accounting, and then use his own public and private keys to get access to the procurement account. The rapscallion can say he's Larry and then prove it by encrypting something with his private key. Then Pencilworld.com can't tell the bandit isn't really Larry. It's yet another reason to keep passwords and private keys very secure.

NOTE: There are, of course, more checks and means of security in e-business Web sites, especially when money is changing hands. But let's follow this example for the sake of explaining how basic SSL works in a Web browser.

To ameliorate this problem, the standards community has come up with an object called a *certificate*. A certificate contains several components that make it unique to each person, for instance:

▼   The certificate issuer's name

■   The entity for which the certificate is being issued

■   The public key of the subject

▲   A number of time stamps

By using certificates, everybody can examine Larry's certificate to make sure it is genuine. Assuming Larry has maintained tight control over his private key and no one has managed to forge it, Figure 12-3 shows how a certificate is used in negotiating a SSL transaction.

Intrusion Detection Systems

Connecting your organization to the Internet not only brings the world to your fingertips, but it can also bring thugs into your organization. Because of this, it is important to ensure that your network is safe and secure. Security can be a very proactive process, including the use of firewalls.

Firewalls are great, but they lack something when it comes to configuration. For a firewall to work, a list must be created that details what individuals can, and cannot, do to be allowed access. In fact, if the firewall is poorly configured, it can do more harm than having no firewall at all by giving everybody a false sense of security. In order to protect your organization, a regular network security audit is called for. Part of the security audit (besides a review of policy, processes, and procedures) is to test the network while running an intrusion detection system (IDS) along with a vulnerability scanner.

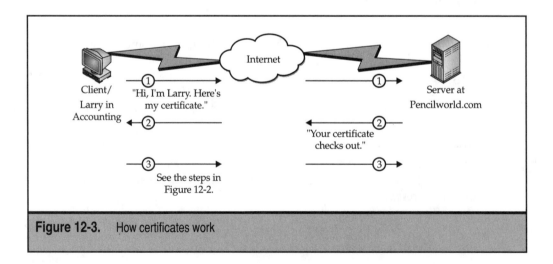

Figure 12-3.   How certificates work

Need

The existence of firewalls might make one wonder why an IDS is even needed. To give an idea of the benefit of an IDS, let's put it in the perspective of home security. Since you want to keep your family safe, you've invested in top-of-the-line locks—double-cylinder deadbolts and even that chain that keeps the door locked from the inside. That level of security can be likened to a firewall. That's fine and dandy, but if a burglar wants to get in, he can still kick the door in or break a window, still gaining access. If you want to kick it up a notch, you can add a burglar alarm with motion sensors and a keypad right next to your bed. Now, if a burglar gets in, an alarm will sound and the next thing he knows he's checking in to the Grey Bar Hotel. IDSs can be likened to a home security alarm.

IDSs and firewalls work hand-in-hand with the knowledge that no system is going to be completely protected. In the event someone makes it past the firewall, an IDS can pick them up before they wreak too much havoc on your system.

The last piece of the security puzzle is the *vulnerability scanner*. This is the same as kindly Officer So-and-So who comes to your house and notes security problems. However, the vulnerability scanner checks your network to let you know where problems exist.

With these features in mind, let's talk about some of the tools at your disposal to help ward off security breaches.

Vulnerability Assessment Scanners

Vulnerability assessment scanners, also known as "risk assessment products," come in two basic forms:

▼ **Passive scanners**   These allow the network administrator to define a security policy for the devices on the network (maybe each device has its own policy). This scanner audits every device on the network and generates a report that details where each machine needs security help.

▲ **Active scanners**   These scanners take a proactive approach to network security and are sometimes thought of as "hackers in a box." Active scanners provide a number of attacks (Web server exploits, DoS, and so forth). This allows the network administrator to probe his or her network resources and get a clear picture of any weaknesses.

These systems take a number of swipes at a network, using information gathered from the early passes to bolster their later attempts. For instance, a scanner might find an open password file in a user's PC during the first pass. In subsequent passes, it might use that password to access restricted resources.

Host IDS

A host IDS (HIDS) uses an agent that resides on each host system that is monitored. The agent analyzes event logs, system files, and other resources looking for unauthorized changes or other records of suspicious activities. In the event something is found out of place, a Simple Network Management Protocol (SNMP) alarm is triggered.

For example, the HIDS will monitor attempted logins. If a password is entered improperly a set number of times, then an alert will be sounded, indicating that someone is trying to illegally access that account, as shown in Figure 12-4.

If an attacker does make it into the system and makes changes to the network configuration, the HIDS will detect this (although it might not happen in real time) and trigger an alarm.

Network IDS

A network IDS (NIDS) monitors traffic in real time. It examines packets in great detail so that it can spot DoS attacks or dangerous payloads before the packets reach their destinations, causing damage. The NIDS does its job by comparing packets against a database of known attack signatures, as Figure 12-5 shows. Like virus protection software, these databases are regularly updated by vendors as new attack signatures are identified.

When attacks are noted, a scanner can both sound an alarm and terminate the connection. In some cases, the NIDS will work in cooperation with the firewall, automatically defining a new rule to shut out the attacker in the future.

Most NIDSs work in what is known as "promiscuous mode." This means that each and every packet that comes through the network is examined. Because of the amount of work that must be done, NIDSs generally require their own dedicated host.

To make the use of a NIDS even more costly and cumbersome, a NIDS sensor will be needed for each segment, because they cannot see across switches or routers. Further, some have problems keeping up with Fast Ethernet segments.

Network Node IDS

Network Node IDSs (NNIDSs) are hybrid IDS agents that overcome some of NIDSs' shortfalls. Such an agent works similarly to a NIDS in that it compares incoming packets against a master database, but it differs in that it concerns itself with packets that are targeted at the network node on which they reside.

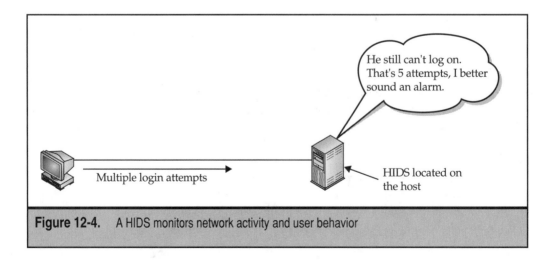

Figure 12-4.   A HIDS monitors network activity and user behavior

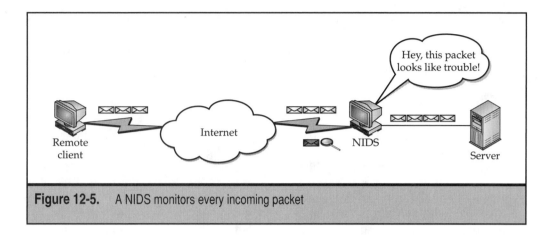

Figure 12-5. A NIDS monitors every incoming packet

A good way to keep IDSs functionality clear is to understand that HIDSs concern themselves with monitoring log files and behavior patterns, while NIDSs and NNIDSs concern themselves with TCP analysis. A NIDS, to be more precise, runs in promiscuous mode, while an NNIDS does not.

Because an NNIDS is not expected to examine each and every packet that comes across the system, it can be faster and use far fewer network resources. As such, it can be installed on existing servers and does not require its own, dedicated machine. Furthermore, it is well suited for heavily loaded segments, switched network environments, or encrypted environments.

The downside is that each server that is to be protected will need its own NNIDS and those will all have to report back to a central control console.

Both HIDSs and NIDSs are well worth the purchase, since they each guard a specific part of your network. NIDSs and NNIDSs monitor incoming packets for attacks. HIDSs are good at watching the key locations within your network.

The Downsides

Of course, installing an IDS isn't the perfect solution to your network security needs. First, it is not enough to simply look at traffic on a packet-by-packet basis, because some attacks are spread out over multiple packets (or deliberately fragmented to fool your IDS). To combat this, packets are buffered (which wastes both time and resources) and state tables are maintained to track individual sessions. This process is more than likely to slow down the detection process.

This must be done while eliminating (or at least minimizing) false positives and setting off alarms. If this is not carefully monitored, the IDS runs the risk of crying wolf. Administrators will be so used to letting harmless packets through that the risk increases of letting through bad packets.

Speed is another factor that can present a problem to IDS systems. IDS products can keep up just fine on Ethernet, but Fast Ethernet and Gigabit Ethernet present a problem. Because there is so much more bandwidth coursing through the line, there are more packets to analyze. Further, a promiscuous-mode sensor can see traffic only on its own segment.

Networks that use VPNs will also run into problems with a NIDS, because the packets will be encrypted, thus making any packet comparisons useless.

Detection

Not every IDS trips an alarm because of database mismatches. There are some products that use a different means to find bad packets. For instance, one means is by completing a full protocol analysis on the data stream. This can highlight anomalies in packet contents much more quickly than searching the packet signature database. It is also much more flexible when capturing new variations on old attacks. These attacks might slip through a traditional IDS, but a full protocol analysis would make them apparent.

Another technique is called *anomaly-based* IDS. This type of detection ignores everything that is deemed "normal." Anything that is an anomaly is considered an intrusion and worthy of analysis.

Anomaly detection is good at detecting previously unknown attacks, because it does not have to worry about what attacks look like. However, this method can run into problems when it comes time to separate noise from natural changes in network traffic. This can occur when a new application is installed somewhere on the network.

OPTICAL CONSIDERATIONS

Though the aforementioned techniques are fit for both electrical and optical networks, there are several issues that are specific to optical networks.

In this section, we examine the features that are unique to optical networks, methods of attack, methods of attack detection, specific optical network vulnerabilities, and some tips to ensure the physical security of your network.

Optical Network Security Features

By virtue of their very nature, optical networks come with built-in security measures. These security features are great at keeping out the bad guys, but they can spell problems when law enforcement needs to monitor telecommunications and data networks.

Consider the trouble law enforcement encounters when trying to do a simple phone tap. According to every movie that comes off the Hollywood cookie cutter, phone taps are simple affairs. Police must simply get a warrant from a sympathetic judge, then tap the line. But with the prevalence of optical fiber, it's not such an easy feat anymore.

Since the 1980s, U.S. telecom carriers have installed an estimated 83 million miles of fiber. That number will more than double between 2001 and 2006, say fiber optics market researchers KMI. Not only are there millions of miles of fiber optic lines to police, but optical device makers are introducing gear than transmits 40Gbps—that's enough to send 10,000 copies of *A Tale of Two Cities* in just one second.

Complex Systems

Another part of network security that is enhanced comes by virtue of the way networks are deployed. Not only does information travel across these lines in the blink of an eye, but they also take sometimes-convoluted paths from Point A to Point B. Consider Figure 12-6.

A single conversation leaving Point A can be broken up, with packets traveling different routes before they arrive at Point B to be rejoined. This mode of communication is meant for the sake of expediency; however, it also makes tapping the line much more difficult. That's good news for the sake of network security and integrity, bad news for law enforcement.

The biggest problem is the sheer amount of data that traverses a network. As we noted earlier, gear is being sold that can send 40Gbps, an impossible task for any human being to sift through. However, one method that has gotten a lot of press lately is the FBI's Carnivore system.

Carnivore, which has been criticized by privacy advocates, is a sniffer that sits on a dedicated PC. Its job is to sift through Web pages, e-mail messages, and other Web content, searching for evidence.

Carnivore looks for evidence by searching traffic for certain keywords. The FBI can connect its own Carnivore to an ISP, or the ISP can elect to use its own version of Carnivore.

The problem with sniffers, like Carnivore, is that they can't sniff fast enough. At most, they can process 50Mbps, which is a far cry from the 40Gbps transmissions that are possible. In essence, sniffers are able to analyze 0.1 percent of the traffic coursing through a 40Gbps network.

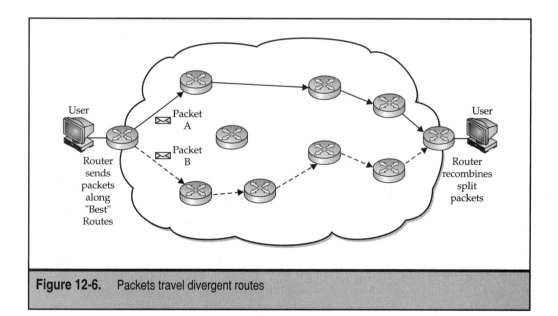

Figure 12-6. Packets travel divergent routes

Tapping Problems

Sniffers aren't the only solution, but they are the easiest and least expensive. Another method is to tap into the fiber optic cable at amplification points, as Figure 12-7 depicts.

At these points, law enforcement can install devices that can trap the optical signal and then translate it into readable information.

Another way to listen in on fiber is to plant underground devices adjacent to fiber optic cables where they make bends. As you remember from earlier discussions, thanks to internal refraction, bends in fiber can cause light to escape from the fiber. At these points, the devices can pick up the light and convert it back into data.

Although this method is possible, it is improbable because of the difficulty associated with getting enough light without immediately being noticed by the system administrator.

Another way to tap into fiber is to cut the fiber; add a connector at each end of the cut; connect the transmitting end to a coupler; split the signal (with a resultant loss of signal strength on the original path); and reconnect the original path to the coupler. The downtime to the path to do this would definitely be noticed by the operator, and use of an OTDR would pinpoint where this action occurred.

Again, this shows a weakness in the fiber that can be exploited by an attacker. For law enforcement, it poses another problem. Whether the information gathered at a bend in the fiber is admissible or even valid is a big problem. Remember, messages are split into different pieces and sent across the best routes. Only when the packets reach the destination router are they reassembled into the original message. The FBI may get portions of a message, or even portions of multiple messages that don't make sense.

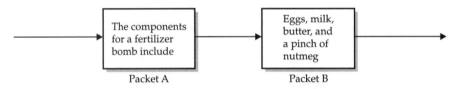

Packets from two sources can pose an
admissibility problem for law enforcement.

Encryption

In the event data traffic is picked up off a fiber, and it consists of complete messages, there is still another hurdle—encryption. Any organization worth their salt is going to use advanced encryption methods to scramble their message. The end result: a message that reads like gibberish. This is bad news for both attackers and law enforcement. This isn't a feature that is inherent to fiber optics. To be sure, it is used in conventional networks all the time and is a very easy way to secure your data.

Naturally, there is some sort of workaround that attackers can attempt. Encryption software is easy enough to download for free off the Internet. But happily enough, encryption algorithms (including Triple DES and Blowfish) are currently very hard to crack—at best it would take at lot of time and a large amount of computing resources to decipher a message.

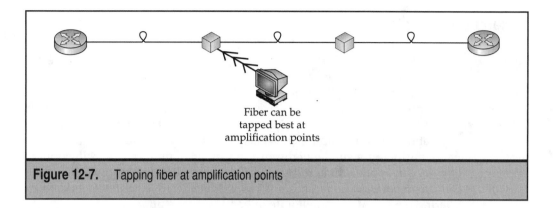

Figure 12-7.   Tapping fiber at amplification points

Interference

Later in this chapter, we'll talk about interference disrupting optical fiber. In those cases, however, the disrupting signal has to be introduced directly into the fiber. By and large, optical fiber is impervious to electromagnetic interference.

Fiber will not pick up noise from nearby electrical cables, nor will it emit noise. Because fiber optics deals in photons and not electrons, it works in the optical range of the electromagnetic spectrum. This is also why error rates are so low in optical fiber.

Monitoring

Fiber networks are constantly monitored for optical loss. The presence of excessive optical loss can indicate not only a problem in the network, but also a tap being placed on the fiber. Unfortunately, fiber can be tapped much like copper wire. The only thing that is needed is an optical coupler. Any fiber can be tapped by bending it and scraping off the outer layers of cladding, although it is extremely difficult.

> **NOTE:**   Though fiber can be tapped and monitored, it is very difficult to introduce a signal onto a fiber.

After the tap has been applied, it is easy to detect the intrusion. An unauthorized optical coupler will cause at least 0.5 dB of signal loss. Normal optical networks will experience a slow, gradual loss of signal over time, but 0.5 dB will be very sudden, and very noticeable.

It is because taps are so easy to detect that the military, banks, and U.S. Government use fiber rather than conventional methods.

Attack Methods

When someone tries to assault an optical network, there are a few options. Though fiber is not as easy to attack as copper wire, there are still a number of places where an optical network needs to shore up its security to prevent attacks.

In-Band Jamming

In-band jamming is another form of a DoS attack. In this case, an attacker inserts a high-powered signal in the optical link, which disrupts the receivers' ability to correctly process the signal. This can either degrade the level of service or bring it completely to a halt. Also, the attacking signal will propagate to other nodes, causing more problems. This is because optical transmissions are transparent, meaning they flow through OADMs without regeneration. SONET/SDH and similar nodes perform OEO conversions, which by definition do reshaping and regeneration of signals (and in most cases, retiming as well). Further, if a single, high-powered signal is used on a specific optical link, it could damage the optical link. In-band jamming is shown in Figure 12-8.

One means to combat in-band jamming is by building a redundant network. Also, blocking or filtering the signal can ameliorate in-band jamming attacks.

Out-of-Band Jamming

Out-of-band jamming is another DoS attack. In this case, the attacker weakens a signal's transmission flow by exploiting components with crosstalk leaks or cross modulation effects. The attacker inject a signal at a different wavelength than the one being used by the network.

An optical amplifier will still accept the malicious wavelength (unless it is filtered out). Because optical amplifiers cannot distinguish between legitimate and attack wavelengths, the wavelength will not be stopped.

The idea behind an out-of-band jamming attack is that the photons the amplifier gives to the malicious wavelength rob power from the legitimate signal (or signals) and provide more power to the attack signal so that it can propagate further. Current attack detection methods would not necessarily detect out-of-band jamming, because the power could be made to decrease (not increase) or remain constant during the attack. This kind of attack could be mounted against an optical amplifier within a node or within an amplified fiber link. Figure 12-9 shows an out-of-band jamming attack.

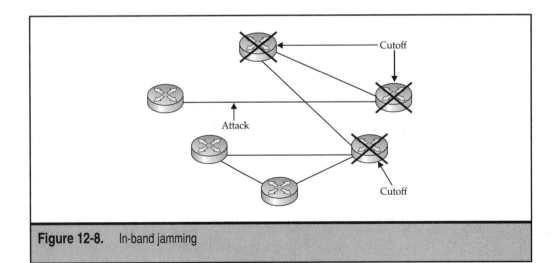

Figure 12-8. In-band jamming

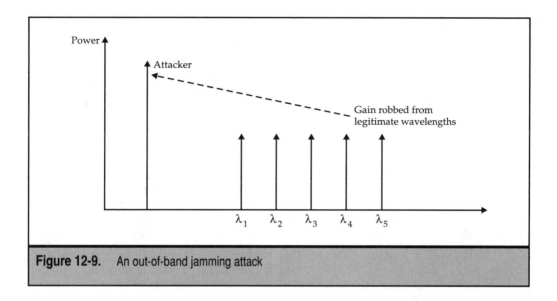

Figure 12-9.   An out-of-band jamming attack

Unauthorized Observation

Unauthorized observation (which is another way to say "eavesdropping") is possible, albeit difficult, in an optical network. There are two places where eavesdropping is most prevalent in an all-optical network:

▼ **Demultiplexer**   Eavesdropping can be accomplished by listening to the crosstalk leaking from an adjacent signal through a shared device, like a demultiplexer. A demultiplexer is meant to divide its component wavelengths into individual signals; however, crosstalk allows a little bit of each wavelength to leak into the wrong path. This crosstalk may be strong enough for an attacker to listen to and recover data from the stream. However, because crosstalk levels in these devices are between 0.03 percent and 1 percent, eavesdropping presents a low-level threat.

▲ **Optical amplifier**   Second, optical amplifiers can be used in eavesdropping attacks. Erbium-doped fiber amplifiers (EDFAs) cause a tiny bit of amplitude modulation between channels because of the presence (or absence) of a signal on an adjacent channel. The attacker can use that modulation to recover a portion of the signal and decipher it. Of course, this requires the attacker to have both intimate knowledge of the circuitry of the EDFA and access, along with the requisite circuitry to decode the signal and decipher it.

Attack Detection

As we noted earlier, an attack on a network (a tap, for instance) can manifest itself to the network operator as signal loss. It is important to be able to differentiate between an actual attack and gophers with the munchies.

Further, it is important to be able to pinpoint the source of an attack and restore the network as fast as possible. If high-capacity networks are "out" thanks to an attack, then a large amount of data can be corrupted or unable to traverse the network at all. Similarly, if an eavesdropping attack is taking place, then a large amount of data can be compromised.

In this section, we'll examine diagnostic tools and techniques that can be used to detect attacks on optical networks. The following sections can be further organized into tools (pilot tone and optical time domain reflectometers) and techniques (wideband power detection and optical spectrum analyzers).

Wideband Power Detection

Power detection is a method of measuring the received optical power over a wide bandwidth. Using this method, a change of bandwidth can be detected when compared against established readings. Since measured power is compared against an established (and therefore *expected*) value, a slight decrease in power may take some time to detect. However, as we noted earlier, gradual losses are not likely to be attacks. Large drops in power (0.5dB at once, for instance) are more than likely attributable to malice.

So that you don't hit the panic button for no reason, it is a good idea to get to know your network and understand what would cause drops in power and how much you are likely to lose on an ongoing, natural basis.

Optical Spectral Analysis

Optical spectral analyzers (OSAs) measure the optical spectrum of a signal. OSAs are useful because they can give a more complete picture than simple power loss. OSAs can detect a change in a spectrum shape, even if the shape does not cause power to increase or decrease.

For example, two different wavelengths can have the same power output, but they will have different spectral shapes. An OSA can differentiate between the two signals, but a power meter will only be able to tell how much power is coming through the glass.

OSAs, though able to tell more than power levels, still need to rely on statistical comparisons between sample averages and statistical averages. As such, OSAs tend to be slower than other detection methods.

Pilot Tones

Pilot tones are signals that travel in the same fiber and nodes in which data travels, but can be differentiated from the data. The main use of pilot tones is to detect transmission disruptions. Pilot tones generally operate at different carrier frequencies than the data signal. In a time division multiplexing (TDM) system (like SONET, for example), they can be put into a different time slot than the data, which helps differentiate between the two.

Pilot signals tend to reside at carrier frequencies within or between wavelength division multiplexing (WDM) lambdas, but they can also exist outside the transmission band. If the pilot tones are present in frequency, and close to the data transmission, they are referred to as *subcarrier multiplexed (SCM)* signals. SCM signals allow a pilot tone to be carried at the same wavelength as the payload signal.

Pilot tones need not be mere "tones" carrying no actual information. They can be set to carry network control information. Pilot tones travel in just one direction.

Optical Time Domain Reflectometry

We talked about *optical time domain reflectometers (OTDRs)* briefly in Chapter 11. OTDRs are a special use of pilot tones. But whereas pilot tones are a one-way signal with the tone being analyzed on the receiving end, OTDRs analyze the reflected pilot tone's signal.

OTDRs are normally used to diagnose problems in fiber, including:

▼ Faults

■ Bends

▲ Loss

As such, they are well suited to detecting fiber attacks.

OTDRs can run into a number of obstacles, however. First, the OTDR signal can be the victim of jamming. Also, because optical isolators are commonly used, it might be necessary to install an OTDR at each amplifier.

NOTE: An optical isolator is a device that reduces optical feedback.

Countermeasures

Finally, it is useful to discuss the mantra of network security. This explains a popular concept for stopping and responding to attacks. The three principles are: prevent, detect, and react.

Prevent   *Preventing* an attack means ensuring that your components are secure from the get-go. That means making sure your components cannot be tampered with, using encryption and using multiple wavelengths. Solid prevention measures go almost without elaboration—if you can prevent attackers from compromising your network, then your network will suffer no ill effects or downtime.

Detect   *Detecting* an attack means not only identifying that, indeed, your network is under attack, but also being able to locate the source of the attack. This is important because it can help you isolate where the attack is coming from, which can help in your response. Is the attack coming from halfway around the globe, or is it a disgruntled employee? Detection is important to help define your response.

React   *Reacting* to an attack means counter-attacking, employing such devices as protection amplifiers and low crosstalk switches, among others. It can also mean that you need to reconfigure your network to enhance safety and security. Another possible reaction comes if the attacker is someone within your organization. Perhaps firing or legal action would be more appropriate steps.

Vulnerabilities

Earlier we talked about the myth that fiber could not be tapped. In reality, however, fiber can be tapped with a coupler; it's just that it is really hard to do. Though fiber is more secure than copper wire, there are still several chinks in fiber's armor. In this section, we take a closer look at some of fiber's weaknesses.

Fiber

Fiber, itself, can be the source of an attack. It's not so much a problem in local area networks (LANs), but fiber is relatively unprotected in wide area networks (WANs) and metropolitan area networks (MANs). As such, fiber is easy to tamper with.

For instance, a potential attacker can tap into fiber without anyone trying to stop him. Also, if an attacker just wanted to stop data flowing on the network, it would be easy enough to dig up the fiber and cut it.

Further, some nodes and devices (like amplifiers and such) could be buried with the fiber. Again, these nodes might not be protected and can find themselves vulnerable to attack.

Crosstalk

Crosstalk is not as much of a problem in optical networks as it is in electrical networks, but it is still present. Crosstalk is the phenomenon where signals from one part of the optical device bleed into another part of the device. Crosstalk can be used for DoS or eavesdropping attacks.

Crosstalk occurs most often in demultiplexers before the lambdas are introduced into their own, unique fibers.

Amplification

EDFAs are prone to jamming. In fact, jammed EDFAs go hand-in-hand with in-band jamming attacks. EDFAs behave differently than electronic amplifiers. By way of a refresher, let's briefly explain how EDFAs work.

Amplifiers are very important in optical networks. They can be used not only near nodes, but also along the path of the fiber. In an EDFA, the optical gain is the result of excited erbium ions that are energized by an optical pump. The resulting excitation can be affected by the signals that are being amplified. This occurs when the signals are intense enough to saturate the gain by extracting energy from the erbium excitation.

The large bandwidth signals will see constant gain; however, if there are large transients in the input signals, the transients can cause large transient changes in the erbium excitation and the resulting gain.

NOTE: Transients are a short-term variation (as opposed to long-term drift) in the characteristics of power delivered to electrical equipment.

Even after the optical transients end, the gain changes can last for dozens of microseconds. As a result, this effect can provide a way for the EDFA to be attacked with an optical signal. Specifically, a low duty cycle can be used to degrade the signal or deny service.

Physical Security

Talk about physical security can seem silly, to say the least. If you remember that Robert Redford movie *Sneakers* from a few years back (it's okay if you don't; no one else does, either), then you'll remember the painful measures that the bad guy took to protect his computer system from attack. At least those measures seemed painful. The truth of the matter is, physical security is every bit as important as encryption or secure amplifiers. Laser and temperature-sensitive intrusion detection systems may not be in your budget, but there are a number of commonsense things you can do to keep the bad guys out of your network.

When we talk about network security, we tend to focus more on stopping the types of attacks that can be initiated by someone at a keyboard a thousand miles away. However, research and statistics show us that more attacks come from inside an organization than from outside.

Network security is not a lopsided issue. Care needs to be taken with firewalls and password protection, as well as ensuring physical security is up to snuff. Physical security is a matter of limiting access to equipment, to prevent tampering and theft—even accidental problems brought on by someone trying to work outside his or her skill set. The results of these actions—be they malicious or just misguided—can end with some serious downtime for your system. That's why it is important to employ solid physical security strategies as part of your overall security plan.

Take a look at your existing system. There are likely already some measures in place that don't even seem like they are physical security. For instance, your server and other networking devices are probably locked away in a server room. This is a good idea because it keeps misguided staff from trying to "help." Later in this chapter, we talk about server room security. This could also apply to any location where fiber comes into a building for amplification, routing, or other tasks.

Tapes

You might also store backup tapes off-site. This is great if there is a fire or some other calamity strikes the building, but what about the tapes, themselves? It's a good idea to make sure they are password protected. If backup tapes fall into the wrong hands, the damage can be just as bad as if prying eyes get into your network (in fact, it would be easier). Truth be told, the safety of backup tapes is a massive weak link. Organizations spend big bucks securing the building, the server room, and the servers themselves, but the backup tapes (complete with the latest data) can walk right out the door with little or no protection.

Server Room

The server room, itself, is an important place to ensure quality security measures are in place. Racks should allow equipment to be stowed behind locked doors. Of course, these locked doors aren't built like those at Fort Knox, but they can serve as a discouragement to would-be attackers.

Though protection can include keeping evildoers out of your equipment, it can also serve to protect your equipment and your network from people who just don't know better. For instance, if your switches and routers are locked away, there is little chance that someone will come in and borrow a cable from a sensitive piece of equipment, or trip over a line.

Next, the servers should be protected with a password. This is available on screen savers, but some administrators don't like them, because they prevent error messages from being posted. However, most server software allows error messages to be sent to an administrator machine. To be safer, a good idea is to put only secure remote monitoring tools in place so the administrator can handle everything from his or her own desktop without compromising security.

For equipment that is not used often, removing the keyboard or mouse is an easy way to keep wandering fingers from being somewhere they shouldn't. True, this can be a pain in the neck for the administrator, but if the device can't be accessed, little harm can come to it.

Windows

The server room, itself, can be selected and built with security in mind. First, you might want to reconsider a room with windows. If the room does have windows, it is worth considering bars and blinds as protective coverings.

If your server room is on an upper floor, you have more safety and security there. However, windows are still a consideration. Someone could still peer in while a password is being entered, thereby compromising that data. Again, it is a good idea to install window blinds or reflective film.

NOTE: Reflective film and blinds serve other good functions as well as keeping the bad guys out. With the server room adequately shaded, the room won't heat up as much, thereby keeping air conditioning costs down.

Walls   Of course, your best bet is an internal room designed with adequate cooling and power and a fully lockable entryway. Additionally, the walls should be from "deck to deck" as opposed to walls that end at a suspended ceiling. It might sound a little over the top, but if someone wants to get at your data badly enough, they might go right over the wall to get at it.

This isn't so much of a problem in downtown locations or in skyscrapers, but in technology parks in the suburbs, the lack of late night activity along with the ground-level access can make this a reality. In some cases, vehicles have punched right through the wall, providing access to the server. This type of attack is known as a *ram raid*.

Visitors

Now that you've got hungry Rottweilers guarding your devices and a moat filled with piranha encircling your server room, it should be all safe and sound. The truth is, there are still vulnerabilities.

It would be nice to think that the server room would be dedicated just to the server and other networking equipment. In reality, however, the server room is likely where telephone systems, air conditioning gear, fire detection equipment, and a bevy of other gear will be collocated. Accordingly, contractors will need to get in and out of that room quite often.

The best procedure is to have the contractor sign in and be issued a security badge. Then, he or she will be escorted by a member of the IT staff who will monitor the contractor's work. However, since your organization likely won't have the manpower to let an IT staffer go every time a contractor walks through the door, a reasonably inexpensive solution is to install video cameras.

If your organization can afford it, another good idea is to build your server room with glass walls. On one hand, it makes everyone aware when someone is in the server room and a contractor is less likely to fiddle with something sensitive. On the other hand, you can feel the cold hard stares of the staff on your back when you're trying to get some work done. Plus, you'll have to be careful that unauthorized persons don't catch a glimpse of the almighty administrator passwords.

It has been said that the difference between Eastern and Western medicine is that in the East, the focus is on wellness—trying to keep people healthy. In the West, on the other hand, the focus is on curing problems once they arise. Physical security is akin to Eastern medicine. If all goes as it's supposed to, you'll never have to worry about a system that has been attacked.

Redundancy

We've talked about the merits of redundancy before, but it is especially worth noting when we talk about physical security. Again, redundancy is having one or more duplicate sets of equipment that house your network's data. In the case of an attack that brings your system down, the backup system can kick in and provide the data.

For example, let's say your networking equipment is housed in your company's main building. This is a reasonable assumption to make for any organization. Now, what happens if your headquarters burns down? Unless you have a redundant system located elsewhere, all your data will be lost.

The same is true for fiber placement. In designing SONET-like loops in a WAN or a MAN, it is a good idea to run the cables in different locations, as Figure 12-10 shows. These logical loops ensure that if the primary fiber is cut (either accidentally or on purpose), then the backup ring won't be cut at the same time.

Fiber

Fiber, itself, can be prone to assault, as we saw earlier in this chapter. But by virtue of the way fiber is designed and constructed, it can ward off attacks and also let authorities know if someone is trying to attack it.

First, there is a popular myth that fiber cannot be tapped into. This is a good myth to perpetuate, because a little bit of disinformation can go a long way. That is, if a green hacker doesn't think he can tap into fiber, he won't even try. However, that will go only

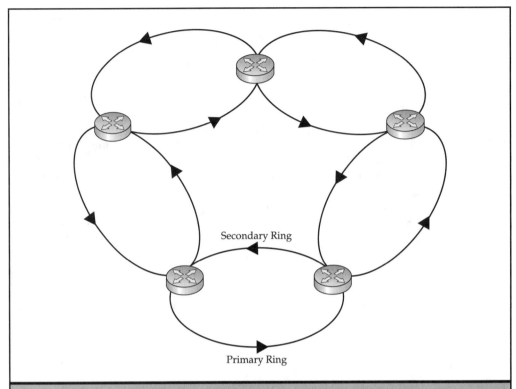

Figure 12-10.   Primary and backup rings should not be physically located together

so far. In the event fiber is tapped into, the signal loss will be so high that authorities will have an easy time detecting the attack.

One measure of security is the way fiber is encased in cabling. As Chapter 11 illustrated, there are many layers in a piece of optical cabling that can serve not only to protect the fiber, but also to discourage all but the most intent attackers. In some cases, the fiber is encased in a metal sheath, which can be a huge pain to get into.

In the event fiber is damaged, a ring system (like SONET) can transfer traffic to the backup ring. In a mesh configuration, routing protocols can sense the fiber cut and re-route traffic away from the severed line.

Network security is a very broad term that refers to a number of issues. However, for ideal security, it is important to address all the facets of network security and ensure that all precautions have been made. This ranges from making sure that users go through the required security checkpoints to ensuring a high level of physical security. As if all these issues weren't challenging enough, optical networks add their own layers of security issues, but with a little planning, many risks can be effectively reduced.

INDEX

G

M

N

P

Q

R

INTERNATIONAL CONTACT INFORMATION

AUSTRALIA
McGraw-Hill Book Company Australia Pty. Ltd.
TEL +61-2-9417-9899
FAX +61-2-9417-5687
http://www.mcgraw-hill.com.au
books-it_sydney@mcgraw-hill.com

CANADA
McGraw-Hill Ryerson Ltd.
TEL +905-430-5000
FAX +905-430-5020
http://www.mcgrawhill.ca

GREECE, MIDDLE EAST,
NORTHERN AFRICA
McGraw-Hill Hellas
TEL +30-1-656-0990-3-4
FAX +30-1-654-5525

MEXICO (Also serving Latin America)
McGraw-Hill Interamericana Editores S.A. de C.V.
TEL +525-117-1583
FAX +525-117-1589
http://www.mcgraw-hill.com.mx
fernando_castellanos@mcgraw-hill.com

SINGAPORE (Serving Asia)
McGraw-Hill Book Company
TEL +65-863-1580
FAX +65-862-3354
http://www.mcgraw-hill.com.sg
mghasia@mcgraw-hill.com

SOUTH AFRICA
McGraw-Hill South Africa
TEL +27-11-622-7512
FAX +27-11-622-9045
robyn_swanepoel@mcgraw-hill.com

UNITED KINGDOM & EUROPE
(Excluding Southern Europe)
McGraw-Hill Education Europe
TEL +44-1-628-502500
FAX +44-1-628-770224
http://www.mcgraw-hill.co.uk
computing_neurope@mcgraw-hill.com

ALL OTHER INQUIRIES Contact:
Osborne/McGraw-Hill
TEL +1-510-549-6600
FAX +1-510-883-7600
http://www.osborne.com
omg_international@mcgraw-hill.com

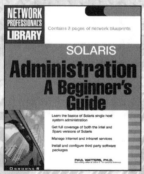

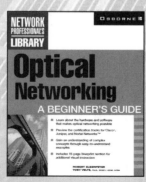